Freedom in the World

Political Rights and Civil Liberties
1983–1984

A FREEDOM HOUSE BOOK

Greenwood Press issues the Freedom House series "Studies in Freedom" in addition to the Freedom House yearbook *Freedom in the World*.

Strategies for the 1980s: Lessons of Cuba, Vietnam, and Afghanistan by Philip van Slyck. Studies in Freedom, Number 1

Freedom in the World

Political Rights and Civil Liberties
1983–1984

Raymond D. Gastil

With Essays by

William A. Douglas
June Teufel Dreyer
Jerome B. Grieder
Liang Heng
Mab Huang
Peter R. Moody, Jr.

Lucian W. Pye
James D. Seymour
Norris Smith
Lawrence R. Sullivan
Leonard R. Sussman
Lindsay M. Wright

GREENWOOD PRESS

Westport, Connecticut • London, England

Copyright © 1984 by Freedom House, Inc.
Freedom House, 20 West 40th Street, New York, New York 10018

ISBN: 0-313-23179-6
ISSN: 0732-6610

First published in 1984

Greenwood Press
A division of Congressional Information Service, Inc.
88 Post Road West
Westport, Connecticut 06881

Printed in the United States of America

10 9 8 7 6 5 4 3 2 1

Contents

Contents

Map

Tables

Preface

Americans have many foreign policy interests. For most citizens our economic and security relations are foremost, and our foreign policy is directed primarily to securing these interests. However, in the long run the future of our country will only be secured in a free and democratic world. From this perspective achieving this world is both a vital interest of Americans and a vital interest of all peoples. To help us in understanding where we are in the struggle to achieve this world and to keep the relevance of this issue before the public, Freedom House has supported the Comparative Survey of Freedom since 1972.

We note that Chile, Poland, South Africa, and Yugoslavia have been placed in the partly free category in the latest revision of the Survey. These changes were made on the basis of assessments of the current situation in these and other countries with comparable levels of freedom. We emphasize, however, that all four countries--Chile, Poland, South Africa, and Yugoslavia--now appear on the bottom rung of partly free countries. These changes reflect, in part, increased assertion of freedom by citizens of these countries, rather than an enlargement of freedom by government action.

It is not Freedom House's intention to give comfort to the four regimes that continue to limit severely the liberties of their people. Rather, we feel obliged to acknowledge that in each of these countries the limits of liberty are currently being stretched by irrepressible forces within the societies. We hope our findings will encourage these forces of freedom. It would be a source of anguish to Freedom House if the new findings were misinterpreted to mean that governmental changes had significantly improved the status of citizens, which they have not.

This yearbook marks the eleventh year of the Comparative Survey and is the sixth edition in the Freedom House series of annual publications. Previous yearbooks, in addition to focusing on the Comparative Survey, have emphasized different aspects of freedom and human rights. The first yearbook, the 1978 edition, examined basic theoretical issues of freedom and democracy and assessed the record of the Year of Human Rights. The second yearbook reported a conference on the potential internal and external factors promoting press and trade union freedoms, the struggle for democracy in

Preface

Iran, elections in Zimbabwe, and the relationship between human rights policy and morality. The 1981 yearbook contained essays and discussions from a Freedom House conference on the prospects for freedom in Muslim Central Asia. The 1982 yearbook emphasized a variety of approaches to economic freedom and its relation to political and civil freedom.

In addition to the material on the Comparative Survey, this 1983-84 yearbook continues the series on the ideological struggle for information freedom. It also addresses the problems of corporatism, both as a competing ideology to traditional democracy and as an academic interpretation of trends in modern democracy. This is followed by a discussion of criteria for estimating the health of democracy in the third world.

This yearbook incorporates the papers and discussions of a conference held at Freedom House on supporting democracy in mainland China and Taiwan. After noting many difficulties and opportunities the conferees agreed that the interest in democracy of the educated youth in both societies was a promising basis for democratic development. The American responsibility in the process was described as continuing to provide a credible alternative to authoritarian institutions through maintaining the present intense level of educational and information exchange and demonstrating our commitment to freedom and human rights.

We acknowledge, once again, the contribution made by the advisory panel for the Comparative Survey. The panel consists of: Robert J. Alexander, Richard W. Cottam, Herbert J. Ellison, Seymour Martin Lipset, Lucian W. Pye, Leslie Rubin, Giovanni Sartori, Robert Scalapino, and Paul Seabury.

We also express our appreciation to those foundations whose grants have made the Survey and the publication of this yearbook possible. We are especially grateful for the continuing primary assistance provided to the Survey by the J. Howard Pew Freedom Trust. We thank the Earhart Foundation for its additional support. The Survey and all Freedom House activities are also assisted by the generous support of individual members of the organization as well as trade unions, corporations, and public foundations which contribute to our general budget. No financial support from any government--now or in the past--has been either solicited or accepted.

We also acknowledge the research and editorial assistance of Jeannette C. Gastil in producing this yearbook.

The Executive Committee of Freedom House

PART I

The Survey in 1983

Introduction: Freedom
in the
Comparative Survey

At first sight many believe that it is foolish to attempt to develop a comparative survey of freedom. There seem to be too many definitions of freedom. Even Americans cannot agree on the meaning of "freedom," let alone people representing the other cultures in the world. However, as is usually the case, the feasibility of a project depends upon the objectives and purposes for which it is designed. From its beginnings in 1972 the purpose of the Survey has been to give the educated public a better grasp of the variations in politically relevant freedoms that exist in the world. By limiting the Survey to only this aspect of the subject, and by emphasizing its heuristic purposes many of the potential problems of the project have been set aside. As the Survey has been repeated over more than a decade an additional purpose has come to be providing a standard by which the educated public can judge trends in these freedoms.

The need for such a survey originally was suggested by the imbalance of the media in favor of reporting catastrophes, their concentration on the problems of the world instead of the accomplishments. To this penchant for the examination of difficulties we should add a natural proclivity to report on relatively open societies, since these are the easiest to investigate. Reporting of the threats to freedom and of the petty and not-so-petty tyrannies that beset the world tends to concentrate on areas of the world where information is relatively available, following the approach of the famous drunk searching for a lost quarter at night under the street lamp. Although he doesn't think he lost it there, this was after all where it was easiest to see.

A further problem of reporting is the tendency of certain fads and "accepted verities" to becloud our understanding of the state of freedom in the world. The inspiration for the Survey goes back to the period of the Vietnam War. Coming to the study of Vietnam under Diem, Thieu, and Ky after a long period of attention to the problems of Iran, I was startled to find newspapers and

3

even academic discussions filled with assumptions about the relative tyranny of our none-too-liberal Vietnamese allies. It was apparent to me that the Iranian regime, especially after 1963, was clearly more oppressive and illiberal than successive regimes in Saigon. Yet the Shah of Iran had a very good press until well into the 1970s, and American government support of his regime was generally applauded. South Vietnam continued to be held to very different standards. The standards of reporters seemed to be those of democracy as it was practiced in Iowa. This was the same period in which reporters and academics often praised, or at least "understood" sympathetically, the regimes of North Vietnam and Communist China, regimes that today most informed people understand quite differently, and understand all too well and too late.

After this background on how the Survey came to be and the kinds of educational problems it addresses, let me outline in more detail the political rights and civil liberties it compares, those issues it considers as relevant but does not place in the center of its rating process, and those issues that are perhaps equally important, but must be reserved for other surveys.

As I pointed out in last year's introduction, **political rights** in the Survey are primarily the rights to participate directly or through freely elected representatives in the determination of the nature of law and its administration in a society. In a large modern state this apparently requires competing political parties and ideally several tiers of elected government. The effectiveness of the political equality promised by the system varies from society to society and can never be perfect. But if reasonably extended by experience and law, and judicially protected, a multi-party democracy provides the nearest approximation to political equality that is attainable--and only political equality respects the dignity of each individual.

Civil Liberties include in the first place those freedoms that make possible the organization and mobilization of new, alternative, or non-official opinions. They include freedom of the news media, and of political, professional, worker, peasant, and other organizations. Civil liberties imply that there should be no prisoners of conscience, and certainly no execution and torture for the expression of beliefs or the organization of opposition where these are not directly related to violence against the system. (Torture and execution may also be condemned legitimately as human rights violations quite separately from considerations of civil liberties or the test of violence--this is one of the points at which consideration of human rights diverges from that of

4

freedom.) Civil liberties extend beyond these more political domains to questions such as religious freedom and freedom of residence. It can be argued that without the autonomous individuality such freedoms imply, the other civil liberties cannot be fully developed.

The two sets of freedoms complement and reinforce one another, and yet they are different conceptually. It is possible, at least for a time, for a society to have a high level of respect for one aspect of freedom but not the other.

The basic material in the Survey, and the "Country Summaries" at the end of these annuals, is organized by independent countries. An independent country may be defined as a political unit with a historical and geographical claim to separate existence that is administered separately from its neighbors, and has its own foreign and defense policies or forces. Criteria such as these lead to obvious difficulties. But they bring us closer to giving a reasonably accurate picture of the world than would adopting any more formal classification, such as UN membership or recognition by the U.S. State Department. They have led to classifying ministates in Europe such as Monaco as dependencies rather than separate states. They have led to the denial of separate status in the Surveys to the Baltic States of Estonia, Lithuania, and Latvia, as well as Tibet in China. They have also led to classifying Transkei as an independent state even though its independence was granted as part of the South African homelands policy that is, in effect, a means of denying the black community a part in South Africa as a whole. They also lead to at least partial recognition of the division of Cyprus into two states. In each case the decisions have no relation to whether the author or Freedom House regards the present condition of a state as desirable or not. Our position on the right of peoples to self-determination has been clear enough: it has been spelled out in several annuals, including the first.

The question is often raised as to the Survey's "objectivity." It is true that the Survey is not based on a group of numerical criteria that automatically produce the ratings through computer manipulation. This could not be true, because there are few criteria that could be quantified satisfactorily--or at least the criteria most likely to be relevant cannot be. There is always a large component of judgment, of discerning patterns, of comparing different countries in which what may be most significant for freedom will vary. For example, well-organized political parties may be decisive in a large, modern democracy, but are a much less important requirement for a small Pacific island.

But the fact that mathematical objectivity cannot be attained does not imply that objectivity is not attained in the sense of qualitative aspiration. The Survey has no ulterior motive beyond the general promotion of free institutions. It supports no political party or ideology or any foreign policy. Every year we do our best to judge what is, even when that is not very comfortable because of its awkward fit with the geopolitical interests of the United States or the traditional interests of Freedom House. Freedom House has faith that in the long run the kind of objectivity the Survey aspires to will do more for freedom than would institutional interference with the ratings.

The tendency of critics to identify the Survey's ratings with the more activist and programmatic objectives of Freedom House remains, however, unfortunate for Freedom House and for the Survey. For example, in a recent exchange on human rights policies, Congressman Wolpe, in criticizing the Survey for previously giving South Africa a partly free rating, sneered that "Freedom House's, shall we say, ambivalence on the subject . . . speaks for its own objectivity."[1] Our return of South Africa this year to "partly free" will no doubt raise new doubts. Yet the doubts are quite misplaced if they reflect on Freedom House's continuing and historic commitment to racial justice in every country, including our own. I personally also believe that it would be self-defeating, and destructive of both blacks and whites, to pretend that there are not hundreds of thousands or millions of blacks and whites in South Africa both able and willing to speak out and organize against the repression and humiliation that they endure.

Any survey at this level of generality is obviously open to many criticisms. The following statement taken from the journal Universal Human Rights is typical of the critical comments that are often made:

> Against this background, a capitalist, liberal democratic undertaking like that of Freedom House, which publishes its annual freedom map, is increasingly scorned as a tool for appraisal because of its ethnocentrism. As Fouad Ajami persuasively argues, any approach to human rights that rates South Africa higher than Cuba or Tanzania is not worth much.[2]

6

Several misapprehensions, mistakes, and characteristic attitudes are included here. As can be seen from the definitions given above, the Survey of Freedom is not a survey of comparative human rights. While there is a great deal of overlap between the two areas of attention, the focuses are quite different. Perhaps there has been more misunderstanding of the Survey through ignoring this distinction than in any other way. Evidently Falk and his authority find aspects of South Africa particularly distasteful, as I do. But there is little question that if we concentrate our attention on the rights being considered here there is a good deal more freedom in South Africa than in either Cuba or Tanzania. This is true in regard to the news media, for example, even if we focus on the black population of South Africa alone. Other topics that mean a great deal from the human rights perspective but little from that of the Survey, except as symbols, are such actions as the expelling of foreign reporters, or the forcing of foreign workers to leave as happened recently in Nigeria. The Survey examines only the degree to which each government lives up to its obligation to respect the political and civil rights of its own citizens.

Equally common is the criticism that the Survey is a "capitalist undertaking." This is evidently attributable to some impressions of Freedom House, which have little to do with its origins and purposes. It is true that we often note the economic system and the degree of government interference in the economy of a country or in the economic life of its citizens. In the 1982 yearbook we explicitly took up the question of economic freedoms and their relation to political and civil liberties; we have also addressed the problem in a variety of other forms over the years. Yet at no time have we said that we used the degree of capitalism in a social system as an indicator or even a considerable factor in our rating of freedom. We have explicitly pointed out that although the freedoms we consider are present only where there is a lack of thorough-going socialism, we do not regard this as necessarily a proof of more than historical association. In the piece by Lindsay Wright in the 1982 annual the point was developed that economic freedom implies the right of a people to decide on the economic system that they desire and to periodically review that decision. Clearly we regard the economic system as important and consider the many people who see economic rights as separate and perhaps prior to political rights have a case to make. But this is not our job; we want only to bring to the attention of readers this other dimension.

7

Introduction: Freedom

The question of ethnocentrism is more difficult. It has been addressed in the 1979 **Freedom in the** World (pages 75-82), but the argument comes in many forms. Liberal democratic rights as we define them developed historically out of Western Civilization. However, the fact that modern civilization is borrowed in large part from the West does not invalidate it or make it inapplicable to other parts of the world. Large parts of Western Civilization were in turn borrowed from other civilizations. The desires that advancing civilization address are universal. Everyone wants better housing, better nutrition, better health, and in some degree better education. Similarly we believe that people everywhere have shown over and over again that they want the basic rights that we include under the rubrics of political and civil liberties. No one really likes oppression and tyranny, although for short periods a tyrannous leader may be applauded. The emphasis put on political and civil rights may vary between peoples with different historical backgrounds, and the form of these rights will surely vary in the democratic world of the future, but we do not feel that the individuals that compose any people anywhere will prefer that they not have a say in the nature and composition of government or that they not be able to express opinions free of fear. Obviously, there are many people in the world who have had so little experience and knowledge of this kind of freedom that they do not conceive that it is actually possible to obtain. Such people will not make strenuous attempts to attain or maintain what we regard as basic freedoms until they have confidence in their possibility.

Falk's statement betrays in its reference to an "annual freedom map" the prevailing ignorance of the critics. Most critics evidently know only fleetingly and indirectly what the Survey is about. Very few even are aware of the yearbooks--or if aware have spent little time reading them.

Finally, the statement that the Survey is "increasingly scorned" is at least no longer true. It might be more correct to say that there is increasing familiarity with the Survey and use of its results. As I write these lines I have just returned from a Council of Europe meeting where I was pleased to note that the Survey was quoted in one of the orienting papers produced for the meeting, and also quoted from the floor. The Survey has become widely used in government and academia. The latest edition of the World Handbook[3] published by Yale University uses the Survey for some of its basic tables, while its conclusions are repeatedly referred to by the Encyclopedia of the Third World[4] and the

Country Reports on Human Rights Practices[5] of the U.S. Department of State. The Survey has also been used for a variety of correlation studies.[6]

In conclusion, the Surveys provide an orientation to one of the critical problems of the world--the attainment of political equality. They are not meant as a source of original information on this problem; many other individuals and organizations have much better facilities for this purpose. Through these annuals I have hoped to use the Surveys as an introduction or framework for the consideration of many special problems that relate to the overall problems of freedom. We hope that you will find both the Surveys and the special analyses and discussions they have inspired of continuing value.

Notes

1. "Human Rights Policies at the Multilateral Development Banks," Joint Hearing, Subcommittee on International Development Institutions and Finance of the Committee on Banking, Finance and Urban Affairs, and the Subcommittee on Africa of the Committee on Foreign Affairs, June 22, 1983 (Washington: Superintendent of Documents, 1983), page 90.

2. Richard Falk, "Comparative Protection of Human Rights in Capitalist and Socialist Third World Countries," Universal Human Rights, April-June 1979, pp. 3-29.

3. Charles L. Taylor and David A. Jodice, World Handbook of Political and Social Indicators, third edition, volume 1 (New Haven: Yale University Press, 1983), pp. 58-65.

4. George T. Kurian, Encyclopedia of the Third World (New York: Facts On File, 1982), three volumes.

5. United States Department of State, Country Reports on Human Rights Practices for 1982, February, 1983.

6. For example, Conway Henderson, "Military Regimes and Rights in Developing Countries: A Comparative Perspective," Human Rights Quarterly, 4,1 (Spring, 1982), pp. 110-123.

Survey Ratings and Tables for 1983

SURVEY RATINGS AND TABLES FOR 1983

Although freedom remained at issue in a large number of states since the last annual, there were no decisive shifts for or against political and civil liberties during the year. Most discouraging was the continuing retreat in Malta, Honduras, and Sri Lanka, resulting in these states falling off the list of free countries. Most encouraging was the overall continued incremental improvement in the "Southern Cone" of Latin America and the further entrenchment of freedom in several countries, most notably Spain.

The Tabulated Ratings

The accompanying Table 1 (Independent Nations) and Table 2 (Related Territories) rate each state or territory on seven-point scales for political and civil freedoms, and then provide an overall judgment of each as "free," "partly free," or "not free." In each scale, a rating of (1) is freest and (7) least free. Instead of using absolute standards, standards are comparative-- that is, most observers would be likely to judge states rated (1) as freer than those rated (2), and so on. No state, of course, is absolutely free or unfree, but the degree of freedom does make a great deal of difference to the quality of life.[1]

In **political rights**, states rated (1) have a fully competitive electoral process and those elected clearly rule. Most West European democracies belong here. Relatively free states may receive a (2) because, although the electoral process works and the elected rule, there are factors which cause us to lower our rating of the effective equality of the process. These factors may include extreme economic inequality, illiteracy, or intimidating violence. They also include the weakening of effective competition that is implied by the absence of periodic shifts in rule from one group or party to another.

11

Comparative Survey: 1983

TABLE 1

INDEPENDENT NATIONS:
COMPARATIVE MEASURES OF FREEDOM

	Political Rights[1]	Civil Liberties[1]	Status of Freedom[2]	Inf.Mort./ GNP/Cap.[3]
Afghanistan	7	7	NF	205/170
Albania	7	7	NF	47/840
Algeria	6	6	NF	118/2100
Angola	7	7	NF	154/800
Antigua & Barbuda	2	3 −	F	NA
Argentina	3 +	3 +	PF +	45/2600
Australia	1	1	F	11/12200
Austria	1	1	F	14/10300
Bahamas	2 −	2	F	32/3600
Bahrain	5	5	PF	53/7500
Bangladesh	6 −	5	PF	136/150
Barbados	1	1	F	25/3500
Belgium	1	1	F	11/12000
Belize	1	2	F	34/1100
Benin	7	6	NF	154/300
Bhutan	5	5	PF	150/80
Bolivia	2 +	3 +	F +	131/600
Botswana	2	3	F	83/900
Brazil	3 +	3	PF	77/2200
Bulgaria	7	7	NF	20/4200
Burma	7	7·	NF	101/200
Burundi	6 +	6	NF	122/250
Cambodia[4]	7	7	NF	212/100
Cameroon	6	6	NF	109/800
Canada	1	1	F	11/11200

Notes to the Table

1. The scales use the numbers 1–7, with 1 comparatively offering the highest level of political or civil rights and 7 the lowest. A plus or minus following a rating indicates an improvement or decline since the last year-book. A rating marked with a raised period (·) has been reevaluated by the author in this time; there may have been little change in the country.

2. A free state is designated by F, a partly free state by PF and a not-free state by NF.

3. Infant mortality per thousand live births over GNP per capita. Figures are from J. P. Lewis and V. Kallab (eds.), U. S. Foreign Policy and the Third World: Agenda 1983 (New York: Praeger 1983), pages 207–221.

4. Also known as Kampuchea.

5. Formerly New Hebrides.

6. See reference to the assessment in the Preface.

	Political Rights[1]	Civil Liberties[1]	Status of Freedom[2]	Inf.Mort./ GNP/Cap.[3]
Cape Verde Islands	6	6	NF	82/300
Central African Rep.	7	5	NF	149/300
Chad	7	6	NF	149/100
Chile	6	5	PF[6]	38/2600
China(Mainland)	6	6	NF	45/300
China(Taiwan)	5	5	PF	24/2500
Colombia	2	3	F	56/1300
Comoros	4	4·	PF	93/300
Congo	7	6	NF	129/1100
Costa Rica	1	1	F	24/1500
Cuba	6	6	NF	19/700
Cyprus(G)	1	2	F	18/3800
Cyprus(T)	4	3	PF	NA
Czechoslovakia	7	6	NF	17/5800
Denmark	1	1	F	9/12800
Djibouti	5	6	NF	NA/500
Dominica	2	2	F	20/750
Dominican Republic	1	2	F	68/1300
Ecuador	2	2	F	82/1200
Egypt	5	5	PF	103/650
El Salvador	4	5	PF	53/650
Equatorial Guinea	7	6	NF	143/200
Ethiopia	7	7	NF	147/150
Fiji	2	2	F	37/1900
Finland	2	2	F	8/10400
France	1	2	F	10/12100
Gabon	6	6	NF	117/3900
Gambia	3	4	PF	198/350
Germany(E)	7	7	NF	12/7200
Germany(W)	1	2	F	13/13500
Ghana	6	5	NF	103/400
Greece	1	2	F	19/4500
Grenada	7 −	6 −	NF	15/900
Guatemala	6	6	NF	70/1200
Guinea	7	7	NF	165/300
Guinea-Bissau	7·	6	NF	149/200
Guyana	5	5 −	PF	44/700
Haiti	7	6	NF	115/300
Honduras	3 −	3	PF −	88/600
Hungary	6	5	NF	23/4200
Iceland	1	1	F	8/12600
India	2	3	F	123/250
Indonesia	5	5	PF	93/500
Iran	6	6	NF	108/1900
Iraq	6	7	NF	78/3000
Ireland	1	1	F	12/5400
Israel	2	2	F	14/5500
Italy	1	2	F	14/6800
Ivory Coast	5	5	PF	127/1200

13

Comparative Survey: 1983

Table 1 (continued)	Political Rights[1]	Civil Liberties[1]	Status of Freedom[2]	Inf.Mort./ GNP/Cap.[3]
Jamaica	2	3	F	16/1200
Japan	1	1	F	7/10300
Jordan	6	6	NF	69/1600
Kenya	5	5	PF	87/400
Kiribati	1·+	2	F	NA
Korea(N)	7	7	NF	34/1100
Korea(S)	5	6 −	PF	34/1700
Kuwait	4	4	PF	39/26000
Laos	7	7	NF	129/100
Lebanon	5	4	PF	41/1900
Lesotho	5	5	PF	115/500
Liberia	5 +	5 +	PF +	154/500
Libya	6	6	NF	100/8600
Luxembourg	1	1	F	12/14000
Madagascar	5 +	6	PF·+	71/350
Malawi	6	7	NF	172/200
Malaysia	3	4	PF	31/1800
Maldives	5	5	PF	120/400
Mali	7	6	NF	154/200
Malta	2	4 −	PF −	16/4000
Mauritania	7	6	NF	143/500
Mauritius	2	2·+	F	33/1300
Mexico	3	4	PF	56/2300
Mongolia	7	7	NF	55/800
Morocco	4	5	PF	107/900
Mozambique	7	6 +	NF	115/250
Nauru	2	2	F	NA
Nepal	3	4	PF	150/150
Netherlands	1	1	F	9/11100
New Zealand	1	1	F	13/7600
Nicaragua	6	5	PF	90/900
Niger	7	6	NF	146/350
Nigeria	2	3	F	135/900
Norway	1	1	F	9/13800
Oman	6	6	NF	128/5900
Pakistan	7	5	NF	126/350
Panama	5	4 +	PF	34/1900
Papua New Guinea	2	2	F	104/800
Paraguay	5	5	PF	47/1600
Peru	2	3	F	88/1100
Philippines	5	5·−	PF	55/800
Poland	6·+	5	PF·+[6]	21/3900
Portugal	1 +	2	F	26/2500
Qatar	5	5	PF	53/28000
Romania	7	6	NF	32/2500
Rwanda	6	6	NF	107/250
St. Kitts & Nevis	2	2	F	NA
St. Lucia	2	2	F	33/850
St. Vincent	2	2	F	38/500

14

	Political Rights[1]	Civil Liberties[1]	Status of Freedom[2]	Inf.Mort./ GNP/Cap.[3]
Sao Tome & Principe	7·	7·	NF	50/400
Saudi Arabia	6	7·	NF	114/12700
Senegal	4	4	PF	147/500
Seychelles	6	6	NF	27/1800
Sierra Leone	5	5	PF	208/400
Singapore	4	5	PF	12/5200
Solomon Islands	2	2	F	78/600
Somalia	7	7	NF	147/300
South Africa	5	6	PF·+6	96/2300
Spain	1 +	2 +	F	11/5800
Sri Lanka	3 −	4 −	PF −	37/300
Sudan	5	5	PF	124/400
Suriname	7	6 −	NF	36/3000
Swaziland	5	5	PF	135/850
Sweden	1	1	F	7/14500
Switzerland	1	1	F	9/17200
Syria	6 −	7	NF	62/1600
Tanzania	6	6	NF	103/300
Thailand	3	4	PF	55/800
Togo	7	6	NF	109/400
Tonga	5	3	PF	21/500
Transkei	5	6	PF	NA
Trinidad & Tobago	1	2	F	26/5300
Tunisia	5	5	PF	100/1400
Turkey	4 +	5	PF	123/1500
Tuvalu	1	2	F	NA
Uganda	4·	5	PF	97/350
USSR	6	7	NF	36/4600
United Arab Emirates	5	5	PF	53/26000
United Kingdom	1	1	F	12/9000
United States	1	1	F	12/12500
Upper Volta	6	5	PF	211/250
Uruguay	5	4 +	PF	37/2800
Vanuatu[5]	2	4 −	PF −	NA
Venezuela	1	2	F	42/4200
Vietnam	7	6	NF	100/200
Western Samoa	4	3	PF	40/850
Yemen(N)	6	5	NF	162/450
Yemen(S)	6	7	NF	146/500
Yugoslavia	6	5	PF·6	33/2800
Zaire	6	7·−	NF	112/200
Zambia	5	6	PF	106/600
Zimbabwe	4·−	5	PF	74/800

15

T A B L E   2

R E L A T E D   T E R R I T O R I E S :

C O M P A R A T I V E   M E A S U R E S   O F   F R E E D O M

	Political Rights[1]	Civil Liberties[1]	Status of Freedom[2]	Inf.Mort./ GNP/Cap.[3]
Australia				
Christmas Island	4	2	PF	NA
Cocos Island	4	2	PF	NA
Norfolk Island	4	2	PF	NA
Chile				
Easter Island	7	5	NF	NA
Denmark				
Faroe Islands	2	1	F	NA
Greenland	2	1	F	NA
France				
French Guiana	3	2	PF	NA
French Polynesia	3	2	PF	38/6500
Guadeloupe	3	2	PF	25/3900
Martinique	3	2	PF	22/4600
Mayotte	2	2	F	NA
Monaco[4]	4	2	PF	NA
New Caledonia	3	2	F	30/7000
Reunion	3	2	PF	20/3800
St. Pierre &				
Miquelon	3	2	PF	NA
Wallis and Futuna	4	3	PF	NA
Israel				
Occupied Territories	5	5	PF	NA
Italy				
San Marino[4]	1	2	F	NA
Netherlands				
Neth. Antilles	2	2	F	25/4300

Notes to the Table

1, 2, 3. See Notes, Table 1.

4. These states are not listed as independent because all have explicit legal forms of dependence on a particular country (or countries in the case of Andorra) in such areas as foreign affairs, defense, or customs.

5. The geography and history of these newly independent "homelands" cause us to consider them dependencies.

6. Now in transition; high degree of self-determination.

	Political Rights[1]	Civil Liberties[1]	Status of Freedom[2]	Inf.Mort./ GNP/Cap.[3]
New Zealand				
Cook Islands	3 –	2	F	NA
Niue	2	2	F	NA
Tokelau Islands	4	2	PF	NA
Portugal				
Azores	2	2	F	NA
Macao	4.	4.	PF	18/2000
Madeira	2	2	F	NA
South Africa				
Bophuthatswana[5]	6	6	NF	NA
Ciskei[5]	6	6	NF	NA
SW Africa (Namibia)	6 –	5	NF –	120/1400
Venda[5]	6	6	NF	NA
Spain				
Canary Islands	1 +	2 +	F	NA
Places of Sovereignty in North Africa	1 +	2 +	F	NA
Switzerland				
Liechtenstein	4	1	PF	NA
United Kingdom				
Anguilla	2	2	F	NA
Bermuda	2	1	F	NA
B. Virgin Islands	3	2	PF	NA
Brunei[4]	6	5	NF	20/11900
Cayman Islands	2	2	F	NA
Channel Islands	2	1	F	11/6800
Falkland Islands	2	2	F	NA
Gibraltar	1	2	F	NA
Hong Kong	4	2	PF	13/5500
Isle of Man	2	2	F	NA
Montserrat	2	2	F	NA
St. Helena	2	2	F	NA
Turks and Caicos	2	2	F	NA
United States				
American Samoa	2	2	F	NA
Belau[6]	2	2	F	(31/920)
Federated States of Micronesia[6]	2	2	F	(31/920)
Guam	3	2	PF	16/7000
Marshall Islands[6]	2	2	F	(31/920)
Northern Marianas[6]	2	2	F	(31/920)
Puerto Rico	2	1	F	20/3000
Virgin Islands	2	3	F	NA
France-Spain Condominium				
Andorra[4]	3	3	PF	NA

Below this level, political ratings of (3) through (5) represent successively less effective implementation of democratic processes. Mexico, for example, has periodic elections and limited opposition, but for many years its governments have been selected outside the public view by the leaders of factions within the one dominant Mexican party. Governments of states rated (5) sometimes have no effective voting processes at all, but strive for consensus among a variety of groups in society in a way weakly analogous to those of the democracies. States at (6) do not allow competitive electoral processes that would give the people a chance to voice their desire for a new ruling party or for a change in policy. The rulers of states at this level assume that one person or a small group has the right to decide what is best for the nation, and that no one should be allowed to challenge that right. Such rulers do respond, however, to popular desire in some areas, or respect (and therefore are constrained by) belief systems (for example, Islam) that are the property of the society as a whole. At (7) the political despots at the top appear by their actions to feel little constraint from either public opinion or popular tradition.

Turning to the scale for **civil liberties**, in countries rated (1) publications are not closed because of the expression of rational political opinion, especially when the intent of the expression is to affect the legitimate political process. No major media are simply conduits for government propaganda. The courts protect the individual; persons are not imprisoned for their opinions; private rights and desires in education, occupation, religion, residence, and so on, are generally respected; law-abiding persons do not fear for their lives because of their rational political activities. States at this level include most traditional democracies. There are, of course, flaws in the liberties of all of these states, and these flaws are significant when measured against the standards these states set themselves.

Movement down from (2) to (7) represents a steady loss of the civil freedoms we have detailed. Compared to (1), the police and courts of states at (2) have more authoritarian traditions. In some cases they may simply have a less institutionalized or secure set of liberties, such as in Portugal or Greece. Those rated (3) or below may have political prisoners and generally varying forms of censorship. Too often their security services practice torture. States rated (6) almost always have political prisoners; usually the legitimate media are completely under government supervision; there is no right of assembly; and, often, travel, residence, and occupation are narrowly restricted. However, at (6) there still may be relative freedom in private conversation, especially in the home; illegal demonstrations do take place; underground literature is published, and so on. At (7) there is pervading fear, little independent expression takes place even in private, almost no public expressions of opposition emerge in the police-state environment, and imprisonment or execution is often swift and sure.

Political terror is an attempt by a government or private group to get its way through the use of murder, torture, exile, prevention of departure, police controls, or threats against the family. These weapons are usually directed against the expression of civil liberties. To this extent they surely are a part of the civil liberty "score." Unfortunately, because of their dramatic and newsworthy nature, such denials of civil liberties often become identified in the minds of informed persons with the whole of civil liberties.

In fact political terror is a tool of revolutionary repression of the right or left. When that repression is no longer necessary to achieve the suppression of civil liberties, then political terror is replaced by implacable and well-organized but often less general and newsworthy controls. Of course, there is a certain unfathomable terror in the sealed totalitarian state, yet life can be lived with a normality in these states that is impossible in the more dramatically terrorized. It would be a mistake to dismiss this apparent anomaly as an expression of a Survey bias. For the fact is there is, with all the blood, a much wider range of organized and personal expression of political opinion and judgment in Lebanon and El Salvador than in many other states.

In making the distinction between political terror and civil liberties as a whole we do not imply that the United States should not be urgently concerned with all violations of human rights and perhaps most urgently with those of political terror. Again it must be emphasized the the Survey is not a rating of relative desirability of societies--but of certain explicit freedoms.

A cumulative judgment of "free," "partly free," or "not free" is made on the basis of the foregoing seven-point ratings, and an understanding of how they were derived. Generally, states rated (1) and (2) will be "free"; those at (3), (4), and (5), "partly free"; and those at (6) and (7), "not free." When the ratings for political rights and civil liberties differ, the status of freedom must be decided by rough averaging. It must be remembered, however, that the ratings are not arithmetical units, but merely

TABLE 3

RANKING NATIONS BY POLITICAL RIGHTS

Most Free	Australia	Dominican	Japan	Sweden
	Austria	Republic	Kiribati	Switzerland
	Barbados	France	Luxembourg	Trinidad and
	Belgium	Germany (W)	Netherlands	Tobago
1	Belize	Greece	New Zealand	Tuvalu
	Canada	Iceland	Norway	United Kingdom
	Costa Rica	Ireland	Portugal	United States
	Cyprus (G)	Italy	Spain	Venezuela
	Denmark			
	Antigua and	Ecuador	Mauritius	St. Kitts and
	Barbuda	Fiji	Nauru	Nevis
	Bahamas	Finland	Nigeria	St. Lucia
2	Bolivia	India	Papua	St. Vincent
	Botswana	Israel	New Guinea	Solomon Isls.
	Colombia	Jamaica	Peru	Vanuatu
	Dominica	Malta		
	Argentina	Honduras	Nepal	Thailand
3	Brazil	Malaysia	Sri Lanka	
	Gambia	Mexico		
	Comoros	Kuwait	Singapore	Western
4	Cyprus(T)	Morocco	Turkey	Samoa
	El Salvador	Senegal	Uganda	Zimbabwe
	Bahrain	Kenya	Paraguay	Transkei
	Bhutan	Korea (S)	Philippines	Tunisia
	China (Taiwan)	Lebanon	Qatar	United Arab
5	Djibouti	Lesotho	Sierra Leone	Emirates
	Egypt	Liberia	South Africa	Uruguay
	Guyana	Madagascar	Sudan	Zambia
	Indonesia	Maldives	Swaziland	
	Ivory Coast	Panama	Tonga	
	Algeria	Cuba	Malawi	USSR
	Bangladesh	Gabon	Nicaragua	Upper Volta
	Burundi	Ghana	Oman	Yemen (N)
	Cameroon	Guatemala	Poland	Yemen (S)
6	Cape Verde	Hungary	Rwanda	Yugoslavia
	Islands	Iran	Saudi Arabia	Zaire
	Chile	Iraq	Seychelles	
	China	Jordan	Syria	
	(Mainland)	Libya	Tanzania	
	Afghanistan	Czechoslovakia	Mali	Somalia
	Albania	Equatorial	Mauritania	Suriname
	Angola	Guinea	Mongolia	Togo
	Benin	Ethiopia	Mozambique	Vietnam
7	Bulgaria	Germany (E)	Niger	
	Burma	Grenada	Pakistan	
	Cambodia	Guinea	Romania	
	Central	Guinea-Bissau	Sao Tome and	
	African Rep.	Haiti	Principe	
Least Free	Chad	Korea (N)		
	Congo	Laos		

TABLE 4
RANKING NATIONS BY CIVIL LIBERTIES

Most Free 1			
Australia	Costa Rica	Luxembourg	Switzerland
Austria	Denmark	Netherlands	United Kingdom
Barbados	Iceland	New Zealand	United States
Belgium	Ireland	Norway	
Canada	Japan	Sweden	

2

Bahamas	Finland	Nauru	Solomon Isls.
Belize	France	Papua	Spain
Cyprus (G)	Germany (W)	New Guinea	Trinidad and
Dominica	Greece	Portugal	Tobago
Dominican	Israel	St. Kitts and	Tuvalu
Republic	Italy	Nevis	Venezuela
Ecuador	Kiribati	St. Lucia	
Fiji	Mauritius	St. Vincent	

3

Antigua and	Botswana	Honduras	Peru
Barbuda	Brazil	India	Tonga
Argentina	Colombia	Jamaica	Western Samoa
Bolivia	Cyprus (T)	Nigeria	

4

Comoros	Malaysia	Panama	Uruguay
Gambia	Malta	Senegal	Vanuatu
Kuwait	Mexico	Sri Lanka	
Lebanon	Nepal	Thailand	

5

Bahrain	Guyana	Nicaragua	Swaziland
Bangladesh	Hungary	Pakistan	Tunisia
Bhutan	Indonesia	Paraguay	Turkey
Central	Ivory	Philippines	Uganda
African Rep.	Coast	Poland	United Arab
Chile	Kenya	Qatar	Emirates
China (Taiwan)	Lesotho	Sierra	Upper Volta
Egypt	Liberia	Leone	Yemen (N)
El Salvador	Maldives	Singapore	Yugoslavia
Ghana	Morocco	Sudan	Zimbabwe

6

Algeria	Czechoslovakia	Jordan	Rwanda
Benin	Djibouti	Korea (S)	Seychelles
Burundi	Equatorial	Libya	South Africa
Cameroon	Guinea	Madagascar	Suriname
Cape Verde Is.	Gabon	Mali	Tanzania
Chad	Grenada	Mauritania	Togo
China	Guatemala	Mozambique	Transkei
(Mainland)	Guinea-Bissau	Niger	Vietnam
Congo	Haiti	Oman	Zambia
Cuba	Iran	Romania	

7 Least Free			
Afghanistan	Ethiopia	Malawi	Syria
Albania	German (E)	Mongolia	USSR
Angola	Guinea	Sao Tome and	Yemen (S)
Bulgaria	Iraq	Principe	Zaire
Burma	Korea (N)	Saudi Arabia	
Cambodia	Laos	Somalia	

categories on arbitrary scales. There are, of course, marginal cases. A (6) and a (5) may lead either to a rating of "not free" or "partly free," depending on whether the (5) and (6) are a high (5) or low (5), a high (6) or low (6).

In place of "outlook" we have added this year a measure juxtoposing the infant mortality rate to the per capita GNP. This offers three pieces of knowledge to the reader in a short compass: the health care and nutrition standard of the population as a whole, the wealth of the society, and the extent to which the wealth is shared to provide the most basic necessities. The use of infant mortality statistics to measure the modernization of a society might have been thought to be outmoded by new measures such as the Physical Quality of Life Index (PQLI), which combines infant mortality, life expectancy, and literacy rates.[2] However, the doubtful comparability of literacy rates introduces an element of incomparability that is likely to make a society appear relatively more modernized or "equalized" than it is. For example, in the Overseas Development Council's table (referenced above) Mongolia, the Philippines, and Thailand have the same GNP/capita and the same infant mortality rates. However, because Mongolia claims 95% literacy its PQLI is given as considerably higher. This suggests either that literacy in Mongolia is incomparable or that literacy in Mongolia is used for purposes of state with little connection to the life of ordinary people. In either case, if we are interested in levels of modernity or "justice," it would seem best to stay away from literacy rates. Doubtless, infant mortality rates may also be "cooked." China's, for example, appears suspiciously low, and we wonder if reported infanticide is included. Yet overall cases of this kind of error appear to be considerably rarer.

We add this data this year as an experiment. It has long been felt that we have paid too little attention to the material correlates, conditions, or context of freedom or non-freedom. While we have argued elsewhere that there is no one-to-one relation between wealth and freedom, and that history has diffused freedom along with economic wealth more than one has produced the other, still the relationship is an important one to ponder and present.

The reporting period covered by this Survey (August 1, 1982, to November, 1983) does not correspond with the calendar of short-term events in the countries rated. For this reason the yearly Survey may mask or play down important events that occur during the year.

Declines in Freedom

Declines in freedom since the last annual were generally small, although in some cases of considerable significance.

The closing of a newspaper in **Antigua and Barbuda** in 1982 reflected a more repressive atmosphere. The 1982 election in the **Bahamas** was accompanied by unnecessary government threats and controversies. The government broadcasting service was also manipulated to affect the result. Continuing military government in **Bangladesh** reduces its freedom.

In **Grenada** a coup in October 1983 further removed the radical left government from the "popular" movement that brought it to power. The rule of law declined further in **Guyana** where government terror has become expected and opposition voices are under threat in so far as they continue to exist. The increased military activity and U.S. involvement in **Honduras** has been accompanied by the reassertion of the leadership role of the military. Freedom has progressively declined in **Malta**. A gerrymandered election victory has been accompanied by further control of the broadcast media to prevent criticism of the government, as well as pressure on the opposition. In the **Philippines** increased violence has led to an increasing lack of press freedom, or freedom to speak out without fear.

The decline in freedom in **Sri Lanka** has been progressive. The incumbent party successfully banned the leader of the opposition from politics. In late 1982 a referendum without full opportunity for debate postponed for six years the need of the recently elected (and largely one-party) parliament to face the ballot. In 1982 riots destroyed the position of the Tamil minority, and their party (the largest opposition group in parliament) was proscribed because of its presumed support of separatism. Moving Sri Lanka to the partly free column is particularly painful because of its strong adherence to democracy and its achievement under regimes of both left and right of a very high "quality of life" relative to income. We had welcomed the intentions of the new government to reduce the high degree of government interference in the economy, but clearly this fails to guarantee the more politically relevant freedoms.

In December 1982 the government of **Suriname** killed fifteen opposition leaders in a general repression of unions, the news media, and all public demonstrations. Violent suppression of traditionalist Muslim opposition in **Syria** has further silenced

23

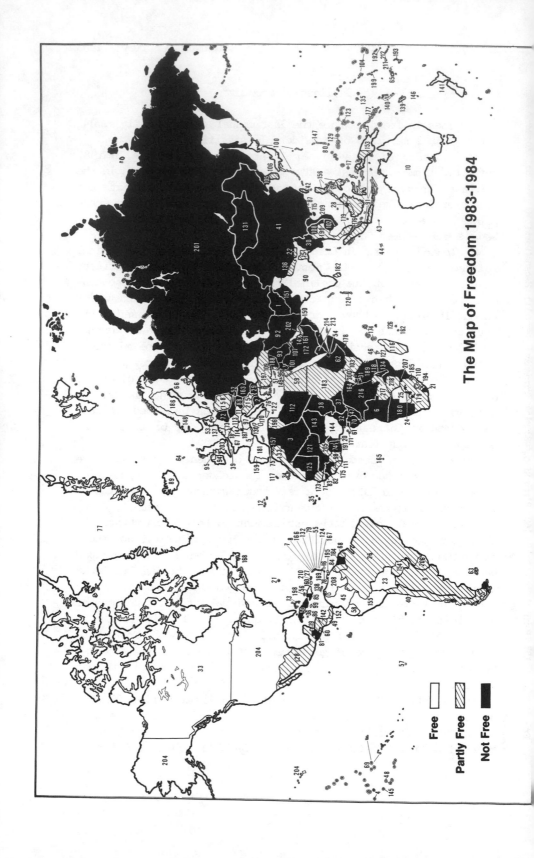

The Map of Freedom 1983-1984

Free

Partly Free

Not Free

Free

Countries

8	Antigua & Barbuda
10	Australia
11	Austria
13	Bahamas
16	Barbados
18	Belgium
19	Belize
23	Bolivia
25	Botswana
33	Canada
45	Colombia
49	Costa Rica
51a	Cyprus(G)
53	Denmark
55	Dominica
56	Dominican Republic
58	Ecuador
65	Fiji
66	Finland
67	France
73	Germany (W)
76	Greece
89	Iceland
90	India
94	Ireland
96	Israel
97	Italy
99	Jamaica
100	Japan
104	Kiribati
114	Luxembourg
126	Mauritius
135	Nauru
137	Netherlands
141	New Zealand
144	Nigeria
148	Norway
153	Papua N. G.
155	Peru
159	Portugal
166	St. Kitts & Nevis
167	St. Lucia
169	St. Vincent
177	Solomon Isls.
181	Spain
186	Sweden
187	Switzerland
195	Trinidad & Tobago
199	Tuvalu
203	U. K.
204	U. S. A.
208	Venezuela

Related Territories

4	Am. Samoa (US)
7	Anguilla (UK)
12	Azores (Port)
17	Belau (US)
21	Bermuda (UK)
34	Canary Isls.(Sp)
36	Cayman Isls.(UK)
39	Channel Isls.(UK)
48	Cook Isls.(NZ)
63	Falkland Isls.(UK)
64	Faroe Isls.(Den)
75	Gibraltar (UK)
77	Greenland (Den)
95	Isle of Man (UK)
117	Madeira (Port)
123	Marshall Isls.(US)
127	Mayotte (Fr)
129	Micronesia (US)
132	Montserrat (UK)
138	Ne. Antilles(Ne)
139	New Caledonia(Fr)
145	Niue (NZ)
147	No. Marianas(US)
157	P.o.S.i.N.Afr.(Sp)
160	P'rto Rico (US)
165	St. Helena (UK)
170	San Marino (It)
198	Turks & Caicos (UK)
210	Virgin Islands (US)

Partly Free

Countries

9	Argentina
14	Bahrain
15	Bangladesh
22	Bhutan
26	Brazil
40	Chile
42	China (Taiwan)
46	Comoros
51b	Cyprus (T)
59	Egypt
60	El Salvador
71	Gambia
84	Guyana
86	Honduras
91	Indonesia
98	Ivory Coast
103	Kenya
106	Korea (South)
107	Kuwait
109	Lebanon
110	Lesotho
111	Liberia
116	Madagascar
119	Malaysia
120	Maldives
122	Malta
128	Mexico
133	Morocco
136	Nepal
142	Nicaragua
152	Panama
154	Paraguay
156	Philippines
158	Poland
161	Qatar
173	Senegal
175	Sierra Leone
176	Singapore
179	So. Africa
182	Sri Lanka
183	Sudan
185	Swaziland
190	Thailand
193	Tonga
194	Transkei
196	Tunisia
197	Turkey
200	Uganda
202	U. A. Ems.
205	Upper Volta
206	Uruguay
140	Vanuatu
212	W. Samoa
215	Yugoslavia
217	Zambia
218	Zimbabwe

Related Territories

5	Andorra (F-S)
27	British Vir.Is.(UK)
43	Christmas Isl. (Aus)
44	Cocos Isls. (Aus)
68	French Guiana (Fr)
69	French Polynesia(Fr)
79	Guadeloupe(Fr)
80	Guam (US)
87	Hong Kong(UK)
113	Liechtenst.(Sw)
115	Macao (Port)
124	Martinique (Fr)
130	Monaco (Fr)
146	Norfolk Is.(Aus)
149	Occupied Terrs.-(Isr)
162	Reunion (Fr)
168	St. Pierre & Miquelon (Fr)
192	Tokelau Is.(NZ)
211	Wallis & Futuna (Fr)

Not Free

Countries

1	Afghanistan
2	Albania
3	Algeria
6	Angola
20	Benin
29	Bulgaria
30	Burma
31	Burundi
102	Cambodia
32	Cameroon
35	Cape Verde Is.
37	Central Afr. Republic
38	Chad
41	China (Mainland)
47	Congo
50	Cuba
52	Czechoslovakia
54	Djibouti
61	Eq. Guinea
62	Ethiopia
70	Gabon
72	Germany (E)
74	Ghana
78	Grenada
81	Guatemala
82	Guinea
83	Guinea-Bissau
85	Haiti
88	Hungary
92	Iran
93	Iraq
101	Jordan
105	Korea (N)
108	Laos
112	Libya
118	Malawi
121	Mali
125	Mauritania
131	Mongolia
134	Mozambique
143	Niger
150	Oman
151	Pakistan
163	Romania
164	Rwanda
171	Sao Tome & Principe
172	Saudi Arabia
174	Seychelles
178	Somalia
184	Suriname
188	Syria
189	Tanzania
191	Togo
201	USSR
209	Vietnam
213	Yemen (N)
214	Yemen (S)
216	Zaire

Related Territories

24	Bophuthatswana (S. Afr.)
28	Brunei (UK)
219	Ciskei (S.Afr.)
57	Easter Is.(Chile)
180	S. West Africa-Namibia (S.Afr.)
207	Venda (S.Africa)

opponents of the regime. **Vanuatu's** troubled transition to independence was further clouded by the closing of its only independent news outlet and the expulsion of its editor. Government
terror and corruption have generally increased in recent years in
Zaire in spite of recurrent attempts at reform. Setting aside the
elected regime in **Namibia** in favor of direct rule by South Africa
represented a setback.

Advances in Freedom

Argentina is again returning to civilian rule, following a
well-contested election on October 30. However, the record of
persistent military intervention and suppressions and its anti-
democratic heritage makes it impossible for the country to emerge
immediately with full freedoms. The situation is similar to that
in **Bolivia** which reestablished democratic forms in 1982. However,
Bolivia did not suffer as harshly under repression, and its democratic institutions appear stronger. **Brazil's** general election
in November 1982 directly affected all positions but the presi-
dency, which remains the center of power. Nevertheless, the
elections were open, hard fought, and have led to a significant
transfer of power.

One-party elections in **Burundi** allowed some choice.

The 1982 presidential election in **Madagascar** allowed limited
but significant opposition. Although this notable move toward
the recreation of competitive politics was followed by the arrest
of the opposition candidate, there is still a variety of accepted
parties within the "front" that compete strongly, as in the 1983
local and legislative elections. Recent events suggest that the
opposition can organize and express its opinions and that the
courts can decide against the government in political cases.
While **Mozambique** continues to deny the civil liberties expected in
the West, its emphasis on response to popular complaint and on
large public meetings with vigorous exchange of opinions requires
additional recognition.

Liberia is well on the way to return to constitutionalism. A
democratic constitution has been drafted and widely reviewed by
representatives of many groups in the society. There are few, if
any, prisoners of conscience and the press represents a variety of
views. Political activity will, however, only be allowed in 1984.

In spite of recurrent setbacks the media in **Panama** have become progressively stronger and more independent, and its party organizations more developed. The initial phase of the military regime in **Poland** is over, and the civilian Party and parliament have regained some of their former power. Recent constitutional change in **Portugal** marked the end of military oversight. It dissolved the Council of the Revolution, the last formal institution for military intervention in the governmental process. **Spain's** 1982 election was remarkably free, both in form, and, by implication, through the results--the ruling party was decisively rejected. All parts of the political spectrum took part, including fascists and anti-democrats such as are denied participation in many European states. The resulting government has resolutely opposed military interference in political policy. This does not imply that democracy is fully secure in Spain, but it has for the time being attained high standards. Rights improved in parallel in the **Canary Islands** and **Places of Sovereignty**--Spain's related territories.

Turkey's constitutional plus presidential election in 1982 and legislative elections in 1983 constituted democratic steps, yet in view of previous democratic achievements by the military in Turkey they were disappointingly small steps. No effective opposition campaigning was allowed in the first instance, while the major parties and major political figures that might have participated in 1983 were largely and systematically excluded. There was an increase in political activity in **Uruguay,** although the political opening was suspended in the last half of 1983.

Other Significant Changes

St. Kitts and Nevis became fully independent in 1983. However, since this former British colony already possessed a fully functioning democratic system this did not involve a marked improvement in rights. St Kitts and Nevis joined a chain of democratic states that had previously emerged from the same background in the eastern Caribbean. The exception has been Grenada. The intervention in **Grenada** by American and Caribbean forces just as this yearbook was put in final form can only be recorded in the Survey as a further diminishment of the rights of Grenadians. However, by the time this book is published we assume that one ostensible objective of this foreign intervention--to restore constitutional democracy--will be well on its way toward achievement. The people of the region are in general sufficiently acquainted with democratic forms to make this outcome probable.

Readers of past Surveys will also note the improvement in the status of **South Africa, Yugoslavia**, and **Poland**, largely on the basis of the Survey's continual **reevaluation.** These states have long hovered on the boundary between free and partly free, with equal numerical scores of 6 and 5 (or 5 and 6) for political and civil rights. In the 1982 yearbook South Africa was moved to the "not free" category primarily because of its forced resettlement of blacks in its "homelands," a policy that still continues.

The reason for placing these three states in the "partly free" category is it will better serve the educational purposes of the Survey. The purpose of the Comparative Survey is to make distinctions--to group together what belongs together and separate what belongs apart. On reviewing the whole Survey it appeared that states grouped together in the "not free" category covered simply too broad a spectrum in terms of their performance in the political and civil rights areas. It seemed therefore to be imperitive that we "break out" some of these states and place them together in a freer category.

South Africa and Yugoslavia are not "not free" for very different reasons. In South Africa there is simply too much publicly aired controversy for a not free state. This has been made especially clear in 1983 through the controversy surrounding the government's plan to grant political rights to the Coloured and Indian communities. Within South Africa this plan has been condemned at major conferences of Black leaders representing hundreds of thousands or millions. The criticism from the White community was equally open and unrestricted, from both right and left.

The reasons for seeing Yugoslavia as not conforming to the "not free" category are entirely different. Freedoms of group organization and expression are much more restricted in Yugoslavia than in South Africa. There is only a cautious degree of criticism and controversy in the press. However, the country is quite open to foreign media of all kinds, and the movement of people into and out of the country is far beyond that allowed in a closed society. Decentralization in industry is extended to the press which uses even American news services. In spite of recent repressions of the Albanian minority, the leaders of the constituent republics have more power and relatively more independence than in other communist states. Yugoslavia's ability to reject Soviet control also adds to its political freedom relative to most of Eastern Europe.

In spite of the continuation of many elements of military rule Poland has retained its position as the only truly embattled communist state. The power of the Catholic Church and the people, symbolized in part by the long periods of relative freedom of Lech Walesa, places Poland in a different category. The amazing vitality and wide distribution of the underground independent press has certainly never been matched in other communist countries.[3] The relatively independent religious publications are also an anomaly, as are repeated public outbursts on a mass scale, and the persistent decline in Party membership under the pressure of popular disapproval of communism.

As a result of these changes the border between partly free and not free societies becomes more clearly that between open and closed societies. Yet there can never be any clear break between countries that fall essentially along a continuum.

In particular it is easy to overestimate what we are saying. South Africa, Poland, and Yugoslavia are still the same repressive societies, societies in which the majority are not given the chance to organize a successful challenge to governing elites. (This is, of course, essentially true of nearly all "partly free" states.) In all three, many hundreds are arrested and often imprisoned for reasons essentially of conscience. Some other societies that continue to be rated "not free," for example Hungary or Tanzania, have many of the attributes of openness that characterize the three, yet they do not have the pluralism and the distribution of power we find in this group. This is a comparative survey and in the final analysis Poland, Yugoslavia, and South Africa have more in common with Singapore, the Philippines (1982), or Paraguay than they have in common with the "not free" Soviet Union, Zaire, or Somalia.

Those surprised or disturbed by the new categorization of South Africa should remember that this is a **comparative** survey. They should ask themselves whether they really consider South Africa to be less free than Chile, a country with an equal rating. Those surprised at the new ratings of Poland or Yugoslavia should ask whether they consider these states less free than South Africa. Unfortunately, these judgments are always made in the flux of events. States at this level are always "clamping down," and thus threatening to become less free. Generally a year later the situation has not changed a great deal, but it is quite possible that just as we change the rating of a state such as Poland, it will indeed move again into a harsher phase.   Freedoms are seldom effectively institutionalized in a partly free state.

Elections and Referenda

Evidence for political freedom is primarily found in the occurrence and nature of elections or referenda.   Therefore, as a supplement to our ratings we have attempted in the accompanying Table 5 to summarize the national elections that we recorded for independent countries since mid-1982.   (Non-national elections are included only in a few instances.)   The reader should assume that the electoral process appeared comparatively open and competitive unless our remarks suggest otherwise; extremely one-sided outcomes imply an unacceptable electoral process.   Voter participation figures are often not comparable, even when available. Many states compel their citizens to vote, in others it is unclear whether participation is a percentage of those registered or of those of voting age.

Political-Economic Systems and Freedom

Table 6 (Political-Economic Systems) fills two needs.   It offers the reader additional information about the countries we have rated.   For example, readers with libertarian views may wish to raise the relative ratings of capitalist countries, while those who place more value on redistributive systems may wish to raise the ratings of countries toward the socialist end of the spectrum. The table also makes possible an analysis of the relation between political and economic forms and the freedom ratings of the Survey.   Perusal of the table will show that freedom is directly related to the existence of multiparty systems: the further a country is from such systems, the less freedom it is likely to have.   This could be considered a trivial result, since a publicly competitive political system is one of the criteria of freedom, and political parties are considered evidence for such competition.   However, the result is not simply determined by our definitions: we searched for evidence of authentic public competition in countries without competitive parties, and seldom found the

TABLE 5
NATIONAL ELECTIONS AND REFERENDA

Nation and Date	Type of Election	Participation	Results and Remarks
Albania 11/14/82	parliamentary	100%	single approved list; one vote against
Argentina 10/30/83	general	NA	heavy and competitive campaigning; civilian cause wins in upset
Australia 3/5/83	parliamentary	NA	ruling coalition defeated
Austria 4/24/83	parliamentary	91%	leads to resignation of leader
Brazil 11/15/82	regional and parliamentary	NA	opposition received more votes; controls some governorships; still minority in assembly
Burundi 10/22/82	parliamentary	95%	single party, choice from selected list
Cameroon 5/29/83	parliamentary	99%	one party, single list
Equatorial Guinea 8/15/82	referendum	NA	nonfree referendum to extend presidential term; 95% approve
8/28/83	legislative	50%?	nonparty; apparently pre-selected
Finland 3/20–21/83	parliamentary	NA	major parties all lose
Germany(W)	parliamentary	89%	government improves position
Iceland 4/23/83	parliamentary	88%	governing coalition loses slightly
Ireland 11/24/82	parlaimentary	NA	new coalition results;no majority
Italy 6/27/83	parliamentary	NA	small parties gain; largest declines
Japan 6/26/83	upper house	57%	government wins by large margin
Kenya 9/26/83	parliamentary	48%	one party; some strongly contested; many replaced; lower participation
Kiribati 1/12–19/83 2/17/83	parliamentary presidential	NA NA	fair, contested, nonparty president wins with 49.6%
Madagascar 11/7/82	presidential	NA	opponent receives over 20%; later arrested
8/28/83	legislative	73%	some real competition within front; defeated presidential candidate elected to assembly
Malawi 6/27–28/83	parliamentary	NA	one party approved choices; no campaigning

Comparative Survey: 1983

Mauritius 8/21/83	parliamentary	NA	ruling coalition wins; partially reversing last election
Morocco 6/10/83 9/ /83	municipal parliamentary	72%	highly competitive; results disputed
Netherlands 9/8/82	parliamentary	81%	coalition loses support; new coalition formed
Nigeria 8/6/83	presidential	40%	president wins; some results disputed
8/13/83	gubernatorial	70%	well-contested; fraud and violence in some areas
8/20/83	senatorial	NA	government wins; court reverses some results
8/27/83	lower house	NA	government wins in bandwagon
9/13/83	state legislative	NA	government wins most areas
Paraguay 2/6/83	general	90%	president and party wins with ninety percent; heavy rigging
Portugal 4/25/83	parliamentary	NA	socialists gain; open contest
Senegal 2/27/83	general	58%	eight parties, coalitions illegal government wins overwhelmingly; fraud in places; open discussion
Seychelles	parliamentary	59%	one-party; most unopposed
South Africa	referendum	NA	whites approve political rights for Coloureds and Indians
Spain 10/28/82 5/8/83	parliamentary regional	80% NA	government overwhelmingly defeated socialists win most assemblies
Sri Lanka 10/20/83 12/22/82	presidential referendum	81% 71% (of regist)	president wins with 53% extended term of parliament another six years; opposition restricted
Sudan 4/14-25/83	presidential	NA	99.6% approve single candidate
Swaziland 10/83	parliamentary		
Sweden 9/19/82	parliamentary	92%	oposition regains government; still a minority
Switzerland 11/28/82	referendum	32%	approve price control authority
Thailand 4/18/83	parliamentary	53%	government coalition wins; many parties compete; army involved

Turkey
| 11/7/82 | referendum | 95% (compulsory) | approve constitution 92% and president for 7 years; restricted campaign |
| 11/6/83 | parliamentary | NA | major traditional parties excluded; most anti-military alternative wins |

| United Kingdom | parliamentary | 73% | government wins open contest with 42% |

United States
| 11/2/82 | legislative & regional | NA | opposition gains |

Uruguay
| 11/28/82 | party | 60% | anti-government factions win |

Vanuatu
| 11/2/83 | parliamentary | NA | government apparently wins |

Western Samoa
| 2/82 | parliamentary | NA | opponent wins; results voided by courts; winner resigns; judge leaves |

Zaire
| 9/18-19/82 | parliamentary | NA | compulsory vote; one party; some choice |

Zambia
| 10/27/83 | general | NA | single party wins easily; only one presidential candidate |

33

search rewarded. Both theoretical and empirical studies indicate the difficulty of effective public political opposition in one-party systems.

The relation between economic systems and freedom is more complicated and, because of our lack of emphasis on economic systems in devising our ratings of freedom, is not predetermined by our methods. Historically, the table suggests that there are three types of societies competing for acceptance in the world. The first, or **traditional** type, is marginal and in retreat, but its adherents have borrowed political and economic bits and pieces from both the other types. The second and third, the **Euro-American** and **Sino-Soviet** types, are strongest near their points of origin, but have spread by diffusion and active propagation all over the world. The Leninist-socialist style of political organization was exported along with the socialist concept of economic organization, just as constitutional democracy had been exported along with capitalist economic concepts. In this interpretation, the relation of economic systems to freedom found in the table may be an expression of historical chance rather than necessary relationships. Clearly, capitalism does not cause nations to be politically free, nor does socialism cause them to be politically unfree.[4] Still, socialists must be concerned by the empirical relationship between the rating of "not free" and socialism that is found in tables such as this.

In the table, economies are roughly grouped in categories from "capitalist" to "socialist." Labeling economies as capitalist or socialist has a fairly clear significance in the developed world, but it may be doubted that it is very useful to label the mostly poor and largely agrarian societies of the third world in this manner. However, third world states with dual economies, that is, with a modern sector and a preindustrial sector, have economic policies or goals that can be placed along the continuum from socialist to capitalist. A socialist third world state has usually nationalized all of the modern sector--except possibly some foreign investment--and claims central government jurisdiction over the land and its products, with only temporary assignment of land to individuals or cooperatives. The capitalist third world state has a capitalist modern sector and a traditionalist agricultural sector, combined in some cases with new agricultural projects either on family farm or agribusiness models. Third world economies that fall between capitalist and socialist do not have the high taxes of their industrialized equivalents, but they have major nationalized industries (for example, oil) in the modern sector, and their agricultural world may include emphasis on cooperatives or large-scale land reform, as well as more traditional forms.

States with **inclusive capitalist** forms are generally developed states that rely on the operation of the market and on private provision for industrial welfare. Taxes may be high, but they are not confiscatory, while government interference is generally limited to subsidy and regulation. States classified as **noninclusive capitalist**, such as Liberia or Thailand, have not over fifty percent of the population included in a capitalist modern economy, with the remainder of the population still living traditionally. In such states the traditional economy may be individual, communal, or feudal, but the direction of change as development proceeds is capitalistic.

Capitalist states grade over into capitalist-statist or capitalist-socialist nations. **Capitalist-statist** nations are those such as Brazil, Turkey, or Saudi Arabia, that have very large government productive enterprises, either because of an elitist development philosophy or major dependence on a key resource such as oil. Government interferes in the economy in a major way in such states, but not primarily because of egalitarian motives. **Mixed capitalist** systems, such as those in Israel, the Netherlands, or Sweden, provide social services on a large scale through governmental or other nonprofit institutions, with the result that private control over property is sacrificed to egalitarian purposes. These nations still see capitalism as legitimate, but its legitimacy is accepted grudgingly by many in government. **Mixed socialist** states, such as Syria or Poland, proclaim themselves to be socialist but in fact allow rather large portions of the economy to remain in the private domain. The terms **inclusive** and **noninclusive** are used to distinguish between societies in which the economic activities of most people are organized in accordance with the dominant system and those dual societies in which fifty percent or more of the population remain largely outside.

Socialist economies, on the other hand, strive programmatically to place an entire national economy under direct or indirect government control. States such as the USSR or Cuba may allow some modest private productive property, but this is only by exception, and rights to such property can be revoked at any time. The leaders of **noninclusive socialist** states have the same goals as the leaders of inclusive socialist states, but their relatively primitive economies or peoples have not yet been effectively included in the socialist system. Such states generally have a

POLITICAL SYSTEM:	Multiparty		Dominant-Party
ECONOMIC SYSTEM:	centralized	decentralized	
Capitalist inclusive	Antigua & Barbuda F; Bahamas F; Barbados F; Belize F; Colombia[4] F; Costa Rica F; Cyprus(G) F; Cyprus(T) PF; Dominica[4] F; Dominican Republic[4] F; El Salvador[1/3] PF; Iceland F; Ireland F; Japan F; Korea(S)[1] PF; Luxembourg F; Mauritius F; New Zealand[3] F; St.Kitts & N. F; St. Lucia[3] F; St. Vincent[3] F; Spain F	Australia F; Belgium F; Canada F; Germany(W)[3] F; Lebanon PF; Switzerland F; United States F	Malaysia PF
non-inclusive	Ecuador F; Fiji[4] F; Gambia[4] PF; Honduras[4] PF; Thailand[1] PF	Botswana F; Papua New Guinea F; Solomon Islands[2] F	Haiti NF; Lesotho PF; Transkei PF
Capitalist-Statist inclusive	Argentina[1] PF; Italy F; Jamaica[3] F; South Africa PF; Sri Lanka PF; Turkey[1/4] PF; Venezuela F	Brazil[1/3/4] PF; Trinidad & Tobago F	China(Taiwan) PF; Mexico PF; Panama[1/3/4] PF
non-inclusive	Bolivia F; Morocco[3] PF; Peru[4] F; Uganda[1/3] PF	India F; Nigeria[3/4] F; Vanuatu PF	Indonesia[1/4] PF; Iran[2/4] NF; Paraguay[1/3/4] PF; Philippines PF; Zimbabwe[4] PF
Mixed Capitalist inclusive	Austria F; Denmark F; Finland F; France F; Greece F; Israel F; Malta PF; Netherlands F; Norway F; Portugal F; Sweden F; U.K.[3] F		Egypt[3/4] PF; Senegal[3/4] PF; Singapore PF; Tunisia[4] PF
Mixed Socialist inclusive			Grenada NF; Guyana PF; Syria[1/4] NF
non-inclusive			Madagascar[1/2] PF
Socialist inclusive			
non-inclusive			

Notes to the Table

1. Military dominated. (All countries in the Nonparty Military column are military dominated.)
2. Party relationships anomalous.
3. Close decision along capitalist-to-socialist continuum.
4. Close decision on inclusive/noninclusive dimension.
5. Noninclusive.

	One-Party		Non-Party		
	socialist	communist	nationalist	military	nonmilitary
			Djibouti NF	Chile[3] PF Suriname NF	Jordan[3/4] NF Western Samoa[2/4] PF
	Sierra Leone PF		Cameroon[3] NF Gabon NF Ivory Coast[4] PF Kenya PF Malawi NF	Chad NF Guatemala NF Liberia PF Niger NF Yemen (N) NF	Bhutan[3] PF Comoros PF Maldives PF Nepal[3] PF Swaziland PF Tonga PF Tuvalu F
				Ghana NF	Bahrain PF Kuwait PF Nauru F Qatar PF S~di Arabia NF U.Arab Ems. PF
			Zaire[1] NF	Bangladesh PF Central Afr. Republic[3] NF Eq. Guinea[3] NF Mauritania NF Pakistan[2] NF	Kiribati F Oman NF
	Burundi[1/5] NF			Uruguay[2] PF	Nicaragua PF
	Libya[1/2/3] NF S~chelles[3] NF	Poland[1] PF Yugoslavia[3] PF			
	Burma[1] NF Cape V[3/4] NF Congo[1/3] NF Somalia[1/3] NF Zambia[3] PF		Mali[1] NF Rwanda[1/3] NF Sudan[1] PF Togo[1] NF	Upper Volta PF	
	Algeria[1] NF Sao Tome & Prin.[3/4] NF	Albania NF Hungary NF Bulgaria NF Korea(N) NF China(M) NF Mongolia NF Cuba NF Romania NF Czechoslovakia NF USSR NF Germany(E) NF Vietnam NF			
	Angola NF Benin[1/3] NF Guinea NF Guinea-Bissau[1/3] NF Iraq[1/3/4] NF Mozambique NF Tanzania NF Yemen(S) NF	Afghanistan NF Cambodia NF Laos NF		Ethiopia[3] NF	

small socialized modern economy and a large preindustrial economy in which the organization of production and trade is still largely traditional. It should be understood that the characterizations in the table are impressionistic; the continuum between capitalist and socialist economies is necessasrily cut arbitrarily into categories for this presentation.

Political systems range from democratic multiparty to absolutist one-party systems. Theoretically, the most democratic countries should be those with **decentralized multiparty systems**, for here important powers are held by the people at two or more levels of the political system, and dissent is legitimated and mobilized by opposition parties. More common are **centralized multiparty systems**, such as France or Japan, in which the central government organizes lower levels of government primarily for reasons of efficiency. **Dominant-party systems** allow the forms of democracy, but structure the political process so that opposition groups do not have a realistic chance of achieving power. Such limitations may be through vote fraud, imprisonment of opposition leaders, or other devices.

The now classical form of **one-party** rule is that in states such as the USSR or Vietnam that proclaim themselves to be **communist**. The slightly larger group of **socialist one-party** states are ruled by elites that use Marxist-Leninist rhetoric, organize ruling parties very much along communist lines, but either do not have the disciplined organization of communist states or have explicitly rejected one or another aspect of communism. A final group of **nationalist one-party** states adopts the political form popularized by the communists (and the fascists in the last generation), but the leaders generally reject the revolutionary ideologies of socialist or communist states and fail to develop the totalitarian controls that characterize these states. There are several borderline states that might be switched between socialist and nationalist categories (for example, Libya). "Socialist" is used here to designate a political rather than economic system. A socialist "vanguard party" established along Marxist-Leninist lines will almost surely develop a socialist economy, but a state with a socialist economy need not be ruled by a vanguard party. It should be pointed out that the totalitarian-libertarian continuum is not directly reflected by the categorization in this table.

Nonparty systems can be democratic, as in the small island of Nauru, but generally they are not. Such systems may be **nonmilitary nonparty systems** ranging from Tonga to Saudi Arabia. Much more important are the many **military nonparty systems**, such as that in Niger or Pakistan.

Economic Systems and Economic Freedom

In the 1982 annual we examined in depth the nature of economic freedoms and their relationship to politico-economic systems and to political and civil rights. This reflected the implicit importance of certain freedoms in the economic sphere to the assessment by many analysts of a country's overall freedom. Table 7 on Economic Freedoms and Economic Systems enables a comparison of the relationship between economic freedoms, rated along a continuum of low to high, and economic systems. It reproduces in a different form some of the information provided in the more comprehensive and lengthy Table on Comparative Economic Measures that appeared in **Freedom in the World: 1982.**[5]

With a few exceptions, the economic freedom ratings remain unchanged from last year. Economic systems tend to change much more slowly than do political leaders or even political systems. Particularly in democracies, changes in economic structures tend to be evolutionary and subject to repeated rationalization and justification at frequent intervals. Conversely, a radical change in political system coupled with a shift in fundamental economic theory may bring few changes to the basic economy despite government pronouncements to the contrary. For these reasons we do not reassess economic freedoms annually.

In our analysis of a country's economic freedom we have tried to take a human rights approach that reflects the desires of individuals and groups in all countries to achieve or maintain control over their own lives. Using several criteria we evaluated the status of four basic economic freedoms on a country-by-country basis within and across politico-economic systems. A scale ranging from **high** to **low** was used to rate each of the four economic freedoms in each country. These individual ratings were then averaged to obtain a single rating of a country's overall economic freedom.

The four economic freedoms on which the overall assessment is based are freedom to have and control property, freedom of association, freedom of movement, and freedom of information, as they

T A B L E   7

ECONOMIC FREEDOM:	High		Medium-High	Medium

ECONOMIC SYSTEM:	Antigua &
	  Barbuda F
	Australia F
	Bahamas F
	Barbados F
	Belgium F
		Ireland F
		Japan F
		Luxembourg F
		Mauritius F
		New Zealand F
		St. Kitts &
			Cyprus(T) PF
			Djibouti NF
			Dominican
			  Republic F
			Lebanon PF
			Western Samoa PF
				Chile PF
				Colombia F
				El Salvador PF
				Jordan NF
				Korea(S) PF
				Malaysia PF

Capitalist inclusive	Belize F Canada F Costa Rica F Cyprus(G) F Dominica F Germany(W) F Iceland F	Nevis F St. Lucia F St. Vincent F Spain F Switzerland F United States F		

non-
inclusive
	Fiji F
	Papua
	  New Guinea F
	Solomon
	  Islands F
			Botswana F
			Ecuador F
			Gambia PF
			Honduras PF
			Kenya PF
			Thailand PF
			Tuvalu F
				Bhutan PF
				Cameroon NF
				Gabon NF
				Haiti NF
				Ivory Coast PF
				Lesotho PF
				Liberia PF
				Maldives PF

Capitalist- **Statist** inclusive	Greece F Italy F Nauru F Trin. & Tob. F Venezuela F		France F Jamaica F Kuwait PF Malta PF Panama PF Sri Lanka PF	Argentina PF Bahrain PF Brazil PF China(T) PF Ghana NF
non- **inclusive**	Kiribati F		Bolivia F Morocco PF Nigeria F Peru F Vanuatu PF	Bangladesh PF Cen. Afr. Rep. NF India F
Mixed **Capitalist** inclusive	Austria F Denmark F Finland F Netherlands F	Norway F Sweden F United Kingdom F	Israel F Portugal F Senegal PF	Nicaragua PF Singapore PF Tunisia PF
non- **inclusive**				Egypt PF
Mixed **Socialist** inclusive				Grenada NF Yugoslavia PF
non- **inclusive**				Cape Verde Islands NF Madagascar PF Rwanda NF
Socialist inclusive				
non- **inclusive**				Guinea-Bissau NF

Medium(cont.)		Low-Medium				Low		
		Suriname	NF					
Nepal	PF	Chad	NF					
Niger	NF	Comoros	PF					
Sierra		Guatemala	NF					
Leone	PF	Malawi	NF					
Swaziland	PF							
Tonga	PF							
Transkei	PF							
Yemen(N)	NF							
Mexico	PF	South Africa	PF					
Qatar	PF							
Turkey	PF							
Saudi Arabia	NF							
U. Arab Ems.	PF							
Indonesia	PF	Equatorial		Pakistan	NF			
Oman	NF	Guinea	NF	Paraguay	PF			
Philippines	PF	Iran	NF	Uganda	PF			
Zimbabwe	PF	Mauritania	NF	Zaire	NF			
		Uruguay	PF					
		Burundi	NF					
		Guyana	PF	Seychelles	NF			
		Libya	NF	Syria	NF			
		Poland	PF					
Sudan	PF	Burma	NF	Togo	NF			
Upper Volta	PF	Congo	NF					
Zambia	PF	Mali	NF					
		Somalia	NF					
		Algeria	NF			Albania	NF	Korea(N)	NF
		Hungary	NF			Bulgaria	NF	Mongolia	NF
		Sao Tome &				China(M)	NF	Romania	NF
		Principe	NF			Cuba	NF	USSR	NF
						Czecho-		Vietnam	NF
						slovakia	NF		
						Germany(E)	NF		
		Benin	NF	Tanzania	NF	Afghanistan	NF	Laos	NF
		Guinea	NF			Angola	NF	Yemen(S)	NF
		Iraq	NF			Cambodia	NF		
		Mozambique	NF			Ethiopia	NF		

relate to economic activities. Our examination of freedom of property in different economic systems emphasizes the degree to which individuals and groups control productive and nonproductive property independent of government restrictions. The analysis of association freedoms focuses on an individual's ability to enter into economic contracts with others, and to form and join organizations in order to pursue personal and group economic interests. Our examination of freedom of movement focuses on physical and socioeconomic mobility, such as freedom from restrictions on internal movement, emigration, and forced employment, and the existence of discriminatory political or cultural practices that inhibit social mobility. The analysis of freedom of information focuses on citizens' ability to discuss, debate, and influence the nature of the economic system and the rate of economic development through formal and informal information channels.

In our evaluations, economic freedoms were not rated according to only one or two criteria; rather a more balanced representation of patterns and trends was attained by examining a broad range of economic features and policies. In many instances, limited information from closed or tightly controlled countries such as Albania and Laos prevented us from acquiring a detailed picture of economic freedoms, but given the general character of life in these countries, it is doubtful that more information would change the ratings significantly. We also attempted to analyze each type of economic freedom separately, but because the freedoms themselves tend to overlap, some of the information acquired was applicable to more than one category. These ratings attempt to reflect trends and patterns--the dynamics of an economy and the political system under which it exists--rather than static conditions.

The disadvantages of using a generalized rather than numeric scale should be noted. Because the overall ratings represent an average, countries with dissimilarities in the protection of particular economic freedoms may be placed in the same overall category. This is true of the medium category, in which combinations of low, medium, and high ratings for the four economic freedoms differ among countries, but may nonetheless result in a "medium" classification of overall economic freedom. Similarly, broad categories applied to a country as a whole tend to obscure variations in economic freedoms within countries. Finally, under conditions of civil war or general anarchy, discussion of relative levels of economic freedom loses much of its relevance. In Chad and Lebanon, and, to a somewhat lesser extent, El Salvador violence among guerrilla and government factions has severely limited the economic activities and endangered the lives of all.

As the table demonstrates, few countries receive low ratings on overall economic freedom, although a breakdown of each country's ratings would show that a significant number of countries are rated low on one or two of the individual economic freedoms. Despite repressive rule, many autocracies of both the left and right allow a degree of economic freedom, most often in the exercise of some types of property and mobility freedoms. Only the well-established, centrally planned communist countries have succeeded in controlling most economic activity, and, even in these countries, private sector and black market activities exist.

Similarly, many of the countries ranked high on overall economic freedom actually are rated medium-high on one or two of the four economic freedoms. Because the ratings are relative, a high assessment neither implies perfection nor suggests an absence of irregularities in protecting the economic freedoms of all groups in society.

The table does not suggest causal relationships, but it does reveal that societies tend to treat freedom similarly across political and economic spheres. Countries that receive high ratings on political rights and civil liberties tend to evidence a high degree of economic freedom; those that show less respect for rights in the political and civil spheres tend to treat economic freedoms similarly.

The relationship between economic freedoms and economic systems supports the argument that the openness of the political system under which economies function influences the degree to which economic freedoms exist and are protected. The disparity in economic freedoms among capitalist economies, which may be surprising to some readers, is a function of our definition under which economic activities become more responsive to the direct and indirect effects of a broad range of interventions, restrictions, and controls. Countries like Chile, South Korea, and the Ivory Coast that restrict freedom of association and information receive lower ratings on overall economic freedom than they might under a narrower definition of economic freedom that focuses primarily on the degree of government intervention and free market enterprise. This variation in economic freedom among capitalist-based countries (including capitalist, capitalist-statist, and mixed capitalist) suggests capitalism alone is not a sufficient guarantor of freedom in the economic sphere. The comparatively high status of economic freedom under capitalist democracies and its lower status in capitalist autocracies seems to support this claim.

Compared to capitalist economies, countries with truly socialist economic systems fall predominantly at the low end of the economic freedom scale. The one-party political structures and centralized economic planning associated with advanced socialism have severely impaired the freedom of economic activity that people might have under a less rigid from of socialism. Mixed socialist countries, which allow greater latitude for private economic activity, fare somewhat better on our scale. On the whole, however, the record of socialist-oriented countries in promoting economic freedoms is discouraging and should be of concern to those who view socialism as a more desirable economic system.

As the table indicates, countries with largely traditional or noninclusive economies are not at a disadvantage in our analysis because of their low economic development. In fact, several socialist noninclusive countries, such as Guinea-Bissau and Mozambique, exhibit slightly more economic freedom than most inclusive socialist countries, in large part because of their governments' inability to incorporate the predominantly subsistence economies into the more socialized modern sectors. However, there does not appear to be any discernible pattern in economic freedom among inclusive economies compared to noninclusive economies when political and economic systems are held constant. Economic development is clearly not a prerequisite for economic freedom, as evidenced by Botswana, Nigeria, and Papua New Guinea. Again, the political system appears to be a critical factor in determining economic freedom.

Conclusion

The struggle for freedom in 1982-83 had its victories and defeats. But we see hope in the fact that there were slightly more gains than losses.

In no country was a democratic system violently overturned, as has happened too often in the recent past. Unfortunately in several countries there was a slow erosion of liberties under the pressure of events or the ambitions of leaders. Particularly saddening were the declines in Sri Lanka and Malta, countries with old and fairly deep democratic traditions. The inability of

Turkey to restore a credible democracy was a major disappointment, although the 1983 election outcome was encouraging. The further destruction of liberty in Guyana, Suriname, and Grenada presaged a regional trend that may now be interrupted.

On the positive side the growth of democracy in the southern part of South America, in Argentina, Brazil, and Uruguay, and especially Bolivia, was particularly welcome. Persistent popular pressure in Chile may soon help to restore democracy there. Beyond this there were many countries, large and small, developed and developing, that quietly deepened their democratic attachment through the exercise or expansion of democratic forms. This was particularly noteworthy in Spain and Portugal, but should also be remarked in Nigeria, Kiribati, Papua New Guinea, Mauritius, and many other states.

Yet democracies, young and old, are beset with many problems. In the long run they will fulfill their promise and stabilize their institutions only if the promise of political equality makes it possible for ordinary people in all countries to have a fair share in the opportunities available in their societies. For this reason once again we set the Survey in the context of considerations of economic freedom and material distribution that must be related, as Douglas points out in the essay below, to the health of democracy in any country.

Notes

1. For more discussion of methodology see R. D. Gastil, Freedom in the World: Political Rights and Civil Liberties, 1978 (New York: Freedom House and G. K. Hall, 1978), especially pp. 7–30.

2. See John P. Lewis and Valeriana Kallab, eds., U.S. Foreign Policy and the Third World: Agenda 1983 (New York: Overseas Development Council, 1983), pp. 206–222 and references cited.

3. See Robert Kostrzewa, "Poland's Free Press," Freedom at Issue, November–December, 1983, pp. 19–23.

4. See Lindsay M. Wright, "A Comparative Survey of Economic Freedoms," in R. D. Gastil, Freedom in the World: Political Rights and Civil Liberties, 1982 (Westport, Conn.: Greenwood Press, 1982), pp. 51–90.

5. Wright, "A Comparative Survey of Economic Freedoms," pp. 78–83.

PART II

Analyzing Specific Issues

Another Year of Struggle for Information Freedom

Leonard R. Sussman

It is eleven years since the Soviet Union formally introduced into
UNESCO the concept that the mass media are tools of the government. Through the good offices of the Byelorussian delegate,
the USSR persuaded the 1972 biennial general conference of the
United Nations Educational, Scientific, and Cultural Organization
to prepare a declaration on "the fundamental principles governing
the use of the mass media . . ." (emphasis added).[1] The norm-
setting mass media resolution did not pass in that form, but the
underlying objectives have been debated increasingly in international forums. In 1977 a related Yugoslav initiative at the
Fourth Summit of the Non-Aligned Movement in Algiers produced
agreement among seventy-five heads of developing countries that
communication channels "inherited from the colonial past" must be
eliminated as "harmful consequences of the colonial era." Three
years later another non-aligned summit in Colombo formally created
the objective and battle cry that became institutionalized at
UNESCO: "A new information order in matters of information and
the mass media is as important as a new international economic
order."

The term has undergone metamorphosis through harsh debates
among representatives of authoritarian and democratic states;
government-controlled and government-free journalists and intellectuals; and the ideologues of the UNESCO secretariat. The latest
consensual expression of the term is the New World Information and
Communication Order.

The NWICO could not be a less felicitous term for those who
remember an earlier "order" that sought to impose on the world
political as well as cultural hegemony that would prevail for a
thousand years. Yet NWICO is the driving force behind UNESCO's
communications program for 1984-89 adopted in December 1982 in the

Medium-Term Plan. The first two-year program and budget of that six-year plan would be fashioned at Paris in November, 1983. At both conferences and at UNESCO ideology sessions such as that convened at Innsbruck in September 1983, the conceptualization of NWICO is kept under constant examination. We shall examine here one of the frankest expositions of NWICO by an academic at the Institute for International Studies of Karl Marx University, Leipzig, East Germany. We shall also report opposite views from the second international conference of independent news media held in October 1983 at Talloires, France. The Talloires-II conference called itself the Voices of Freedom '83. It produced the "List of Talloires" which is a global inventory of some 300 programs to provide for journalists from the developing countries programs of education, training, exchange, and internships. This list was released shortly after UNESCO's International Program for the Development of Communications approved some nineteen grants totaling $629,000 for government-run information programs in fifteen countries. One independent newspaper in Botswana was minimally supported--$14,000 granted after $228,000 was requested--after great controversy, but the funds will be spent for UNESCO field work with government approval.

Are Press Restrictions Inspired at UNESCO?

Clearly, UNESCO for more than a decade has provided the principal forum in which the domestic as well as international flow of news and information has been examined and debated. Those who sought to alter the content of that flow have credited the organization with raising the issue and keeping it on national and international agendas. Others who fear governmental and intergovernmental participation in determining the content particularly of the news media regard the UNESCO initiatives as a dangerous intrusion. Some who believe there has been a need to improve the quality of news media coverage of the developing countries, mainly by enlarging their own capacities to exchange news and information, and not at the expense of anyone's freedom, are also concerned over the authoritarian influence in proposals for changes in the flow.

The question arises: Are press restrictions inspired by debates at UNESCO?

UNESCO did not invent press restrictions. The itch to censor was government's first instinctive reaction to the threat it perceived from the printed word. Germany began censoring in 1529, and three decades later the British limited printing to presses in London licensed by the Crown. That was in 1557, some 388 years before UNESCO received its charter. Restriction is the seemingly easy road governments follow when they mistrust their own people. Such mistrust has been rampant throughout history. It is unlikely that censors 400 years ago, however, served their people elaborate rationalizations for restrictions on printing. Today, sociological studies and intergovernmental programs on communications are conducted year-round. These activities are ostensibly intended to advance the quality of news flow. Both the totalitarian and the democrat readily speak the same words: "freedom," "democratic," "balance"; but the speakers have vastly different objectives--as different as totalitarianism and democracy.[3]

UNESCO's Director-General Amadou Mahtar M'Bow told an interviewer[4] that he would act always in support of democracy and the freedom of the press. Mr. M'Bow has stated privately, however, that he is an international civil servant and must operate within his mandate; that is to say, he is expected to follow the objectives of governments. This he does. Where, then, is the majority of that governmental constituency leading UNESCO? For, in the real world--not the consensual world of resolution writing--the majority inevitably impresses its will. The majority of countries, by a large margin, determine what their domestic journalists can see, hear, or report, and how (see Table 8, page 52).

This reality feeds the fears that UNESCO has been a clearinghouse, perhaps the coordinator, of carefully conceived proposals to alter the content of the worldwide news flow. The fact that seven countries in Latin America restrict journalists by licensing them--and the number of licensing countries may soon rise to ten--is not the direct result of UNESCO resolutions.[5] Yet UNESCO indirectly sustains the trend toward licensing as well as other forms of government influence over press content. UNESCO began its coordinated move into the news field in 1974. An intergovernmental conference on communications in Latin America became the forerunner of major conferences on news and information in Africa and Asia. UNESCO's working papers and planning conferences laid on the table the most radical press-control proposals by defining "the ideological context of a communications policy: role of the State in the formulation of a national, coherent and corrective policy" (emphasis added).

UNESCO's "experts" told the delegates that "a national communications policy is a set of prescriptions and norms laid down to

TABLE 8

NEWS MEDIA CONTROL BY COUNTRIES

	Generally Free[1]	Partly Free[1]	Generally Not Free[1]	Gov't News Agency[2]	Civil Liberties[3]
Afghanistan			PB	X	7
Albania			PB	X	7
Algeria			PB	X	6
Angola			PB	X	7
Antigua and Barbuda		PB			3
Argentina	P	B		X	3
Australia	PB			X	1
Austria	PB			X	1
Bahamas	P	B			2
Bahrain			PB	X	5
Bangladesh		PB		X	5
Barbados	P	B		X	1
Belgium	PB			X	1
Belize	P	B			2
Benin			PB	X	6
Bhutan			P		5
Bolivia	P	B		X	3
Botswana	P	B			3
Brazil	P	B		X	3
Bulgaria			PB	X	7
Burma			PB	X	7
Burundi			PB	X	6
Cameroon			PB	X	6
Canada	PB				1
Cape Verde Isls.			PB		6
Central African Rep.		PB			5
Chad			PB	X	6
Chile		PB		X	5
China (Mainland)			PB	X	6
China (Taiwan)		PB			5
Colombia	PB			X	3
Congo			PB	X	6
Costa Rica	PB				1
Cuba			PB	X	6
Cyprus (G)	P	B		X	2

Notes to the Table

1. P designates print media; B designates broadcast (radio and TV) media. Print media refers primarily to domestic newspapers and news magazines. Countries with undeveloped media or for which there is insufficient information include: Comoros, Djibouti, Kiribati, Rwanda, St. Kitts and Nevis, Solomon Islands, Tuvalu, Vanuatu, and Western Samoa.

2. X designates the presence of a government news agency, with or without the availability of private news services.

3. See Table 1, pages 13–16.

	Generally Free[1]	Partly Free[1]	Generally Not Free[1]	Gov't News Agency[2]	Civil Liberties[3]
Cyprus (T)	P	B			3
Czechoslovakia			PB	X	6
Denmark	PB			X	1
Dominica	PB				2
Dominican Rep.	P	B			2
Ecuador	PB			X	2
Egypt		P	B	X	5
El Salvador		PB			5
Equatorial Guinea			PB		6
Ethiopia			PB	X	7
Fiji	PB				2
Finland	P	B		X	2
France	P	B		X	2
Gabon			PB	X	6
Gambia	PB				4
Germany (E)			PB	X	7
Germany (W)	PB			X	2
Ghana			PB	X	5
Greece	PB?			X	2
Grenada			PB		5
Guatemala		P	B	X	6
Guinea			PB		7
Guinea-Bissau			PB		6
Guyana		P	B	X	5
Haiti			PB		6
Honduras	PB				3
Hungary			PB	X	5
Iceland	PB				1
India	P	B		X	3
Indonesia		P	B	X	5
Iran			PB	X	6
Iraq			PB	X	7
Ireland	PB				1
Israel	PB				2
Italy	PB			X	2
Ivory Coast		P	B	X	5
Jamaica	P	B			3
Japan	PB			X	1
Jordan			PB	X	6
Kampuchea (Cambodia)			PB	X	7
Kenya		P	B	X	5
Korea (N)			PB	X	7
Korea (S)		P	B	X	5
Kuwait		P	B	X	4
Laos			PB	X	7
Lebanon		PB		X	4
Lesotho		PB			5
Liberia		P	B		5
Libya			PB	X	6
Luxembourg	PB				1

Information Freedom

	Generally Free[1]	Partly Free[1]	Generally Not Free[1]	Gov't News Agency[2]	Civil Liberties[3]
Madagascar			PB	X	6
Malawi			PB	X	7
Malaysia		P	B	X	4
Maldives		P	B		5
Mali			PB	X	6
Malta	P		B	X	4
Mauritania			PB	X	6
Mauritius	PB				2
Mexico		PB		X	4
Mongolia			PB	X	7
Morocco		P	B?	X	5
Mozambique			PB	X	6
Nauru	PB				2
Nepal		P	B	X	4
Netherlands	PB			X	1
New Zealand	PB			X	1
Nicaragua		P	B		5
Niger			PB		6
Nigeria	P	B		X	3
Norway	PB			X	1
Oman			PB		6
Pakistan			PB	X	5
Panama		PB		X	4
Papua New Guinea	PB				2
Paraguay		PB			5
Peru	PB			X	3
Philippines		P	B	X	5
Poland		P	B	X	5
Portugal	PB			X	2
Qatar			PB	X	5
Romania			PB	X	6
St. Lucia	PB				2
St. Vincent	P	B			2
Sao Tome & Principe			PB		6
Saudi Arabia			PB	X	7
Senegal		PB		X	4
Seychelles			PB		6
Sierra Leone		P	B		5
Singapore			PB		5
Somalia			PB	X	7
South Africa		P	B		6
Spain	PB			X	2
Sri Lanka		PB		X	4
Sudan			PB	X	5
Suriname			PB		6
Swaziland			PB		5
Sweden	PB			X	1
Switzerland	PB			X	1
Syria			PB	X	7
Tanzania			PB	X	6

	Generally Free[1]	Partly Free[1]	Generally Not Free[1]	Gov't News Agency[2]	Civil Liberties[3]
Thailand		P	B	X	4
Togo			PB	X	6
Tonga		PB			3
Transkei			PB		6
Trinidad & Tobago	PB				2
Tunisia		P	B	X	5
Turkey		P	B	X	5
Uganda			PB	X	5
USSR			PB	X	7
United Arab Emirates		P	B	X	5
United Kingdom	PB			X	1
United States	PB				1
Upper Volta		P	B	X	5
Uruguay		PB			4
Venezuela	PB			X	2
Vietnam			PB	X	6
Yemen (N)			PB	X	5
Yemen (S)			PB	X	7
Yugoslavia			PB	X	5
Zaire			PB	X	7
Zambia		P	B	X	6
Zimbabwe		P	B		5

Table Summary for Countries

	General Rating		Print Media		Broadcast Media	
	No.	%	No.	%	No.	%
Free	48	31	53	34	36	23
Partly free	53	34	40	25	31	20
Not free	56	36	64	41	89	57

Governments in three-fourths of the world have a significant or dominant voice in determining what does and what does not appear in the media. This definition of control does not include regulation such as that practiced by the FCC: it means control over newspaper or broadcast content. In some countries particular media (often broadcasting) may be government financed and indirectly government managed like the BBC, but are still largely free of government control of content.

In only one-fourth of the countries are both the print and broadcast media generally free: the press is generally free in one-third. Newspapers tend to be freer than radio or TV.

Nearly a half century ago there were thirty-nine national news services in twenty-eight countries. Seventy percent of these were at least nominally independent of government (Robert Desmond, The Press and World Affairs, Appleton-Century, 1937). Today there are 105. The number of government-operated news services has increased rapidly in the past five years in consequence of recommendations made by UNESCO. Sixty-eight percent of the countries have a government news agency: eighty-one percent of the "not free," sixty-eight percent of the "partly free," and fifty-seven percent of the "free" countries. Of nations with the lowest civil liberties rating (7), ninety-five percent operate government news agencies. National news agencies often use the world news services of the transnational Western media or TASS. They may then decide what world news may be distributed inside the country. Some national news agencies assign themselves the sole right to secure domestic news for distribution inside or outside the country.

guide the behavior of communications institutions in a country."
It was declared "necessary to stress the role of the government or
the state." It was thus said to be "apparent that a communications policy is always inseparable from an ideological framework."

Little room is left for objective reporting, professional
integrity, or proper balancing of news.

It was acknowledged that "governments which are interested in
regulating the communications systems in their countries . . . have met with strong resistance on the part of the
owners of . . . 'private enterprises'." Consequently, "since the
pernicious effects of the purely commercial orientation of radio
and television programming are obvious, it is important that
governments should assert a policy of national interest for the
benefit of the entire population." UNESCO, it was added, should
provide a "general guide with its respective alternatives," for
"governments alone can determine their own communications policies." For, it was said, news media are a "public utility."

That term appeared in the debates in India in 1983 on the findings of a second governmental Press Commission. India is a good
example of a national government's desire to influence the content
of the domestic and international news media, and also the government's interplay with UNESCO over this objective. Before,
during, and after the 1975 Indira Gandhi-declared "emergency," a
variety of press-control measures were contrived inside India, and
still harsher measures supported by Indians in the Non-Aligned
Press Agencies Pool, and in debates at UNESCO. Indian delegates
have stimulated news-content-changing and accepted UNESCO's rationale for such activities. Ending the 1975 emergency was a tribute
to the good sense of the Indian people. The reversal was aided by
a few persistent journalists who invoked the remaining power of
the courts to delay the application of stringent economic, political, and legal controls over the independent press of India.

These controls took forms that had been repeatedly discussed--
if not specifically approved by resolutions--in UNESCO and related
meetings. For example, UNESCO's MacBride Commission decried the
so-called "commercialization" of the news media. That commission
in 1980 recommended that future expansion of the news media avoid
commercial influences. Soon afterward (April 3, 1982) the Indian
Press Commission presented, among many recommendations, placing
trustees over editors to separate them from management; setting a
price/page schedule; fixing a news-to-advertisement rate; and
imposing a punitive import duty on daily newspapers whose average
page level exceeds twelve per day. Other proposals sought further

to weaken the financial structure of the major newspapers by separating them from other business enterprises, and leaving the press more open to editorial suasion from government. This in India is called "delinking." It is argued that the sensationalizing of news would thereby be ended, though it is difficult to understand how weakening the financial base of a newspaper will cause it to pursue more sedate and responsible editorial policies. The minority report[6] of the Press Commission declared: "We believe it would be tragic beyond words if in trying to turn the press into a public utility its viability as an industry were to be destroyed" (emphasis reflects the term used in UNESCO's 1974 "experts" paper). The minority also said the report "shows disregard for economic considerations without any understanding of the nexus between the freedom of the press and its commercial soundness."

The commission's majority supported pre-censorship as an "extreme necessity in the national interest." That step could be taken without a constitutional declaration of a national emergency, the commission argued. It also proposed that the newspaper-publishing industry be regulated in diverse ways as other manufacturing industries. The commission did not call for creating a code of ethics for the press, but it did propose penal powers for the existing press council. Penal powers--including denial of newsprint--would inevitably require setting forth some code against which to judge violations deserving penalties. Press codes, councils, and penalties have repeatedly been discussed at UNESCO meetings on communications.

The commission did come out "in favor of daily newspapers being left in the private sector." But they would be severely weakened if the commission's other proposals were adopted. The commission realistically noted that the Indian government sometimes uses payments for advertising space "as an instrument for punishing or rewarding a newspaper for its (editorial) policy."

The commission's report deals at length with the Right of Reply, a subject increasingly appearing on UNESCO's agendas. This implies an inherent right of an individual, group, or even government, to have a response published. The imposing of a statement on a publisher or editor would result in a clear abridgement of press freedom. The commission proposed granting penal powers to a press council to implement the right of reply.

It is not surprising that the Press Commission invoked for its recommendation the term New International Information Order, the hallmark of discussions at UNESCO over changing the content of news flow. The Indians, however, used "international" as the modifier of the order (suggesting governmental intervention) rather than "world" (encompassing independent media as well), as used at UNESCO after many trade-offs.

Perhaps the clearest example this year of a direct causal link between debates at UNESCO and actions in the real world is the case of Malaysia. Its government in June 1983 approved a plan to make the government-dominated news agency, Bernama, the sole distributor in Malaysia of all news entering or leaving the country. After next May, the world-news services could no longer distribute directly to the Malaysian press. Bernama would be the monopoly for selecting, editing, and distributing all foreign news. This is in line with a recommendation made at the creation of the Organization of Asian News Agencies (OANA). Bernama is reported to have conceded that it already practices self-censorship and omits news reports on instruction from government officials. Information Minister Adib Adam provided a rationale often heard at UNESCO: The takeover, he said, will be "an exercise in national sovereignty." The application of governmental controls, he said further, "will help correct the imbalance in the flow" of information between the developing and developed countries. This will be assisted, he added, by using material from national agencies in Asia, presumably through OANA, the non-aligned pool, and the Islamic agencies. Tass is now a regular exchange agency on the Asia-Pacific news network.

Malaysian newspaper publishers and editors oppose the government's decision.[7] They believe Bernama wants to control the news. The multiracial, nonpartisan reform movement, Aliran, saw the plan as "impinging upon the right of a citizen in a democracy to make up his own mind about world events on the basis of the full facts available to him." Aliran, as had many in UNESCO, earlier criticized the Western press for "information imperialism." They decried "monopolization" of the news flow attributed to the four world-news services.

Yet the ultimate in monopolization is governmental control of the news. UNESCO was directly involved in Malaysia's decision to crown Bernama. The issue of a new information order was heatedly debated at a 1981 UNESCO conference in Kuala Lumpur. There Malaysia's present Prime Minister strongly attacked the Western news media: "It is because the exercise of the free press is so loaded in favor of the developed countries that we have tried to fight for a new . . . order. UNESCO is very well aware of this. All the principles of the UN," said the Prime Minister, "were written by developed countries before the developing countries were admitted as members. Now . . . some of the loaded principles should be reviewed."

Clearly, the Prime Minister is developing a "national communications policy"--an objective repeatedly urged at UNESCO--and such centralized policies lead rather naturally to central control of news media.

Such policies are sometimes supported by Western observers. The Sandinist regime in Nicaragua has implemented stringent censorship, arrests, and harassment of independent journalists since the General Law of the Mass Media of Social Communications was approved by the revolutionary junta in August 1979. One North American scholar has commented sympathetically: "Whether the degree and nature of press controls in Nicaragua are appropriate depends on the unique combination of economic, political, historical and cultural conditions in the country and should be gauged on a case by case basis, and not on some arbitrary international standard."[8]

Such a relativistic evaluation of press controls is similar to the defense of public whipping or amputation because they are local traditions. Censoring or harassing journalists violates international standards precisely because communication is a vital civil liberty that is protected in international covenants. The Inter-American Convention on this subject bolsters the Universal Declaration of Human Rights and its specific Article 19.

While no resolution passed at UNESCO calls for censorship or licensing, it is also accurate to say that the late President Somoza never openly called for killing journalists. Yet he effectively labeled his enemies--whether politician or journalist--as foreign, corrupt communists. The American television journalist Bill Stewart was executed before his own cameras in June 1979 by Somoza guardsmen imbued with the conviction that the likes of Bill Stewart were foreign, corrupt communists. Somoza's successors tell their people that opposition journalists are still the enemy. The climate of hate is pervasive.

UNESCO, too, has been used to create a certain repressive climate in international communications. UNESCO officials frequently recall the American-coined phrase in the UNESCO charter: "wars begin in the minds of men." Repressive ideas also begin there, and are often more difficult to detect. Such ideas can masquerade as "protection of journalists" though they end by shackling the labors or the bodies of reporters.

Tension is inevitable between government officials who withhold information from the public, and the journalists who seek to share it with the people. The official of even the smallest country is the Goliath, and the journalist the David. It is an unequal match. Yet the UNESCO debates often portray the journalist--even the domestic journalist--as the intruder acting against a nation's interests, and the all-powerful government as the defender of the people.

What goes on in the minds of men who hear journalism charged with blame, saddled with specific tasks, and told that someone must make journalists act "responsibly?" A climate of doubt and suspicion of the press provides a fertile field for the press-controllers to do their work--and justify it to other governments willing to accept repression of news media once the ground has been properly nurtured.

It is, therefore, useful to examine UNESCO's own climate-setting structure. The principal mechanism for the six-year period ahead was the Extraordinary General Conference that approved in December 1982 the Medium-Term Plan (1984-89). We shall examine Major Program III, Communications in the Service of Man. Eleven tightly printed pages provided an analyses of "problems" and strategy of action and program on studies in communication, a freer and more balanced flow of information and increased exchanges of news and programs, and the development of communications.

The debate over the communications resolution and annex--both presumably setting UNESCO's course for six years--reveals the intention of the drafters (the secretariat under Mr. M'Bow), the degree to which consensus seeking produces compromises for delegates from the democracies, and the control of the final text by both the secretariat and the majority intent on altering the content of the news and information flow. This last was clearly illustrated in the debate of paragraph 3035 which begins, "freedom implies a heavy responsibility on the part of communicators, be these individuals or corporate bodies." The original thrust of the section was to remind private communicators of their "responsibility" to act "in accordance with professional principle and ethics" and, as well, the intergovernmental objectives presumably set for them in UNESCO's 1978 declaration on the news media. This latter was the closest dictum so far by a UNESCO conference in setting forth "uses" of the independent news media. The new paragraph would introduce such objectives as "a heavy responsibility." Western delegates, however, managed to insert the term "public and private" wherever the news media were mentioned in the document. That added no new restraint on governments whose own "public" communicators already accept responsibilities set forth by governments. Nor was it much of a gain to specify that "administrators of government media and other officials with authority over the media" also exercise professional integrity. The next sentence, however, was an innovation. It stated clearly:

> The mass media can make an important contribution in scrutinizing activities of authorities and in preventing abuse of power. (Emphasis added.)

Instead, an earlier version of this sentence had referred to the "watchdog" role of the press as exemplary. That Western term was eliminated and, by consensus, the above version adopted. By the time the final resolution of the conference was published, however, the UNESCO secretariat had changed the wording of the crucial sentence of 3035 to read:

> The mass media could make an important contribution in scrutinizing all actions which might lead to abuses of power.

In this version, independent news media could be the subjects charged with "abuses." In the version approved earlier by consensus, and supporting the legislative history, the watchdog role of the news media was directed at the abuse of power by governments. Knowing this legislative history U.S. Ambassador Jean Gerard applauded the "positive contribution that the media can make in scrutinizing activities which might lead to abuse of power." She hailed the reference in the Medium-Term Plan to censorship and self-censorship "among the obstacles to freedom of expression," and noted the repeated reference that other obstacles might be posed by "either governments or private entities." She disagreed "heartily," however, with the concept in the plan that the international community must concern itself with—a new slogan—"messages and what they say." That, as originally posed, was more ominous. It stated governments "cannot ignore the problem of the content" of messages passing through modern telecommunications channels. It would be a small step from translating concern for those messages into judgments about them, Ambassador Gerard noted. "And from there it would be only one step to trying to control their content through censorship of the worst sort," she added.

Information Freedom

Similarly, references in the text to a supposed right of "participation" of the public in the decision-making process of the independent press is a "concept fraught with danger," said the American, "because it could be a short step from there to 'public' or
state control of the media."

Response from Talloires II

The inclination of some professional journalists from both
developed and developing countries who met at Talloires in October
was to make the most of this new UNESCO agreement "scrutinizing . . . abuse of power"--though the watchdog had its teeth
extracted. The Talloires report welcomed such scrutinizing. The
UNESCO statement was called "an important step forward by the
international community recognizing the positive contribution that
the independent press can make to safeguarding individual liberties and strengthening a free society."

The Talloires conferees--independent news men and women from
the Americas, Europe, Asia, and Africa--reaffirmed the Talloires
Declaration of May 1981 (see the text of the 1983 report in
Freedom at Issue (Nov.-Dec. 1983). The conference condemned proposals to define a "right to communicate," procedures imposed or
inspired by governments or intergovernmental bodies for "democratization of communication," and for "participation in communication," governmental imposition of "codes of conduct" for the news
media, proposals advanced in the name of "national sovereignty" to
block cross-border newsreporting or broadcasting, and efforts in
the name of "protection of journalists" to introduce journalistic
licensing, sanction the surveillance of journalists, or place
conditions on their entitlement to protection.

The conference encouraged recognition of the importance of private and independent news media, exploring ways to assure the
editorial independence of state-owned news media, improving newsreporting within and for the developing countries and strengthening the press as a guardian against abuses of power.

The conference concluded:

. . . international debates on communications should
cease the emphasis on recrimination, repression, and pessi-
mism. Unparalleled expansion of all manner of communications is under way--benefiting the near and the distant,
the poor and the prosperous nations.

New communications technologies should be welcomed, not feared. No one people, nation, or group of nations can monopolize these technologies or the content they will convey, any more than one nation monopolized the arts of reading or printing. Yet by restricting the flow of communications--or even threatening to do so--governments can delay their own people's access to new technologies.

Let us welcome the era of great communications possibilities, and allow the communications revolution to proceed, without harassment, in recognition that where the press is free, people are free.

Ken Gordon, director of the Caribbean News Agency, told the Talloires assembly how the independent press in his part of the world has recently been affected, especially where the courts--despite their British inheritance--"no longer dispense justice and are regarded as an extension of the political arm." Governments, he said, do not become corrupt or dictatorial overnight. The process is "insidious" and "develops its own momentum" if not put into public focus by the press. Gordon said the press was "totally emasculated in Guyana by subterfuge that was greatly assisted by foreign ownership which had neither the will nor the stomach to resist." In Grenada, he said, "it was less subtle for the ideological imperatives were both impatient and deep." He saw some victories: in Jamaica, the Daily Gleaner played "an historic role in turning the tide of public opinion against the then government in power which was moving increasingly into the sphere of Cuban/Soviet influence; in Barbados, the Nation averted the purchase of what was then the only daily newspaper on the island by the then government. . . . In Trinidad the draconian laws proposed in the Public Order Act were withdrawn when the Express mounted a public campaign. . . . The Prime Minister of St. Lucia recently made a public statement announcing that intelligence reports had confirmed that Libya had been making large sums of money available for political activity in the Eastern Caribbean [including the training of twenty-six persons for terrorism] and the sudden growth of a radical fortnightly newspaper in Dominica." Gordon argued that "the Dominicas of his world, small though they be, assume a new and significant importance . . . [for] the political pressure against the free press builds."

"Areas of need" for Third World newspapers were described by Harold Hoyte, managing director of the Nation Barbados. Developing-country journalists when harassed or their media abused need the public support of their developed-world colleagues. "Our role strikes at the evil which keeps our people in ignorance and mental slavery," he said, and "we are therefore a target for official assault by governments." He included in the need for "full and unconditional support," material assistance and technical training.

The conference particularly welcomed the initiatives being taken to extend private and public multilateral and bilateral communications assistance to the news media in developing countries. Discussions at Talloires underscored the sensitive nature of the issues. Walter Cronkite in a keynote address suggested that communications-technology assistance to developing countries be tied to assurances that the news media would be free of government restrictions. A journalist from Africa and another from Asia urged the conference to avoid such acts that might cause the recipient-journalists to be perceived as puppets of "foreigners."

The "List of Talloires,"[10] distributed at the conference, tabulated "the impressive number of programs currently offered by the independent media of the developed world to their colleagues in the developing world." The list had been prepared by George Krimsky, world news editor of the Associated Press. The Talloires report did not mention by name the communications-transfer session of UNESCO's IPDC that had concluded at Tashkent, USSR, two weeks earlier.

The Trade-Offs at Tashkent

The third IPDC grant-making session again demonstrated the ideological motivations that lie just beneath the surface of this UNESCO program. The Western delegations were relieved because press-control objectives and programs did not surface more blatantly. There seemed to be general agreement that projects elaborating ideological principles of the NWICO in the name of journalism training were not acceptable. Funds-in-trust and bilateral aid would hereafter be reported and invited, thereby sustaining the American preference to fund aid bilaterally rather than by placing U.S. dollars in the IPDC bank. By giving a small grant to an independent newspaper in Botswana the principle was established that aid could be given to nongovernmental media. Strong opposition was shown to continuing in Rome "development journalism" training for a Latin American governmental consortium. Such training would be held instead in the Third World. And, finally, the Western participants' response to the Soviet downing of a Korean passenger plane produced a salutary conclusion. The condemnation of the attack on the plane was kept out of the IPDC final report, thereby setting a precedent of not introducing political issues at IPDC.

Three regional projects were approved: development of personnel in graphic arts (Latin American/Caribbean), $40,000; seminar for journalists in government agencies (Latin American/Caribbean), $40,000; and development of a distribution system for Andean television programs, $40,000.

Sixteen national projects were funded: Benin, documentation center, $40,000; Burundi, creating regional communications centers, $40,000; Ethiopia, mass media training center, $31,000; Kenya, supporting trainees for the Institute of Mass Communications, $15,000; Madagascar, aid to the national news agency, $20,000; Mozambique, aid to the national news agency, $20,000; Chad, rebuilding information facilities, $40,000; Zimbabwe, telecommunications training, $14,000; Somalia, training to introduce television, $40,000; Sudan, rural TV development, $40,000; Mexico, curriculum designing for consumer education in TV, $40,000; Jamaica, radio and TV production and training center, $40,000; Botswana, development of the Examiner newspaper, $14,000; Tunisia, refresher course for the non-aligned press pool, $40,000; India, non-aligned pool improvement, $40,000; and Mozambique, communications school, $35,000.

The United States pledged $850,000 for training in the U.S. ($350,000) and for funds-in-trust projects ($500,000) approved jointly by IPDC and Washington. To date, none of the earlier U.S. pledges of nearly $500,000 have been spent. The Soviet delegation repeatedly mentioned this, and tried to bar the American representatives from participating in the division of IPDC allocations.

Revelation at Innsbruck

The secretariat of UNESCO arranged a week-long conference at Innsbruck in September to discuss the NWICO presumably in preparation for further implementation of the "order" at the general conference two months later. The usual geopolitical spectrum was represented, but one speaker in particular produced an important, revealing paper. Wolfgang Kleinwachter of the Institute for International Studies at Karl Marx University, Leipzig, East Germany, provided a frank statement of the objectives of many--not only in the Soviet bloc--who support a new "order" in news and information. Kleinwachter's topic was "Conceptualization of a New International Information Order: Perspectives of Discussions."

He began by noting the increased role of the mass media in international relations, the heightened "fierceness" of the ideological struggle, and the "autonomous province" that communications have come to assume in international relations. Clearly, he did not favor such autonomousness. He described it as "a global problem of mankind, a challenge." Tackling it, he said, "admits no further delay."

It is timely, then, to examine the international legal foundation for installing a "new order." The author argues it is in the competence of states and, therefore, intergovernmental bodies to regulate the international flow of information. This he terms "democratization and decolonization." This would mean, in the words of a Soviet authority: "to establish international norms which would make it a duty for states to tolerate no propaganda of certain specified conceptions and to make use, in the international ideological struggle, only of such means as are admissable under international law."[11] That formula would hardly permit any cross-border transmissions not acceptable to the regime of the receiving country (for example, broadcasts from Radio-Free Europe/Radio Liberty, Voice of America, Deutsche Welle, BBC, Kol Israel, and others).

The author cites existing international instruments--the Helsinki accords, UNESCO's 1978 mass media declaration, the 1980 UNESCO resolution accepting the MacBride report, and the 1982 UN resolution banning direct-broadcast satellites--as "milestones in the process of formulating fundamental principles for international information and communications."

This contention demonstrates the interconnectedness of several instruments fashioned in different forums. It reveals the persistence of those who introduce these diverse resolutions in varied contexts but with singleminded purpose. The debates in UNESCO, the UN Committee on Information, and the Political Committee are not unrelated. The objectives are clearly revealed post facto in such clear, legalistic argumentations as in Kleinwachter's paper.

He stresses his last conclusion: "It emerges from these documents that international mass media activities may only take place in conformity with the basic principles of international laws" (emphasis added). As added "proof," the author quotes extensively from the 1980 resolution on the NWICO adopted by the Intergovernmental Coordinating Council for Cooperation of the Non-Aligned Countries. The "new order," they said, should be based on "(a) the fundamental principles of international law, notably self-determination of peoples, sovereign equality of state and non-interference in internal affairs of states; (b) the right of every nation to develop its own independent information system . . . in particular of regulating the activities of the transnational [information] corporations; . . . (f) the responsibility of various actors in the process of information for its truthfulness and objectivity as well as for the particular social objectives to which the information activities are dedicated" (emphasis added).

To continue the pressure for the "new order," these principles and objectives were to be reintroduced for discussion at the 1983 general conference of UNESCO, and the Innsbruck conference was Mr. M'Bow's way of preparing for further discussions at Paris.

Kleinwachter then outlines the elements that should be included in further UNESCO initiatives leading toward the elaboration of international law as "information principles." He lists these and describes them in this fashion:

1) The "role" of fundamental principles of international law: International law is the "basis" for NWICO because--says the author--the MacBride report and the resolution accepting it says so. The MacBride report, however, was not an official UNESCO document. It was a special report to the director-general. The resolution acknowledging that report included the perfunctory advice that the NWICO should have a basis in law. Kleinwachter, however, turns this around and declares that "this interlinkage"-- references in many documents to the NWICO and a new economic order--makes it "obvious" that international law already provides "the basis" for the NWICO. He then reinterprets seven fundamental principles of international law to sustain an international legal standard for information. None must be construed apart from others, he insists. He paraphrases them: "Prohibition of the propaganda of force, the right of each nation to determine its own national information system, the equal sovereign right of every state to participate in international information relations, and the prohibition of information interference in the affairs of other states."

This body of legal restrictions provides a statist basis for all international news and information flows. It allows for no international news flow apart from government control. It demands a standard of editorial judgment and performance that is keyed not to the reporting of each event as a subject projecting its own meaning; rather each event would be reported to fulfill a predetermined objective set forth by one government and admissable to other governments. The news and information available to the people of the world would be only what the most restrictive government would permit as non-interference in its internal affairs.

2) Human rights and international information: Kleinwachter argues that "information is aimed at influencing the attitudes of people" (emphasis added)--an interesting revelation of the author's intentions!--and information is, thus, a matter of human rights; and since human rights are the subject of international instruments, "freedom in the information sphere is inseparably linked with responsibilities, rights and duties constituting a unity" (emphasis added). That means, says the author, that free expression is "not a right conferring unlimited freedoms." The absolute character of Article 19 of the Universal Declaration of Human Rights, he says, is qualified by Article 29 which cites "duties to the community." It was no accident, he adds, that the MacBride resolution cited both articles of the declaration. The International Convention on Civil and Political Rights also assigns "special duties and special responsibilities" to the free dissemination of information, Kleinwachter says. Nowhere, he adds, is there an absolutely free flow of information. Capitalist states have libel laws and restrictions on incitement, though, he adds, they are not enforced "when incitement and slander have anticommunist motivations."

Information rights, he holds, can only be implemented in conjunction with other rights, such as the right to work. Thus, the state must guarantee economic and social foundations as "a precondition for the dissemination of information." No state can "dictate to another state its internal legislation, not even in the field of information dissemination." That would justify repeated Soviet-bloc efforts to make all states responsible for the activities of mass news media under their jurisdiction. Kleinwachter refers here to the currently discussed "right to communicate." There is no clear definition yet, he acknowledges, but the key element should be "the broad participation of the masses in the national communication process, and the democratic participation of all nations in the international communications flow."

3) Information content: Since content of communication determines whether it "promotes" the desired objectives, rules must
spell out the "prohibition of certain types of propaganda" (emphasis in original), and the range of these prohibitions "could be
widened," the author says. It is also possible, he adds, to
define "desirable goals for the flow of information."

4) Information sovereignty: National sovereignty is increasingly threatened by the "nonviolent means of 'information'," says
Kleinwachter. In diverse ways, therefore, he clearly emphasizes
that statist defenses and objectives are the primary concern in
the international flow of news and information.

5) Cooperation: He praises the programs of the IPDC but warns
that there must be more research of transnational cooperation on
the information field.

6) Responsibility: He holds that a state's public media must
comply with the demand to change their content "if another state
looks upon such actions as interference in its internal affairs."

As Kleinwachter moves to his conclusions, he drops most euphe-
misms and speaks frankly of "the regulation of journalistic work."
It is an "internal affair" he says, but implies that their work is
too important to go unregulated on the international scene. He
disavows making journalists the direct subjects of international
law. Instead, the content and form of their communications are,
indeed, to be strictly defined, with the responsibility for providing standards, monitoring journalistic output, and presumably
penalizing code-breakers--all that placed directly in the hands of
states.

Finally, the author recommends a pattern for establishing norms
in international news, information, and communications. He acknowledges that states are subjects of international law and the
mass media are not. He would merge the two--presently distinct--
areas of jurisdiction. That would require creating a "complex
fabric of norms":

political norms, setting forth recommended objectives for
journalists;

norms of international law, legally binding international
conventions on the rights and duties of the state with
regard to international news and information;

ethical-moral norms, codes of ethics set by professional organizations.

There are obvious pitfalls in all this for the continued freedom of the independent communicator. First, the setting of "norms" in itself acknowledges a higher authority for reporting than the innate commitment to truth seeking by the individual journalist or communicator. Second, the linkage of the three "norms" suggest the creeping intrusion of governments and intergovernmental organizations into the judgments of content and style that must be the prerogative of the communicator if freedom of information as a human right is to have meaning.

Most important, the author has provided the framework by which those who would control the content of the international flow of news and information can use international legal forms and international organizations, step by step, to build a structure that would enhance repression-under-law.

This frank statement of restrictive goals and tactics may not per se alter international rules and rights. With the active assistance of the UNESCO secretariat, Soviet-bloc delegates, and many other authoritarians, the ocean in which all the fish swim is being further salted.

Will the U.S. Leave UNESCO?

The running debates at UNESCO continue to anger the Reagan administration. The ideological differences between the United States and UNESCO's secretariat have been aired for years. A letter from the President to the Congress supporting a Congressional initiative in 1982 led to passage of the Beard Amendment. It requires the United States to end financial support of UNESCO if that organization acts to license or in other ways harass journalists. Financing of UNESCO programs--the steadily rising budgets and alleged misapplication of funds--became in 1983 another source of strong U.S. irritation.

During a meeting with Director-General M'Bow in Paris in the spring, Ambassador Gerard and Gregory J. Newell, Assistant Secretary of State for International Organizations, raised these budgetary issues. They pointed out that UNESCO had retained a large unbudgeted windfall from the exchange earned when the organization received U.S. dollars and paid expenses in devalued French francs. M'Bow responded angrily accusing Washington of sending incompetent representatives, and displaying a psychological sickness where UNESCO is concerned.

Ambassador Gerard was recalled to Washington for a time. Soon afterward, the State Department initiated an extensive reassessment of UNESCO. The Department asked the U.S. National Commission for UNESCO and others to provide independent estimates of each of the sectors in which UNESCO operates--education, natural sciences, social sciences, culture, communications, and human rights. The review would assess the effectiveness of UNESCO as a vehicle for promoting U.S. interests, international cooperation, and development. It would seek to determine the impact of politicization of the organization's budget, "statism," and U.S. participation. In the last regard, a range of policy options would be examined: "(1) acceptance of the status quo; (2) more selective U.S. participation; (3) increased participation under certain circumstances; (4) adjustments of U.S. payments; and (5) withdrawal."

The reassessment was not expected to be completed until early in 1984. The threat of withdrawal would, therefore, hang over the UNESCO general conference the previous November.

Not only UNESCO faced American withdrawal. The UN Committee on Information (UNCI) has been an increasing source of contention over the NWICO and related matters, as well as the size of the UN's information budget. The UNCI report prepared for the UN Special Political Committee in October included proposals not approved by the usual consensual format. The United States found several of these objectionable including one introduced by the Soviet Union that would prohibit broadcasts that mar international understanding.

Withdrawing from the UNCI would simply mean not attending meetings. By being present, the United States often must trade off something it wants for wording it really does not want. Then it must repeat that process over the same terminology in the Political Committee. Finally, then, the United States tends to inscribe its name on declarations it does not generally approve. The question arises, however, whether it is better to remain part of the damage-limitation process, than not; and, indeed, whether more initiative should be taken to introduce (or having others introduce) imaginative and constructive proposals we would wholeheartedly support.

That, after all, is the crucial argument for remaining in any intergovernmental organization including the United Nations itself.

Notes

1. See Leonard R. Sussman, "Freedom of the Press: Problems in Restructuring the Flow of International News," in Raymond D. Gastil, Freedom in the World, 1980, pp. 53–98, for an overview by this author of the history of recent communications issues at UNESCO and elsewhere, and the 1981 and 1982 yearbooks for continuing reports and analysis.

2. This section includes some material from "UNESCO: Getting Down to Cases," September 30, 1983 (mimeo), prepared by the author for Voices of Freedom '83, the conference at Talloires, France, cosponsored by the Murrow Center of Tufts University's Fletcher School for Law and Diplomacy and the World Press Freedom Committee.

3. See Leonard R. Sussman, Glossary of International Communications: Warning of a Bloodless Dialect, (Washington: The Media Institute, 1983). Sets of four definitions of words and terms often used in international communications debates; as used in the First, Second (Marxist), and Third Worlds and at UNESCO; available from Freedom House.

4. South, November 1981, p. 11, interview by Altaf Gauhar.

5. Three Latin American countries—Brazil, Costa Rica, and Ecuador—had introduced licensing of journalists as the news media issues were arising in UNESCO. Four countries in the region adopted licensing after the 1974–76 discussions—Colombia, Honduras, Panama, and Venezuela—and three countries in the area are considering licensing: Argentina, Dominican Republic, and Nicaragua.

6. In Defence of Press Freedom, Minutes of Dissent to the Report of the Second Press Commission, Calcutta: A Statesman publication, pp. 12, 16, 36.

7. Wall Street Journal, by Barry Wain, 9/1/83; and Bangkok Post, "Malaysia Treading a Dangerous Path," p. 4, 7/9/83.

8. John Spicer Nichols, paper for the Tenth National Meeting of the Latin American Studies Association, Washington, March 3–6, 1982; (mimeo).

9. Fourth Extraordinary Session, Paris 1982 4XC/4, Second Part; and Records of the General Conference, Paris, March 23 to December 3, 1982, Volume 1, Resolutions.

10. "The List of Talloires," a global inventory of education, training, exchange, and intern programs for journalists from the developing world; compiled by George A. Krimsky, world news editor of the Associated Press (New York: The Associated Press, 1983).

11. Volossov: Massovaya informatsia i mezhdunarodnoye pravo, Moscow 1974, p. 24; as quoted by Kleinwachter.

The Future of
Democracy:
Corporatist or Pluralist

Lindsay M. Wright

Introduction

The advanced democracies of Western Europe, North America and
Japan are reeling under the pressures brought on by unconstrained
political demands and rapidly changing economic conditions.
Government is no longer capable of controlling societal claims for
benefits. It can neither meet all claims, because its resources
are finite, nor can it make the politically painful decisions of
who shall lose and who shall gain. Economic collapse looms on the
horizon as governments struggle to cope with the structural changes that are transforming the world economy. The political and
economic instability of our time has numerous causes. We witness
the debt crisis in the international economy, rising competition
to industries in the advanced democracies by newly industrializing
developing countries, and the emergence of new and vociferous
special interest groups challenging once again the compatibility
of social justice and economic prosperity, collective interests
and individual freedom.

These are the opinions of many observers within and outside
academia concerned with the political economies of the advanced
industrial democracies. Impending doom has been the theme of much
scholarly and popular literature since the early seventies, but
the alarm over the future of liberal democracy in Western Europe,
North America, and Japan deepened in the early eighties. For
example, Robert B. Reich, a liberal political economist from
Harvard, opens his new book, The New American Frontier, with these
dramatic and pointed words:

Since the late 1960s America's economy has been slowly
unraveling. The economic decline has been marked by

growing unemployment, mounting business failures, and falling productivity. Since about the same time America's politics have been in chronic disarray. The political decline has been marked by the triumph of narrow interest groups, the demise of broad-based political parties, a succession of one-term presidents, and a series of tax revolts.[1]

Other American writers on the same subject, such as Lester Thurow, Paul Hawken, and Richard Cornuelle have joined a long list of European scholars including Samuel Brittan and Michel Crozier,[2] who have been urging governments and civic leaders to acknowledge the severity of these problems and look for new ways of solving them before we witness the breakdown of our democratic systems.

These perceptions of increasing political and economic crisis have compelled scholars and observers alike to seek theoretical and practical solutions to the critical problems facing the advanced industrial democracies.

Those concerned with freedom must also be concerned with the current theoretical discussions in academia and with the implications of this work for public policy-making. On a theoretical level, many scholars have begun to question seriously the pluralist model of interest group politics that underpinned the last generation's academic understanding of political democracy. Pluralism they claim no longer provides an accurate framework in which to view either the process or the structure of policy-making in North America and Western Europe. Political relations between society and the state do not seem to fit the roles that the pluralist model assigns each actor: the state as a neutral, impartial mediator among competing groups with conflicting interests. Instead, critics of pluralism argue that in many countries the major interest groups, particularly business and labor, have with the state's encouragement begun to institutionalize their relations with the state, resulting in a more cooperative structure for decision-making based on mutual exchanges and tradeoffs. In Sweden, for example, the national industry and labor associations work closely with the government to shape public policy affecting their sectors to ensure an atmosphere of stability for continued economic prosperity.

The political model that appears to many political scientists to capture these new relationships is called "corporatism." It has become the new theory of political relationships in the advanced democracies. Increasing acceptance of this theory raises serious questions about the current state of democratic politics as well as the direction in which the political structure of the advanced democracies is evolving.

Some analysts also see corporatism as a pragmatic solution to the political and economic crises which reappear with disturbing regularity in the advanced democracies. Declining legitimacy for traditional sources of authority, stagnating capacity of governments to process and meet unrestrained demands for benefits, as well as continuing inflation and rising unemployment, balance of payments deficits, increasing public debt, and irreversible structural changes in the economy are seen as both the causes and outcomes of deep-seated crisis. For some, these phenomena are evidence of the need to restructure state-society relations to improve the capacity of the advanced democracies to govern. Such corporatists would integrate major interest associations into the policy-making process, making them equally responsible for the benefits and costs arising from policy decisions and implementation. Corporatism is seen as a way to stem the quantity of demands being made on government and to seek through tandem efforts by the public and private sectors acceptable and effective solutions to economic problems.

Without question the political systems of Western Europe, North America, and Japan are straining under the pressures of a rapidly changing, increasingly interdependent political and economic environment. Although it is not clear that the collapse of democracy is imminent, the alarm raised by its critics is healthy. It forces us to question the myths that shape our views of the ideal and actual roles of the state and interest groups in democratic politics. It can illuminate the sources and processes of change that inevitably will transform the manner in which policy is made and effected. Corporatism may be neither the best descriptive nor ideological framework on which to base an assessment of contemporary political relationships in the advanced democracies. Nevertheless it can provide us with a starting point for trying to determine whether and how we should revamp the procedures and improve the processes of democratic decision-making while protecting the basic principles of equal representation, participation, and freedom on which democracy is based.

Until the 1970s there was a tendency for both academic and popular writers to focus on the multifaceted problems of building and preserving democracy in the less-developed countries to the virtual neglect of the equally complex and serious dilemmas facing the democracies of the more-advanced countries. We now realize this was a serious oversight: the maintenance and stability of our international political and economic institutions are dependent on the strength and survival of the advanced democracies. We must be aware of the pressures, conflicts, and tensions that are likely to arise from external and internal sources of change and what alternatives are available to the advanced democracies for dealing with these pressures. By providing an overview of some of the issues raised above, this essay attempts to redress the inattention in previous yearbooks to the problems confronting the advanced industrial democracies.

We will first look at the nature and possible causes of the political and economic crises which generally afflict Western Europe, North American and Japan. We will then discuss the major tenets of the pluralist perspective on democratic politics with which we are so familiar. We will examine why pluralism has been attacked and why it no longer describes convincingly the interplay between state and society in the advanced democracies. Against this background we will discuss briefly corporatist theory which has for many become a viable theoretical alternative to pluralism and a possible solution to continuing political and economic debility. Finally we examine the conflicts that could arise from the conjuncture of corporatism and democracy: the moral implications of corporatism for popular participation and the practical implications of corporatism as a viable policy-making process in a system based on the primacy of individual rights.

The Crisis of Governability

The advanced democracies are experiencing a crisis of democracy and governability, claim many political observers, including British commentator and political economist Samuel Brittan, MIT economist Lester Thurow, and Harvard political scientist Samuel Huntington.[3] They argue that the slower economic growth of the past decade has not been matched by a parallel reduction in interest group demands on the government for goods and services. Demands for a larger share of declining resources have escalated, overtaking the capacity of government institutions to process let alone meet these demands. As demands have continued unabated and unmet, government has steadily lost its authority and ability to impose unilaterally policies that might adversely affect the lives of some citizens. The multitude of interest groups luxuriate in and lobby to preserve the benefits received. Those who have been previously neglected press for an equal share. The political economies of the advanced democracies cannot sustain the onslaught, but no one is willing to soften their demands or bear the costs. The result in one writer's opinion is "anomic democracy": the political system becomes a lawless arena for asserting conflicting claims rather than a means for striving to achieve common purposes.[4]

There are numerous hypotheses concerning the probable causes of this deterioration in governability. Each is closely related to the next. None alone is sufficient to explain the complexity of the forces that have rapidly transformed the democratic process in Europe and North America. Among these possible causes are the breakdown of traditional sources of authority, the impact of sustained economic prosperity, the transformation of mass communication, the universality of education, demographic changes, and the politicization of the economic marketplace.

Huntington along with the French political scientist Michel Crozier[5] argue that the breakdown in legitimacy of any type of hierarchy in contemporary society has led to a decline in the moral authority of government to impose its will on the citizenry to reach common goals. Authority in traditional institutions such as the church, the military, the university (particularly evident in the sixties and early seventies), and the family has collapsed under the pressures of demographic shifts, increased social, economic and geographical mobility, and broader freedom of choice for the individual outside these conventional networks. The decrease in respect for authority in political institutions is a natural consequence of these developments.

Another possible source of the crisis of democracy is the impact that long-term economic growth and prosperity have had on the public psyche. Rather than satiating the populace's demands for goods and services, the prosperity of the post World War II era has led to escalating expectations for less expensive, higher quality consumer goods, more efficient and equitable services, and a constantly improving quality of life secured if necessary through public provision. Thus the character of claims on government seems to have changed. The problem is not only that the demand for greater quantities of goods has continued unabated. New demands concerning the quality of life have arisen, such as those for a "nuclear free society," protection from environmental and work-place health hazards, and full equality for the handicapped. The state, if it wants to maintain its authority, must develop new ways of sorting and processing these claims.

The transformation of mass communications is cited as another source of the political crisis in the advanced democracies. According to Crozier and Huntington, the spread of information technology has had immeasurable positive benefits, but it has also contributed to the breakdown of traditional institutions and values. With the help of the mass communications revolution new opportunities for employment and different cultural experiences have been opened and mobility away from traditional institutions has been greatly facilitated.

Changes in communication have also given rise to mass media which, although a necessary component in the democratic system, have transformed in positive and negative ways the manner in which government processes societal claims. One negative consequence of the development of mass media has been a reduction in the conventional distance between elected political officials and the citizenry which helped in the past to maintain governing authority and capacity. Government activities are open to immediate public scrutiny and criticism; officials have lost the benefit of time lags between policy proposal and public reaction. Indeed, media critics of various political persuasions fear that the mass media, particularly in the United States, are becoming a powerful, organized interest group in their own right, shaping and influencing the type of issues that come before the public and how those issues should be resolved.

In a positive sense, government may in some ways be more responsive and sensitive to public wishes, particularly elected officials who may feel compelled, under the threat of vote-losing publicity, to carry out their duties more conscientiously. Nonetheless government is also less able to make hard decisions--those involving long-term goals with immediate costs--because of public pressures, intensified through the media, for gratification of short-term claims. Sensitivity of elected officials is only one side of the coin in the policy-making process. The other side is the bureaucracy whose languorous procedures operate against those of the politicians by inhibiting speedy reaction to the public's demands and effective implementation of policy. The positive advantages of the reduction in distance between elected officials and the public have been considerably offset by the growth of an impersonal bureaucracy. This phenomenon has moved a different but equally important portion of the government apparatus further away from the reach and control of the populace.[6]

The advent of national media combined with the universality of education have, according to Huntington, encouraged the formation of new groups that pursue specialized interests zealously and often stridently. Political polarization has been the general consequence of the spread of information and education: people are less willing to adopt without question the policies of traditional parties and more prone to accept alternatives. The rise in the late seventies and early eighties of neo-fascist groups, the anti-nuclear movement, abortion foes and proponents in the United States, and others may be partially attributed to the inability of existing parties to absorb and represent these interests. Individuals with special interests have sought more responsive outlets for expressing their concerns.

Demographic changes may be another significant force behind the rise of new demands on the governments of the advanced democracies. The gradual aging of the population has created a need for sustained health and income-related services placing an additional burden on the working population to provide the revenues to finance these services. The subsequent demand for a fair exchange by the burdened segment of the populace forces the government to make promises that cannot be kept or policies that cannot be sustained.

Another demographic shift that has contributed to the pressures on government involves the emergence of a mature work force with a greater ability to engage in "distributional dissent . . . and a readiness to challenge the prevailing pattern of income inequalities."[7] While this mature labor force, especially evident in Great Britain according to British political economist John Goldthorpe, is not revolutionary, neither is it willing to accept unquestioningly the notion that free market forces should determine individuals' welfare. The growth and reinforcement of political and civil rights in the advanced democracies, especially those of association and representation, have strengthened the legitimacy of organizations through which the labor movement has achieved its gains. Most of these gains, primarily in living standards, have been the consequence of concerted, persistent organizational pressure on government to move toward direct intervention and establishment of the welfare state. Governments are now faced with the task of trying to mediate and resolve the conflicts arising from the collision of a declining acquiescence in economic inequalities under capitalism with increasing institutionalization of equality under social democracy.

The Crisis of Economic Management

Perceptions of a breakdown in governability in the advanced democracies is paralleled by similar perceptions of economic crisis evidenced by the longevity of monetary and fiscal problems which the democracies have been unable to resolve either singly or jointly.[8] One of the clearest formulations of the advanced democracies' economic crisis has been made by Samuel Brittan[9] who sees the double phenomenon of high inflation and unemployment as the most serious symptom of a weakened, politically disabled state. In a democracy, he argues, there is supposed to be a consensus on taxes and spending. Inflation should be less prevalent because the state should have the authority to establish acceptable parameters for the expression and resolution of societal demands.

In the advanced democracies however two phenomena have occurred that work to reduce governmental ability or willingness to impose constraints on demands. First, governments have recognized that inflation can operate in their self-interest as a tax on moneyholders, as a mechanism for decreasing the value of the public debt, as a means of fiscal drag (commonly known as tax bracket creep), and as a time lag providing breathing space between policy implementation and economic response. The gains from inflation tend to be concentrated, whereas the costs are spread broadly and for the most part well hidden.

Second, political electoral cycles, particularly in the United States which has an invariable four-year cycle, have promoted the adoption of expansionary economic policies before elections with only a partial slowdown following elections. Brittan claims that this pattern leads to a steady upward movement of inflation and unemployment regardless of the party in power, leaving each successive government with a limited margin within which to maneuver. The problem seems inherent in the democratic political process: politicians press to stimulate the economy and strive to meet constituent claims for benefits in order to maintain their positions in office. No natural force appears to exist to counteract this trend.

Expanding politicization of the economic marketplace lies at the root of the economic crisis of democracy, according to writers such as British sociologist Colin Crouch and Canadian political scientist Thomas Courchene.[10] Individualism and atomism are the core of perfect competition under capitalism. But perfect competition in most sectors tends to disappear as economic interests become organized, enabling them to pursue their goals in the market through direct, controlled action. Gradually this direct action has moved beyond the economic realm and into the political sphere.

This phenomenon, as John Kenneth Galbraith has argued, is now the pattern in the advanced industrial countries as high-technology and capital-intensive industries require, in fact demand, protection through beneficial regulation from the unpredictability and vicissitudes of unfettered capitalism.[11] Instead of being forced to restrict their activities to automatic regulation by the marketplace, organized economic interests have been integrated into the political system. Similarly, those groups that have not been able to pursue their goals through the market have also turned to direct political action. This is natural for some groups since much social action cannot be adequately or appropriately dealt with through market regulation. The cumulative result however is that the political system is burdened with the task of making distributional and allocative decisions once made by the market.[12] Moreover, once state intervention into an area previously in the private domain takes place, there is an inherent tendency for the process to expand because of the vested interests that arise to protect the benefits received from intervention. In essence, the economic role of the state has changed enormously in the past century from facilitative to supportive to interventionist, and it is highly improbable that the trend can be permanently reversed during the term of a particular president or prime minister.

Structural changes in the modern industrial economies, that is "long-standing basic trends unlikely to be reversed in the immediate future,"[13] have been a primary force behind the declining importance of market allocation of costs and benefits and the expanding role of the government in industrial planning and the regulation of prices and costs. According to many writers,[14] much of the economic crisis can be attributed to the inability of advanced industrial democracies to adjust to structural changes in their economies induced by industrial concentration, declining profitability, rapid technological development, and intensified international competition. British economist J. T. Winkler argues that market concentration in certain industrial sectors or product markets has presented the state with a difficult dilemma. Pragmatically, declining industries or large firms cannot be allowed to fail because of probable adverse effects on regional economies. Morally, the state cannot allow oligopolies to plunder the consumer through excessive profit maximizing.[15]

Rapid technological change has also contributed to the heightened complexity of economic issues. For instance, many new and existing groups have made demands for protection against the social costs (for example, toxic waste, air pollution, acid rain, nuclear waste disposal) produced by adverse technological change. The rapidity and extent of technological change has increased the need for technological expertise to solve problems and make decisions. The state has become more reliant on the private sector for expert knowledge as direct inputs into government policy-making.[16] How governments choose to, or are forced to respond to, these structural economic changes may lead to a further blurring of the division between the public and private sectors and may transform the manner in which policy is made.

The Breakdown of the Pluralist Explanation of Democracy

For decades pluralist theory has been the foundation of our democratic system. It has dominated and colored our perceptions of the actual and ideal roles of the state and interest groups in the political sphere. It has been used not only to describe the actual dynamics of democratic politics, but also to prescribe the manner in which the state and civil society should interact. Myths are difficult to dispel, and since the mid-sixties, pluralism has been under attack as the dominant theory of interest group politics in the advanced industrial democracies. Fears of escalating political and economic crisis have caused many to question the efficacy of the pluralist model of problem-solving. Relationships between interest groups and the state are changing in a direction that raises doubts about the accuracy and validity of the pluralist explanation. In the scholarly literature on interest group politics, concern has gradually shifted from a focus on the process of policy-making to an emphasis on its structure, raising new empirical and normative questions. Many ask not only whether pluralism accurately describes the manner in which policies are formulated, but also whether pluralism is "an appropriate procedural and institutional mechanism for public policy-making."[17] The implication is that other institutional arrangements might better enable society to confront and resolve either more effectively or justly the complex, multifaceted problems confronting the advanced democracies.

According to pluralist theory as developed by Bentley, Truman, Dahl, and others,[18] democratic society is comprised of groups that

check and balance each other, thereby preventing any single interest from gaining and exercising undue power. Pluralism holds
that all interests--economic, ethnic, regional, and political
alike--can be organized by people of all economic levels in confidence that they have a reasonable chance to compete with others
for votes and influence. This view of politics is analogous to the
perfect competition of the free market in which firms (interest
groups) form spontaneously and their numbers proliferate and contract as a result of natural market forces over which no one firm
or group of firms has monopoly influence and control. In this
view the pluralist political system is an open, fluid process,
both "self-regulating and self-correcting."[19]

Pluralism also holds that the state's role in politics is to
act as an impartial mediator of competing and conflicting interests. Policy outcomes reflect the public's policy preferences
because they result from the state's neutral resolution of contending pressures. In the pluralist view, the state is not an active
participant in the political process, that is, it has no interests
of its own pursued independently of other groups. The role of the
state is to seek an equilibrium, however temporary, among the
conflicting interests.[20]

In ideological terms, the underlying assumption of pluralism is
that political power is and should be exercised by several interest groups and not by any single set of interests. Multiple
centers of power with overlapping memberships are necessary to
prevent abuses of others' rights as well as to inhibit misuse of
governmental authority. Government is viewed as a "benevolent
umpire."[21] Supporters of pluralism believe, as one observer
notes, that the "interplay of interest enhances individual
freedom" and encourages rational, even creative policy-making,[22]
for the state is compelled to seek consensus among divergent
interests.

Much criticism has been levied against these principles of
pluralism. The notion of politics as a self-regulating, competitive process similar to that of the economic market has been
criticized as particularly fallacious. Perfect competition is an
ideal which exists only in theory. Contemporary mixed capitalist
economies are characterized by oligopoly, barriers to market entry
imposed by both the private and public sectors, and extensive
government regulation. Critics of pluralism claim that, like
advanced capitalism, political competition in the advanced industrial democracies has also become oligopolistic. The equal competition construct of interest group politics ignores the highly

uneven distribution of political, economic, and organizational resources evident among groups in most Western democracies. Critics further assert that some interests are poorly represented or not represented at all (consumers, the poor, and the elderly are among the least well organized largely due to their heterogeneous composition) so that the "public interest" often tends to reflect the demands and goals of small but highly organized segments of society.

The notion of the neutral state has also been assailed by critics. They contend that the state frequently plays an active, self-interested, quasi-autonomous role in the policy-making process. The state is one actor among many in the political system. Moreover, the state tends to be biased at specific times or on certain issues toward a particular group or class. It also tends to take an active role in initiating policies and attempting to structure responses to those initiatives.

Ideologically, critics argue that by dispersing rather than concentrating power, pluralism prevents the state from dealing with important issues through centralized, comprehensive planning. Pluralism reduces the efficiency of decision-making, rendering government unable to process the variety and quantity of demands emanating from organized interests. Critics also claim that dispersion of power has contributed to the rise of entrenched private oligarchies whose leadership is unresponsive to the demands of the rank-and-file membership and whose power rivals that of the state. Internally these associations are only superficially democratic and no longer serve as an effective means through which individual members can pursue common interests. Given these conditions, the power of the private sector, some critics claim, should be matched by an equal amount of power concentrated in the hands of the state.[23]

Corporatism Examined

The weaknesses of pluralism as a model of interest group politics along with fears of prolonged political and economic crisis have been the major forces behind the search for an alternative, more realistic explanation of politics in the advanced industrial democracies. The theory that has received the most attention in recent years is known as "corporatism." The enthusiasm with which the corporatist perspective on state-society relations has been adopted has led to an enormous outpouring of writings, and increasingly critiques, creating a virtual "growth industry" in corporatism as a subfield in comparative politics.[24] Accompanying this literary profusion has been heightened confusion over what the term "corporatism" actually means. In general terms, corporatism as applied to the advanced democracies purports to describe a cooperative, symbiotic relationship between major nationwide associations (usually of business and labor) and the state which facilitates policy-making and implementation through mutual arrangements and tradeoffs. In a corporatist society legislative institutions no longer play the primary role in regulating state-society relations; instead the state interacts directly through its agencies with organized interests.

However, since each writer in this field presents his own definition of corporatism, even the most experienced reader of corporatist literature can be overwhelmed by the assortment of meanings ascribed to the same term. Philippe Schmitter, whose seminal writings have been highly influential in this field, himself complains that the "concept of corporatism suffers from being either too broadly defined so that relationships that it purports to describe can be found everywhere or too narrowly defined so that it becomes unique and not analytically or comparatively useful."[25] Corporatist theory is as diverse as the varieties of corporatist thought from which it is derived. Nonetheless, contemporary theories share assumptions of unity, class harmony, cooperation, and consensus which originate from common threads in corporatist thought.

The theoretical origins of corporatism lie in a branch of late nineteenth and early twentieth century social theory that rejected both the individualism and competitive capitalism of classic liberals and the class conflict and collectivism of Marx. The goal of the theory's proponents was to establish a society founded on class harmony and organic unity in which hierarchically and functionally organized socioeconomic groups worked together for the good of the whole while maintaining their own autonomy. Representation of the interests of individuals was to occur through the functional group of which he was a member. The word corporatism itself derives from the Latin "corpus" (body) reflecting the belief that the disparate elements of society should be united in a mutually interdependent manner into a whole.

Despite this common goal, the methods by which an ideal corporatist society would be achieved in practice varied among the different models that emerged from corporatist thinking. In practice, although corporatist thought constituted the theoretical foundation for fascism in the 1930s its functional groups were completely subordinated to the state. In many ways the corporatist concept still suffers from this heritage.

However, Schmitter has made significant strides toward ridding corporatism of its ideological overtones and connections with particular political systems. He urges the objective use of the corporatist concept as one of several possible explanations of contemporary political trends. Toward this end he has identified two subtypes of corporatism: "state corporatism" and "societal corporatism." These are distinguished by the different roles that the state assumes in the transformation of a fragmented society into an organic, corporate whole.[26] In theory, state corporatism describes a system in which the direction of the flow of power, control, and manipulation is from the state to society. The different economic interests (obviously central players in the development of class harmony) are organized by the state into singular, non-competitive, hierarchically stratified groups subordinate to and dependent on the state. These groups are granted special representational privileges and are included in the policy-making process in exchange for exerting certain controls over the expression of demands by their members.

According to many scholars, state corporatism has been evident in varying degrees in Peru under the liberal military rule of Juan Velasco Alvarado from 1968 to 1975. During this period many organizations, such as the National Agrarian Confederation and the National Industrial Community Commission, were established as the sole legitimate organizations for their sectors. A more overtly repressive form of state corporatism has been practiced in Brazil, particularly during the decade following the 1964 military coup. Brazilian labor groups were severely repressed; those that continued to function did so under the thumb of the government. Since 1973, the Pinochet government in Chile has listened half-heartedly to corporatist philosophers, known as "Integralists," while pursuing its own brand of enforced corporatism through replacement of many existing groups with state-controlled organizations. Features of state corporatism have been present in Mexico since 1940 and in Spain under Franco from 1936 until 1975.[27]

While the organizational structure under societal corporatism is superficially similar to that of state corporatism, its groups are in theory autonomous and tend to penetrate the state. Organizations cooperate with the state and work closely with other groups because of their mutual interdependence.[28] The actual configuration of interest groups (that is, noncompetitive, hierarchical, singular) is not imposed by the state. It evolves out of the efforts of interest groups to institutionalize their relationships with the state which the state may actively encourage. Cooperation with the state, not domination by the state, is strongly emphasized. According to Schmitter, this evolution can occur in several ways such as through spontaneous or voluntary agreements among groups, through the natural consolidating tendencies of bureaucratic processes, or increasingly through the efforts of political leaders to improve the efficiency of the policy-making process.[29] In the view of some observers, elements of societal corporatism have been identified in many of the advanced industrial democracies of Western Europe (most strongly evident in Scandinavia, Switzerland, Holland, and Austria) and, to a lesser extent, North America, with Great Britain, France, and West Germany occupying a middle stage of development.

Corporatist Theory as Response to Pluralism's Inadequacies

The weaknesses of pluralism as viewed by its critics has led many to consider corporatism as a more appropriate theoretical framework for examining contemporary relationships between the state and civil society. In many advanced democracies the relationships among interest groups are not marked by competitive interaction, but by "complementary interdependence."[30] This is illustrated, corporatists claim, by the close collaboration in company and industry policy between labor and management in most large corporations in Japan, West Germany, and Sweden.

Corporatists also assert that the state in the advanced democracies is no longer (if it ever was) a neutral bystander. The state frequently acts as an autonomous actor in the political process with interests of its own and independent capacity to achieve its goals, although this capacity may vary depending on the particular issues that are being debated.[31] The state often openly encourages the development of strong, centralized national associations as a means of limiting the number of groups and consequently the quantity of demands with which it must deal. An example of this is the British government's efforts in 1965 to promote the formation of the Confederation of British Industry (CBI), now considered the principle organization representing British business interests.[32] The Swedish model of politics also appears to follow this pattern. Leaders of social democratic governments have promoted highly centralized labor and industry organizations (the Swedish Trade Union Confederation--LO, and the Swedish Employers' Confederation--SAF), giving large wage and work welfare-related concessions to labor in exchange for stability in labor-business relations.

Finally, corporatists argue that the development of industrial capitalism and the subsequent rise of centers of power rivaling the state have been paralleled by the creation of symbiotic, collaborative arrangements between the bureaucracy and the private sector which does not fit the pluralist model. Government "regulatory bodies . . . [such as the Environmental Protection Agency, and the Departments of Energy and Commerce in the United States] . . . tend to become the captives of the firms that ostensibly they regulate," making it difficult for government either to control or challenge them.[33]

The concept of the state in the corporatist literature seems unrealistically one-sided and as out of place today as pluralism's notion of the passive mediator-state. But in fact most of the major writings on corporatism avoid proposing a concrete definition of the state. One writer suggests that the state does not include parties and the parliamentary system because these institutions tend to be bypassed in the salient policy-making issue areas.[34] Does the state then include only the administrative agencies and bureaucracies? It seems to assume that these are consistent and congruent interests that seldom conflict and that enable the state to act as a "single, monolithic unit." At least one critic of corporatism suggests that it is "nonsense to assume that the state is a monolithic unity. . . . The state is as complex and fractionated as the economic sphere in its financial, commercial, and productive and labor sectors, and these divisions ensure conflicts within the bureaucracy and the state apparatus over policy."[35]

There is another problematic aspect of corporatism that raises serious questions about the theory's perspective on interest group-state relations. There is an assumption in corporatist theory that apparent tendencies toward corporatism in the Western democracies are a direct consequence of the evolution of advanced industrial capitalism in which the state assumes a central role to ensure the continuity of the capitalist system.[36] While the arguments are complex and neo-Marxist in origin and need not be reviewed here, the implications of this assumption are straightforward. By deriving societal corporatism from the economic system within which it operates, the corporatist model becomes a static one consisting only of economically (that is, class-) based

groups that interact corporatively with the state only over economic policy issues. Non-economic groups such as environmental
organizations, senior citizens, blacks in the U.S., and ethnic
groups in Europe, that may have a direct and significant influence
on a variety of economic policies, are virtually ignored. Thus,
interest groups in the corporatist model are characterized as
fixed, never changing, and internally cohesive, obscuring the
fluid, competitive, and highly complex interactions that characterize inter- and intra-group relations in the advanced industrial
democracies.

In spite of these and other criticisms, corporatism's core
propositions concerning close cooperative relationships between
interest groups and the state appear to describe realistically
patterns that are emerging in some of the advanced democracies.
Despite its shortcomings, corporatism's usefulness lies in its
ability to provide us with an alternative perspective for viewing
democratic politics and to compel us either to question further
the relevance of the pluralist viewpoint or to strengthen our
commitment to the theory and practice of pluralist democracy.

Corporatism as Response to Political and Economic Crisis

On a more practical level, unease about the capacity of governments to respond efficiently and adequately to continuing political and economic crisis has convinced many to take a closer look
at the practical advantages that corporatist arrangements between
state and interest groups can offer. At least partial adoption of
corporatist decision-making procedures is being advocated by many
as a solution to the apparent failures of the advanced democracies
to cope with the challenges facing their authority and capacity to
govern and to deal with the increasing political burdens that
society is forcing them to bear. Some corporatist theorists like
Schmitter believe that corporatism and pluralism can co-exist,
albeit in different policy-making arenas. Corporatism in this
view is simply a technique of mediating and minimizing conflict
among groups and between groups and the state as a means of controlling escalating demands on the state. Another writer sees
corporatism as a more efficient, pragmatic method of building
consensus and making policy in the face of a general collapse in
the competence of party systems to facilitate speedy and rational
decisions.[37] Still a third writer views corporatist practices,
particularly the deliberate promotion of organized social inte-

rests, as a means of forcing groups to play by the rules of the political system, thereby preserving social order in a period of impending chaos.[38]

Corporatism is also being advocated as a likely solution to the inability of governments to resolve economic crises through conventional processes and methods. The emergence of corporatist features in state-society relations is being hailed as a pragmatic, administratively necessary and efficient solution to managing societal adjustment to structural economic changes. If the state is politically incapable of directly imposing constraints on societal demands, which it appears to be, it can develop explicit alliances with the major economic interests seeking support for and cooperation with economic policies in exchange for participation in the policy-making process. For example, institutionalized consultation can occur between the government and major labor organizations to obtain wage restraints as a means of holding down inflation. One advantage of corporatism as envisioned by its advocates is that such arrangements can be beneficial to all participants, and are just as likely to be initiated and encouraged by the private sector as they are by the public.

West Germany and Japan have been most explicit and successful in institutionalizing cooperative, corporatist relations between business and the state as a means of encouraging readjustment to industry-related structural change. Assistance to troubled firms and industries has been given on the condition that plants be retooled and labor and management retrained to compete effectively on the world market. Japan's Structurally Depressed Industries Law provides subsidies to firms that agree to scrap their excess capacity thereby encouraging uncompetitive firms to leave the industry. It also stipulates that redundant workers be retrained to assist their relocation to more competitive industries. West Germany has set up a system through private regional banks for subsidizing resource shifts from declining to growing industries.[39] Also since 1969 every West German adult has been offered up to two years of job training or retraining at full government expense. In Sweden, a reemployment program matching industry needs with worker skills has existed for several decades, financed jointly by government, business, and labor.[40] Although an industrial policy with these features has never existed in the United States, adoption of a coherent industrial adjustment policy is now being urged on several political and economic fronts. Corporatism, though seldom mentioned, is an essential ingredient of such efforts.

Conclusion: Conflicts between Corporatism and Democracy

Although "crisis" may be an extreme way of describing conditions in the advanced democracies today, the political and economic pressures under which governments are trying to operate are
considerable.   If the development of corporatist relations between
the state and civil society is a viable means of controlling and
processing demands and facilitating economic adjustment to structural change, perhaps we should applaud and encourage rather than
resist and condemn such efforts.   Even if we wanted to it is not
clear that we can resist creeping tendencies toward corporatism.
Certain features of pluralist democracy and the mixed economy
actively encourage the development of corporatism.   For example,
pluralism promotes and supports participation by individuals
through groups that perform specific functions, such as trade
unions, and veterans organizations.   Interest groups are a legitimate, vital and necessary part of the democratic process, and
have been given the authority to represent their members' interests over against both competing groups and the state.   It is
natural that interest groups should turn to the state for favors
just as the state should call upon and receive cooperation from
the major interests. In the advanced democracies demands for
benefits have run up against a finite source.   Ultimately governments must seek concessions in return for benefits if the democratic system is be to preserved.

The nature of the mixed economy and the problems of planning
that go along with it also seem to be pushing governments and
groups in the direction of societal corporatism.   Keynesian
efforts to manipulate overall demand as a means of controlling the
vagaries of the market economy have failed and been replaced in
much of Western Europe by sectoral planning that requires a
greater degree of consultation between the state and affected
groups than ever before.   Institutionalized consultation can easily acquire a corporatist character.[41]

If corporatism is merely cooperation and consensus-building,
surely this form of state-society interaction has been going on
for decades without adverse effects on the democratic system.   The
new writings on corporatism may be simply giving a new name to an
old practice.   As one writer notes, institutionalized consultation
"is not of itself corporatist.   It can be public, representative
and participatory, and allow for competition."   What we must be

concerned about is the "secret, non-competitive, oligarchic" type of corporatism.[42]

The rise of forms of decision-making that are removed from direct public influence and the legal constraints which govern the political process is an explicit challenge to representative democracy. As British political scientist H. M. Drucker explains:

> In a corporate society all important decisions are meant to be made in private negotiation between the representatives of the powerful functional groups. Government is, of course, one such powerful group; but only one. The hallmark of corporatist decision-making . . . is the **extra-legal, extra-constitutional** way government has to deal with the other functional groups. . . . In a corporate society the constitutional forms, and most especially the legislative parts of these forms, are radically devalued (emphasis added).[43]

Another British political scientist warns that the development of corporatism creates problems for liberal democracies "in which the accountability of government to elected assemblies is a cardinal rule. For where the government and private experts agree on a solution, there is a tendency to presume that this is not open to question."[44]

Corporatism in practice poses a danger to democratic modes of policy-making if commitment by the leadership to conventional procedures for defining policy declines and the role of representative legislatures is perceived as less central to the policy process. Direct interaction and consultation between the state and interest groups need not be anti-democratic and exclusionary. It becomes so when such forms of policy-making take precedence over and actually circumvent legislative procedures. In the advanced democracies legislatures provide a forum however imperfect for the expression of many disparate interests. The importance of this forum is eclipsed when certain groups in society are bestowed with uneven advantages through special access to the policy-making process. In this way, groups which are not part of the elected decision-making apparatus are given joint responsibility for policy decisions and implementation. The process becomes isolated from the influence of politics; participants are not held accountable for their decisions as are elected officials.

Moreover, explicit recognition of one group over another assumes that these chosen groups best represent the spectrum of interests in their sector, leaving little room for consideration of minority or opposing viewpoints. Dissent within any given sector might go unheard, or worse, be suppressed. There are also disadvantages for the recognized groups: close ties to government may eventually result in less autonomy and some loss in their representative status.

The moral dilemmas posed by the conjuncture of corporatism and democracy are paralleled by the practical problems of whether corporatism can improve the efficiency of government policy-making. Samuel Brittan points out that corporatist practices might exacerbate inefficiencies and further undermine market functions. These inefficiencies result from what he calls "a fair exchange of restrictive practices: a tariff for one industry in exchange for quotas for another and a government subsidy for a third." Moreover, the benefits derived from restraint by interest groups are diffused across a broad segment of the population, whereas the costs are concentrated among the self- or government-restrained groups. Thus some corporatist relations may be inherently doomed to fail for group leaders are unlikely to commit political suicide by focusing on long-term benefits while members see only the short-term costs of restraint.[45]

There are bound to develop other moral and practical problems if corporatist tendencies especially evident in some Western European countries become more permanent features of those societies. As theory, corporatism in many ways more accurately portrays contemporary state-civil society relations than does pluralism. But we must make a clear distinction between the usefulness of a theory (its explanatory power) and our ideological adoption of it as the way society should be organized. While corporatist theory may sometimes better explain the actual structure of interest group politics than pluralism, it is not clear that we should then encourage complete restructuring of our political system along corporatist lines. Prolonged political and economic crisis may push us unavoidably in this direction, but we must ensure that close consultation and cooperation remain open to political influence from the general population and operate within the constitutional framework of our legislative processes. The price of adoption of corporatism as a preferred system of politics will almost certainly be a loss of freedom.

Notes

1. Robert B. Reich, The Next American Frontier (New York: Times Books, 1983), p. 3.

2. Lester Thurow, The Zero-Sum Society (New York: Basic Books, 1980); Paul Hawken, The Next Economy (New York: Holt, Rinehart and Winston, 1983); Richard Cornuelle, Healing America: What Can be Done About the Continuing Economic Crisis (New York: G.P. Putnam's Sons, 1983); Samuel Brittan, "Can Democracy Manage an Economy?" in Robert Skidelsky, The End of the Keynesian Era (London: MacMillan Press Ltd., 1977); Michel Crozier, Samuel P. Huntington, and Joji Watanuki, The Crisis of Democracy: Report on the Governability of Democracies to the Trilateral Commission (New York: New York University Press, 1975).

3. Brittan, "Can Democracy Manage an Economy?"; Thurow, The Zero-Sum Society; Samuel P. Huntington, "The United States" in Crozier, et al., The Crisis of Democracy.

4. Crozier, The Crisis of Democracy, Conclusion.

5. Crozier.

6. Reginald J. Harrison, Pluralism and Corporatism: The Political Evolution of Modern Democracies (London: George Allen and Unwin, 1980), p. 9.

7. John H. Goldthorpe, "The Current Inflation: Towards a Sociological Account" in Fred Hirsch and John H. Goldthorpe (editors), The Political Economy of Inflation (Cambridge: Harvard University Press, 1978), p. 193. See particularly pp. 204–210 for a general discussion.

8. Several books have recently been published on this subject. See, note 2.

9. Samuel Brittan, "Inflation and Democracy," in Hirsch and Goldthorpe (editors), The Political Economy of Inflation.

10. Colin Crouch, "Inflation and the Political Organization of Economic Interests," in Hirsch and Goldthorpe (editors), The Political Economy of Inflation; Thomas J. Courchene, "Towards a Protected Society: The Politicization of Economic Life," Canadian Journal of Economics, November 1980.

11. John Kenneth Galbraith, Economics and the Public Purpose (Harmondsworth: Pelican Books, 1975).

12. It can be argued that with the decline in the legitimate authority of traditional institutions, the state has also assumed a normative role in many of its interventions. See, Crouch, "Inflation and the Political Organization of Economic Interest," p. 225.

13. J. T. Winkler, "Corporatism," Archives Europeenes Sociologique XVII (1976), p. 117.

14. Winkler. Also, Harrison, Pluralism and Corporatism.

15. Winkler, "Corporatism," p. 121.

16. See, for example, Harrison, Pluralism and Corporatism, pp. 6–8.

17. Charles W. Anderson, "Political Design and the Representation of Interests," Comparative Political Studies 10:1 (April 1977), p. 129.

18. A. F. Bentley, The Process of Government (Cambridge: Harvard University Press, 1967); David Truman, The Governmental Process (New York: Knopf, 1951); Robert A. Dahl, A Preface to Democratic Theory (Chicago: The University of Chicago Press, 1956).

19. William A. Kelso, American Democratic Theory: Pluralism and its Critics (Westport, CT: Greenwood Press, 1978), p. 14.

20. There is of course a similar debate in the Marxist literature about the nature of the state and whether it is anything but a tool used by the dominant class to achieve its goals.

21. David Nicholls, Three Varieties of Pluralism (New York: St. Martin's Press, 1974), p. 25.

22. Kelso, American Democratic Theory, p. 12.

23. See E. E. Schattschneider, The Semi-Sovereign People (New York: Holt, Rinehart and Winston, 1960); Henry Kariel, The Decline of American Pluralism (Stanford: Stanford University Press, 1961); Grant McConnell, Private Power and American Democracy (New York: Knopf, 1966); Theodore J. Lowi, The End of Liberalism: Ideology, Policy and the Crisis of Public Authority (New York: Norton, 1969).

24. Leo Panitch, "Recent Theorizations of Corporatism: reflections on a growth industry," British Journal of Sociology 31 (June 1980).

25. Philippe C. Schmitter, "Still the Century of Corporatism?" in Frederick B. Pike and Thomas Stritch (editors), The New Corporatism (Notre Dame and London: University of Notre Dame Press, 1974), p. 86. Panitch, "Recent Theorizations of Corporatism," and Winkler, "Corporatism," also support this view.

26. Schmitter, "Still the Century of Corporatism?"

27. James M. Malloy, "Authoritarianism, Corporatism and Mobilization in Peru," in Pike and Stritch (editors), The New Corporatism; Kenneth Paul Erikson, The Brazilian Corporative State and Working Class Politics (Berkeley: University of California Press, 1977); Frederick B. Pike, "The New Corporatism in Franco's Spain and Some Latin American Perspectives," in Pike and Stritch (editors), The New Corporatism; Alfred Stepan, The State and Society: Peru in Comparative Perspective (Princeton: Princeton University Press, 1978). Stepan identifies two types of state corporatism: inclusionary, such as that practiced in Peru under which existing groups are incorporated into the corporatist structure, and exclusionary, such as practiced in Brazil and Chile, under which existing groups are dissolved and new ones created by the state in their place.

28. David Marsh and Wyn Grant, "Tripartism: Reality or Myth?," Government and Opposition 12 (1977), p. 196.

29. Schmitter, "Still the Century of Corporatism?".

30. Schmitter. p. 97.

31. Lehmbruch's model stipulates that the state's power varies by issue area. See Gerhard Lehmbruch, "Liberal Corporatism and Party Government," Comparative Political Studies 10:1 (April 1977). Winkler however holds that the state has

considerable though not completely omnipotent power. See Winkler, "Corporatism." Schmitter sees group-state power relations as more fluid and changeable. See Schmitter, "Still the Century of Corporatism?" and his "Modes of Interest Intermediation and Models of Societal Change in Western Europe," Comparative Political Studies 10:1 (April 1977). There is a fourth view of the state in the neo-Marxist corporatist literature which ascribes little autonomy to the state and near-total power to private monopoly capital. The state is said to be "privatized" by the monopoly sector. See James O'Connor, The Fiscal Crisis of the State (New York: St. Martin's Press, 1973).

32. Crouch, "Inflation and the Political Organization of Economic Interests," p. 222.

33. Galbraith, Economics and the Public Purpose, p. 176; see also McConnell, Private Power and American Democracy for an even more extreme view of U.S. state-group relations.

34. See Lehmbruch, "Liberal Corporatism and Party Government."

35. Andrew Cox, "Corporatism as Reductionism: The Analytic Limits of the Corporatist Thesis," Government and Opposition 16 (Winter 1981), p. 90.

36. See for example, Winkler, "Corporatism."

37. See Lehmbruch, "Liberal Corporatism and Party Government."

38. Crouch, "Inflation and the Political Organization of Economic Interests," p. 222.

39. Reich, The Next American Frontier, p. 199.

40. Reich, p. 220.

41. Harrison, Pluralism and Corporatism, p. 61.

42. Harrison, p. 88.

43. H. M. Drucker, "Devolution and Corporatism," Government and Opposition 12 (1977), p. 179.

44. Harrison, Pluralism and Corporatism, p. 8.

45. Samuel Brittan, "Towards a Corporate State?," Encounter 44 (1975), pp. 61-62.

Judging the Health of
a Democratic System

William A. Douglas

If we wish to play the role of physicians of politics, and give a democratic political system a "physical examination," what indicators should we use to determine if the system is healthy or diseased? The question is one with practical importance. Many corporations and banks employ political scientists to do "risk analysis," and in relation to democratic countries, the corporations want to know whether the democratic system is viable or about to collapse. Governments must make similar calculations. Recently a U.S. diplomat stationed in the Dominican Republic complained that back at the State Department in Washington the key decision-makers were assuming that there were no political problems in the Dominican Republic, because the nation has successfully carried out two democratic elections. What indicators should the diplomat cite to make the point that beneath the surface the Dominican democratic polity remains very shaky? Administrators of foreign assistance programs must make similar judgments about the health of democracies. Aid institutions engaged in assisting political development, such as the West German Ebert, Adenauer, and Naumann Foundations, or the American AFL-CIO's three regional labor-development institutes, need to identify the weak spots in democratic polities so these aid organizations know where the priority needs lie. Thus, just as a physician has a checklist when giving a physical examination (blood pressure, weight, etc.), so does the analyst of democracies' health need his own checklist.

The checklist developed below (and summarized at the end of the chapter) is designed to apply to political systems in which the principal leaders of the national government are chosen periodically in free, seriously contested elections held under conditions in which the freedoms of speech, press, and association prevail.[1]

The considerations that led to selection of the indicators cited arose during the author's work in developing countries, so the checklist will be most applicable in the developing areas, but many of the same indicators would also be useful in judging the health of industrialized democracies. In fact, many United States and European writers decrying certain weaknesses in democratic polities of Asia or Latin America often fail to note that democracy in their own industrialized homelands may exhibit precisely these same weaknesses! (Either the viability of the industrialized democracies despite the weaknesses should offer some hope to the developing democracies, or the danger of collapse of the latter due to the weaknesses should be taken as a warning signal in the industrialized democracies.) Thus there is utility in applying the same checklist to both developing and industrialized democracies.

The Electoral Process.

The most immediate and obvious item for the evaluator of a democracy's health to note is the election system itself. This requires little comment. Let it suffice to say that three main questions should be asked about the elections:

First, are they really free? The manipulation of "election" procedures by dictatorial regimes for purposes other than choosing national leaders is so commonplace today that no claim of "free elections" should be taken at face value. In many dictatorships that hold elections several opposition parties are allowed to present candidates, and these candidates frequently win a significant number of votes. However, opposition parties and candidates with enough support that they might actually win control of the government are not allowed in such systems, and the elections are not really free, because they do not determine who will govern the country. Elections under the Somoza regime in Nicaragua, and the 1981 elections in South Korea are examples. Deciding whether elections in a given country are truly free requires considerable knowledge of the political forces in that country, and may sometimes be a "judgment call." One useful thing to note is whether, before the elections, there is avid speculation in the free press and in conversations among citizens about who is going to win. If bets are being offered and accepted, the elections probably really will determine who will govern. Uncertainty over the outcome is the hallmark of a free election.

Secondly, are the votes counted, and the results reported, honestly? Probably no democratic election has ever occurred in which no citizen voted twice, everyone who voted was alive, and the results reported at every single polling place corresponded precisely to the actual contents of the ballot box. President Kennedy often noted that the first political slogan he heard as a child in Boston was "Vote early and often!" Thus the question should be, not whether any electoral fraud occurred, but whether it was enough to alter substantially the percentage of the vote won by each candidate or party. (Elections so close that a tiny amount of fraud determine who won should still be considered honest. The 1960 Kennedy-Nixon contest in the United States is widely thought to have been so close that had all the votes in Cook County, Illinois, been counted accurately, Kennedy might have lost. It is also widely believed that the reason Republicans did not contest the count in Cook County was that they did not wish to invite close scrutiny of the remarkably high Republican total in southern Illinois.)

Finally, did most of the electorate vote? A high rate of voter abstention is often an indication that the democratic political system is in trouble. Voters who have no faith in the system may stay home on election day as an act of rejection or of protest. The rate of abstention in Colombia, sometimes as high as sixty percent of the electorate, is often cited as an indicator of deep-seated trouble in Colombia's democratic polity.[2] A high percentage of blank ballots, cast in protest, is a similar way of showing voter alienation from the prevailing political system.

The Political Parties.

First, one must ask: Are the nation's political parties personalistic or programmatic? Many political parties in developing countries are simply conglomerations of local political factions. Often the factions are rural-based, and they are led by politicians from the families traditionally powerful and influential in each area. Each faction consists of a political patron and his loyal clients. The clients offer loyalty and support to the patron, and he provides protection and favors to the clients. Small patrons in local areas, in turn are clients of bigger patrons at the regional level, who in turn join in political parties at the national level. Patronage, cronyism, and the dispensation of favors are the political coin of such a political system.

It is sometimes difficult for a foreigner to tell that a nation's parties are merely coalitions of personal groups, because the parties often have impressive, modern-sounding names, seemingly based on some ideology or program. One indication of personalistic politics may be the names of factions or groupings within a party: if they are known as "Mr. X's faction," or "Mr. Y's faction," rather than "progressive," "socialist," or "pro-business" groups, then the party itself is probably also personalistic. Another hint is the stability of factional membership in each party. If factions leave their parties between elections, and recombine in different groupings, this is another indicator of personalistic politics continuing behind the facade of modern party names. Another indication is the presence of only one strong leader in a given party or faction. Where teamwork among two or more strong leadership personalities is evident in a political grouping, some bond is keeping the leaders cooperating-- usually common belief in an ideology. In personalistic politics, each faction is the machine of one person. In case of competition between two leaders in an inner-group or party election, the winner will award all the positions in the group to his own followers, purging all the followers of his defeated challenger. The latter, of course, then secedes and founds a separate faction identified only with him. Personalistic politics thus inevitably result in division and fragmentation of democratic political movements. In Honduras, for example, there are now twelve democratic peasant organizations, each led by one, and only one, strong leadership personality.

Another common consequence of personalistic democratic parties is corruption. If each political group is led by one leader, and he entered politics mainly for careerist reasons--to advance his own position and prestige--then he has little reason to refrain from taking bribes, or demanding kickbacks, or profiting from inside information, whenever the opportunity presents itself. He has no other goal in politics than the advancement of his personal interests. Personalistic democratic politics is thus often not only factional, but also corrupt politics.

Personalistic democratic parties can function adequately in a democratic electoral system. The big-city machines in the United States lasted for many decades, and they were certainly characterized by personalism, factionalism, patronage, favor-trading, and corruption.   In Panama and the Philippines,[3] a similar kind of politics functioned for many years, and it is still surviving as of this writing in Colombia. When democratic systems based on personalistic politics fall, it is not so much because of their sins of commission--factionalism and corruption--as their sins of omission--their inability to lead their nations to rapid economic growth with equitable social conditions.[4]

Successful economic development requires changing a nation: changing the social structure, changing the way people think, and changing social customs. Personalistic parties cannot change a nation because the basis for the survival of such parties is the continuation of the old ways of the personalistic, traditional society. Unless they evolve into more modern forms, democratic polities based on personalistic parties will usually collapse to be replaced with some form of dictatorship: often military, sometimes totalitarian.

To industrialize and modernize a society, programmatic parties are needed, based not on personal careerism, but on commitment to an ideology and a program for national modernization. In such movements personal ambition is of course present, but it is supplemented by the commitment of political leaders to a goal going beyond their own personal careers and fortunes: modernizing the nation. Factionalism is more easily restrained in programmatic parties, for two or more strong leaders, all committed to the same ideology and program, have a basis for working together as a team. Their rivalries and struggles can be limited and contained within the framework of the party, instead of splitting the party. Corruption can also be more easily controlled, for leaders have reasons besides personal advancement for entering politics, and thus have more ethical restraints on their actions. Most important of all, programmatic parties are committed to national development and have a plan for bringing it about. Their cohesion depends on progress toward their goal of change, for their ideology of development is the cement holding their organization together, not just personal ties of political patron and client. The most basic question to ask about parties, then is: Are they personalistic or programmatic?

Having an ideology and program, and leaders committed to them, is of course not enough for success. To change a nation, the party must reach the entire nation. To carry through its program, the party must mobilize the population. This requires organization--mass organization. Geographically, the party must reach into every district in the countryside and every neighborhood in the city.   Socially, it must be a multi-class party; that is, if conservative it must reach from the wealthy families at least down into the upper-middle class, or if progressive, it must reach from the impoverished up through at least the lower-middle class. (Coverage of all social classes by each party would be the ideal, but has seldom if ever been attained once national independence has been won. Only during anti-colonial struggles do all classes of a nation have a mutual interest strong enough to maintain them all within a given party.) To staff all these party branches, the party will need thousands, often hundreds of thousands, of members. Political cliques of intellectuals may have ideologies and programs, but without mass organization their political reach is limited to the cafes of the capital city.

The mass membership of a programmatic democratic party must have enough internal discipline that the party branches present more or less the same program throughout the nation, and mobilize popular support for the same efforts. Personalistic democratic parties, if they comprise enough factions, may have a large membership, and may cover the nation geographically, but they are so disunited that they deliver little if any message, and certainly not a common message throughout the country. To reach an entire society with the party's program of change, the movement needs a mass membership, all accepting and trying to popularize the same ideology and platform.

The party's activists--both its fulltime staff and its part-time volunteers--to operate an impersonal, modern, program-based movement, must themselves have a modern outlook and some prior experience in other modern, impersonal organizations. Such experience is seldom possessed by the political patrons who preside over the local units of personalistic parties. They often go directly from their locally prominent family into the university, and from there into full-time politics. Their outlook and social attitudes are those of the personal, face-to-face, patron-client relationships of traditional rural society, even though they may hold a degree from a U.S. or European university.

Programmatic democratic parties must recruit their local leaders from among persons who have already worked in large modern organizations. Conservative parties will look for young business executives, government "technocrats," or former military officers, who are comfortable in the milieu of the modern corporation or the professionalized army. Progressive parties must look to the lower-income groups ('the popular classes') for their activists, and will depend mainly on members with prior experience in such modern organizations as trade unions and cooperatives. The majority of progressive, programmatic democratic parties in the developing nations have a trade-union base as a training ground for party workers. In Latin America, for example, the Venezuelan Accion Democratica Party has its base in the CTV labor federation, as does the Peruvian APRA Party in the CTP, and the Mexican PRI in the CTM. In regard to a party's membership, then, the political analyst should note whether the middle leaders have begun their careers as professional politicians, or whether they are now or have been within modern corporations, government bureaucracies, trade unions, or cooperatives.

To contrast progammatic democratic parties with traditional, personalistic ones that rely on dispensing patronage and trading favors is not to indicate that the modern parties confine themselves only to popularizing their ideas. Favors and services to constituents are always a major part of democratic politics. The services which the programmatic parties provide, however, are part and parcel of their effort to modernize their societies. Most of the successful programmatic democratic parties, such as the APRA in Peru or the Congress Party in India, use their mass organizations not only for political tasks, but also to bring modern skills and attitudes to the people.[5] In the countryside they teach hygiene, reading, nutrition, and crop rotation. In the city they aid the migrants arriving from the rural areas, providing cafeterias, dormitories, employment agencies, and vocational training. All these services may seem far from the political role of a modern party in spreading its ideology and winning votes in election campaigns. However, these social services are part and parcel of modern politics. Providing them enables the programmatic parties to compete with the personalistic parties' offerings of patronage jobs and personal favors, as well as with totalitarian parties and military forces, both of which also offer the people similar services. In sum, the provision of social services makes the programmatic parties channels of modern influence in the society, and thus makes them, like armies, dominant forces in the nation during the modernization process. Political analysts, then, should ask not only how well the democratic parties are doing their work of political propaganda and electioneering, but also if they are providing practical social services to the citizens as well.

Programmatic parties, with mass organizations, staffed with activists at home in impersonal organizational settings, and performing both political and social services to the public, clearly need widely comprehensive ideologies to provide guidelines for a party's program and its varied activities. A few slogans about nationalism and progress will not suffice; even the traditional personalistic parties can come up with verbiage at this general level. Modernization is a confusing process, and the party's members and voters need some general pattern to which they can relate all the changes in their lives. Four areas in particular should be covered by a comprehensive ideology of a democratic party:

1. The nation's political system. The ideology should explain how the nation is governed at present, why political democracy is the best system of government, and how the nation's social structure relates to national politics. (If no one else offers an explanation of this last point to the voters, one can rest assured that anti-democrats such as the communists will.)

2. The nation's economic system. How are the factories, banks, stores, and farms owned? How are wages determined, and how does the market set prices? What changes, if any, does the party advocate in these existing ownership and market systems? What is the present distribution of income? If the party advocates income redistribution, what social reforms does it propose through which to achieve such a redistribution?

3. The nation's role in international affairs. Where is the nation located in the world power balance--with the Eastern bloc, with the West, or non-aligned? Does the party advocate any change in this alignment? What is the nation's role in the international economy? What are its major trading patterns? How much foreign investment is coming into the nation? Does the party advocate changes in the nation's foreign trade or investment positions?

4. An economic development strategy for the nation. How does the party propose to provide enough jobs to absorb the growing labor force? What types of industry, using what kinds of technology, does the party feel the nation should emphasize? What measures, social and technical, does the party advocate for increasing agricultural productivity? How does the development strategy recommended by

the party fit the democratic political system it supports?
In judging the strength of parties in a democracy, then,
another question we should ask is: Do the parties' ideologies cover these four key areas?

We can conclude that if the democratic parties are programmatic, possess mass organization, have modernized middle-level leadership, perform both political and social-service functions, and
have comprehensive ideologies, political democracy in a nation
will be strengthened. If the parties lack a significant number of
these characteristics, democracy will probably fail.

Party Coverage of the Electorate.

The peoples of nation-states are seldom homogeneous. They are
divided by race (as in Guyana), by geographic region (as in
Ecuador or Colombia), by language (as in India), by tribe (as in
Nigeria), and in almost any nation, by social class (management
versus labor, or "the oligarchy" versus "the popular classes").
The central purposes of democracy are to maintain peace in a
nation by giving each group the political means to defend itself
against oppression by others, and to attain social justice by
giving each group channels for demanding its fair share of the
wealth. For a healthy democracy, every major group must have
political power and political channels through which to apply it.
Even the existence of modern, programmatic parties is not
always sufficient to maintain a democratic polity if those parties
do not represent some of the major groups in the society. Those
with no party channel will remain excluded from the democratic
political system, and fail to support it. They are open to the
appeals of dictatorial forces of the right or the left.
In a nation with a history of antagonism between racial, religious, or linguistic groups, how supportive will a given citizen
be of democracy if he enters the voting booth and finds on the
ballot only candidates from the groups that are his historical
adversaries? If a nation has long been riven by geographic regional rivalries, how can one region defend its interests through
democratic elections if all the political parties are based in the
other regions? How much value will a businessman place on elections if only working-class parties exist? Won't a poor peasant
or an underpaid worker listen with interest to appeals of the
totalitarian left if all the parties in his democratic country are

dominated by what he regards as "the oligarchy?" This last situation points up an extreme case of exclusion of important groups from the party spectrum. In a society with a small wealthy class and a majority of propertyless citizens, democracy with only parties favoring the wealthy excludes the majority of the population. Its economic interests will not be served. People's expectations that political democracy will pay off in social reforms will not be fulfilled unless the struggle for votes is able to lead to a fundamental change in the interests of one or more parties. When democracy does not represent the majority, it will fail, for its basic purpose is not being fulfilled. Unfortunately, this situation of monopoly of democratic party politics by parties of the rich is common among those developing countries that have democratic polities. Consequently, those systems are in serious danger of collapse. Colombia and Honduras are examples in Latin America. In both countries the poor majority expects political democracy to produce social reform, but in both countries the two major parties continue to represent the interests of what many workers regard as "the oligarchy." These workers refer to this situation as "formal democracy", or "bourgeois democracy." With marxist theory relating so closely to the workers' reality, democrats should not be surprised that communists are gaining ground in the labor movements of both nations. If the party spectra in Honduras and Colombia are not soon broadened to provide progressive parties representing the economic interests of the lower-income groups, democracy in both nations is doomed.

Thus, when we judge the health of a democracy, we must make an inventory of all the major groups in the society, and then see whether each group has one or more parties representing its interests. If important groups are excluded, problems in the polity can be expected. If groups forming a majority of the population are excluded, political collapse is likely.

The matter of party coverage of the electorate seems obvious, but for some reason this point is often overlooked by foreign-office analysts of conditions in democratic countries. They see electoral systems functioning, note the existence of some large political parties, and assume all is well. So do many of the "risk analysts" employed by banks and multinational corporations. For Western organizations involved in aiding democratic political development, overlooking the matter of party coverage would be even more serious, for the limited resources such groups have available should be focused on the developing democracy's greatest needs. It would be of little help in Colombia, for example, to sharpen up the campaigning skill of activists from the existing parties while the majority of the voters continue to feel excluded from the democratic process. The West German political foundations, the U.S. labor-aid institutes, and whatever entity emerges from President Reagan's proposal for a U.S. program to aid democratic movements, should all pay particular attention to the problem of democratic party systems that do not cover the entire electorate.

Upper-income groups have money, education, and connections. They usually make sure parties exist to represent them. Only after social revolutions do the upper-income groups sometimes remain without party spokesmen in the resultant polity. As far as divisions of social class are concerned, it is most often the poorer classes that remain unrepresented by a party. To fill this threatening gap, two approaches should be considered: the poorer classes can organize a new party or parties to compete with the existing economically conservative parties, or one of the traditional parties may be permeable enough that worker and peasant leaders can enter its organization, shifting the party to a more populist position. Whatever strategy is followed, in the long run it is in the interest of the traditional parties that progressive parties appear to represent popular interests, because progressive parties, like conservative ones, are necessary parts of a healthy democratic party system. If the system dies, because it was too unrepresentative, the conservative democratic parties will die with it when the generals or the commissars take over. It takes two teams to have a soccer game, two sides to the bargaining table to conduct labor-management relations, and both progressive and conservative parties to have stable democratic politics.

Interest Groups.

Along with programmatic mass parties covering all major parts of the electorate, a comprehensive system of competent interest groups is another necessary component of a healthy democratic political system. As has long been noted, parties seldom articulate the demands of particular groups in the first instance; rather, the parties try to aggregate the demands voiced by the various interest groups.[6] The citizen of a democracy thus needs two channels through which to advance his interests: his interest group, and his party. If one or the other means is missing, then he is entering into the democratic political fray with one hand

107

tied behind him. The worker needs his trade union, the peasant his association of agricultural cooperatives, the businessman needs the Chamber of Commerce, and the middle-class needs civic associations and consumer organizations. Once the interest groups voice the various demands, the parties must play a mediating role, for many of the demands will conflict. Urban groups want low food prices, farm groups want the prices higher. Importers want low tariffs while domestic producers want high tariffs, and so on.

(In most countries a given political party does not really mediate among all society's interest groups. Each party has its base in a certain coalition of some of the interest groups, and competes against parties with other coalitions of other groups. Usually, the conservative parties speak for the interest groups among the wealthier classes, with progressive parties putting together coalitions of groups from the poorer classes. The national election then determines which interest-group/party team will win. The interest-aggregating done by the parties, then, is among the interest groups within its particular coalition of supporters. For example, a progressive party always has the problem of finding a balance on food prices between the needs of urban workers and rural peasant producers.)

As with the party spectrum, one key question the analyst must ask is whether all major social groups have organized themselves into effective interest groups. The democratic system will not adequately service those who have no organizational voice in the chorus of demands heard by the political parties. Unfortunately, in many developing nations, the poor majority of the population is poorly organized. Forming an interest group and keeping it operating effectively is a complex task, requiring education, experience, connections, and time. By the very nature of underdevelopment, the poor majority often has only the latter. In Latin America before the Second World War it was often noted that there was a crust of social organization at the top of society, with a great organizational void below, where most of the people lived. Only in the last thirty-five years have trade unions and peasant organizations grown enough to fill much of that gap. In the Andean countries and in Central America, even today the Indians remain outside modern society, with few trade union or cooperative associations to speak for them in the modern polity. Where major social sectors have no interest groups, democracy is correspondingly weakened.

Assuming interest groups do exist and have comprehensive coverage of the society, there are other questions that need to be
asked to determine how much strength those groups contribute to
the democratic polity. One crucial consideration is whether the
interest groups are under democratic leadership, or are led by
pro-dictatorial elements. In many countries, and by no means only
in developing nations, the dictatorial left has considerable
strength in the interest groups of the lower-income strata, while
the dictatorial right is strong in the organizations of those who
are better off. Throughout southern Europe the Communists have
control of the greater part of the labor movement, and in Latin
America they have considerable importance in the trade unions of
Colombia, Peru, Honduras, Ecuador, Panama, Costa Rica, the Dominican Republic, and Bolivia. In the "southern cone" countries of
Uruguay, Chile, and southern Brazil, Communist labor strength was
eliminated only by brutal repression, and could easily recur in
the future, strengthened indeed by the reaction to that
repression.

The dictatorial right is equally threatening in many developing
nations. Often the landowners' association, the Society of Industries, and the Chamber of Commerce are dominated by conservative
elements that judge political systems by one criterion: Can they
prevent social reforms and income redistribution? They have no
ideological commitment to political democracy, or to any other
form of government. Knowing that there are more poor voters than
rich voters in any country, these elements may invite a military
coup to prevent democracy from putting into practice its inherent
tendencies towards social justice. Obviously, interest groups led
by dictatorial forces undermine the democratic system.

Where the interest groups are under democratic leadership, they
provide a solid foundation for democratic politics. Where social
democrats or Christian democrats dominate the labor movement, as
in Venezuela, or the farmer's organizations, as in the northern
valleys of Peru, these groups make a great contribution to democratic strength. Similar contributions are made by business
groups when their leadership is democratic. One factor that has
so far enabled Honduras to escape the socio-political disasters
that have befallen all her neighbors is the democratic, flexible
outlook of business groups on the country's north coast. Similarly, Venezuela's Christian Democratic party (the Copei) is in
great part based on business elements that are firmly democratic
in their political outlook; this fact helps explain how democracy
flourished after 1958 in what was initially an unpromising set-

ting. In summary, the analyst must not only see whether interest groups exist, and how extensively they cover the social spectrum, but must also note whether they are led by friends of democracy.

A subsidiary point worth noting is whether the democratic-led interest groups actively promote democratic theory among their members. Interest groups can function only in the free play of pluralism, and that social condition virtually requires political democracy. This fact is recognized by democratic labor leaders, who frequently comment in speeches that trade unions can function fully only where democratic politics prevail. Unfortunately, few democratic trade unions or democratic business groups have programs to spread the democratic gospel among their own members. Trade union education courses usually limit their content to bargaining techniques, dues structures, and so forth, and seldom provide a grounding in the basic concepts of political democracy. Democratic trade union leaders seem to just assume that their members already know democratic thought.

Business groups do even less to imbue their members with democratic belief, even when the groups' leaders are themselves staunch democrats. How many Chambers of Commerce, especially in developing nations, provide basic courses in democratic principles for their members?[7] Businessmen in Nicaragua recently, faced with the problem of presenting a democratic alternative to the Sandinista's incipient totalitarianism, have been complaining ruefully, "But we don't know what we believe!"

Given that the interest groups' self-preservation requires political democracy, it is odd that they are not more active in making their members confident and articulate spokesmen for democratic ideas. The American Bar Association does offer programs and seminars for the public, especially for young people, on the rule of law, due process, and the role of the legal system in a democracy. By doing so, the A.B.A. has made a useful contribution to the strength of U.S. democracy. Where interest groups do undertake such educational efforts, the analyst of democratic politics should give a plus mark to the strength of democracy.

Even where interest groups cover all major social sectors, and are mostly under democratic leadership, all may still not be well for democracy in the interest-group area if those groups do not accept each other's legitimacy. They should, because as was mentioned above, an interest group needs democracy if it is to flourish, and democracy in turn needs full coverage of the society by interest groups if it is to remain strong. Logically, where unions are weak, employers should be out encouraging their formation, and where Chambers of Commerce are weak, unions should help strengthen them. Unfortunately, this is expecting more enlightened self-interest than most of us can muster.

It is much more common for democratic businessmen to view trade unions as illegitimate bodies that interfere with management's prerogatives, reduce corporate flexibility, and threaten the business with bankruptcy by demanding wage increases in excess of productivity gains. Such thoughts may weaken the businessman's will to resist a military coup; in the back of his mind he may think "Well, at least the generals will sit on the unions." On the workers' side, a similar rejection may occur: democratic socialist unions, rejecting the private ownership of the means of production, look on private corporations as illegitimate entities. This ideological viewpoint may weaken the democratic trade unionists' opposition to totalitarianism. They may muse, "Well, at least the communists will destroy the corporations."

Regardless of the merits of anti-union or anti-capitalist views, a democratic polity is obviously stronger if there is a national consensus on what kind of economic ownership system should exist, and on what array of interest groups are legitimate. Such a consensus does exist in the United States where labor and business can be relied on to form a common front against enemies of democratic pluralism. Unfortunately, there are few societies with such broad agreement on the proper economic system, and in many nations democratic interest groups may spend more energy fighting each other than countering their mutual dictatorial adversaries.

A final--though controversial--feature of the interest-group system that analysts should note when gauging the strength of democracies is the degree of autonomy the interest groups have in relation to other bodies. In theory, most democrats agree that an interest group should be controlled only by its own members. That way it will be sure to fulfill its proper function: voicing the members particular demands. In practice, however, some interest groups, or their leaders as individuals, are often under the discipline of other organizations, usually the government or a political party.

While admitting in the abstract that a fusion of interest group and party violates the principles of democratic pluralism, confusing the roles of articulators and aggregators of interests, most democrats involved in such arrangements stoutly defend them as necessary and useful in their specific setting. In Britain, trade unions are part of the Labour Party. In Mexico they form one sector of the Partido Revolucionario Institucional. In many developing countries labor leaders operate in their unions under the policy discipline of their political parties, and are in fact elected to union office on the party ticket, formally or informally. The same party-interest group intermingling is often found with agricultural groups. With business associations, the tie is usually in the other direction: conservative political parties often follow policies dictated by the Chamber of Commerce or the national association of industries. In any event, analysts of democracy should take note of the degree to which interest groups are autonomous from political parties, even though there is no agreement among either practitioners or students of politics on whether a partial lack of autonomy is really damaging to the democratic system in a given case.[8]

There is much more agreement that interest groups should definitely be autonomous from the government. Unfortunately, in many countries, especially developing ones, when the government changes, so does the leadership of many chambers of commerce, trade unions, agricultural associations, and civic groups. This certainly raises some doubt about which way the demands are flowing when interest groups act as channels between citizens and the government. Particularly in the "single-party democracies" of Africa, interest groups are so much under government control that it becomes questionable whether democratic pluralism can really be said to exist in these countries. If they are considered democratic, then certainly their democracy is weakened to the extent that the interest groups are under government influence. (One indicator of the relationship between governments and interest groups is how government, management, and labor delegates from a given country vote in the annual meetings of the tripartite International Labor Organization. If all three always vote the same way, there may be a lack of interest group autonomy. If the three sets of delegates commonly go off in different directions, there is almost certainly full interest-group autonomy.) In general, since interest group autonomy from government almost always goes hand-in-hand with free, competitive national elections, autonomy is a factor which should be closely observed in judging a democracy's strength.

The Electorate's Level of Political Consciousness.

Finally, along with appropriate election mechanisms, parties, and interest groups, there is yet another ingredient for a strong democracy: voters who know how to use their vote effectively.[9] In several democratic developing countries the absence of long-term, rational calculations by voters is a serious problem.

Voting on the basis of family tradition is one difficulty. This is especially pronounced in Honduras and Colombia, and was a problem in the Philippines when democracy prevailed there. In such countries one is born, for example, into a "Conservative Party family," or a "Liberal Party family." One votes for the family's party, even if that party over the years comes to represent a social class that is one's adversary. In these countries masses of poor people regularly vote for parties favoring the rich. It does little good to organize a new progressive party to represent the popular classes if no one will vote for it.

Another problem may be that voters sell their votes; in Latin America it may be for a peso or a drink. This vitiates the democratic process: the resulting government represents those who paid for votes, and not the voters. Where parts of the electorate remain unrepresented in the political party spectrum, vote-selling may not come from ignorance as much as from an all-too-clear understanding of alternatives. The selling of one's vote may be an act of protest or alienation. It has the advantage over casting a blank ballot in that the voter at least receives an immediate reward. However, often vote-selling occurs simply because the voters do not really understand the connection between voting and obtaining a government that represents them.

Voting in order to obtain a personal favor from a politician or party is another common phenomenon, and not only in developing countries. Often conservative candidates will promise a town a school house, or a voter a scholarship for his nephew, and thus secure the votes of poor people whose class interests really do not lie with that candidate or party. Again, the connection between voting and having one's long-term interests represented is broken. When democracy does not produce governments that serve the people there is no point to democracy.

To resolve all these problems, major campaigns of voter education are necessary. Voters must be shown that their vote is their share of the political power, and must be warned against such specific errors as voting by tradition, vote-selling, and trading votes for short-term favors. Fortunately, experience in such areas as Puerto Rico and Venezuela shows that voter education campaigns can be effective in changing a populace's voting habits over a short period of time.

In judging the strength of a democratic system, one must be alert to problems in the public's grasp of the democratic process. Where voting habits tend to disconnect the electoral process from the formation of responsible government, the observer should note whether civic education campaigns are under way to correct the problems. Labor movements, student organizations, and religious groups often undertake such campaigns, using volunteers. If problems of voting behavior exist, and nothing is being done about it, democracy is correspondingly weakened.

Summary: A Checklist of Indicators of Democratic Strength

The electoral process:

> Are the elections really free?
> Is there substantial electoral fraud?
> How large was the voter turn-out?

The political parties:

> Are they personalistic or programmatic?
> Do they have mass organization, with party discipline?
> Are party workers experienced in modern, impersonal organizations?
> Do the parties have both political and social-service functions?
> Do they have comprehensive ideologies?

Party coverage of the electorate:

Are there parties representing:

> All major ethnic groups?
> All major religious groups?
> All geographic regions of the country?
> All social classes?

Interest groups:

Are all major social sectors organized into such groups?
Are the interest groups under democratic leadership?
Do interest groups teach democratic principles to their
  members?
Do the major interest groups accept each other as legitimate
  bodies?
Are the interest groups autonomous:

From political parties?
From the government?

The electorate's level of political consciousness:

Are the following problems in voting behavior prevalent:

Voting by family tradition?
Vote selling?
Trading of votes for personal favors?

Are voter-education campaigns being conducted?

Notes

1. This formulation follows closely Raymond Gastil's definition of democracy quoted in the Interim Report of the Democracy Program, Washington, D.C., April 18, 1983, p. 27. See also Myron Weiner's definition, quoted in Peter Berger, "Democracy for Everyone?", Commentary, September 1983, p. 32.

2. See Howard I. Blutstein, Area Handbook for Colombia (Washington, D.C.: U.S. Government Printing Office, 1977), pp. 87, 89, 283, and especially pp. 304–305.

3. On personalism, factionalism, and corruption in the Philippines, see Jean Grossholtz, Politics in the Philippines (Boston: Little, Brown and Co., 1964), pp. 159, 163–164.

4. On clientelistic politics in Latin America, see Gary Wynia, The Politics of Latin American Development (New York: Cambridge University Press, 1978), pp. 12–13.

5. On the Indian case, see Pran Chopra, Uncertain India (Cambridge: The MIT Press, 1968), p. 359.

6. One classic exposition of this categorization is in Gabriel A. Almond and James S. Coleman, eds., The Politics of the Developing Areas (Princeton: Princeton University Press, 1960), pp. 33–45.

7. One activity foreseen for business under the proposed "National Endowment for Democracy" would provide such courses. See the Interim Report of the Democracy Program, Washington, D.C., April 18, 1983, pp. 40-43.

8. For an early defense of close ties between unions and parties, see Bruce Millen, The Political Role of Labor in Developing Countries (Washington, D.C.: Brookings, 1963), Chapter 7. For a discussion of present union-party relationships see Everett Kassalow, Trade Unions and Industrial Relations, New York: Random House, 1969, Chapters II and III, and pp. 297-302.

9. For a fascinating analysis of how peoples develop democratic political skills, see A. H. Somjee, Political Capacity in Developing Societies (New York: St. Martin's Press, 1982).

PART III

Supporting the Development of Democracy in China

Foreword

On May 6 and 7, 1983, a conference was held at Freedom House on "Supporting Democracy in the People's Republic of China and the Republic of China (Taiwan). This conference was the third in a series. Previous conferences have been held on supporting freedom and liberalization in the Soviet Union and Muslim Central Asia. (See the 1979 and 1981 editions of Freedom in the World.)

The purpose of the conference and the general issues to be addressed were sketched in the first paper included below. This is followed by the full texts of papers that were delivered in summary form at the conference. Following each paper we have included a presentation of the discussion it inspired. A personal summary and conclusion concludes the discussion.

In addition to the editor the participants were:

Richard Bernstein of the New York Times. Mr. Bernstein is a reporter and well-known authority on China.

June Teufel Dreyer of the Center for Advanced International Studies of the University of Miami. Professor Dreyer is a specialist on the Chinese army, security services, and ethnic minorities.

Jerome B. Grieder of the Department of History, Brown University. Professor Grieder is particularly known for his work on the modern intellectual history of China.

Liang Heng, a graduate student from the People's Republic of China.

Liao Xueqian, a graduate student from the Republic of China (Taiwan).

Mab Huang of New York State University at Oswego. Professor Huang is a lifelong student of politics and human rights in both Taiwan and the mainland.

William R. Kintner is Director Emeritus of the Foreign Policy Research Institute of the University of Pennsylvania. Dr. Kintner has served in many governmental positions, including Ambassador to Thailand.

119

Margot E. Landman after three and one-half years working and studying in China is currently with AFS International/Intercultural Programs in New York.

Peter R. Moody of the Department of Government and International Studies, University of Notre Dame. Professor Moody has made a particular study of recent dissident movements.

Andrew Nathan of the Political Science Department, Columbia University. Professor Nathan is an authority on Chinese constitutions, democratic theory, and dissent.

Lucian W. Pye of the Department of Political Science, Massachusetts Institute of Technology. Professor Pye has been particularly concerned with Chinese political culture. (Unfortunately Professor Pye was unable to attend the conference in person.)

James D. Seymour of the East Asian Institute, Columbia University, and Director of the Society for the Protection of East Asians' Human Rights.

Norris P. Smith retired in 1983 after twenty-five years with the United States Information Agency. Mr. Smith's last position was in Beijing.

Lawrence R. Sullivan of the East Asian Institute, Columbia University, and Adelphi University. Professor Sullivan is a specialist on modern Chinese politics.

Zhu Xiao is a graduate student from the People's Republic of China.

Supporting Democracy in the People's Republic of China and the Republic of China (Taiwan): General Considerations for the Freedom House Conference

Raymond D. Gastil and James D. Seymour

This conference was called to assist Freedom House in its efforts to defend, expand, and deepen freedom in the world. Freedom is defined as liberal democratic rights: political equality and civil liberty under law. Put another way, freedom is seen as deriving from the right of all people to determine the nature of their own lives, and to live by their own symbols and values. In principle, this applies to nations as well as individuals. "Democracy" implies the absence of oppression from both native and foreign rulers. But tension can arise between the demand for liberal democracy on the one hand, and the interest of both individuals and states on the other. This is especially true when there are overlapping claims to nationhood. Often competing demands have legitimacy. Whatever the claim, let us confine our deliberations to individuals, ethnic groups, and nation states, and avoid the elitist concept of "masses."

Freedom has been given increased importance in recent American foreign policy, through the emphasis on human rights by Congress and the administration of Jimmy Carter. After an uncertain start, President Reagan appears to be continuing to incorporate human rights into his administration's foreign policy, though the degree, methods, and political focus are different from President Carter's. The main thrust in support of freedom has been through increased efforts to combat the expansion of communism. Recently, Washington has made some proposals for the more general promotion of democracy, both by the U.S. government and the private sector.

China: Supporting Democracy

Whereas the qualitative (if not quantitative) requirements of national defense in support of American and allied freedoms are relatively easy to determine, the requirements of promoting the expansion of freedom (particularly in the most closed societies) are simply not known. Certainly the U. S. government has often been misguided (or at any rate unsuccessful) in its efforts to influence change for the better in such different countries as Chile, Iran, Haiti, Nicaragua, or Poland. Some would say the United States tried too hard, others that the effort was too little. The Philippines, which was once held up as a model of the transfer of democracy, cannot even be influenced to maintain a constitutional order, at least given the limited pressure that we seem willing to apply. Private organizations, of course, are not capable of applying as much pressure as is the government. But even such efforts are sometimes capable of doing more harm than good--especially in countries characterized by anti-Western sentiment. With these considerations in mind, the conferees were asked to address the following questions:

1. What substratum of attitudes do these lands' proponents of democratic evolution confront, and what is the probable evolution in these attitudes?

2. What has been and may be the influence of outside models on Chinese political culture during the modernization process? What are the present and possible future interrelationships of the PRC and Taiwan? What is the relevance of each to the successful democratization of Japan?

3. What are the steps by which the two undemocratic regimes could make sustained progress toward democracy?

4. To what extent is self-determination for minority peoples feasible, and what is the relation of such possibilities to the question of freedom for the whole society?

5. Around 1979 there were impressive outbursts of democratic sentiment in both the PRC and Taiwan. How important were these movements, and what is the likelihood of their recurrence or enhanced effectiveness?

6. What are the cultural barriers to democratization, and how might these be overcome?

7. What aspects of the political cultures are favorable to democratic development, and how might these be enhanced?

We should be able to learn from the experience of democratic movements in other countries of the non-Western world. All these countries have in common that liberal constitutional democracy is widely perceived as alien because it developed in Europe and North America. Democracy's spread from those centers, though slow, has still been remarkably steady if seen in historical perspective. Only in the late 1970s did it at last become accepted in all non-communist Europe. Beyond Europe, the acceptance of democratic concepts has been most general in Latin America; here the influence of democratic countries has been relatively intense. Although the continent has been notorious for its juntas, essential concepts such as the possibility of a loyal opposition and freedom of the press are popularly accepted, and have often been institutionalized. However, political institutions there (even more than elsewhere) are fragile. The example of Chile reminds us that the most stable-appearing democracy is vulnerable; while the case of Brazil suggests it is possible for the most brutal dictatorial situation to evolve toward democracy.

Alone among regions, the Middle East has seen democracy retreat. The area has been bedeviled by the Palestine question and the resurgence of a fundamentalist version of Islam. Even Israel, a transplanted European democracy, has seen some movement away from liberal democratic precepts in recent years, at least in the administered territories.

At least as mixed is the picture in Asia. One of the poorest states, India, has a functioning democracy, probably because of intense and long association with Britain. Japan's democratic institutions may have a similar explanation. Although the country enjoyed some democratic development in the early part of the twentieth century, today's stable democracy was imposed by the United States following World War II. Still, the Japanese case suggests that a society with some of the same cultural traditions as China can successfully operate as a democracy. The case of Thailand demonstrates that at least limited democracy can evolve in Asia in a country that has experienced only marginal institutional pressures from abroad.

China: Supporting Democracy

Problems and Opportunities in China.

There are four separate polities dominated by "Han" people
(ethnic Chinese). Because of its lack of geographic proximity, we
shall not be examining Singapore at this conference. Likewise,
Hong Kong is too special a case to be useful for our purposes.
Though its people give every sign of desiring democracy, they know
that China does not permit it. The nature of all four polities is
not such as to automatically create optimism about the prospects
for democracy under Chinese rule.

Certainly neither Taiwan nor the PRC has made much progress
toward achieving democracy. Although (as we shall see) the two
cultures and two systems have a good deal in common, they also
have their differences (as both ruling groups insist). In theory,
and to some extent in practice, Taiwan is less absolutist. This
is primarily because economic activity is generally freer of
government control. As for politics, although no genuine opposition is tolerated in either place, Taiwan's most moderate opposition elements (personified by Legislator K'ang Ning-hsiang) have
been treated with more consistent respect than have their counter-
parts in the PRC. The pressures to offer positive affirmation of
the political order are not as severe on Taiwan. Although the
island's Chinese Nationalist (Kuomintang/KMT) rulers claim to
reflect traditional political Chinese virtues, more apt analogues
seem to be found among their chosen allies such as South Korea and
South Africa. Other exemplars of this limited-pluralist system
are Singapore and Indonesia.

When it comes to the prospects for liberalizing the PRC, many
of the problems faced are similar to those in all other dictatorships, but others are peculiar to Leninist regimes. In a sense,
we may include Taiwan in this category, because the Kuomintang was
organized by Leninists in the 1920s as an elite, centralized
organization, and it retains many of its original characteristics
to this day. To the extent that the two Chinese regimes are sui
generis, the special problems of democratization presumably relate
to (1) Chinese political culture, (2) a peculiar historical situation, or (3) parallel national interest or fears regarding the
future. These are not conclusions, but offered hypothetically for
acceptance, modification, or rejection.

In examining the question of outside support for democracy in
these lands, we will be faced with some common assumptions that,
if true, cast doubt on the practicality or legitimacy of the
effort. Many view Chinese political culture as essentially

unchanging, and by extension unchangeable. (Even the official PRC media complains about the persistence of "feudal" attitudes.) Others view any attempt to "export democracy" as a misguided attempt to impose an alien system on a people perfectly comfortable under the system and in the culture in which they have grown up. Actually, such caveats are raised in defense of most undemocratic orders, and are easily dismissed. Let us briefly discuss some of the reasons that we doubt these claims for the two Chinese regimes.

Both political orders are products of the traditional political culture (and to some extent, traditional political system), on top of which have been imposed Soviet-style institutions. In the PRC, there are the standard array of communist forms: an omnipresent state; an elite-vanguard single party; parallel state and party structures radiating from the center down to the villages; a small, aging, but rarely challenged politburo; a privileged "new class" based on party membership of techno-bureaucratic standing; homogeneous information media; and state socialism (with pragmatic unsocialist concessions where necessary for incentive purposes).

Yet, there have been times when the Chinese communist political order has looked very different from other communist countries. Though disunity within a communist movement is not unusual, it is usually muted if not completely hidden from the public. In China, on the other hand, there have been times when a sector of the public was mobilized to support one faction against another. Sometimes this has led to mob action. Although the Cultural Revolution was costly to the nation, and at least appears to have been universally repudiated, many people came to accept the notion that they had a right--even a duty--to take direct action in the name of revolution when those in control of the government engaged in backsliding. This attitude may explain the 1976 demonstrations at Tienanmen Square, and also the 1978-1979 movement centered around Xidan Democracy Wall. Of course, the Cultural Revolution had been personally instigated and legitimized by Mao Zedong, whereas the other movements were spontaneous and not legitimized by the leadership. Nonetheless, there are repeated examples of large numbers of people expressing unorthodox opinions, usually at the expense of the establishment. The myth of the sacrosanct "party line" had been exposed. Now, ordinary people took it upon themselves not only to have independent political thoughts (this in itself was not new), but also to express them.

To be sure, several Eastern European countries have seen spontaneous uprisings, but those governments owe their existence to

125

the Soviet Union; there is an obvious question about their legitimacy, and nothing novel about the idea that the local people's political activities were legitimate (much as this is denied by the ruling groups). But the PRC is no satellite; its leaders no running dogs of foreigners. Indeed, the nation's rulers owe their own legitimacy largely to the fact that they have stood up to the "imperialists" and "social imperialists" as no Chinese government had been able to do for centuries. Since nationalism is not now a genuine issue, it is all the more difficult to dismiss dissension as irrelevant to the question of what type of political order is compatible with Chinese culture and Chinese realities.

Taiwan is more comparable to Eastern Europe, in that the Nationalist regime owes its existence to the United States. Its legitimacy is further questioned because of its carpet-bag nature, with the Taiwanese (at least eighty-five percent of the population) having little say in the affairs of state. Thus, dissent is treated much as it is in parts of Eastern Europe; there is some toleration of criticism, but those who question the legitimacy of the regime are severely repressed. It would have been inconceivable for Chiang Kai-shek to call on the public to rise up against the establishment the way Mao did. No one questioned Mao's legitimacy; Chiang would not have been so fortunate. The legitimacy crisis is even more grave now. Because of official intransigence regarding the "Republic of China" myth, the handling of foreign policy has been so bungled that the regime is officially recognized by almost no other government--a fact that cannot be lost on many Taiwanese. But at issue is not so much the legitimacy of the Chiang family (of undoubted popularity), as their means of perpetuating their tenure in office.

It is important for our purposes to note that both Chinese leaderships give lip-service to the need for democracy. The Nationalists' lip-service seems largely for foreign consumption. Internally, there is little embarrassment about the continuance of martial law and the suspension of the constitution. In the PRC, however, the domestic media have been filled with praise for democracy, despite the term's bourgeois connotations. An example from People's Daily at the time of the promulgation of the revised Constitution in December:

The new constitution . . . was drawn up by the party on the basis of both positive and negative experience gained in the past 32 years by the people under its leadership, especially the bitter lessons of the 10 years of internal

disorder [Cultural Revolution] during which socialist democracy and the legal system were seriously damaged. Without
democracy, there will be no socialism. . . .

The fundamental rights and duties of citizens have been
given greater importance and the guarantee of citizens'
personal rights has been strengthened. In the new constitution, the fundamental rights and duties of citizens are
arraigned in the second chapter. [It had been in the
third.] . . . This shows that out country now attaches
greater importance to the fundamental rights and duties of
its citizens and that our state organs of the people's
democratic dictatorship have been established entirely for
the people's interests. Thus, the concept of "all powers
belong to the people" has been better displayed. In the
chapter, "Fundamental Rights and Duties of Citizens," the
citizens' personal rights are more extensively guaranteed.
Besides the provisions of the previous constitutions on the
inviolability of citizens' personal freedom and homes,
there are additional provisions in the new constitution,
for instance: that the personal dignity of citizens is
inviolable; insulting, slandering, falsely charging or
framing citizens through any means is outlawed; citizens
have the right to demand compensation, according to law,
for losses due to violation of their rights by any state
organ or functionary, and so forth.[1]

In the face of such impressive language (which is virtually
required reading for Chinese), the arguments that freedom and
democracy are illegitimate or hopelessly alien are certainly
called into question. Still, we are left with the feeling that
these words have little real meaning.

Democracy requires free elections. In the past, elections in
China were totally controlled exercises. In recent years there
have been some experiments with somewhat freer elections at the
local level. Usually the voters appear to have been almost as
non-plused as the cadres who were supposed to carry them out.
Having learned all their lives that elections were to gratify the
decisions of higher authority, they found it awkward (even scary)
to make real choices. But in some places (university communities,
factories in more cosmopolitan centers) the elections turned into
exciting affairs. Sometimes charismatic figures emerged, now
fighting for the rights of constituents, now defending the leftist
ancien regime, but more commonly defending the idea of liberal

democracy.[2] In Taiwan elections have been held more frequently. Although it is required that campaigns be short, they are lively affairs. True, sometimes candidates who overreach themselves are imprisoned. But sometimes non-party people are allowed to take office. Although in both Taiwan and the PRC such elective offices are powerless, they can (especially in Taiwan) provide a platform for further political activity.

All this might suggest that the primary barriers to democracy are political, not cultural or systemic, and that all that would be required for both lands to have governments elected is for the present rulers to allow it to happen. But even if this assumption (which many will certainly challenge) is correct, it does not necessarily follow that democracy, once established, could be sustained in the long run.

It is true that democratic institutions, like all political institutions, tend to benefit certain elements in society more than others. Thus, official spokespersons in China tend to insist on socialism first, and democracy a distant second (with the "dictatorship of the proletariat" properly intervening in any democratic process that goes the "wrong" way). We argue that there is more apt to be net exploitation of the working class in a closed system where the workers cannot organize to demand their share of the pie from the "new class." In China they have not been free to so organize, though in the late 1970s peasants did come to the capital to openly demand their rights and an improvement in their conditions. A worker's question at Xidan, "Why is it that factory workers can elect their unit leaders by secret ballot, but when the leaders of our country are chosen, we can have no say whatsoever?,"[3] suggests that many workers understand democracy at the factory level, and some have an expectation (or at least hope) of expanding democracy on the basis of experience under communism.

Although those involved in making such demands were subsequently arrested, the hesitancy of the repression may indicate that the leadership was in some way unsure of itself. Perhaps it suggests a leadership painfully aware of the contradictions of ideology and reality. Or maybe the elite's regard for the Confucian concept of the responsibility of leaders to followers made the leadership think twice before they finally cracked down. Cynics, though, would say that Deng Xiaoping had only been unsure of himself vis-a-vis his opponents on the left; when the liberals had served his purposes in helping in the battle against them, they could be dispensed with.

Dissident rallies in the Soviet Union have always been poorly attended affairs, with at most a dozen protesters. Perhaps Soviet repression is invariably so quick and effective that hope has simply vanished. Yet, those experienced with the USSR believe that there is not much sympathy for dissidents. Witnesses of crowds at Xidan and other dissident events in China paint a different picture. They report, for example, that Canton's Li-Yi-Zhe group are well known and honored. True, we cannot say that a majority of Chinese approve of dissension. Still, many Chinese perceive the difference between rabble-rousing and pointing out shortcomings of the system. After all, most Chinese must have experienced, and resented, the arbitrary exercise of authority, and many a soul must have wondered why he or she was so powerless to set things right. For some, the Cultural Revolution was a revelation for it taught people that rebellion is justified; for others, the lesson was that challenging authority harms society. Perhaps even more compelling is the legacy of Confucianism, with its emphasis on social harmony and prohibition of insubordination. This is one of several congruencies between Leninism and Confucianism. Although "correct" criticism is always meritorious, under neither philosophy is opposition legitimate. The rulers of Taiwan and Singapore seem to find the idea of a "loyal opposition" as difficult to understand as those in Beijing and Moscow. Politics is monolithic and all-encompassing, with economic and religious structures relegated to a secondary and dependent position. However, there have been countercurrents in Chinese history, and the more the Communist Party has identified its legitimacy with tradition and nationalism, the more it has opened itself to these currents.

One countercurrent is the right of "the people" (however defined) to revolt (implicit in the concept of the Mandate of Heaven). Another is the traditional contradiction between the absolute power of the central government on paper, and the lack of integration of the centralized apparatus with village China. There was also an undercurrent of philosophical anarchism, and the principle of governmental non-action (wu wei). The lineage (clan) was also an institution which countervailed the power of the state. Confucian arguments may be used to defend authoritarianism (as they are on Taiwan), but they may also be cited to deny the superiority of the state to family loyalty. The more modern legacy of Sun Yat-sen is equally ambiguous, and Taiwanese dissidents are fond of turning the good doctor's more democratic precepts against his self-styled disciples in the KMT.

Chinese attitudes toward law are colored in a most unfortunate way by tradition and semantics. The first Chinese rulers who acted in the name of "law" (fa) were extremely oppressive, and the legacy of these "Legalists" has been to prejudice the nation against the rule of law. The more sophisticated Chinese realize that "law" in the old Chinese sense has nothing to do with real law. (When the democrat Hu Ping complains that the traditional Chinese political system was "Confucianism in form and Legalism in substance,"[4] and that "Legalism" still poisons Chinese politics, he is obviously not arguing against the rule of law.) There have been some, such as the seventeenth century political philosopher Huang Zongxi, who argued for rule of law rather than men. But this was a distinctly minority view. Today, the PRC is placing great emphasis on the need to establish a system of law, but it is an uphill battle. On Taiwan, the population (with its experience under Japanese administration) is amenable to modern legal institutions. But the usual practice in both the PRC and Taiwan is to exempt political offenders from the protections of the legal system.[5]

Ideology in both the Confucian and communist traditions has placed high value on the generalist. (This is less true with the Chinese Nationalists, whose state is dominated by militarists and techno-bureaucrats.) The traditional generalist was the ru, or Confucian scholar/philosopher/poet. Communists see the ru as effete parasites, a perception which gave rise to intense anti-intellectualism after 1949. But for all Mao Zedong's efforts to "resolve the contradiction between mental and manual labor," and the recruitment of somewhat more rustic types during the Cultural Revolution, cadres today still have much in common with the mandarins. They must be steeped in philosophy (Marxism), and also know a little about various professions. But there is bound to be some tension between these two sides of cadres; the better educated they become, the less tied to Marxist simplicities and rigidities they are apt to be.

The peasantry's role in any democratization is fundamental, but probably not decisive. Rural people do not normally determine the nature of governments. In a democracy, however, they can be a powerful force, as the example of Japan demonstrates. This suggests that China's peasantry will not determine whether the PRC "goes democratic," but if the country does, they will be the major beneficiary.[6] This, in turn, reduces the likelihood of democratization, because under the circumstances democracy would probably result in a shift from the "haves" to the "have nots." And it is the "haves" who have the power to determine the nature of the system.

Unlike other third world countries, peasants in the PRC are almost never allowed to change their residence from rural to urban. Thus, even though city people have been forced into the countryside, there is perhaps less interplay between city attitudes and rural attitudes in China than in other countries. Recent developments point to a great deal of hostility between city and country, with the enforced sojourns of city youth exacerbating as much as reducing this hostility. One suspects that the result is that we outside observers have an especially poor understanding of what peasants (eighty percent of the population) really think of the system. It may also be uncommonly difficult to estimate the degree of their potential support for, or opposition to, possible democratic change. We find it disconcerting that many of China's "democrats" seem little concerned with bringing democracy to the countryside. Their idea of democracy is often Mencian: Power to "the people"--who are defined as the intellectuals. Perhaps this is unsurprising. After all, a truly democratic China would be controlled by those who till the land, and neither the communists nor the intellectuals see themselves as benefiting from this.

Certainly the present regime is no more inclined to listen to the peasantry than are the dissidents. On December 10, the National Peoples Congress adopted a revised electoral law (regarding delegates to the NPC and local congresses). Instead of one-person-one-vote, the system is strongly weighted against the rural population. "The number of deputies to the NPC to be elected [by province-level congresses] shall be . . . in accordance with the principle that the number of people represented by each rural deputy is eight times the number of people represented by each urban deputy."[7]

Chinese peasants, we suspect, are like peasants elsewhere. If we are right in this, they value family or individual control over their production, income, and way of life. We know, however, that Chinese peasants are accustomed to outside agents telling them what to do; when one must, one bends with the wind. The degree that this interference is perceived as legitimate is unknowable. But the petitioning peasants led by Fu Yuehua in 1979 represented an old tradition. The tradition suggests that when people see a chance for redress, they will grab it--perhaps especially those, such as peasants, who have little to lose.

An argument can be made that Chinese peasants have good reasons to support the communist system. They know that much-needed peace (as well as some equalization of status) followed the "Liberation." Recently, Deng Xiaoping has introduced more autonomy and incentives in agriculture. Will this make the peasants more pro-government? Or will it cause them to want democracy? The answer probably hinges on the amount of education they can gain. Today, it is probable that roughly half of China's rural people are functionally illiterate. When this situation improves, peasants (who are mostly under thirty-five) are increasingly apt to ask their leaders: "What have you done for me lately?" Still, such dissent is unlikely to threaten the system, particularly since there is no alternative power structure available to organize and focus dissent (as there was in Poland and Iran). Only a rural-based revolution, such as the Taiping of the nineteenth century or the communists of the 1930s, could perform that function. This would entail a civil war that no one wants.

In Taiwan, the land reform carried out by the Chinese Nationalists in the 1950s was a key to KMT success. However, in more recent years the government has kept crop prices so artificially low that farm families have to send members to work in factories in order for the family to survive financially. Typically, farming has not been profitable, and is engaged in by many farmers to hold on to the land. Given this situation, it is not surprising that some of the leading dissidents live and work in rural areas. This fact, combined with economic realities and the experience of Japan, suggests that farmers would be active participants in a democratizing process.

The party "reformers" see a close connection between intellectuals and the rural condition. As former science czar Nie Rongzhen put it in the party journal last year, even though the recent incentive system has improved the picture in agriculture, "there is a limit to giving full play to the initiative of the peasants, and someday the 'saturation point' will be reached." Thus, further gains must come from improved technology, that is, from the work of intellectuals. He writes:

There are some people who say that "our [positive] evaluation of intellectuals is exaggerated," and that intellectuals are "cocky once again." These words are groundless. At present our implementation of the policies related to the intellectuals has just begun and the resistance we are encountering both within and outside the Party is not small and can be regarded as quite stubborn. I had a talk with a **Guangming Daily** reporter in August. Most people approved of this talk when it was published in the newspaper. There were also people who opposed this talk, criticizing the comrades in Guangming for this bourgeois stand. I have indeed offended some people on this issue. However, what is to be done? We must continue to fight for the interests of the party and state, for the four modernizations and for the overall implementation of our policies regarding intellectuals.

On the question of implementing this policy, it is still necessary for the media to make a loud public appeal. It is no good to talk about this in general terms; open criticism must be made. It is also no good to make mild criticism; it is necessary to make sharp criticism. Sometimes it is even necessary to conduct some struggles. Neither Marx nor Engels said that all intellectuals are reactionary.[8]

These remarks indicate that the status of the intellectuals is a hot issue in China. Nie's main concern is maximizing the intellectuals contribution to economic modernization. But it cannot be lost on people like him that the first to perceive government policies as mistaken, and the most articulate critics of such perceived mistakes, will be the intellectuals. One suspects that this is why his critics in the party fear their "cockiness." In other words, how the "problem" of the intellectuals is dealt with is extremely important, and may determine what chance China has of becoming democratic.

Alternatives for the Future.

With the above considerations in mind, we should be able to consider a range of alternative futures for the PRC and Taiwan. The alternatives should set forth scenarios of change or stability that we might imagine for the next generation. The problem for the conferees then becomes how to estimate the probability of each, the desirability of each, and the ways in which relevant outsiders might act to promote the most desirable and prevent the less desirable scenarios.

China: Supporting Democracy

I.   PRC SCENARIOS

   A.   Repeat of mid-1970s to present.[9]

   B.   Political modernization leading to:
       B-1.   Yugoslav model (production-unit democracy)
       B-2.   Thai/Japanese models (liberal democracy)

   C.   Violent factionalism leading to military government
       and authoritarianism on the South Korean or Polish
       (post Solidarity) model.

   D.   Violent factionalism leading to anarchy, widespread
       destruction, and finally:
       D-1.   Restored oppressive authority
       D-2.   A pluralistic, more decentralized order

   E.   Authoritarian regime on KMT model, perhaps followed
       by (B) or (C).

II.   TAIWAN SCENARIOS

   A.   Repeat of mid-1970s to present.

   B.   Iberian-style transformation to a democratic system
       (perhaps with KMT becoming a Japanese-style Liberal-
       Democratic Party).

   C.   The military/techno-bureaucratic balance shifts in
       favor of the military to prevent shift to Taiwanese
       control.

   D.   Violent overthrow of KMT; power shift to Taiwanese:
       D-1.   A new dictatorship
       D-2.   A democratic system

   E.   Retrocession to PRC (then following one or more of
       the scenarios under I):
       E-1.   By conquest
       E-2.   Gradual absorption

Merely listing these scenarios (and many more might be suggested) points to the likelihood that the futures of the PRC and Taiwan are open-ended, and that there are dynamic elements of change that may render the standard scenario (A) less plausible.

The next generation in the PRC and Taiwan will not be like the last. The old verities and enthusiasms have been dulled and often destroyed by experience. Many people will be looking for new opportunities and new solutions, at the same time fearing the chaos that any change may bring in its train.

As we try to think out the details of the various scenarios, we must wonder what the influence of United States policies might be. What kinds of information should the U.S. be imparting to the two peoples, and in what ways? Does it help when foreigners struggle against violations of human rights, or is this merely a way to make us feel better? How often does it really (1) help individuals, or (2) advance the cause of democracy? Should we attempt to publicize the development of dissent and the ideas and heroism of individuals such as Wang Xizhe and Wei Jingsheng, Li Ch'ing-jung and Shih Ming-teh? Can this be done without appearing to be partisan? Should the fight be waged primarily by foreign governments, or by private organizations? Openly or quietly? What is the potential leverage of Western military or economic relations? Do alliances or good relations give us an opportunity to promote change, or do they merely strengthen the existing order, and thus oppression? Can the more democratic Asian states, such as Japan, India, or Thailand, be encouraged to play a part in promoting concrete models that would help to liberalize life in the PRC or Taiwan?

Although dramatic change in Taiwan is conceivable, the PRC will not liberalize overnight. Until the Chinese people feel that there is a possibility for authentic change, most will live within the assumptions of their existing system. Our task is to respect their humanity by assuming their oppressions to be as keenly felt as those of other similarly situated peoples, and their potential desires for freedom to be as great. The Chinese are not a separate breed of humanity, gathered into an undifferentiated mass with mass interests. They are people, and people with individual and changing concerns.

Notes

1. Yu Haocheng, "The New Constitution Has Developed Socialist Democracy," Renmin Ribao, 20 December 1982, p. 2, FBIS I:249.

2. See, for example, the brilliant essay on the subject by a candidate at Peking University, Hu Ping, "On Freedom of Speech," translated in SPEAHRhead (P.O. Box 1212, New York 10025), nos. 12–15.

3. John Fraser, The Chinese: Portrait of a People, New York: Summit Books, p. 237.

4. SPEAHRhead 12/13, p. 51.

5. Recently, under pressure from the United States following the murder of interrogation-victim Carnegie-Mellon Professor Ch'en Wen-ch'eng, the law in Taiwan was changed to provide for a lawyer to be present while a suspect is questioned—a development noted in the State Department's Human Rights Report for 1982 (p. 692). What is not noted is that this provision applies only to civil cases, not to martial law cases. It is precisely under the latter that most of the abuses have occurred.

6. That peasants suffer from the absence of political freedom was tacitly admitted by Gansu's provincial radio station in 1977. Before that time, we are told, local people realized that the agricultural policies carried out in the province were erroneous. One member of a county party committee had "put forward some dissenting opinions, but the leaders slandered him, saying that he did not believe in putting politics in command. They also stirred up a cold wind, and suppressed the people's revolution. . . . Their efforts put all cadres in a dilemma. When they emphasized production, they feared that [bad political] labels would be stuck on them. If they neglected production [in favor of politics], they feared that the people would starve. . . . [Nonetheless, those in power] did not allow people to reveal the truth" (emphasis added). Quoted in SPEAHRhead 1, p. 21.

7. New China News Agency, text of Electoral Law, Section 14, FBIS I:243. The people electing these delegates are themselves elected by a weighted process. At the sub-provincial level, "the number of people represented by each rural deputy is four times the number of people represented by each urban deputy;" middle-level congresses "may" be more representative (Section 10).

8. Nie Rongzhen, "Strive to Create a New Situation in China's Science and Technology Work," Hongqi #13, December 19, 1982, FBIS I:247.

9. In this scenario, the history of the post-Mao/post-Chiang (Kai-shek) years would be repeated. There would be fluctuations in freedom and human rights, but little real progress. Clearly, Scenario A is probably everyone's choice in terms of probability, at least for the PRC. (For a variety of reasons the probability of "A" is somewhat lower for Taiwan.)

Before the discussion of this paper began **Gastil** added that among the particular aspects of China that differentiate it historically from other countries in the third world secularism is particularly important. The weakness of a church or an analogous institution is striking in Chinese history. This is in sharp contrast to Islamic countries or Russia where there was a large, well-organized institution acting as a counterpole to the political institution. Since China never had such a counterpole, what is happening now in Poland is inconceivable in this form in China. What is happening in Poland happens in Argentina, Chile and El Salvador--in most oppressive societies there is a struggle between the religious and political institutions. We won't find this struggle on the national level in China, although we may find it at local levels. The Confucian hierarchy that might be analogous was actually a part of the government.

One could argue that the lack of a religious institution might have a positive effect on modernization because the system can move more rapidly in a modern direction without religious opposition. But in Gastil's opinion the reduction in the chance for pluralism has an overall negative effect on the chance for democracy.

In regard to the paper as a whole Gastil added that we are not just asking these questions for the fun of it. The question at the end is always, what then should we be doing? Should we have more exchange of students? Should we be giving more information to the Chinese? If so, in what form? What should we be doing about American policies in regard to Taiwan that might affect this issue? Increasingly there are Chinese dissident movements developing in the United States and elsewhere. Should we be helping these groups? If so, what would be useful ways of offering such help?

Seymour added that the paper had not pointed out that the question "Can we help democracy?" is different from the question

"Should we help democracy?" So there are four possible answers: we can and we should, we can't and shouldn't, we can but shouldn't, and we can't but should. He personally did not know if we could, but he thought the West should at least make the effort in a small way. There are a number of reasons, not the least is that we should be consistent in the application of our principles. We should not act as though we believe democracy and self-government are relevant only for one part of the world or for certain races.

He said the concept of political culture permeated the paper even when the authors tried to separate it out. On page 124, for example, the three special problems of democratization are all really related to political culture. The particular historical situation is actually reducible to culture: the ideas that linger on from historical experience are, after all, culture.

They also did not emphasize as much as they should have the fact that there was not just one or two cultures in these two places: each has many cultures. This conference will discuss cultures of ethnic minorities in this conference, but he meant more than that. The cultures of the intellectuals and that of the rural peoples are quite different. In Taiwan there is the culture of the mainlanders and the culture of the Taiwanese with their long experience under the Japanese. One could slice these cakes many ways into subcultures.

As far as the problems of democratization are concerned, most discussions center around the role of the intellectuals. The banner of democracy appears to be held, if held at all, by intellectuals. It always seemed to Seymour that in a country eighty percent peasant, like the PRC, democracy by definition means turning the country over to the peasants. This is not a prospect that Chinese intellectuals, including democratic activists, seem to relish.

Chinese peasants, after all, are conservative and have a relatively low educational level. Recent statistics on the literacy rate are surprising. In his naivete Seymour had assumed that the rationale for dictatorship is that when dictators set out to accomplish a particular goal, such as teaching everyone to read, they can accomplish it. The Chinese government now says that twenty-five percent of the population remains functionally illiterate. When one looks beyond this he finds there is a double standard in the statistics. Literacy in rural China is defined as knowing 1500 characters, and most foreign students of Chinese probably passed the 1500-character mark in the first year of

learning Chinese--yet they knew they were not literate at that
point.   In addition, Chinese statistics only include those twelve
to forty-five years old.   Those over forty-five are ignored. Since
just about everybody in the cities probably reads, this suggests
that perhaps half of the rural population is essentially illiterate. **Dreyer** added that recently it has been reported that the
number of children leaving school early has increased because now
they can stay home and earn money on agricultural tasks. Illiteracy might actually be increasing for those under twelve.

The preliminary open discussion then turned briefly to consideration of two related issues. First, the group as a whole empha-
tically did not think that literacy would be easier to attain if
the use of Chinese characters was replaced by romanized letters.
The example of Japan with an even more difficult character-based
writing system was cited as proof that literacy is not related to
the system. It was also pointed out that there has been a democratization of the writing system through simplification and
through use of the vernacular language, baihua.

Gastil pointed out that as democracy developed in Europe dialects became more and more important. Most recently this has led
to new television programs in Welsh. Democracy seems to go along
with more and more emphasis on actual spoken languages as opposed
to more universal, dominant languages. He wondered if this would
occur in China?

Seymour found a tension in China between democracy and nationalism. However,the Chinese people seem in the name of patriotism
to be willing to put up with a great deal of human rights depri-
vation; they avoid standing up and saying the emperor wears no
clothes. The great advantage of ideographs is that one can write
any language in them. The dialects can be written in more or less
the same language. Although today the written language is based on
the Peking dialect, literate people all over China can still look
at the ideographs and know what they mean. **Gastil** asked if they
listen to Peking radio and understand it. How much of the country
is cut off from understanding the radio? **Seymour** pointed out that
the Han children generally learn the Peking dialect in school.
But non-Hans and even many Hans (such as most Cantonese) can
generally not understand it. **Bernstein** added that people generally appear to understand the standard language even if they
can't speak it. The people understand a much greater range of
dialect than foreign students of Chinese, the same way Americans
can understand deep South dialects. He would think the most
important and believed single source of information about the

outside world is the Voice of America, through broadcasts in the standard Peking dialect.

Gastil wondered whether, if China moved in a more democratic direction, there would be demands for more regional broadcasting.

In answer **Smith** pointed to the interplay in Guangdong between Cantonese and standard Chinese. In the last couple of years they have increased the amount of Cantonese broadcasting, both radio and television, and it is extremely popular, but it is supplementing rather than supplanting Mandarin (the standard Peking dialect). It is somewhat the way minority languages are in parts of Europe or the Soviet Union; they coexist without necessarily having serious conflict.

As an aside he added that he was glad the Voice of America had been mentioned. One of the most important actions affecting internal communication or the flow of ideas that the authorities of China had taken, and in this case primarily by default, was to permit people to listen to foreign broadcasts. It is not just Voice of America, although it has the widest accessibility. They don't jam it. As far as he knew there was no official discouragement of listening, although it may be criticized on the local level at times. **Bernstein** said that Deng Xiaoping, when introduced in Peking to Wendel Corey (VOA Peking correspondent), said, "Oh, I listen to you every morning." **Smith** added that the Voice had an enormous impact in ways we can't understand because we aren't the people at the other end listening to it.

Returning to regional dialects, **Dreyer** suggested that we cannot tell very much about pluralism in China from the spread of regional broadcasting or its lack. During the height of the Cultural Revolution when minority broadcasts all but disappeared, there were still Cantonese dialect broadcasts for two hours out of Peking. One among many explanations was that the PRC government wanted the people in Hong Kong to get the cultural revolution news the way the government wanted them to hear it. If you could show that more regional broadcasts have been added because of a demand from below, this would of course indicate pluralism. But this doesn't seem to be the way it has worked in the last couple of years, but the other way around.

Gastil concluded by saying that he was looking for the possible development of a democratic attitude. Moody differentiates in his paper (below) two different attitudes toward democracy. The elitist believes that the people who know more should get more power, or according to Norris Smith's paper, the "people of the word" should have more power. He is unlikely to support more regional broadcasts. Those with more populist attitudes would be more likely to support regional broadcasting.

Critique of Gastil-Seymour Paper by Jerome Grieder.

In preparation for the conference Professor Jerome Grieder had been asked to critique the Gastil-Seymour paper. His remarks follow:

My function is to comment on what seem to me to be the more important issues raised in the Gastil-Seymour paper, to suggest a few general questions that might provoke further discussion, and, as an historian whose field of expertise is pre-communist (or pre-1949) China, to offer some historical generalizations as background. Some of what follows may apply to the ROC (Republic of China) on Taiwan; but whenever I descend to specifics, it is the People's Republic that I have in mind.

One crucial issue that must be clarified as the discussion goes forward is the question of whether we are talking about demo-cracy/freedom as a potentiality inherent in the indigenous politi-cal-social culture, a style of government and political life that may emerge from the Chinese background. Or are we talking about democracy/freedom as a transplant, the product of an alien cull-ture with an alien history, and hence, essentially, an import or an imposition? Obviously we would like to feel that we are embra-cing both of these possibilities--what might evolve out of the indigenous culture, and what might be injected into it. But in our discussion we must clearly distinguish between them: on the one hand, evolution, and on the other, transubstantiation; on the one hand, inherent capacity, on the other, receptivity; on the one hand, the message that Radio Beijing might someday convey; on the other hand, the message that the Voice of America now broadcasts.

The Gastil-Seymour paper tends toward the transformationist view. It talks about the transfer of democracy as though demo-cracy were a complex of skills that could somehow be packaged and marketed. It identifies democracy/freedom with the West and with westernization, suggesting that in some areas of the world the transfer of democracy has been made difficult by the prevalence of anti-Western feeling, a victim of the struggle against imperia-lism. The paper does not satisfactorily address the relationship between "westernization" and "modernization." "Westernization" is

141

a catch-phrase for many normative values which may, in certain contexts, facilitate "modernization" as a long-range strategy, while in other contexts conflict with it.

A second important issue flows from the first. Are we to assume, for the purposes of this discussion, that democratization is by definition subversive of the regimes in question? Are we to assume that freedom/democracy--viewed as being unambiguously a good thing, from the perspective of popular interest--is fundamentally antithetical to the interests of these governments? The Gastil-Seymour paper asks, for example, whether the reforms currently underway in the PRC (such as the introduction of the responsibility system in agriculture, and the establishment on the periphery of the state economic system of urban cooperatives to absorb some of the surplus labor that has returned to the cities) will strengthen allegiance to the government, or will strengthen the demand for democracy? As I read it, this is put to us as an either/or proposition: the possibilities are mutually exclusive and essentially incompatible.

I would prefer, on the other hand, to use this discussion as a way of gaining a clearer understanding of the evolutionary possibilities in these cases. Short of the forceful overthrow or drastic restructuring of the existing governments, how may existing institutions and principles of political organization evolve into more broadly based political systems? Or is it a prospect beyond reasonable expectation?

A third issue--perhaps the central issue, one touched upon in Peter Moody's paper (below) and several others--involves the question of our understanding of the correspondence between freedom and democracy. The Gastil-Seymour paper uses these as though they are synonymous, interchangeable, and co-extensive terms, but I would not. Freedom is a normative term, descriptive of a condition of political life. Democracy is not a normative term; it describes a system of political organization or mobilization by no means contingent upon the existence of a pluralistic social and political culture. Democracy may be synonymous with participatory politics; but in itself, participatory politics is not an adequate definition of the normative values implicit in the Gastil-Seymour paper. China's revolutionary history has certainly demonstrated that an extraordinary degree of political participation can not only coincide with but be the instrument of social coercion, political oppression, and fundamental anti-liberalism.

Liberal democracy--which is what the Gastil-Seymour paper is really talking about--is a normative term: it describes a poli-

tical system in which participatory opportunity is institutionalized in an environment sufficiently pluralistic to allow for
individual choice, and the existence of sufficiently distinct
alternatives in respect to political and social modes of behavior
to render the exercise of this freedom of choice significant.

This leads me, however circuitously, to another question that
is central to any attempt to arrive at a reasonable prognosis as
to the prospects for freeom/liberal democracy in China. Is the
"Fifth Modernization" (as the idiom of the moment has it) really
compatible with the original Four? In other words, is liberal
democracy even a possibility in the general context of social and
economic programs that virtually necessitate large-scale planning
and (to varying degrees in different areas) the centralization of
planning authority?

I rather doubt that any of us would be inclined to challenge
the necessity for planning in China. We might well take exception
to this or that example of the way in which it has been done; we
might well lament its social and political consequences. But,
given the economic and demographic conditions with which the
Chinese are contending, it is next to impossible to contend
seriously that their goals can be achieved without large-scale
planning in the shaping of policies for the control of population
growth or economic policies having to do with the accumulation and
allocation of resources. Any credible "scenario" for China must,
it seems to me, encompass the inevitability of more or less
centralized planning.

Planning at any level means the subordination of the nonexpert
to the expert. Obviously as the scale, measured either in size or
in degree of technical specialization, increases, so does the
distance between expert and nonexpert. Planning also means the
subordination of individual interests to the collective interest--
or, to put it in somewhat different terms, it makes it impossible
to define the collective interest as the aggregation of individual
interests, the traditional liberal definition.

By "expertise" I don't mean only technical expertise, the
expertise of the laboratory or the research institute. I mean
more broadly the ability to manipulate political and/or cultural
symbols with authority. Of course, individual and expert interests can coincide--they do coincide in the intellectual. This is,
I think, one of the reasons why, in addressing the kinds of issues
that a discussion of this kind raises, we find ourselves preoccu-
pied with the role of the intellectuals and the conditions of
intellectual life. It is also a reason why, in a discussion of

this kind, we come almost inevitably to an essentially elitist view of the peasants as the beneficiaries, but not the agents, of democratization or liberalization. The intellectuals' claim to participatory rights dominates our attention; it is perhaps reasonable to assume that what is done at the instigation and for the benefit of the twenty percent will in the end improve the conditions of life of the other eighty percent. But when we relagate the peasants to the status of passive beneficiaries, are we still talking, in any meaningful way, about democracy?

In On Representative Government, John Stuart Mill justifies the extension of political rights to the greatest number possible, "Not in order that they may govern, but in order that they may not be misgoverned." In the "Democracy Movement" of recent years there has been, it seems to me, a strong element of protest against misgovernment--and a strong desire to insure that those who suffered most acutely the outrageous abuses of the "Ten Lost Years" cannot again be so victimized. This is certainly understandable; but I think we must be clear on the fact that, in talking about political rights as a defense against bad government rather than as a structuring of opportunity to shape government, we are not talking about democratization of China's political culture. In the end, this approach would leave the ancient distinction between ruler and ruled--or ruling elite and ruled masses--intact and unchallenged.

(If only to be contentious, let me suggest that the only genuinely democratic episode in the history of China's long revolution--noncommunist and communist--occurred during the coming-to-power phase of the Communist revolution when, briefly, the peasants were the "experts." During the land reform movements of the forties, it was the peasants' experience, the peasants' wisdom, that was being sought, through the mechanism of the Mass Line in the effort to shape policies that would maintain political coherence and the momentum of social change. It is certainly possible to dismiss this proposition as no more than the residue of the romanticization of the revolution in the reporting of Edgar Snow, Jack Belden, the Crooks, William Hinton, et al. The Communists themselves make something of a romantic conceit of it, in their nostalgic retrospectives; and it was an aspect of the radical chic romanticism that was attached to the "Thought of Mao Tse-tung" on American campuses a decade or so ago. Nevertheless, as one reads back through that literature the evidence accumulates that at that time--and only at that time--the revolution **was** in the hands of the people, as never before nor since. "A constitution is not the

act of a government," wrote Tom Paine, "but of a people constituting a government. . . . A constitution is a thing antecedent to a
government, and a government is only the creature of a constitution." Perhaps this was what was happening, from village to
village throughout the Liberated Areas in 1947-48-49 . . . ? Perhaps this was, at least in part, why the government that came to
power in 1949 wore so comfortably, for a few years, the mantle of
legitimacy . . .?)

I mentioned earlier the durability of the distinction between
ruler and ruled. This brings me to the larger question of the
influence of the past upon China's revolutionary present. No one
would seriously uphold the view that the Chinese Communists are
simply Confucians, or Legalists, in Mao jackets. There are,
however, some intriguing and more than superficial parallels that
can be drawn between Confucian political culture and Communist
political culture. Gastil and Seymour have mentioned some of
these in their paper. Let me review the list, and briefly elaborate on it:

(1) Both "old" and "new" China are dominated by a comprehensive sociopolitical vision that encompasses cultural
and moral values.

(2) These are, in each case, "secular" ideologies, that
is, not dependent on an authority derived from supermundane
sanctions, and addressed largely to problems of social
organization, that is, the problems of this world.

(3) In each case, the distinction between "orthodox" and
"unorthodox" thought is clearly delineated. Neither tole-
rates a pluralistic intellectual culture. In both, acceptance of orthodoxy is the key to status and privilege, the
pathway to political and social authority.

(4) Both are, in a sense, "populist" ideologies: stres-
sing the importance of "the people," emphasizing the moral
obligation to serve society, investing heavily in large-
scale public works.

(5) Both Confucianism and Chinese Communism assume an
environment of economic scarcity and rationalize its perpe-
tuation--partly by extolling the virtue of austerity, and
insisting upon a fairly even distribution of poverty (a
least in theory). Both denegrate individual profit as a
worthy purpose, and are hostile to the mercantile-entrepre-
neurial accumulation of wealth.

(6) As already mentioned, both distinguish clearly between "ruler" and "ruled" (a distinction admittedly blurred in some of the more extremist expressions of Maoist doctrine.) This common elitism in turn produces similar characteristics attributed to the respective elites:

- as communicants of the established orthodoxy, the members of the ruling elite share (or are supposed to share) an identical outlook on the world whose governance is in their charge.

- by virtue of their education and the quality of the character thus instilled, the members of the ruling elite are (or are supposed to be) omnicompetent--able to move from task to task, from assignment to assignment, confident in their ability to deal with whatever problems may confront them by reason of their understanding of human or social nature.

- as representatives of both a ruling ideology and an indivisible political authority, the members of the ruling elite are extensions of the center--Emperor or Politburo--both administratively and ideologically; under no circumstances can they legitimately serve as the representatives of particular constituencies.

Joseph Levenson once shrewdly obvserved that however seductive such similarities may seem, we must not lose sight of the fact that the categories of Confucianism and Marxism are not the same. It is memorable advice.   For one thing, Marxism/Leninism/Maoism is far more complex, far more comprehensive in its social analysis, than was Confucianism. It defines social roles in adamant and exclusive terms. It is far more demanding, and much less tolerant: acceptance of the reigning ideology is compulsory. The old notion that one could be--indeed, perhaps should be--"A Confucian in office, a Daoist out of office" is untranslatable: "A Communist in office and a Social Democrat out of office" simply does not make sense--much less a liberal democrat, or an anarchist!

Compulsory allegiance to the ideology, and compulsory participation in the political process, generates the need to vulgarize Communist ideology in order to bring it down to the level--more or less--of the "common" man: whether or not he could read it, whether or not its precepts were applicable to the problems of pig raising or an infestation of locusts, it was considered prudent if not essential by every peasant to have his picture taken with the Little Red Book in hand. The "Sacred Edicts" of the Ch'ing, or the hortatory xiangyu sermons, are hardly analogous in effect, whatever may have been their intent. No one ever treated Confucius and Mencius except as the objects of ritualistic veneration on the part of the peasants.

Despite its very real sense of social concern, moreover, Confucianism was motivated by different emotions. The acceptance of Marxism, historically, can be accounted for largely by either a sense of social victimization on the part of the oppressed (or those who identify with the cause of the oppressed), or by a sense of social guilt on the part of those who see themselves as "oppressors." Guilt is not a sentiment indigenous to traditional Chinese social thought: it cost the Communists much effort, in the 1950s, to inculcate among the progeny of the old social elite the conviction that they must bear the burden of guilt for their sins, or the sins of their fathers, or of their "class." Such subjective analysis of their role presented the remnants of the old elite with an unprecedented and, in some instances, an intolerable challenge.

Finally, for our purposes, the Marxist/Maoist emphasis on conflict, tension, and contradiction may be contrasted (as it has often been) to the Confucian ideal of a harmonious, frictionless, tensionless society. Beyond this, the Marxist/Maoist notion of ongoing class struggle implies the need for activism: shaping history, not just enduring it; moving with purpose toward goals that lie in the future. The Maoist definition of such goals became increasingly obscure, or utopian; but the goals of the present regime, epitomized in the "Four Modernizations" slogan and linked to the symbolism of the year 2000, are reasonably concrete and specific, whether or not we think they are realistic.

Such differences between the inherited social/political culture and the social/political culture of Communist China are extremely significant in respect to the question of the inherent evolutionary capacities of the present regime. Whether they are conducive to "liberalization" I am not really sure--but on balance I am inclined to think not. On balance it appears that a morally authoritarian ideal of governance has been transformed into a morally authoritarian and politically totalitarian structure of government.

In several fundamental ways, moreover, it seems to me that the direction in which the Chinese will move, and the limits of such movement, will continue to be determined by inherited political and cultural precedents, or habits, or instincts. Let me conclude by suggesting, in broad terms, what these limits may be.

I cannot imagine a political/social transformation in China that would result in the subordination of the collective interest to individual interests. The collective interest may be defined in different ways at different times--indeed, the collective itself may be differently defined as circumstances change--but the collective interest will always take precedence over the individual.

No more can I envision a transformation so sweeping as to challenge the centralization of authority, especially intellectual or ideological authority--what Mao called "the centralism of correct ideas." In the future as in the past--under the imperial system, the Nationalists, or the Communists in the earlier phases of their revolution--every effort will be made to maintain a centralized ideological/political authority while at the same time regionalizing or localizing administrative authority.

In the future as in the past, the tensions and ambiguities generated by the effort to maintain control from the center while regionalizing or localizing administrative authority will be reconciled, insofar as possible, through the instrumentality of a politicized, ideologically committed bureaucray--thus contradicting the Weberian notion that a bureaucracy is by definition politically neutral.

I cannot imagine a transformation of the Chinese political culture so far-reaching as to allow the claims of an autonomous, pluralistic intellectual culture to be heard--much less to take precedence over the demand for a uniform political culture.

Finally, and most pessimistically, I cannot foresee the evolution of the Chinese political culture in a direction that would give more encouragement in the future than in the past to the emergence of, or even an understanding of the concept of, limited government. From its inception, and into the present day, the Chinese political tradition has encompassed only two responses to the idea of government. Government has been viewed either as the generator of culture and ethics, both public and private, and therefore legitimately comprehensive in its claim upon the lives and minds of the people; or it has been viewed (as in the profound skepticism of the anarchist-Daoist tradition) as essentially irrelevant to the real problems that lie at the heart of the attempt to understand the human dilemma. The idea that government can be essential, powerful, and important, but still limited in its legitimate authority, is entirely alien to the Chinese tradition. But such an idea is absolutely fundamental to any hopes we might entertain for the liberalization, the genuine "democratization," of the regime.

George Santayana once remarked that "In a hearty and sound democracy all questions at issue must be minor matters; fundamentals must have been silently agreed upon and taken for granted when the democracy arose." I must observe in closing--with profound regret--that, as I view it, the Chinese situation, or, just as important, the Chinese perception of the Chinese situation, must be seen in terms of continuing extremes, continuing polarities, that render the hope of any kind of consensual politics a very slim hope indeed.

Further Discussion on the Gastil-Seymour Paper.

In resuming the discussion in light of Grieder's critique **Seymour** advanced four points. On the question of transfer of democracy, we cannot get away from the historical fact that with very few exceptions--Thailand was perhaps an exception--the way non-European countries became democratic was by having it transferred to them, in some cases imposed on them. If you trace it back, most democracy in non-Western countries goes back to England. For example, we imposed democracy on Japan, and we got ours from England. He saw the problem of transfer as a given, as the most common road to democracy. On the question of democracy being subversive, he thought that in a sense democracy was subversive. It may not be true in China but certainly in Taiwan it is the judgment of the Chiang family that democracy is subversive. They know very well that it would be a real feather in their caps if they could win a free election. But they have very good reasons for not holding free elections: they are worried about what the outcome would be. In fact the reason most governments do not hold free elections is that they are afraid they cannot control the process. They realize it is very important to seem to be democratic, so they hold rigged elections, as in both the PRC and Taiwan.

Seymour identified Grieder's most significant question as the coextensivity or lack of coextensivity between democracy and freedom. He would more or less disagree. He did not see how you could have a "democracy" unless you have a free flow of information and ideas. Whoever controls the flow of information and ideas controls the country. People are simply going to be manipulated unless there is a free flow. Perceptions of facts and ideas are so limited that people become politically "incompetent."

The problem isn't whether collective interests or a multitude of individual interests will prevail. The question is who will decide what the collective interests are. If you have a very small group that controls the information media making the decisions, then you don't have a democracy. But it seemed to him, theoretically as well as practically, that one could let the public freely choose to let collective interests prevail and to define these interests. This is no problem for democracy.

There must be an opportunity to participate, but the participation must be meaningful, it must be based on knowledge. **Gastil** asked if Seymour would agree with Grieder's point that in a real democracy you have to be able to non-participate as well as participate. **Seymour** agreed, but added that if too many people choose not to participate you don't have a democracy anymore because too few people are calling the shots.

Referring to the earlier discussion **Huang** reminded the group that Seymour had said that democracy in the PRC would mean turning power over to the peasant and went on to say the peasant was illiterate, uneducated, and so forth. Huang found this an astonishing statement. He reminded us that in nineteenth century England the working class gained the right to vote but they were quite deferential in their exercise of power. He did not see why democracy in the PRC meant turning power over to the peasants. The issue here was one of leadership. Certainly the peasant may be given the right to vote, and political parties might compete for their support. But this does not necessitate turning over power. He thought that for the next few decades intellectuals would play a critical role in the PRC and on Taiwan.

He found Grieder's critique both exciting and profoundly pessimistic. It was as though nothing has changed in China in the last fifty years. This is not quite the case. Huang stated that he had been arguing that for the past fifty to seventy years there has been a struggle for democracy and human rights in China. The obsession with the struggle for power between the National and Communist parties is too narrow a focus; we must take into account the simultaneous struggle for democracy and human rights. He agreed with Seymour that the ideas of freedom and democracy were imported into China, but did not wish to get into the argument about the indigenous contribution. Certainly for the past fifty to seventy years the Chinese intellectuals have been attracted to both ideas. Of course one group might emphasize freedom and another participatory democracy--Moody's paper also takes up that issue. But Huang did not see an absolute dichotomy.

In responding to Seymour, **Grieder** agreed with the subversive threat of democracy. The example of the Chiang family was very well taken. But this is a conference around the question of what can we do? If we work on the assumption that yes, democratization is essentially subversive to the stability, to the established sense of priorities, or to established policies, then this will very much color what we can do. Obviously we cannot work through the established order for such goals. We will be working against it. We will be working with--if we can get access to them--the tiny group of dissidents, hoping that they will be sufficient yeast to leaven the whole. He thought this was a basic distinction. Are we going to try to modify or are we going to try to replace? Maybe there are grades in between: he would like to see them articulated.

On the question Huang raised concerning the "power to the peasants" statement, **Grieder** wondered if we could imagine a "democratization of China" based on a franchise limited to a minority. If the eight hundred million peasants are enfranchised then they do have the power.

Gastil agreed with Huang on the possibility of an in-between position. If you look at American history, in many states, for example Massachusetts, most people voted right from the beginning and most were "peasants," or at least farmers. Nevertheless, for a long time there was a small, rather intellectual elite that ran the country, at least up until the time of Jackson, and, in other ways, up until the time of the introduction of the initiative and referendum and the popular election of senators. So there are periods when people have the franchise and there still is effective rule by an elite, or much smaller group. Certainly this is one thing that could happen in China. The actual, effective, populist takeover might be much later than the extension of the franchise.

Sullivan wondered if it was proper to refer to those eight hundred million as "peasants" or as "farmers"? He would never refer to Americans in the eighteenth century as "peasants;" they were "farmers." These terms conjure up sets of attitudes, of orientations toward the market, and ways of living. If he understood the anthropological literature correctly, peasants need lords. America didn't have lords, therefore it never had peasants.

China: Comments and Discussion

The word peasant suggests certain characteristics--dependency, subordination, communalism, parochialism, probably illiteracy, lack of orientation toward a market, but also self-sufficiency and self-reliance. The word farmer means something else. But he only meant to raise the question whether the Chinese agriculturist is properly called a "peasant." Does the word "nong min" mean peasant or farmer? Some people in China may fit what anthropologists would define as peasants while today some would better be called farmers. If we go back to Evelyn Rawski's work there may have been some people even in the Ming dynasty better referred to as farmers. If we perceive the rural people negatively, we may take the view the peasants will throw up leaders who are populist demagogues. Maybe Mao's despotic leadership was representative of the Chinese peasants. Maybe what Grieder says about the peasants is true earlier in the revolution. If that was the time the peasants were really in control, who was leading them? Naturally their leader ends up being a real autocrat. If the peasants were not peasants, then we must look elsewhere for an explanation.

Seymour said he used "peasant" because every one else did. It was a semantic problem that exists in English, and not really in Chinese, and will not tell us too much about China. We should avoid both terms; they are neither peasants or farmers. If a farmer owns a farm, then these folks really are not farmers. They are also not peasants in the sense of the history of Western feudalism. He might have written rural people or agricultural people and not "peasant."

Gastil seconded Sullivan's suggestion that people in rural China live in a variety of different situations. Apparently those living near cities live very much like the evolved agriculturists of parts of India and lower Egypt. They are coming to live an essentially urban life. It would be interesting to know how large a group belongs here, probably millions at any rate. They are urbanized people earning their living on the land. They are literate, have radios, even televisions. It will be helpful if we differentiate our views of agriculturists at least to this degree.

Nathan said the term "peasant" involved a question of usage among anthropologists, and they were very confused about it. In common anthropological usage the term peasant is applied to much of the world's population. It is a very loose term. Peasants are distinguished from tribesmen, from plantation workers, ranch hands, and farmers. In most anthropological writing all other agriculturists are referred to as peasants. Distinguishing farmers and peasants is a problem, but the term "farmers" usually refers to agriculturists who hold large parcels of land and use modern technology. They are also not a politically subordinated class in the society. In these terms the collectivized, slightly modernized, market-oriented agriculturists of the socialist world are usually considered "peasants" by anthropologists, so we should not apologize for using the term. **Gastil** pointed out that many rural people in Taiwan that might have been called peasants in a previous generation are now, even on small farms, probably better called farmers. He also believed we could no longer apply Redfield's classic anthropological discussion of peasants to the people of rural Japan. **Nathan** suggested we need two terms: one for suburban farmers and one for the rest.

Kintner could not understand why Seymour had denied the Chinese had a feudal system. He had visited collective farms where the ruling council for a group of sixty to seventy thousand people consisted of about ten people. The people were controlled much like Sullivan described peasants. He felt that like peasants elsewhere they had very little control over their own lives; no freedom to move from the place. **Seymour** did not feel we should ipso facto call every rural person in totalitarian countries a "peasant."

Bernstein saw the discussion getting to the heart of Grieder's question as to whether democracy was subversive. Kintner visited these collectives a couple of years ago. If he went to a collective farm now, he would be shown something else. They would want to show him the responsibility system, with the "agriculturists" being given considerable freedom of choice in the economic sphere. They don't vote for much of anything. They do not seem to have much choice as to whether they are going to practice the responsibility system or retain the old collectivized system. Certainly they do now have meaningful choices in the way they farm their land and allocate their labor, as to whether members of the family will stay on the land or go into the city and look for a job. In Beijing there were women from Anhui becoming maids. They have been freed from the feudal elements of the work-point system because the family can now obtain grain by growing it and keeping a portion. So a certain element of freedom has been introduced which the regime apparently does not regard as subversive to itself. Obviously in other areas in urban life the government has been encouraging "small freedoms" because it thought these were necessary for political stability. Improvements such as those in the marriage law, in expanding the private sphere, in personal choice, in increasing predictability, these are seen as freedoms

that are countersubversive. But if you look at the large freedoms
we generally think of, political and civil rights, those are what
are considered subversive. We ought to consider how meaningful
these small freedoms are that are nonsubversive. This would help
us understand the extent to which communism in any form is incompatible with real improvements in the human rights situation in a
place like China.

Moody agreed with Huang that on Taiwan democratization by
definition would be subversive. The Kuomintang's legitimacy, if
it has any, is based on its claim to rule all of China. The fact
it doesn't make sense as the government of an independent Taiwan
curbs democratization. On the mainland it depends on what we mean
by the "regime." If it remains a revolutionary regime dedicated
to the total transformation of the human being, then it will
amount to some people doing something to others. It is not going
to be democratic. If it settles down, as it might be doing, to
simply a group of people ruling other people and staying in power
as best they can, then there is a possibility of some democratic
evolution. It might be easier to rule people if you let them
alone or let them have a little influence over the laws they
should live by.

In this there is a link with the question of the rural people.
In his paper Larry Sullivan talks about the way communists have
been discussing "peasant" interests, and that it is the peasant
background of the party that leads to extreme egalitarian approaches, the millenarian peasant position where they want to split
everything up, until everyone is the same except for the king.
There is this element in peasant culture, but their other side is
suggested by the responsibility system that indulges peasants as
rational economic workers. People are perfectly happy with inequality if the person who works harder gets more. What is fairer
than that? In this way the question just might not be that of
turning the power over to "the peasants" as a social category.
The issue isn't one of giving power to a class, but whether people
are going to have some control over the way they live their lives
in the small sense or the big sense. It is not obvious what
choices they would make.

Turning to Grieder's discussion of the need for planning, we
can all agree planning is necessary and ask whether it is compatible with democracy. The expert is supposedly going to have to
have power over the nonexpert. One response is that Western
societies and Japan have a considerable amount of planning. We
could argue how really democratic they are, but considerable

planning is compatible with democracy defined as political rights and civil liberties. We should also remember that often the most effective planning would be letting people do what they want to do. This made a link with his earlier comments. Planning need not mean bossing people around. It could mean setting goals and allowing people to work toward these goals. Here there could be quite a bit of liberty without any popular control over rulers. A relatively passive government could stay in power without being questioned on its legitimacy.

Gastil pointed out that in the nineteenth century the United States under a democratic system engaged in some enormous planning projects--for example, the building of the railroads to the West Coast, the Homestead Act, and the Land Grant Colleges. **Grieder** thought this was in an utterly different socioeconomic context. **Gastil** thought this suggested that we do not have to set democracy aside to achieve long-range planning. **Sullivan** added that there was a considerable economic planning apparatus in India. However, he agreed with Grieder that the obstacle to democracy wasn't so much the necessity of planning as China's very large bureaucracy.

Liang wished to reconsider Bernstein's discussion of the small freedoms in the countryside today. He disagreed with Seymour's point about democracy giving power to the peasants. That was one way but not the only way. The situation now was that the Chinese government and party control the people even more than under Chairman Mao: they control the people's thought more closely. Yet in the countryside the Party has very open policies and very good policies. The new responsibility system includes elements of freedom. Under this new policy peasants have more power to manage how and what to produce. Before only the political cadres, the officials controlled everything; they made the plans, and said how much and how to plant. Today the peasants can really manage by themselves. He would not claim this is democracy, but the Party has given the people power. In the countryside the Party now emphasizes its political work and its political control. They are giving some economic freedom but not political freedom.

Dreyer asked Bernstein what mechanism the maids from Anhui used to get to Beijing, given the continued requirement for government-issued residence permits. Do people advertise for maids and therefore they are allowed to transfer their residence permit? **Bernstein** did not think their moves were unusual. **Dreyer** reminded us of the xiafang youth (young urbanites sent to live in rural areas, generally as peasants. The movement began with volunteers in the middle 1950s, but most xiafang were moved compulsorily in the period of the Cultural Revolution.) who would like to come back to the city. **Bernstein** thought that most, or at least a high percentage, of the xiafang youth had returned through a combination of bribery and policy. As for maids, he thought it a matter of personal connections. The ones he knew of came through relatives and friends writing letters. All they needed was train fare. **Dreyer** felt that a substantial number of the xiafang youth remained in rural areas.

Seymour wondered what they did about ration coupons, for that was the key way people were kept in the countryside. **Bernstein** said that although it is more expensive urban people can now buy grain on the open market. Lots of maids have left their work unit. They have what is called "pocket hukou." Their registration is not with any of the local police where it should be. There are millions of people living in the cities without registration in the city they live in. They borrow their train fare in the village--paying maybe ten percent interest a month. They send back their whole first month's pay and then they are free and clear. A typical wage might be twenty to twenty-five yuan a month, and they may send most of it back to their relatives. The family they work for provides all the necessities.

Gastil wondered if this was a new policy or were they just not enforcing the regulations. **Bernstein** thought that China's tolerance for victimless crime had increased. There was more tolerance for doing things that were technically illegal. The police and government recognize that to try to enforce many rules would lead to too much reaction. Of course, there is always the possibility that this change will not endure in the countryside. The local party cadres that are losing power and authority may counter attack; there may be a re-radicalization and re-collectivization of the countryside. But as of now labor power can be freely allocated by the family. So you can send your people to be carpenters or tailors or maids or any number of things.

Dreyer found this fascinating because one of the PRC's accomplishments that the PRC has been most consistently credited with by foreign analysts has been its ability to control the flow of peasantry into cities where there were no, or few, jobs; thus it could prevent the development of unhealthy or subversive barrios. She thought it likely that the government can accept this change as long as people find employment in the city. If they can't find work, then the government will crack down. **Bernstein** thought the most difficult thing to find was housing. **Smith** saw the system working primarily through housing. You must get yourself attached to a housing unit (hukou means household or gate) through family ties, or sometimes just by purchasing a slot in someone's house-- they rent you a room and then you get a de facto hukou status. This is essentially the way movement to the city is controlled in other countries without formal controls.

Gastil asked if there were parasite laws similar to those in the USSR and Cuba. **Smith** said there were certainly antiparasitic practices by the police, but not really any laws. **Nathan** added that you could be given a labor reeducation term for being a vagrant.

Seymour returned to the "big issue" of whether democracy meant turning power over to the peasantry. He found it interesting that we had heard from two Chinese intellectuals so far in this conference, and they both very conveniently confirmed his thesis that Chinese intellectuals do not see democracy as meaning turning over political power to the rural eighty percent. He thought this interesting and important. **Huang** said this was not quite the point. The point was that he didn't see turning power over to the peasant as a block of rights or goods that will be given the peasant.

Kintner felt that there must have been a great liberalization in the countryside. When he was there in September 1980 in Xian among other places, he took a trip 100 miles north and a hundred miles south, and he watched the roadbuilding. There were about 3,500 men and women moving a great deal of gravel and they would practically haul it on their backs. Somebody had to be giving the orders. The countryside was very poor. Burma was the only other place in Asia he had been that looked that bad. There was nothing to pay them with there. It was deplorable countryside, and back-breaking work for ten hours. How much freedom of action could there be if you can impress that many people daily to work on a project like that? He wondered if this system of tight control had disappeared.

Seymour thought we had nicely juxtaposed what Bernstein was talking about and what Kintner was talking about--corvee labor. They are both going on at the same time. He believed what Kintner was describing was much more common for the average person. What Bernstein was talking about was exceptional--only a few managed to get themselves illegally to the city.

Bernstein agreed that moving to the city was not a basic change, but the introduction of the responsibility system was. (The consensus of the group was that 75 to 85 percent of the rural production teams have adopted the responsibility system.)

Seymour added that they still had to get the roads fixed. **Sullivan** suspected it was more a matter of when you were in Xian. But he wondered if it was more difficult to impress people for corvee labor when they can be off raising vegetables for their own account. There must be considerable tension between the demands of the state for basically laudable purposes such as the repair of infrastructure, and individual desires for profit. He noted that Bernstein and Liang had pointed out that, in many ways, the biggest problem the party faced is controlling the large group of rural cadres who have spent the last twenty-five years ordering people about. Now they are frustrated with nothing to do, and the possibility of their taking action is a real one.

Grieder wished to explore the suggestion someone made that the responsibility system was a concession to the peasantry or agriculturists. The peasant's rational decisions as to what to plant and what to plan for are accepted as valid. But how important are concessions of this kind at this level in this context to the larger questions? How can one connect the Xidan (Democracy Wall) protests with the implications of the responsibility system? Are there common interests, or are we really talking about two very different things?

Zhu believed, as Liang mentioned, the government has made many economic reforms in the last few years, especially in the countryside. He believed ninety percent of the production teams have adopted the responsibility system. This was very important for agriculture. But he wondered how long the government would be able to balance agriculture on a decentralized basis and the economy on a centralized basis? How can the government make the political development, especially after the middle of 1980, conform with its basic principles? The commune organization was a political as well as economic organization. Since the government is destroying its own political organization in the countryside, it will have difficulty keeping its stability. Even before he left China he had read internal documents in which many local cadres criticized the government for capitalist restoration. Maybe in the short run it is possible for the government to have it both ways, decentralized agriculture and centralized industry, as the Soviet Union did in the 1920s with NEP (New Economic Plan). The existence of conflicting policies also fuels inflation, because there are two markets, the free market and state market. The government is emphasizing light industry and agriculture, but when peasants are given freedom they do two things: they develop agriculture, but they also develop small-scale factories, mostly to process agricultural products. So there develops competition between private and state light industry in the cities. The city factories, such as cigarette factories in Shanghai, can no longer get enough for production. How long can this contradiction be maintained?

The Democracy Wall experience is not totally unrelated to the peasants. Most peasants do worry about future changes in policy. Some people writing in the Democracy Wall Movement thought the government should give peasants more freedom. There have been points of contact.

As to this imbalance between freer agriculture and the rest of the system, **Grieder** wondered if Zhu believed tighter controls would again be put on agriculture or whether industry would become freer. **Zhu** thought that in the near future it would be difficult for government to decentralize more. They have tried, but are retreating: for example, the internal economic literature four years ago discussed Yugoslavia; two years ago the writers discovered Hungary; this year they discovered the Soviet Union. In his judgment Soviet methods were increasingly attractive, especially in the political area.

Nathan thought we should talk more about the limits to freedom under the responsibility system. The peasant is still tied to the land. His residence registration is inherited from his mother, who is more likely to have remained in the countryside even if his father went to work in the city. One cannot legally move without changing his registration, and it is hard to get permission. (Although he knew nothing about the Anhui maids before, he now had a theory to explain their movement. Contract labor has always been a feature of the Chinese system. In this spirit, a peasant might go into the cities temporarily--although this could be for years--but without permanently changing his registration. It is possible to get a temporary registration from the police in such cases. He believed the Anhui maids may well have such temporary registrations.) Nathan also pointed out that the peasant family under the most free version of the responsibility system has to sign a contract with his production team in order to receive permission to use the land or whatever other facilities were involved. The land continues to be collectively owned. The peasant can produce what he wants to produce within the limits of the contract he signs. The team must still fulfill the state plan in regard to grain production. It is not completely free. The team still has to sell quota grain to the government at a government-controlled price. (Nathan asked whether excess grain also had to

be sold to the state at a higher fixed price.   In answer **Bernstein**
and **Zhu** agreed that excess grain no longer had to be sold at a
higher fixed price: the government encourages further sales to
the government, but they are not compulsory.)

Nathan also pointed out that agricultural prices on the "free
market" were generally regulated: they must be within a fixed
range.   Through all these means the government continued to control the rural surplus. It chose now to allow the peasants to get
richer and to lower the prices of inputs to the countryside, but
all these factors of exchange remained under the control of the
state.

Returning to the abstract level and Grieder's discussion,
Nathan agreed with Huang that democracy was an idea that had come
to China in the last hundred years.   It didn't really exist
before.   Change does and has occurred. When foreign ideas come
into China, the Chinese accept from among the foreign ideas those
that are most compatible with their previous way of thinking, and
then reinterpret even these ideas in their own way.   What they end
up with is an idea of democracy that is insistently democratic but
is very, very different from our idea.   The core of it is the idea
of mobilizing the energy of the people to help enlarge the power
of the state.   This is true of both of the Chinas. In the twentieth century, when Chinese philosophers and thinkers studied
foreign ideas, they accepted foreign ideas that:

1)   Justified the idea that the power of the state cannot
be limited.   They chose from among available Western ideas
doctrines that said that natural rights do not exist, that
law is what the state decrees, and that it can decree anything because it is sovereign.

2)   Supported their idea of the supremacy of the collective interest.   This idea is central to Marxism, but also
nationalism.

3)   Rights are justified by their utility for social ends
and can be justified in accordance with what makes them
most useful.   This is combined with the idea that many
rights that will be useful later are not very useful now
because China is still a backward country.   Gradualism is
necessary.

So Chinese governments in this century, Kuomintang as well as
the others, have recognized popular sovereignty, but as a theoretical basis for state legitimacy rather than as a basis for the

people's institutional power over or against the state. In this theory elections express popular sovereignty but do not exercise popular power. In taking these positions China has aligned itself with most of the countries of the world; this includes the socialist and most of the authoritarian countries. So China has developed a modern "democratic" idea that is both international and profoundly rooted in Chinese culture. Nathan agreed with Grieder that it was not very likely to change.

Another reason to be pessimistic about change was the obvious power interests of the ruling party and of ruling groups within the party. We could talk about future scenarios of political disorder in China, but none of them are likely to lead to a long-term liberalization or downward distribution of power (although this may be a temporary outcome of struggle within the party elite).

There are forces in China that yearn for certain aspects of what we define as democracy. Especially the young people and some of the workers--and the workers are predominantly young (sixty percent under the age of thirty-five in state-owned factories)--would like more freedom of speech just because they want the sense of being able to talk. These groups and many other groups would like to see more predictability in government; they want the rule of law. But if the Chinese government were to respond in some degree to these desires--which it seems particularly inclined to do in regard to the rule of law--he agreed with Zhu that it would go in a Soviet direction. The Soviet government has total power yet it agrees to obey certain rules and regulations. So when it wants to suppress a particular individual the regime may go through complicated legal maneuvers to get the person to the point where they can legitimately lock him up. The United States can help China evolve in this particular direction through the Voice of America and cultural exchanges. We can move it in the direction of the Soviet model; he supposed we would want to.

Nathan did not know any significant constituency in China that supported such ideas as limited government, the propriety of interest groups making demands on government, or the propriety of individualistic behavior that doesn't bow to collective interest. He did not think that the American government or people could do anything to move China in these directions.

Dreyer agreed with Nathan that rights were given in order to enhance the mobilization of the Chinese people. In fact she could recall Deng Xiaoping saying in effect: The economy is stagnant and repressed, so we are going to give the people freedom so they will go out and produce more. As soon as the rights given appeared counterproductive--for example, too many people were spending their time demonstrating or writing wall posters--the rights were rescinded.

As to the question of democracy for the intellectuals versus democracy for the peasants, Dreyer did not recall intellectuals ever saying, "We ought to receive power because we are intellectuals." Instead they have set themselves up as spokespersons for the people at large. She could imagine a scenario where the intellectuals were leading a movement for increased rights for the peasants. The Economist's analysis of the reason for the arrest for Fu Yuehua was that here was an intellectual forming an alliance with the peasants. This was too dangerous; she had to have her thought reformed immediately. She was arrested. Someone may try the same in the future. Bernstein's idea was a very interesting one--could the small freedoms eventually be enlarged into the big freedoms? People given a certain amount of economic democracy may then begin to assert their rights to other freedoms. Although she had been a professional pessimist most of her life, she felt a little odd being the optimist of this group, but she did feel some evolution was possible as long as the changes were not too sudden.

Huang had been taught that a distinguishing characteristic of the American people was optimism. Yet now he had to defend the possibility of democracy and human rights in China. On the whole he agreed with Nathan's comments. Democracy and human rights will be difficult to come by in China. But he would not be so absolutist. Again and again through the decades a group in China, including intellectuals, has demanded democracy and human rights. They did not get very far. But what has happened in Taiwan should give us pause before we get so pessimistic. In the past thirty years an organized group in Taiwan has supported limited government. He was thinking of a slogan used for some years now by the Tang-Wai (the opposition grouping): "Democracy relies on check and balance, and check and balance relies on Tang-Wai." Because of economic development the political culture of Taiwan has not been so powerful and unchanging. Opinion and attitudes have changed. A middle class has emerged. So developing a real democracy is hard but the case is not hopeless.

Even if the idea of democracy has been brought into China primarily to mobilize energy and power, in the European experience the mobilization of the people for mobilization and power led eventually to the government making concessions in other regards. So the rule of law and other freedoms have closely followed mobilization by the ruler to accomplish his purposes. So, when it comes to China, Huang did not see such absolute dichotomies between liberal democracy and participatory democracy, or the negative freedoms and participation in decision making--he agreed on the tension that Moody described, but he found movement: the pendulum goes one way and then another.

Bernstein thought that the situation on Taiwan offered some hope. In fact he was uncomfortable talking about the PRC and Taiwan in the same conference because the human rights situation, respect for law, and degree of personal freedom were so different. Although he did not agree that the idea of limited government was firmly entrenched on Taiwan, it was a government that has been forced to give more options and meaningful choices to people than that of the PRC. If a country starts with a free enterprise system, which Taiwan has always promoted, then the government has to give more freedom of action in the economic realm than it would with a planned economy. Bernstein related Nathan's discussion to the difference between an authoritarian and totalitarian system. Nathan had established limits on how far China could go toward the Western concept of democracy, yet he left open areas of change such as increase in the rule of law and predictability. Was this a movement from a totalitarian toward a more authoritarian system? He did not like either very much and did not know where one stopped and the other began, but the difference was very important.

In the subsequent discussion Bernstein thought the Soviet Union totalitarian, but **Sullivan** thought there had also been a fundamental change there. Under Stalin the legal structure did not mean much, while today, particularly for people who are not labeled as primary political threats to the system, the government works through a fairly legalized structure to deal with all kinds of problems. He did not think the word "totalitarian" was accurate since 1953. He gave the example of an episode four years ago when the government tried to get the Georgians to adopt Russian. There was almost a popular uprising. The central government finally agreed the Georgians could go back to teaching their own language in the schools. Sullivan added that what has happened in China with the responsibility system could not happen in the Soviet Union for some complex reasons. We may look back on this as a basic change. Poland cannot be called totalitarian, when, for example, Western news reporters are allowed to interview Lech Walesa as he walks out of his apartment in the morning.

China: Comments and Discussion

Grieder and **Gastil** both thought that to describe the process of minimizing random, abusive intrusion into the lives of people as implementation of the rule of law is questionable.

The Controversy over Popular Political Culture in China: 1978-1982

Lawrence R. Sullivan

In the aftermath of the December 1978 Third Party Plenum, a debate emerged in Chinese media on the nature of China's popular political culture. Throughout 1979 and 1980 in particular, spokesmen for the Chinese Communist Party and non-party intellectuals argued over the basic character of the values, customs, and habits of the Chinese people that influence their political attitudes and behavior.[1] Was China's political culture essentially backward and traditional with the Chinese people, especially the peasantry, overwhelmed by authoritarian sentiments rooted in the past? Or were they characterized by a political maturity and sophistication that prepared them for meaningful participation in political affairs? After experiencing decades of dictatorship from both the political right and left, were China's people ready for some measure of self-government?

The basic stimulus for this "debate" came from the decisions of the Third Party Plenum, which raised fundamental questions of China's political history since the 1950's.[2] According to the official plenary communique and speeches by party leaders, such as Deng Xiaoping and Ye Jianying, the Communist Party had just emerged from nearly twenty years of "despotic" rule by Mao Zedong, supported by Lin Biao and the Gang of Four.[3] From 1958 on, Mao had accumulated enormous personal power backed by a "personality cult," and, contrary to the principle of "collective leadership," he had ruled the party with an iron hand. Though Mao had died in September, 1976, with the Gang arrested soon after, the plenary communique indicated that the party still suffered from an "over-concentration of authority" as some party leaders attempted to replicate the Maoist leadership style.

Much of this criticism was, of course, directed by Deng Xiaoping against his opponents on the left, especially Wang Dongxing and members of the pro-Maoist "whatever" faction, who attempted to cast the leadership of the then chairman Huo Guofeng in the Maoist mold. But beyond purely partisan politics, there was considerable interest and controversy within the party and among intellectuals over explaining the social basis of Mao's "patriarchal despotism" (jiazhang zhuanzhi). Mao, and especially Lin Biao and the Gang, were assigned primary responsibility for the two decades of despotism, and the disastrous policies of the Great Leap Forward and the Cultural Revolution.[4] But the question also arose about what role the people had played in the degeneration of Chinese politics into "despotism." Did they support Mao and the Gang's creation of a Hitler-like leader principle? And were they, therefore, potential supporters of aspiring despots like Huo Guofeng? Or were the Chinese people anti-despotic and anti-authoritarian in their basic political attitudes and values? Were they now ready for political democratization, particularly after the experience of the last twenty years?

This paper outlines the major arguments on the nature of popular political culture that appeared in the party press and intellectual or academic journals from December 1978 to the Twelfth Party Congress in September, 1982. Section One presents two radically different interpretations of the basic political character of the Chinese people that were supported by two opinion groups within the Chinese Communist Party (CCP) and among Chinese intellectuals. As demonstrated below, these views were tied to more practical policy positions within the CCP, especially on the question of Party reform. In section two, the analysis examines the views of Chinese historians on the role of the Chinese people in the long historical formation of "feudal despotism" in China's dynastic era. Once again, two contrary interpretations emerged that were evidently used to justify different programs of contemporary political reform. The controversy over China's political culture and history was more than just an academic exercise: It was a debate over the future of the Chinese political system.

On the Nature of People Under Socialism.

The dominant view in the party press was that the Chinese people were characterized by a profoundly "slavish" political culture that led to an absolute obedience before powerful politi-

cal figures like Mao Zedong. Supported, I believe, by Deng Xiaoping and other "orthodox Leninists" in the party leadership,
proponents of this view argued that "backward" conditions in
Chinese society and the masses' general contentment with "arbitrary but 'orderly' rule," had contributed, at least indirectly,
to the long period of Mao's despotism.[5] Rather than checking the
excesses of the leader, the Chinese people had served as a com-
pliant, and even supportive audience for the despot. With few
exceptions, the press saw China's population immersed in an intri-
cate web of "feudal" social relations and "customs," such as the
"patrilinial" family, and heavily influenced by traditional
beliefs, such as the "mandate of heaven."[6] Instilled with par-
triarchal and pro-monarchial sentiments, China's vast majority
accepted the "great leader" as a necessary component in the "natural political order."[7]

Responsibility for this "underdeveloped" state of popular political consciousness was, in part, directed at Lin Biao and the
Gang. By advocating "the idealist theory of innate genius and
[forcing] the people to worship their leader as an infallible
god," the radicals had "swayed public opinion to accept the idea"
of "blind faith" in the leader.[8] But the impact of the Gang's
"god-creating movement" had been to reinforce, rather than create
the "force of habit deeply rooted in the masses' minds" that the
leader possesses absolute authority.[9] Similar to seventeenth
century England, when as Christopher Hill notes "the strength of
the monarchy's appeal to ordinary people" was rooted in mystical
practices like the royal touch, China's post-Third Plenum leadership saw China's "overwhelming majority" locked into a pre-politi-
cal and pre-rational state of mind that provided fertile soil for
the despot.[10]

This view was cogently expressed by Li Honglin in a September
1980 article on "The Leader and the People."[11] On the one hand,
Li attacked Lin Biao and the Gang for promoting the "modern superstition" of "'loyalty to the great leader,'" and for making any
criticism or "disrespect" of the leader a counterrevolutionary
crime. On the other hand, Li also suggested that the Chinese
people had contributed to the Gang's scheme. In response to his
own rhetorical question--"What kind of society gives rise to and
needs such a political relationship [of absolute loyalty to the
great leader]?"--Li answered: "a feudal society. The economic
system in the feudal society," he continued, "gives rise to a
relationship of personal dependency. Peasants are dependent on
the landlords and residents of the whole country are dependent on

the supreme feudal lord--the emperor." Li noted, of course, that China was no longer a purely feudal society, it was a "socialist society" in which "the relationship of personal dependency---has long been broken. . . ." But there were significant "backward and reactionary ideas" in the popular culture that the Gang had managed to resurrect "to an unprecedented degree" in the Cultural Revolution when Mao's personality cult had peaked.[12] Thus, Li concluded: "It is the people who make the great man. . . ."

Examples of the people's profound cultural "backwardness" were readily apparent in extant "feudal superstitions," especially religion. Widespread beliefs in the sanctifying role of "heaven" and in the material power of spirits, such as the kitchen god, were powerful "mental shackles," particularly among the peasantry, that maintained the people's identity with the anthropomorphic authority of the despot.[13] Shaanxi Daily, for instance, pointed out that such superstitions as belief in the '"signs given under divine guidance,' [were] gradually spreading from the rural areas into the towns" and that "some enterprise workers and state cadres [were] also taking part in [traditional festivals]."[14] In Guangdong, the provincial press also noted that rural festivals were heavily ladened with patriarchal themes, such as the '"great king and father' touring the villages and driving away the evil spirits."[15] This resurrected traditional culture had even infected the local CCP, for as Nanfang Daily noted, "those who carried the sedan chair [in the festival] were all members of the Communist Party." Despite economic progress since 1949, the popular culture that had helped sustain the imperial monarchy and then encouraged modern despots, from Yuan Shikai to Mao Zedong, was far from dissipated. China's people, workers and peasants alike, were still incapable of breaking out of an enveloping, pro-despotic culture.[16]

This negative image of the popular political culture was not, however, universally shared by all commentary in the press. Although Red Flag (December 1981) criticized the radical left for having "exaggerated the consciousness of the masses," some articles in 1979 and early 1980 painted a more positive picture of the popular political mind. In a discussion of party and government elections, for instance, People's Daily (September 17, 1979) emphasized the masses' innate capacity for choosing good leaders. Citing the example of "Bo Le (an ancient horse expert)" who was adept at selecting "thoroughbreds," the newspaper suggested that the "masses especially are [able] 'Bo Le's' because of their ability to judge leaders."[17] Although "leading comrades" and "cadre workers," were also lauded for their ability to select good leaders, the article maintained that the "masses are in the best position to know whether or not a comrade has both the ability and the political integrity . . . of being a leader."

Of course, the communist leadership has always attributed positive political qualities to the Chinese people, while denying them meaningful political participation. But in the post-Third Plenum period, some Chinese political and intellectual leaders, which I have labeled "party reformers" and "proto-democrats," appeared to challenge the dominant image of the pro-despotic population, to justify their proposals for fundamental political reform. Although these two opinion groups apparently admitted that the "backward" mentality of the people had, in the past, played an important role in propping up despotic leaders, they also argued that China's population had undergone a significant change in political consciousness since the Cultural Revolution. After experiencing the disastrous consequences of political movements promoted by Mao and the Gang, the Chinese people, they believe, are now driven by an anti-despotic impulse that lends support to political liberalization.

In this sense, some party officials, and, especially, intellectuals outside the party apparatus, believed that political events have had the greatest impact on creating a more politically mature population. Contrary to the orthodox Marxist position that links the formation of a radically new "world view" to substantial material transformations and to the emergence of new social classes, some Chinese, associated with the "reformers" and "proto-democrats," came closer to a Hegelian formula in analyzing the emergence of a politically aware people who now reject despotism and demand a measure of liberty.[18] In his **Phenomenology of Spirit**, specifically the section on "Leadership and Bondage," Hegel saw the "bondsman" gradually gaining recognition of his own servitude through a process of intellectual growth which ends in a "rational consciousness," that is a knowledge that political inferiority has no moral basis, and that men accept subjugation solely on the basis of belief and not necessity.[19] In other words, as Richard Sennet points out, for Hegel "consciousness of lordship and bondage is all"; once the bondsman reacts to his servitude and adopts a new pattern of belief, then absolutist authority structures are doomed.[20] For Marx, such profound changes in thought could only occur with the development of certain material conditions, but in Hegel's view the creation of radically new patterns of thought grew out of certain "crises of authority" that were not

necessarily materially determined. Although Hegel, in a proto-
Marxist vein, saw the bondsman become "conscious of what he truly
is . . . through work," the "crises of authority" that changed the
bondsman's beliefs were less dramatic than the rise and fall of
complete social-economic systems, as was suggested by Marx. Recognition, the basis of liberty and freedom for Hegel, was a reaction to events that fell considerably short of great historical
transformations.

In China, post-1978 analyses of changes in popular consciousness were made in a similar mode, especially, it appears, among
supporters of significant political reform.[21] From their view,
the Chinese people have formed a more sophisticated and mature
political awareness, even though Chinese society has not undergone
a fundamental historical transition, at least in the orthodox
Marxist sense. In Hegelian terms, the Cultural Revolution constituted a "crisis of authority" that created a people who are now
willing to criticize despotic leaders, as they did not do in the
1960s and early 70s. In some press reports, emphasis was given to
the population's cynical and critical view of powerful party
officials. In one account, for example, the press indicated that
the masses were now openly contemptuous of such arrogant political
practices as extravagant "welcoming ceremonies" for top party
officials:

> As soon as the locals see the welcome posters then they
> comment critically: "the old official patriarchs are
> coming."[22]

Similarly, when village-level cadres reportedly neglected their
political duties for such "feudal" customs as extended mourning
for a deceased father, the "lower and middle peasants" supposedly
commented: "What difference is there between this and the officials of the old society?"[23] The critical faculties which are
necessary for a rational participation in politics, are seen to
exist in the popular mind, at least in embryonic form.[24]

On balance such positive views of the people were not, we must
emphasize, a major theme in the party press, even during the
"liberal" period of 1979. Instead of praising an emerging political rationality and anti-despotism among the masses, most commentary stressed the population's profound "cultural backwardness,"
especially among the peasantry. Contrary to the interpretation
that the Cultural Revolution had generated a more politically
prepared people, the prevailing view was that it had caused a

dramatic loss of confidence among the people, which, in turn, had actually produced a stronger belief in fate and a restoraton of religion and superstition. With the "influence of a petty producer . . . and peasant mentality" still strong, the Chinese people have not yet reached the stage of a "rational consciousness."[25] On the contrary, as a Xinhua commentator noted, "conditions in China today are very similar to those prevailing in Russia" after the Bolshevik Revolution when, according to Lenin, "cultural backwardness . . . held back the Soviet regime."[26] More than thirty years after the CCP's assumption of power, China's people still lack the basic elements of "civil society," that is the internal cohesion, the desire for progress, and the informed and critical judgment necessary for an active role in political affairs. Therefore, a long, arduous process of material development and political education under party leadership is necessary to alter fundamentally the masses' consciousness.[27]

For Deng Xiaoping and his "orthodox Leninist" supporters in the party, this emphasis on the people's political incapacity, rooted in cultural, and ultimately economic "backwardness," was used to justify a continuation of the CCP's one-party dictatorship. This was apparent, for example, in Deng's description of China as a "tray of loose sand," which indicated his belief that little progress had been made in imparting to the Chinese people a social cohesiveness and autonomous political will since Sun Yat-sen first used the phrase in the 1910s.[28] Although Deng shares the opinion that the population's pro-despotic sentiments reflect, in part, the impact of past political leaders like the Gang, his position, and that of "orthodox Leninists" in the party, also places considerable emphasis on the influence of China's "small-scale production" in shaping popular political beliefs. For this group, China's archaic modes of production keep the people mired in old "feudal superstitions." In a culture heavily influenced by powerful "feudal remnants," Chinese society is seen as "restorationist." That is, without the guidance of a party which is now firmly committed to "collective leadership," the Chinese people would spontaneously support another great leader, a "savior" that would repeat the disastrous policies of the past. But by continuing the party's dictatorship, Deng argued, China could avoid yet another deterioration into despotic rule, as the protracted process of industrialization gradually transformed "peasant" and "petty bourgeois" thinking into proletarian consciousness.

In sum, the press presented two images of the Chinese people's political character which were prompted by different political

opinion groups in the CCP. Where the masses' spontaneous rejection of despotism was stressed, the people were seen as forming an
inchoate rational consciousness that could provide a solid social
basis for significant political reform.[29] But where a deep-seated
"cultural backwardness," rooted in "small-scale" production was
emphasized, the need to maintain the party's dictatorship over
Chinese society was the prevailing theme.[30] Deng's arguments for
maintaining political dictatorship long after significant industrialization were supported by declaring that "ideology changes
much slower than does the mode of production."[31]

Feudalism and Despotism.

The controversy over the political character of the people was
also apparent in Chinese historiography. As in previous political
disputes, historiographical analogy and debate were used in the
1978-82 period to support particular ideological positions and
programs. Contrary to the Gang era when Yao Wenyuan had argued
that "capitalism" was the major threat to the Chinese revolution
and that bourgeois interests were represented in the party, since
1978 party leaders generally agreed that the "restoration" of
"feudalism" was the major problem confronting the Party and Chinese society.[32] The origins of the patriarchal leader in the CCP
was inseparable from China's historical evolution that, since the
Qin dynasty (221-207B.C.), has been locked into "feudalism." But
as we demonstrate in this section, there was considerable conflict
in the historiographical treatment of Chinese feudalism over the
source of China's stagnation in the feudal stage, and the structural relationship of feudalism to despotism. These issues, we will
argue, were also closely tied to the question of China's popular
political culture and of political reform in contemporary Chinese
society.

On the Material Basis of Despotism.

The dominant line of historiographical argument, supported we
believe by Deng Xiaoping and "orthodox Leninists" in the CCP,
stressed a deterministic relationship between "feudal small-scale
production" and "patriarchal despotism." In addition, it considered despotic rule an inevitable by-product of China''s feudal
economy. In contrast to the West, where the emergence of capita-

lism had produced political movements against the **ancien regime**, China has stagnated in a backward, feudal mode of production which gave rise to powerful despotic political forces from the Qin dynasty to the present.[33]

Examining modern Chinese history since the late nineteenth century, proponents of this historiographical line emphasized that "feudal" ideology and practice have consistently won out in the struggle with emerging bourgeois and proletarian forces, especially in the realm of political leadership. While the "sprouts of capitalism," rooted in the late Ming, produced political movements with anti-feudal and anti-despotic purposes, ultimately the overwhelming power of feudalism encouraged even the most progressive leaders to revert to a "patriarchal" leadership style. The Taipings and Hong Xiuquan, for instance, were praised for their "anti-feudal thinking" and for waging a revolutionary struggle against the "four great ropes--feudal divine right, political power, clan authority, and the authority of the husband.[34] But the Taiping movement failed because "it theoretically based itself on the religious thinking of the 'divine right of kings' and the feudal theory of 'l'etat c'est moi.' The 'king' was the representative of god on earth, holding absolute power over people's life and property." Drawing an obvious parallel to Mao and the CCP, Hong and the Taipings were criticized for having initially opposed feudalism in their struggle for power, but then using "feudal notions," heavily ladened with religious sentiments, to solidify their own political position. "Hong's thinking emerged to meet the needs of the laboring people's revolution," but he defeated his original revolutionary purposes by appearing "[u]nder the banner of the revolutionary personification of the sovereign god."

This contradiction of ideology and practice was not attributed to Hong's personal political opportunism; but to the inherent limitations of a political movement dominated by a peasant constituency. According to the article quoted above, "peasant war alone cannot overthrow feudal rule. . . . Hong Xiuquan represented the peasants who were small producers" imbued "with an inevitable sense of historical limitations. They were unable to have a field of vision that transcended the feudal system. . . . The ideology was only able to borrow forces from religion to mobilize and organize the peasant." Even with the best intentions, Hong (and by implication Mao) was eventually forced by political circumstances to adopt a leadership style that fit the feudal ideology of his "backward" peasant constituency.

Similar analyses were also made of the 1898 Reform Movement, the 1911 Revolution, the May Fourth Movement, and even the Communist Revolution. Though the 100 Days of Reform was declared to be a "fierce onslaught on feudal despotism" which "took the reform of feudal autocracy as the point of departure and demanded 'people's democratic rights'," the movement was also judged a failure because it represented a "national bourgeoisie" that was too weak to counter feudalism in the political realm.[35] Like Hong Xiuquan, Kang Youwei was praised for attacking "feudal despotism, demanding parliamentary rule, and a constitutional monarchy," and along with Yen Fu, for promoting a "bourgeois ideological enlightenment movement" that established the "theoretical basis of his reform concepts." "For the first time in modern China," Guangming Daily (July 17, 1979) asserted, "the movement gave rise to the emancipation of the mind" and "it educated and influenced the people . . . and prepared conditions for the revolution of 1911." But, in the end, the influence of this "enlightenment" was restricted to the intellectuals, while the reformist movement as a whole remained "divorced from the masses," dooming it to defeat at the hands of the Empress Dowager. Confronted by the overwhelming power of feudalism, Kang abandoned a progressive political role and "degenerated into a diehard royalist."[36]

By 1911, the collapse of the monarchy and the "equalization of land ownership" had weakened the political and economic underpinnings of the feudal system. And yet, the verdict on the revolution was also negative, because "it did nothing about remaining feudal vestiges." 1911 was a lesson that it is "impossible to eliminate feudal concepts overnight."[37] Even with the fundamental political and economic changes accomplished in 1911, feudalism remained the dominant force "exerting great pressures on the bourgeoisie whose ideology was 'crooked,' 'transformed,' and at times even distorted beyond recognition."[38] Bourgeois leaders, such as Sun Yat-sen and Zhang Binglin were not imperial despots, but they were tainted by a feudal leadership style that was "based on the theory of innate genius," and that "regarded the broad masses as the 'common herd' who were 'imperceptible'." Sun, in particular, was accused of rejecting democracy and, like the Gang, of promoting rule by "supermen of foresight."

Finally, in an analysis of the May Fourth Movement and the CCP, the regenerative power of feudalism was cited as the primary cause for the persistence of despotism into the revolutionary era. Like 1898, May Fourth was praised for its attacks on despotic leadership by such cultural iconoclasts as Wu Yu (who in 1978 was canonized in the press for his critique of the patriarchal structure of the Chinese family).[39] But, on balance, the long-range effect of May Fourth was minimized: it "lost momentum and petered out existing only in name."[40] Intellectual movements, like May Fourth, were an insufficient transformative force in a sea of peasant-based feudalism molded by backward material conditions. For the "orthodox Leninists" in the CCP, the economic base still determines the political "superstructure."

In similar terms, the press suggested that the Chinese Communist Party has had limited success in fighting feudalism in its sixty-year history. In the 1921-1949 revolutionary era, the CCP was unable "to thoroughly eliminate the influence of feudal forces that had built up over 2000 years."[41] Contrary to the view of Western scholars who argue that the party's insulation from Chinese society enhanced its transformative power, Chinese interpretations now view the party as profoundly affected by its feudal surroundings.[42] The admission that "there has always been a very high ratio of comrades with petty bourgeois backgrounds in the party" illustrates the post-1978 leadership's belief that the "vanguard of the proletariat" is still heavily influenced by the society's backward conditions.[43] Thus in a pessimistic judgment on the party's political influence over China's historical development, People's Daily (June 1979) noted: "Even now we can only stress the criticism of feudalism, [we] are in no position to eliminate it."[44] Since feudal and petty bourgeois forces are still dominant in Chinese society, and represented in the party, the task of preventing new despotism must remain in the hands of the party elite, with political reforms restricted to refurbishing Leninist practices of "collective leadership."

In sum, this first historiographical line interpreted Chinese history, and especially the Chinese revolution, in "linear," deterministic terms. In China's past, intellectual and political movements have opposed feudalism, and its political manifestation of despotic leadership, but the entrenched small-producer economy encased in feudal social formations consistently inhibited fundamental political reform. Beginning with the Qin dynasty, the objective force of "feudal production" has been the dominant motive force in China's historical development. Moreover, since the Taiping rebellion, every revolutionary movement including the CCP, degenerated into despotism, a trend that was not accidental but "traced to the material conditions of society."[45] All China's modern despots, from Yuan Shikai to Chiang Kai-shek to Mao, have found a secure political base, especially among the peasantry for whom "the subsistence economy forms the real foundation of their monarchical thought."[46] According to an article in Research on Chinese History:

> The peasants' production methods do not lead to mutual contact but separation. Each family produces most of its needs, and the things they need to survive on come from nature, not society. The ties that bring together families and households do not derive from economic relationships but instead depend on a non-secular clan power. The clan head of one or many clans is the brains of the entire village and is the leader in guiding the people to ancestor worship. . . . In China's feudal society, the patriarchal system and monarchism are closely linked . . . monarchism is simply the patriarch writ-large.[47]

China's peasants, in other words, are still predisposed to support a powerful leader because of their backward production, a condition that has not substantially changed since 1949. "Although the Chinese revolution has had a profound effect on the village--land reform and collectivization for example--and because agricultural labor organization is still arranged around one village or clan, agricultural cadres are most comfortable with using the patriarchal system to direct production. . . . This then provided the basis for Lin Biao and the gang's feudal despotic system."[48]

This situation, moreover, was not considered radically different in urban areas: "In industry progress has been slow such that most labor is still manual. The small-scale production still exists . . . while the working class is by and large only recently of peasant origin."[49] In the cities and countryside, the "superstitious practices of Lin Biao and the 'gang' caught on because many people were prone to superstitious beliefs."[50] Local society influencing the CCP's grassroots organization fostered a despotic politics which then gradually overwhelmed the party's upper-levels, a process which continued to plague the party after Mao's death.[51]

The lesson of Chinese history, then, is that an underdeveloped China provides fertile soil for the despot. Until full-scale industrialization "transforms the peasantry into working class," Chinese society remains a repository of pro-despotic sentiments.[52]

On the Political Basis of Feudalism.

A second historiographical line which appeared in the party press, and especially in academic journals, suggested that political factors were primarily responsible for creating and sustaining despotism throughout Chinese history. This argument, we believe, was used to support limited democratic reforms in the CCP and Chinese society as a whole. Without denying the material basis of feudalism and political autocracy in general, this interpretation treated despotism as a particularly extreme form of autocratic rule that China's elites, from Ming Taizu to Mao Zedong, had created within a general feudal context. Here despotic politics was not considered an inevitable by-product of the feudal economy; nor was its genesis and strength rooted in the people, even the peasantry. Instead, the emphasis was on the political determination of despotism in which the **primum mobile** was the ruler's pursuit of absolute authority. Throughout Chinese history, dynastic and modern, the despot imposed his arbitrary will on Chinese society "from above," stupefying the masses and leaving them unprepared for political participation. From this perspective, the people, including the peasantry, are largely absolved from responsibility in creating a social basis of despotic politics.

An example of this approach was the historian Wang Cengyu's analysis of China's "feudal cultural autocraticism."[53] Focusing almost exclusively on radical changes in the political "superstructure," which occurred within the broad historical stage of feudalism and largely independent of economic forces, Wang argued that before the Song dynasty China lacked a "full-fledged feudal autocracy" in both political thought and practice.[54] Although Confucius had established the foundation of a pro-despotic philosophy with such phrases as "The people can follow, but cannot know," overall, Wang argued that the master's attitude toward loyalty (zhung) "was not an absolute, unconditional one." Similarly, from the Han to the Tang, China's emperors had not aspired to a total concentration of power; nor had they attempted to manipulate philosophy and religion for despotic purposes. Contrary to their post-tenth century successors, these "rulers had a sense of self-confidence, and their minds were relatively lively." Even Qin Shihuang, traditionally the most notorious despot in Chinese history, possessed positive characteristics, for, according to Wang, "he was very much out in the open and frank. He merely wanted to believe in law, he did not want to promote benevolence [that is, the tool of feudal despotism]."[55]

However, by the Song (960-1279 A.D.), China's imperial system, and society in general, moved in the direction of a fully developed feudal-system despotism. But, contrary to the argument discussed above, this fundamental transformation was not rooted in material conditions. Rather, Wang argued, it was the result of political machinations by powerful elites who, in establishing imperial dominance over philosophical and political thought, created a despotic autocracy. In the Song, Wang Anshi and Zhu Xi solidified their autocracy by imposing on the political order strict interpretations of the Confucian classics, which replaced the more vigorous and creative interpretations of the classics that had supposedly existed since the period of the hundred schools. The greatest contribution to an imperial despotism, however, came from Ming Taizu:

> [Before the Song] religion and government were basically separated . . . and the emperor was not the leader of a sect. By and large he relied on Confucius, Mencius, and Zhu Xi to provide the substance of belief, while he himself did not promote a specific belief. However, during the Ming and Qing . . . there was a tendency of the emperor to serve the function of a religious leader. Thus, for example, Ming Taizu recognized that Mencius' belief that "the people are valuable and the emperor is light" . . . was not in the interest of autocratic dictatorship. So he quickly set about eliminating Mencius from the Confucian temple and ordered a revision of the Mencius compilation.

In Wang's view, the emperor Taizu attacked the realm of autonomous thought, crushed independent thinking, including scientific innovation, and linked religion to politics solely for absolutizing his own personal power. The "so-called 'imperial compilations' used selections from the classics to create a deeper sense of literary slavishness; they used the emperor's name for promotion to satisfy Kang Xi and Qian Long's desires for self-aggrandizement as Confucian prophets. Consequently, intellectual and cultural debates became a plaything in the hands of imperial power. . . . [Moreover] these rulers sought out spirits and ghosts in order to strengthen their dictatorship. This period [Ming to Qing] was worse than previous ones." The result, according to Wang, was a "stupefaction of the people" and of "the scholar officials," with the emperor as the sole beneficiary. In Ming-Qing China, imperial despotism was implanted at the expense of the bureaucratic class, as well as the Chinese people.[56]

In a similar analysis, the historian Qiu Hansheng posited a direct influence of Song-Ming New-Confucianism (lixue) on the increasingly despotic cast of the family and the clan.[57] Just as Zhu Xi was accused by Wang Cengyu of manipulating the Confucian classics for the purpose of absolutizing the emperor's authority, so too was he faulted by Qui for expanding the authority of clan heads to enforce an arbitrarily severe discipline through his rendering of "village rules" (xiangyue). For Qiu, the creation of despotic clan patriarchs at the local level, was not a natural outgrowth of small-scale production, nor did it originate in the peasant family. It was the conscious creation of the state, which by the Song was totally committed to imposing pro-despotic values on the entire society. Once the conventions on clan organization gained acceptance among the elite strata of the landlord class, their adoption and promulgation through ancestral halls, clan registers, and family codes granted enormous discretionary power to clan heads well beyond customary precedent. With the quasi-legal nature of the village rules, backed by the Neo-Confucian theory that the five cardinal relationships were ordained in heaven and imbued with cosmological potency, the state transformed the local social structure into a mere appanage of centralized, monarchical power. Beginning with the Song, the structure of authority in local society assumed a pronounced pro-despotic character that was not intrinsic to its "organic" nature. For instance, the subordinate status of women, a necessary component in the patriarchal structure of the family and clan, became much more oppressive than anything in Han times. By the time of Wang Shouren (1472-1528), who also contributed to this process with his own delineation of harsh village rules in the Nangan Xiangyue, Chinese society mirrored the state's structure of absolutist authority.[58] Despotism had become a pervasive influence in both the "great" and "little" traditions of Chinese culture, with the clan and family heads mere agents of the ruler's will.

In sum, for this second historiographical line, imperial despotism was not the mechanical reflection of China's backward feudal economy, inextricably wedded to small-scale production. Nor was feudal ideology, embedded in the people's minds, the major factor contributing to the prevalence of the despot in post-Song Chinese history. Instead, it was political leaders pursuing absolute authority who had created the conditions for mass obedience to despotism.[59] The essential foundations of despotic rule, the political control of thought and religious sanctification of imperial and clan authority, did not emerge from within Chinese society, but were imposed by elites on the people.[60]

For some members of the CCP leadership, we believe this historiographical argument was used to support limited democratization of party and society that went beyond orthodox Leninist values. By focusing on the political and ideological machinations of a few leaders as the primary cause of despotism, the implication drawn was that it is necessary to break this long cycle of despotism by the creation of a more democratic political machinery, with substantial participation of rank-and-file cadres in the decision-making process, with limited popular input into the CCP and the government. If despotism is the creation of a power-hungry elite, then the only effective means for reforming the party is to expand political controls from below. And, though economic backwardness may still limit the growth of a mature popular consciousness and the formation of civil society in China, the argument of the reformists and proto-democrats was that the extension of some democratic reforms to the population should not wait on industrialization. Since the despot is as much the cause of China's underdevelopment as its consequence, they argued that "without political democratization, there will be no economic modernization."[61]

Conclusion.

This paper has outlined two major interpretations of China's popular political culture that appeared after the Third Plenum in December 1978. On the one hand, defenders of the CCP's one-party dictatorship painted a highly negative image of the Chinese peasantry and working class that, in the historicist framework of Marxism-Leninism, denied a transfer of political power to the people until their transformation by material forces. On the other hand, some commentary on contemporary politics and history portrayed the Chinese people in more positive terms, and suggested that the horrors of the Cultural Revolution and China's long history of despotism, were the responsibility of political leaders who were unaccountable to popular control. For supporters of this argument the only effective means to avoid a repeat of despotic rule is to take absolute political power out of the hands of China's political elite. Unfortunately, by late 1981, this viewpoint gradually disappeared from public forums as the party leadership cracked down on unorthodox opinion. Like the participants in the Democracy Wall Movement, supporters of substantial political reform in the CCP, and gradual democratization in the direction of perhaps a two-party system, prepared for a long winter, after a very brief "spring."

Notes

1. Richard H. Solomon, Mao's Revolution and the Chinese Political Culture (Berkeley: University of California Press, 1971), p. 2.

2. "Communique of the Third Plenary Session of the 11th Central Committee of the Communist Party of China," NCNA, December 23, 1978.

3. Ye Jianying, Xinhua 29 (September 1979). Deng Xiaoping, "18 August [1980] Speech to Politburo," Chang Wang 461 (April 16, 1981.)

4. Besides Mao, Lin, and the Gang, unnamed "senior cadres" and even rank-and-file cadres were accused of supporting Mao's "despotism."

5. People's Daily, August 10, 1979. This article, which actually defended a more positive view of the people's political culture, noted that negative judgments on the people were, in the past and present, linked to the concept of the "state of the nation" (guoqing). "For many years the Chinese people, influenced by views on the state of the nation, appeared content with arbitrary but orderly rule." Although the authors challenge this view, they note that from 1898 to the present, this argument was used by political elites, from Yuan Shikai to the Gang to resist the introduction of modern political ideas, such as democracy, and also Marxism-Leninism. According to the article, "some people" in China still believe that "because of its large population and differing opinions . . . practicing democracy will give rise to great disorder. . . ."

6. Quangming Daily, January 21, 1979, Shanxi Daily, October 11, 1980, noted that the frenzy of "superstitions" in China was the same as in the post-liberation period.

7. See, for example, the analysis in People's Daily, December 11, 1979, in which the author tied the despotic authority of emperors, and then the Gang, to the patrilineal system (zongfa) and to the tradition of avoiding (hui) names of past ancestors in the family.

8. Beijing Domestic Service 29 (November 1979). The Gang was also accused of having encouraged religious fervor which accounted for the continued affection for strong leaders among the masses. See, Hunan Radio, November 28, 1979.

9. Guangming Daily, January 21, 1979.

10. Christopher Hill, Some Intellectual Consequences of the English Revolution (Madison: University of Wisconsin Press, 1980), p. 27. An article in Historical Research, September 15, 1979, noted, for instance, that the "passivity [of the mass of the people] . . . today still constitutes the objective foundation that has given rise to careerists and schemers like Lin Biao and the Gang of Four."

11. People's Daily, September 18, 1980.

12. This focus on China's feudal society also provoked a debate over whether the "feudal influence in our country is not a mere vestige but actually a kind of force." Philosophical Trends in China (Guonei Zhexue Dongtai) 3 (1981), as reported in Cheng Ming 47 (September 1, 1981).

13. One article also noted that a reliance on "dependency" (gao) in the party was rooted in traditional Chinese conceptions of the kitchen god's power to grant favors and benefits. People's Daily, May 15, 1979.

14. Shaanxi Daily, November 9, 1980.

15. Nanfang Daily, May 5, 1981.

16. Fudan Journal 5 (September 5, 1979) in discussing the limitations of the peasantry and the role of peasant ideology in promoting heroic leaders, also noted that the "working class is basically born out of peasants."

17. People's Daily, September 7, 1979. This article used the Bo Le adage to support reforms of the party's electoral system, specifically the proposal to allow several candidates to compete for party posts. It also noted that "the past practice of holding party elections with the number of candidates equal to the number to be elected," had opened the door to Lin Biao and the Gang's takeover of the party apparatus.

18. Interest in Hegel's philosophy blossomed after the Third Plenum, even though the party's campaign to "seek truth from facts" was at odds with Hegel's idealism. Specifically, the emphasis in Hegel on "objective truth" and on the importance of seeking the "truth" in a diversity of philosophies, had significant appeal in the post-Mao era. See, "Preliminary Examination of Hegel's Philosophy of History and Its Method," Philosophical Research (Zhexue Yanjiu) 4 (April 1979).

19. G. W. F. Hegel, Phenomenology of Spirit, translated by A. V. Miller (Oxford: Clarendon Press, 1977), pp. 111-119.

20. Richard Sennett, Authority (New York: Alfred A. Knopf, 1980), p. 129.

21. There was also considerable interest among this group in early Western democratic theory, specifically Locke and Rousseau. See, "Locke's Criticism of Feudalism," World History (Shijie Lishi) 6 (December 20, 1979), and "Rousseau's Democratic Thought," World History 1 (February 2, 1980).

22. See, "Letter to the Editor" in the "Party Life" column, People's Daily May 17, 1979, and May 23, 1979. The authors of both letters, who were local cadre, expressed dissatisfaction over the persistence of such practices, more than two years after the Gang's demise.

23. People's Daily, April 18, 1979.

24. Yet, even spokesmen for the democracy movement recognized the profound limitations of popular consciousness. According to an article in the magazine Sea Spray (hailanghua): "The big shot could be big only because the small people belittled themselves," a view which the author accounted for by the "lack of a democratic revolution in China." Sea Spray 1 (August 31, 1979).

25. "CC Communique," December 22, 1978, and Guangming Daily, March 11, 1979. The latter noted: "Small production can be regarded as a factor constantly engendering patriarchy."

26. Xinhua, January 20, 1980.

27. Nanfang Daily, May 5, 1981 and Red Flag (March 6, 1979). Beijing Daily, March 10, 1979, emphasized that even Mao had to undergo a thorough transformation in his thinking. Brought up in feudal society, his thought had to go through a change—"there had to be a process"—especially in eliminating the influence of religion which, quoting Engels, had as its ultimate goal, the "deification of man."

28. "Report on the Current Situation and Tasks," March 1979, in Zheng Ming (January 1, 1980). In another speech, Deng noted that "the citizens have a weak concept of their rights and duties. . . ." "18 August [1980] Speech to Polit- buro," Chan Wang 461 (April 16, 1981).

29. Major reform proposals for the CCP, that involved limited internal "democratization" of the party and government were advanced by Liao Gailong, an advisor to the Central Committee. See, "The '1980 Reform' Program of China," The Seventies 134 (March 1, 1981).

30. This was, in fact, the major theme of the internal party 'rectification' which Deng and his orthodox supporters promoted as an alternative to more radical party reforms.

31. People's Daily, June 5, 1979.

32. Guangming Daily, January 21, 1979.

33. Wen Huibao, July 10, 1980. This "linear" view of Chinese history was not, we note below, universally held among historians.

34. Guangming Daily, November 30, 1979. Also, see Nanfang Daily, March 30, 1981, and People's Daily, December 23, 1980.

35. Guangming Daily, July 17, 1979, and November 30, 1979. Historiographical interpretations of the 1898 Reform Movement were not, however, without contro- versy. One article, for instance, highlighted the positive results of 1898 and noted that in the Cultural Revolution, radical historians, like Qi Benyu, had used criticism of the reform movement "to eulogize the peasants' revolution." People's Daily, November 14, 1979. Also, see People's Daily, January 11, 1982.

36. Guangming Daily, May 8, 1979.

37. Red Flag,3 (March 6, 1979). For a contrary view of the 1911 Revolution, see People's Daily, April 13, 1979, in which the critical importance of over- throwing the monarchy was stressed.

38. People's Daily, January 24, 1980. This view was strongly promoted by the historian Li Zehou.

39. See Wu Yu's original article, "The Family System as the Root of Despotism," in New Youth (Xin Qingnian) 6 (February 1917). Wen Huibao 15 (September 1979) called on its readers to evaluate the "antifeudal pioneers of sixty years ago."

40. Guangming Daily, January 21, 1979.

41. Guangming Daily, January 21, 1979.

42. See, in particular, Kenneth Jowitt, Revolutionary Breakthroughs and National Development (Berkeley: University of California Press, 1971) where he emphasizes the importance of "formative isolation" in the development of communist parties and their ability to "create cadres with few commitments to the external environment." pp. 60–61.

43. Red Flag 9 (September 2, 1979). Also, see Deng Xiaoping's analysis of the impact on the CCP of peasant ideology, such as the belief that "whoever conquers the world is entitled to dominate it," Historical Research (Lishi yanjiou) 10 (October 15, 1979). The press also stressed the linkage of "petty bourgeois" and "feudal" social patterns: "The individual private ownership of the petty bourgeoisie is associated with both the outmoded feudal patriarchal system and capitalism." Xinhua, January 20, 1980.

44. People's Daily, June 5, 1979.

45. Workers' Daily, February 24, 1979.

46. Li Guihai, "The Peasantry's Monarchist Thought," Research on Chinese History (Zhongguoshi yanjiou) 1 (1979).

47. Li Guahi. Li's analysis of the peasantry borrowed heavily from Marx's The Eighteenth Brumaire of Louis Bonaparte.

48. Li Guahi. Also, see Pang Zhuoheng, "Comparative Research on the Feudal Despotic Systems of China and the West," Historical Research 2 (1981).

49. Philosophical Research, March 25, 1979, Fudan Journal (Fudan Xuebao) 5 (September 1979), and Academic Monthly (Xueshu Yuebao) 128 (January 20, 1980).

50. People's Daily, April 13, 1979.

51. According to an article by Wang Xiaoqiang in Historical Research, October 15, 1979, "the work style of the small producers and the feudal patriarchal system could find a wide market in the ranks of our party and have a profound influence on its members."

52. People's Daily, April 13, 1979.

53. Wang Cengyu, "China's Feudal Cultural Autocraticism," Research on Chinese History 2 (1979).

54. In this sense, Wang adhered to a curvilinear view of Chinese history in which despotism did not emerge as a dominant force until the Song. After the tenth century, China was increasingly burdened by despotic rulers and pro-despotic cultural values, but before the Song the political system and society as a whole was less affected by despotism.

55. For another "revisionist" view on Qin, see "Criticism of the Gang of Four's Mystification of Qin Shihuang." Research on Chinese History 1 (1979).

56. For a similar historical argument, see Guangming Daily's report on an "academic seminar on the criticism of feudalism." November 13, 1979.

57. Qui Hansheng, "Song-Ming Neo-Confucianism and Patriarchal Thought." Historical Research (November 1979).

58. For a competing analysis, which locates the historical roots of the patriarchal family system in the Western Zhou, see Red Flag 20 (October 16, 1980).

59. Similar analyses were also made for the Taiping Rebellion, the 1898 Reforms and the Cultural Revolution, in which despotism was viewed less as predetermination of the feudal economy and more as an outcome of purely political factors among elites. See, for instance, Red Flag 3 (March 6, 1979) and Historical Research (September 15, 1979).

60.   Besides the historiographical analysis presented here, other historians presented radically new views of the Zhou dynasty which suggested that it had been a period of "original democracy" (**yuan shi minzhu**) comparable to the direct demo- cracy of the Athenian city state.   See, for instance, Xu Hongxiu, "The Residue of Original Democracy in the Aristocracy of the Zhou Period." **Chinese Social Science** (Zhongguo shehui Kexue) 2 (1981).

61.   This phrase is attributed to Ye Jianying, hardly a supporter of democratic reform.   However, I believe that it was seized upon by more "liberal" members of the party to argue against the dominant view of the "orthodox Leninists" that substantial economic change needs to precede any political liberalization.   Xinhua (January 20, 1980).

In introducing his paper, **Sullivan** said that essentially what he had tried to say in this basically empirical paper was that from the Third Party Plenum in 1978 to the Twelfth Party Congress in 1982, many of the issues we are talking about were discussed in China. His focus was not on the Democracy Wall writers: although there was some overlap between the materials he discussed and what they were saying, his focus was on the Party press and the intellectual or academic press, for example, the Journal of Historical Studies and Philosophical Research, as well as many of the university journals that have become available. Since at last count there were 120, this research has become somewhat difficult. By now almost every university has its own journal, and many have become forums for arguing out these issues.

In the course of his presentation Sullivan added that the Chinese have never been able themselves to say that the Cultural Revolution was created solely by Mao. He had been trying to compare the analysis of Stalinism in Khrushchev's secret speech with the kind of analysis that has recently been made in China. In both cases, because of certain political reasons the failings could not be blamed on the single leader. The regime still needs Mao even if he is dead. That raises the question of why his despotism occurred. Many issues emerged from this discussion in China, but in the paper he was only looking at two.

In two asides to the paper Sullivan pointed out that there were many things in the open press in 1979 that have not been seen before or since; for a brief period it was a very open press. He also explained that many Chinese intellectuals who condemn the Cultural Revolution also see it as having created a more critical and less servile population.

In an expansion Sullivan suggested that the "proto-democrats" must be important because Deng Xiaoping spent a good deal of time in his speeches condemning them. Why would he spend all this time if they were unimportant? He found a continuum in political

187

thinking both within and outside the Party. He felt that perhaps the most likely kind of change would be a process of gradual reduction in the power of the central party apparatus.

Gastil asked how many writers supported the minority viewpoint he mentioned in the paper. **Sullivan** thought about nine out of ten supported the orthodox position. It varied: in the intellectual press there was more of a balance, particularly in the historiographic arguments and in 1979. Debates were often carried out in such esoteric terms that one did not know what the arguments were really about. In the party press you had to search for articles that took issue with the majority view, and then they were elliptical and circumspect. But there were dissident voices in the Party as well as outside. The leadership had opened a pandora's box. By 1981 disagreement had died down. He had noticed in the proceedings of a 1981 academic conference that even though some of the nonorthodox historians attended, they were given almost no forum for expressing their views.

Gastil pointed out that so far the conferees had emphasized two points about the nature of Chinese political culture. One was the lack of a concept of a legitimate opposition, and the other was the idea that limited government was foreign to Chinese traditions. What Sullivan was saying was that there were important intellectual groups even in the Party, that opposed both of these traditional ideas.

Sullivan replied that he thought there were many people in the Party who believed the structure had to undergo some form of transformation. Some may argue only that party elections be meaningful. This isn't much of a change, but they want more than just a presentation of names, they want some sort of internal campaigning and exchange of views on various issues. Others are obviously calling for the establishment of an effective two-party system. There is also the Liao Gailong reform program. (Attached to the Central Committee of the CCP, Liao Gailong proposed around 1980 very liberal changes. Some of the economic proposals have been implemented.) This program would lead to substantial changes. He did not find much on the idea of limiting governmental authority. However, there was considerable interest in the concept of separation of powers, which can be seen as a kind of limitation.

Sullivan also mentioned a remarkable debate on whether pre-Qin China, that is the Western Zhou dynasty, was comparable to Athenian democracy.

Smith said that one practical thing that comes up again and

again in conversation in terms of limits to power is the desirability of a fixed tenure with early retirement. It seems trivial
but in fact its impact would be considerable if it were consistently adopted. **Sullivan** did not think it trivial at all. It is
very important, particularly if we realize one of the arguments is
that Mao was able to build up his power because he could appeal to
the desire of people around him to hold on to power. Breaking
this cycle of despotism, where people are willing to sell their
souls to maintain their positions, is critical.

Smith noted that as far as he could see the idea of personal
rights that are real rights, in effect unlimited, had been totally
missing from any serious, quasi-official discussion. **Sullivan**
agreed but said they did talk about certain "rights" of Party
members. But this was very different--it is also discussed by
Lenin.

Zhu added some footnotes. In his understanding there was
controversy, even within the party, in the period of late 1978 and
early 1979. There were three basic reasons why liberal factions
should arise in the party: 1) Some people in the party had a very
hard time during the cultural revolution. 2) During the cultural
revolution very high ranking cadres, especially intellectual
cadres, had more contact with the countryside, they learned how
bad things really were. That is one important reason why some
developed such a very liberal policy for agriculture. They really
saw the problems. Chinese peasants had waited thirty years for
gains from the revolution, and they asked how long they could
wait. 3) Especially after Mao's death a lot of information began
coming into China from outside. People learned how other developing countries had been developing their economies. This was not
just a crisis for the intellectuals and young generation, but also
a crisis for high level cadres. They began to ask the question,
"What really is socialism?" **Sullivan** said Hong Yung Lee of Yale
argues that this is one of the factors pushing for reform. In
contrast to the USSR, there are now many returned cadres pushing
for reform.

Zhu said that when people talk about the system, they talk
about being economically backward. In early 1979 an important
article in People's Daily raised the question as to whether the
system in China was a socialist system or not. The author concluded China was not a socialist country, but one in transition to
socialism. The author was deputy director of the Institute of
Marxism-Leninism and Modern Thought. After he published his article some high-ranking cadres like Hu Qiaomu tried to organize a

group of scholars to criticize him, but no one wanted to do it. Then in the democracy movement they used his argument that China was not socialist; they asked what kind of system China had and concluded it was a bureaucratic system. They developed his argument. Even inside of the Party there has been a great deal of discussion, especially in "internal publications," that introduced Western political thought and that of dissidents from Eastern Europe.

Sullivan added that they even had serious discussions on Locke, Rousseau, and Montesquieu. Of course, in the first paragraph of such articles the author would say that Locke, for example, was from the bourgeoisie and so forth, but then the author would go into a very astute discussion. The point here was also to remember who Locke was arguing against. He was arguing against the supporters of absolute monarchy. The Chinese officials admit they had something like monarchy; England was feudal, and they admit China is also feudal.

Zhu said they also introduced Western political and economic thought by translations for internal publications. They published many pieces, for example, by nonorthodox East European economists because they thought them important for the Chinese people.

Dreyer added in confirmation of Sullivan that there was disagreement in the Party about how it should be run. Some people were definitely in favor of more checks on leaders. There was a speech of Deng Xiaoping, after the crackdown on the democracy movement, in which he asked in regard to the continuing trickle of criticisms, "How is it that these criticisms continue to be printed on high quality paper on good printing presses?" Obviously he was admitting serious dissent within the party.

Nathan agreed that there were those in the party who supported the democracy movement, but thought that both in the democracy movement and in the party we needed to make some fine distinctions. Much of what was said in the party and the democracy movement by way of reform sentiment fell well within the central tradition of Marxism-Leninism. It had to do with such concerns as restoring democratic centralism, that is the right of party members to express their views until the party has made a decision, and doing away with bureaucratism, which has always been viewed as a serious problem in the Soviet Union and China. So we must look for something more remarkable than this, such as accusations that the system overcentralizes power; views that would tie the emergence of despotism by one or more individuals to the very structure of one-party rule; positions that imply there ought to be more than one political party; or statements suggesting that the people are more progressive than the Party leaders and hence should be allowed truly to influence the direction of policy, not just be led, through institutions that permit actual influence by the people, or through freedom of the press. These are the ideas we have to search for if we wish to gauge the extent of dissent from Marxism-Leninism. He believed such ideas existed but often in rudimentary and truncated forms. When he talks with academic people from China he finds strong sentiments in these directions, but the scholars find it hard to express such ideas directly. Academics will, for example, write an extremely scholarly analysis of the fu form of poetry in Tang literature, and then they will tack onto it a paragraph saying that literature flourished in the Tang because there was a relatively high level of freedom. Similar hints can be found in the literature on the peasants or on feudalism. We should not read too much into it, but there is obviously a yearning for more freedom.

Nathan found a problem with Sullivan's discussion of the literature on the peasants. He doubted that there were many intellectuals in China who really believed the peasants were progressive. He noticed the references to them in the paper were thin, and doubted they represented a significant group. All schools of intelligentsia in China believe the peasants are backward. The issue really is what they plan to do about it. One idea is to change the peasants through a very long-term process of cultural reform, the classic liberal approach of Hu Shi.

Gastil said it seemed to him that Wei Jingsheng implicitly made the point in his writings that if you let the peasants do what they want to do, the country would be in better shape. That seems to be similar to the idea of letting the peasants go economically; it assumes that they are potentially progressive. The "Fifth Modernization" argument is based on the idea democracy can be defended for practical reasons. Wei believes that modernization is impossible without democracy because without democracy it is impossible to organize the economy effectively and efficiently to produce an economic takeoff.

Nathan and others did not see this in Wei. **Seymour** added that because Wei held up the "right wing" of the democratic movement, his perspective would be somewhat different from that of most of the other democrats. **Grieder** thought Wei's argument could be used to justify something like the responsibility system but not as license to let the peasant get ahead of the cart.

Moody said the radical Marxists are the last people one would expect overtly to doubt the progressiveness of the peasants. The traditional criticism of **Water Margin**, the novel about banditry in which the bandit chief joins the government and fights hard, is that this was a great book showing both peasant rebellion and the class limits of the peasants that they could not transcend. Around 1975 the Maoists said that peasant rebellion is in itself progressive. The peasants had not read Marx and they didn't have the Party to lead them, but in itself peasant rebellion leads to historical development. The trouble is that people like Deng Xiaoping take over these movements and transform them. In these papers being discussed the peasant rebellions are seen as not very useful, they essentially restore the same system. Marx had this figured out correctly. By 1981 this was being revised and people began saying that everything should not be blamed on the peasant, the peasant rebellion is actually progressive.

To **Nathan** it was necessary to understand that now when a Chinese speaks of peasant rebellion he is in a disguised form talking about Mao. The people Sullivan cites are really saying that Mao was a peasant dictator, and that what he carried out was not communism or socialism. So after the Sixth Plenum decided to affirm much of what Mao had done, it became necessary to say good things about peasant rebellion.

Sullivan replied that the issues do get mixed up. This is one reason he had not used much material after the Sixth Plenum (June 1981). The discussion was then too often implicitly concerned with the legacy of Mao. (Incidentally, Sun Yat-sen is criticized for being a peasant leader just like Mao.) He agreed that most intellectuals view China's peasantry negatively. But positive views were held by more than one or two. Even if purely for political reasons, many of those supporting reform realized they have to present a very different picture of the population. For example, the People's **Daily** (September 17, 1979) in discussing the traditional adage of a man especially adept at selecting thoroughbreds wrote: "The masses are like this man because of their ability to judge leaders. In comparison to the leading cadres or party workers, the masses are best able to tell whether a comrade has both the ability and the political integrity to be a leader."

Nathan voiced three objections. First, this was "the masses" rather than the peasants. Secondly, Sullivan was overreading. Nathan remembered this article to be a very minor one. The author was only making the simple point that people can select leaders. Thirdly, the article doesn't say anything about the role of peasants in leading. It is just a question of selecting the leader.

Bernstein was not clear on the importance of this. Sullivan writes that after the Cultural Revolution there was a majority group blaming the Cultural Revolution on the peasants because they were feudal. But how does that correspond to the historical reality of the Cultural Revolution, which was largely an urban movement of supercharged youth who fought against each other. They were the promoters of the little red book. Where did the peasantry come into this?

Sullivan agrees. This was exactly what Professor Edward Friedman asked while he was in China two years ago when this was the line given to him by some Party members. It is not a question of objective reality. After the Third Plenum it was in the political interest of the Party to paint as negative a picture of the peasantry as it could. Their answer would be that peasant society was so backward and overwhelming in size that even urban areas were highly peasantized. The peasant mentality even affects the Party, which is the reason it would be dangerous to have too much decentralization in the Party. Power would then be in the hands of the semi-feudal Party leaders who do things like participate in village rituals--the example given was a village festival in which the cadres carried the sedan chair. In these terms the reformers tried to link a more positive view of peasants to their overall program.

Bernstein asked, "So these groups, the conservatives, the restorationists, they talked about going back to the fine old tradition of party rule?"

Sullivan said, "Yes, Deng talks of the Chinese people as a 'tray of loose sand' that needs the party to pull it together. The reformers, or proto-democrats, begin their argument with a different image of the people."

Dreyer pointed out that Deng talking about the Chinese people as a tray of loose sand echoed Sun Yat-sen's original statement in 1906. This would seem to be a shocking admission of what has not happened in the last seventy-five years.

Grieder thought Nathan had made a good point when he said they were talking about the "masses." The "masses" is one of those terms that dissolves everything you throw into it. It moves away from a sociological or political category and appeals to the "great pumpkin." This makes a difference. The Chinese people, the ruled, have always been given credit in the political mythology to tell a good ruler from a bad ruler, a good magistrate from a bad magistrate--they clap when he leaves, or weep. This is nothing new. **Sullivan** says that in fact the reformers quote

Mencius to back up what they are saying. In the same way they go back and ask what the character shu ("masses") meant in the Zhou dynasty.

Nathan noted that Mencius says that in a well-ruled kingdom when the king has someone put to death, it is said "the people killed him"--this is because the king wants to kill any minister the people do not like. But this doesn't mean that the king--or the party--ceases to rule. This particular article is one defending the county-level elections and supporting the right of the people to vote on People's Congress deputies. Sullivan writes that the emphasis of Deng and his supporters on the people's incapacity was used to justify continuation of the CCP's (Chinese Communist Party) one-party dictatorship, and meanwhile the transfer of power from the Party to the people is postponed into the indefinite future. In fact there isn't ever going to be such a transfer. The justification of one-party rule is not based on any temporary factor like the people's backwardness. It is a permanent necessity because the party is the vanguard. The implication in the paper is that once they are less backward, they won't need the dictatorship, but this is not really the theory of one-party dictatorship. **Sullivan** adds that it solidifies the necessity. He agrees that it all goes back to Lenin and his discussion of trade-union consciousness. The people need the Party.

Kintner remarked that Sullivan wrote that Mao was necessary even if dead. The Chinese don't have a Lenin so they have to have someone at the beginning of the party that they can look to as their god, so to speak. He wondered if Sullivan thought there was a possibility of a restoration of Mao like the restoration that is apparently taking place with respect to Stalin inside the Soviet Union.

Sullivan said he had no answer. What the current leadership claims to want is a restoration of what existed in the fifties, that is, an orthodox communist party without the bureaucratism. (Sullivan did not believe this had actually existed in the fifties, however.) There is a concern that another Mao-type will arise and circumvent the party by appealing directly to the "masses." The present leadership sees itself as a kind of compromise. Mao went too far in one direction, but democracy would go too far in the other direction.

Sullivan disagreed with Lucian Pye on the importance of Mao's personality type, on Mao per se. What the leadership is saying is that they don't fear Mao per se, but a Mao-type, and there are probably many Mao-types around. People have said that it was the structure of the party itself and of the economic planning system that created an environment that allowed Mao to rise to the top. So there was a specific linkage made between the party organizations and the system. **Kintner** compared this to the argument that Stalinism came out of Leninism. **Smith** added that for this reason there has been a lot of effort made to build up an iconography of Zhou Enlai in particular, as well as Zhu De and Liu Shaoqi. All are characterized as very moderate leaders.

Liang asserted that while the personality of Chairman Mao was very important for him to maintain his power, a communist is a communist. Even though Deng Xiaoping and Zhou Enlai are different than Chairman Mao they are communists. From 1979 to 1980 or 1981 Deng Xiaoping needed the young people to support him, just as in East European socialist parties when a reform faction wanted to change Party policies and got the people to support them. As to democracy wall in Xidan, of course, many high Party leaders or their children were involved, but their effect was to attack Wang Dongxing, Wu De, and Hua Guofeng. Mao received information about the bureaucracy through his spy system on the conflict between the bureaucracy and the masses. (Liang's father was a newspaper reporter in China; and the newspapers senior reporters have a special responsibility to investigate what people are thinking and any anti-party policies. He wrote Rui Tan or internal reviews. He always did this job. His reports which Liang sometimes saw were accurate. He would write down what people said, including even criticism of Chairman Mao himself. Then he would send two copies of the Rui Tan to the appropriate bureaus. In this way Mao learned of the conflict between the bureaucracy and the masses. He attempted to resolve this conflict through the Cultural Revolution.) So Deng Xiaoping also gets Rui Tan from different provinces. He again understood in the seventies that the big problem was to resolve the conflict of the bureaucracy and the masses. He was very smart; he used the elite news media first and then moved later to the masses. This gave the people a good chance to show their hatred of the Party. He asked the red scholars in the party to write articles supporting his ideas, for example, Yu Guangyan and Huan Xiang. He is a communist, he wants to build a socialist system. He thinks it is very different from Mao's system, but he never thinks of his own system as a democracy. Notice that when Lin Biao wanted to escape, he went to Russia, because it was a socialist country. When Deng got power he sent an emissary to visit Yugoslavia. Today, this week, Hu Yaobang is in Romania and is planning visits to other Eastern European countries.

195

The ideas of the younger generation are very different from those of the Deng Xiaopings. It does not want to be used again by the Party as Deng used them. When he discovered the young were building organizations and publishing magazines, he saw this as trouble, as going beyond limits. The democratic faction developed a different line. This is where Wang Xizhe wrote his famous article at the end of which he said Deng Xiaoping put our democratic young in jail. Some day he may need us again and will ask us to support him again.

Zhu preferred to emphasize the differences among communists and communist countries. Khrushchev and Stalin were very different. The USSR is still communist but there are important changes. The problem is not just individuals. Many leaders after Mao's death felt pressure from the people to change the system. **Liang** wondered if Zhu thought the party leaders would allow the people to build an independent organization. **Zhu** agreed this was impossible, for there can be no independent political forces as we see with Solidarity in Poland.

Gastil thought this was a critical issue for the whole conference. As Grieder had asked, were we seeing democracy as subversive or were we talking about it as the outcome of an evolutionary change. Obviously, most of us would agree that someone like Wei Jingsheng who wants to throw out the whole system and start over is appealing. This is the way to go if it is possible to do it. Yet this seems an unlikely option in the short term, and maybe there are options for evolution that can be supported. Many believe, for example, that Solidarity simply pushed too fast, that it could have attained a good deal of what it wanted if it had not become a political movement, and had been willing to remain a labor movement. There is something in this argument. There are many people in Poland, even in the top of the Communist Party, that are not enamored of a Stalinist state. They would like to see something else. Yet they are also scared of the collapse of the system and their role in it. China has the same problem.

Bernstein saw a fundamental difference in the fact China did not have to worry about the Soviet Union in the same way as Poland. He thought what our two friends from the PRC were telling us was that we shouldn't be too bedazzled by improvements from the absolute depths of Maoism to believe that the next step will be democracy. There are many scholars and journalists who make too much of the political changes. But as Liang and Zhu say, they are still communists, and they are not going to tolerate competing organizations. This is a real dilemma for those wanting to support democratization. The "big freedoms" remain subject to communist control. There is an extraordinary parallel between the Soviet experience after Stalin and the Chinese experience after Mao. Given the difference between the two countries **Bernstein** had come to believe there was a natural course to communist movements that overrode cultural and historical differences. What happened in both countries, and this was not his original theory, is that a larger than life figure passed from the scene for biological causes leaving the Party without a symbol of legitimacy. It did not have immediately an equivalent figure. So it had to turn to something else. It restored rules, regulations, and procedures; impersonal authority took the place of the personal authority of the leader. There was even a refinement common to both countries. In the short-term aftermath of the death of the great leader and the euphoria that accompanied the introduction of laws and procedures, there was a tendency toward a genuine liberalization. They called it the "thaw" in the Soviet Union. Solzhenitsyn's One Day in the Life of Ivan Denisovich and Bulgakof's Master and Margarita were published at this time. It was an exciting time. Many Russians thought the death of Stalin had eliminated the barrier to democratization. But then there has been a re-Stalinization, a new imposition of controls, a new crackdown. Andropov became the head of the KGB and introduced psychiatric hospitals as an informal mechanism for dealing with dissidents. This allowed them to incarcerate people who had not committed any crimes. They could put people like Shcharansky in jail because he has done and said enough that they can pin a crime on him. But somebody like General Grigorenko had not done enough. Analogously, the Chinese Public Security Bureau has "educational reform." They can send anyone to three years plus an additional year to prison in this way without any procedures. That is how they had gotten rid of most of the people publishing unofficial journals. Thus, the same periods occurred in China. A thaw, artistic flowering, democracy wall, then a modest re-Maoization and party reassumption of control. The purpose in both cases, personal or impersonal control, is to maintain absolute Party control.

Smith agreed, but he added that in the case of China there had been some solid and lasting institutional changes. He believed the changes in the educational system that he described in his paper (below) could be very significant in the long run. Emphasis on study abroad, as well as changes in the availability of information within the system, have made a real difference in the general intellectual atmosphere in which people work. He understood this was not true in the Soviet Union. Their educational system has not changed since the time of the Czars. **Gastil** added that there were also never crowds in the streets in the USSR. But Bernstein's parallel was a close one.

Huang again questioned the neat conceptualization of democracy as subversion or evolution. He thought it might be better to speak of "subversive evolution." It is evolutionary but at the same time subversive. This explains the twist and turn, the movements forward and backward that have occurred in both Soviet Russia and China. There have been pulls in different directions. We talk about disagreement within the party, about different factions in the democracy movement pulling in different directions. We talk of a greater degree of liberty permitted by the Party and then again crackdowns. So is it useful to think of subversive evolution, a complicated movement or process that will take a very long time, particularly in the PRC. Even in Taiwan we can speak of this. The Tang-Wai has been compromising with the authorities as well as fighting them.

Dreyer thought that a movement toward democracy was always subversive. There cannot be a change of power without someone's ox being gored, and the person doing the goring is always seen as subversive of power. As Bernstein said, there has been a movement backward from the freedoms allowed in 1978 and 1979. It is very much to prevent the emergence of competing centers of power. She noted that the Jesuits who were let out of prison recently after fifteen years have now been put back into prison. This was not because of anything positive they had done, but simply because they refused to foreswear trying to make contacts with Rome. They were not accused of trying, but simply of not being willing to say they would not. Another interesting example is what happened to Wei Guoqing in October. Wei had a remarkable career. She thought he was the only first party secretary to survive the Cultural Revolution intact. He also survived the purge of Lin Biao and that of the "Gang of Four." Yet recently he was removed from his position as head of the army's General Political Department because he dared to criticize Deng for going too far in liberalization of the arts. The issue here is not as much ideological as the possibility of a competing center of power.

Bernstein wondered if Dreyer really had evidence. She seemed very sure this was the reason Wei was eliminated, but he thought there were many who thought Deng was going too far. **Dreyer** answered that there was a journal (Shidai de baogao) controlled by the General Political Department of the PLA (People's Liberation

Army), and hence by Wei, which consistently criticized Deng. The journal had its editorial board completely changed and was taken out from under the control of the General Political Department. At the same time, the official army newspaper, Jiefang Junbao, which was also under Wei's control and which had also been critical of Deng's policies toward literature and art, made a public self-criticism. The General Political Department itself was reorganized. All this happened at the same time Wei was removed as head of the GPD. Deng will not admit he got rid of Wei to silence criticism, but the evidence is not in doubt.

Zhu thought the question was not whether or not Deng or others wanted to support reforms. The problem is how far they can go in the present political and economic situation in China. If the changes fail, and many actions are going to fail, what kind of political situation will come up? If we are talking about whether or not the people should support the evolutionary process in China, the question is how do we evaluate the possibility for the process to succeed? If it is going to fail, it does not matter if people support it or not.

Sullivan suggested that one of the essential conditions for the evolution of democracy in the history of the West and perhaps even of Japan appeared to be a split in the ruling elite. When there is a major split, then each group in the elite seeks out supporters below. They pull people into politics that politicizes new segments of the population. This is the critical starting point. If you want to draw a very rough parallel with England, it was the split between aristocracy, the monarchy, and the church that allowed democratic rule to take root. It is more difficult when the institutions and elites are united as they were in nineteenth century Russia.

Dreyer asked if this could be crucial, because there was already a split at the top. **Sullivan** thought it not yet deep enough. As Dreyer and Nathan have said, what is really critical is what is going to happen over the next ten years. To prevent economic collapse the Chinese had to go to the responsibility system. They knew that a system that really falls on its face creates divisiveness at the top--the division exists today, but it is controlled because things are not bad enough yet.

A big gap in our knowledge of China is what is going on with workers and unions. We talk of Solidarity, yet five years ago we would never have thought Solidarity would have gotten as far as it did. In China the events in Poland have always been either denounced or ignored. At the height of liberalization the one area where they were not willing to talk of significant change was that of unions. In his files on press coverage of the reform program Sullivan could only find three references to the desirability of independent unions.

In any event there was not yet a major split at the top. The twelfth party congress was in fact one of the more somnolent congresses. There was not much debate or real discussion on issues. He was still looking for splits on policy reflecting deep problems in society. Others in the group suggested there were some splits now although they remained obscured.

Zhu thought that such a crisis would depend very heavily on the economic situation. In the next four or five years there could be a serious succession crisis. These two factors would heavily determine China's near future. He did not see the international aspect as very important--China had too many internal problems.

Gastil mentioned that Khrushchev was unable to maintain himself and his very modest reforms partly because he did not reach down. There was never an attempt in the Soviet Union to involve the people as a support mechanism. Power stayed within a very narrow top elite. **Sullivan** pointed out that Khrushchev did try to involve the activists in the party; he invited them to Party meetings, Central Committee meetings, and involved them in decision making. In doing so he challenged the Party strongmen. **Gastil** repeated that Khrushchev never had a group of people that would take to the streets in his defense.

Liang thought that if the government carried out the responsibility system in the countryside for three or four years, then the whole society and the political structure could change. Because the commune in China is not only an economic unit; it is also a political unit. So today in factories the team unit is changing. The leader of the team, the duizhang won't easily allow his power to be taken away by the new economic regulations. The Party's power in the countryside will also be weakened if the new program is continued--but the cadres don't want to lose power. As Zhu says this will be a problem, as well as the continued centralization of industry.

Sullivan recalled that in the Soviet Union when it was obvious that the contradictions Zhu talks about were emerging as a result of the Libermann reforms, which were never pushed all that far anyhow, they retreated. They knew contradictions were emerging, not just in politics versus economics but in the Plan where they had two market systems and price systems emerging. They sacrificed the reforms.

Gastil suggested that if it had been to someone's advantage to go the other way, they might have. He recalled two hopeful stories that modify the implications of Dreyer's statement that democracy is always subversive. Nagy in Hungary tried to overthrow a communist system although he was himself a communist. Dubcek in Czechoslovakia tried to radically democratize a communist system even though he also was a communist. So there are cases where people who have been good communists for a long time decide that it is in their interest to sponsor radical change. In both cases the Soviet Union stepped in, but this does not affect China, because intervention is much less likely.

Zhu noted several differences between China, Eastern Europe, and the Soviet Union. In Czechoslovakia most of the party cadres were well educated; in China they are not, and this is a serious problem for Deng. A second difference is that in China the army is very deeply involved in politics. This was not true in Czechoslovakia, especially in 1968; the army was not much involved in the power struggle in the Central Committee. The reform faction in China is also much weaker than in 1968 in Czechoslovakia. **Gastil** said that he wasn't suggesting something similar was going to happen, but only that it could. He also wanted to offer evidence that an evolution of communism to democracy was possible.

Bernstein pointed out that Poland was an authoritarian society. It was a communist society only because of the existence of the Soviet Union, just as Czechoslovakia was in 1968. Czechoslovakia was also an essentially Western European country. It is argued that the Chinese system will allow for political evolution because after all if it had not been for the Soviet Union there would have been evolutions in Hungary, Czechoslovakia, and Poland. But in this case he agreed with the Chinese conservatives: There is a deeply feudal strength to the Party based on the backwardness of the people.

Bernstein also raised the question, a very important one for thinking about the possibility for change in China, of the extent to which the security apparatus can operate outside of the control and will of the party. The security apparatus is almost by definition very conservative and interested in control; it may have maintained its independence of the drive of the political leaders to be reformist or moderate. He reminded us of the case of the Frenchman Bellefroid who was engaged to marry Li Shuang. The foreign ministry had more or less approved of it; they were just waiting for the papers to come through. Bellefroid only had to prove he was divorced. But in the meantime the security people stepped in and created a fait accompli that China's leadership would not repudiate. So here is an example of the more moderate, permissive side being blocked by the conservative, repressive, puritanical, orthodox Leninist side. This Frenchman had smuggled dissident documents out of China. For him to be able to marry a Chinese girl and then go to Hong Kong where he taught at the University and stir up more trouble could not be accepted by the security forces. There is the PLA, the Ministry of Public Security, and all of the elaborate bureaucracy, and the police, who are by and large of peasant origin. They are terribly conservative, and steeped in traditionalism. The kind of people that came from rural Sichuan and Shaanxi, joined the revolutionary armies when they were sixteen in 1937, stayed with the party their whole lives, and now are in charge of security for a county or a province. This is an important conservative force resisting any change toward democracy. He was not saying it could not be overcome. Clever moves by the political leadership might weaken their power.

Prospects for
Democracy in China

Peter R. Moody, Jr.

Liberal democracy developed first in the Western cultural context, and it has not developed spontaneously anywhere else. Explanations of politics that focus on culture may sometimes explain too much (since culture would seem to include the totality of a society's life); but cultures vary and it would be surprising if these variations did not matter for politics. Chinese culture has not produced liberal democracy. This does not mean that Chinese culture cannot support democracy: both Indian and Japanese culture would seem to be inherently less hospitable to democracy than China's, yet India and Japan are democratic countries.

Because political culture is such a broad concept, we must be careful how we use it. The term sometimes refers to the individual attitudes toward politics current in a particular society. Richard Solomon, in his influential work on Chinese political culture, argues that Chinese are raised to be timid, dependent, submissive to authority. They may dislike some of the consequences of strong rule, but they fear that any loosening of rule will lead to the dreaded luan or chaos. Many Chinese thinkers from the nineteenth century reformers through the radicals of the May Fourth period up to the dissidents on Taiwan and the mainland today have blamed alleged character deficiencies of the Chinese people for China's lack of democracy. Western visitors to China in the early 1970s, when it was still the thing to look upon Maoist totalitarianism and pronounce it good, reasoned in basically the same way: because of cultural differences which only the most benighted ethnocentric bigot could overlook, the Chinese people actively rejoice in practices which "we in the West" could never tolerate. Solomon, of course, does not argue like this. Yet he does hypothesize that if China becomes democratic, it will be only thanks to Maoism: By diluting the authority of the stern family head, the totalitarian state would foster the rearing of new generations which would not have in their personalities the emotional inhibitions which were the basis of political submissiveness."[1]

Chinese society may encourage psychological inhibitions to democracy. But it also seems clear that liberal democracy has been the preferred political position of most educated Chinese this century, including those in the People's Republic. The Taiwan opposition is almost entirely liberal. Opposition and dissent in the People's Republic, whether anti-communist, Marxian humanist, or radical, has tended to converge toward support for law and democracy. Beyond this, one can wonder how politically submissive the Chinese people as a whole have been historically, whatever scores they may make on personality tests. Some twelve decades ago T. T. Meadows asserted that while the Chinese may be the least revolutionary people on earth, they are easily among the most rebellious. The character traits Solomon identifies among the Chinese seem similar to many Ruth Benedict, in The Chrysanthemum and the Sword, finds among the Japanese, but the traits do not have the same consequences in Japan as in China. Solomon says that being carried by grown-ups or big sisters after they are able to walk helps make Chinese children dependent.[2] Miss Benedict says the same practice in Japan produces poised, self-confident little chaps. Both may, of course, be right; but the layman is inclined to wonder whether there might be some problem here with the methodology.

The notion that Maoism may be a precondition to later liberalization is not in itself absurd. Part of the point is that both democracy and totalitarianism are modern, and thus closer to each other in temperament than either is to more traditional forms of authoritarianism, with its stern family heads. Maoist totalitarianism in its later phases also inculcated a defiance of authority, which later turned against the Maoist order. This is not, however, on its face the kind of defiance which leads to the sense of civility and self-restraint one tends to associate with stable democracy. Such defiance of authority, in any case, is not something missing in China until Mao came along; Maoism can be interpreted as the latest manifestation of a perennial theme in Chinese culture.[3] In fact, many Chinese dissidents and even part of the dominant segment within the present ruling structure of the regime interpret the Maoist system as regressive, "feudal," and a negation of modernity. It is one thing to say that Maoism has the potential to evolve in a democratic direction; it is something else to claim that China can become democratic only because it has been totalitarian. To see totalitarianism in itself as anything other than an obstacle to liberal democracy is perverse.

Cultural explanations of politics must be pitched at the right level, and that level is probably the social structure rather than the individual psyche. It may be significant that Chinese are afraid that loosening the grip of power over society will produce chaos. It is probably more significant that in China such loosenings have in fact produced chaos regardless of individual desires, hopes, or fears. The Chinese people themselves are probably not culturally unsuited to democracy, but the cultural configurations of Chinese society, together with China's specific historical experience and the nature of the forces interested in democratization, hinder its growth.

Democracy has been thrown around as if it were obvious what the term means. It is, of course, a notoriously ambiguous and equivocal concept. We need not concern ourselves here with usages which make it a transparent synonym for tyranny: democracy as the dictatorship of the proletariat, or as rule in the interest of the vast majority of the people, or as government by the best qualified or the like. Even in ordinary Western usage there would seem to be at least two potentially antagonistic implications to the term. Democracy can mean popular participation in the making of political decisions, or it can mean limiting the power of the state by subjecting the state to control by the social order. Democracy in its first aspect might be called radical; it stresses liberation: freedom from the constraint of custom, social openness. Radical democracy can be a way of bringing about social change as the desires and values of social majorities, or articulate and committed minorities, change. It is hard to know what to call the second aspect of democracy: authoritarian might be apt, although the seemingly opposite term, liberal, might do as well. Authoritarian democracy tends to support the status quo. It protects valued ways of life from outside forces, forces which often but not always work through the state. It generally stresses limitations of state power, although it may also value legal enforcement of conventional morality--of, say, the authority of parents over their children. Authoritarian democracy may well tolerate severe restraint on the behavior of individuals through social mechanisms. Radical democracy is willing to use the state as an instrument to break those restrictions. The sexual liberation movements, for example, break up the authority of custom and of family, but increase the scope of political power over what had previously been considered to be private life.

A healthy democracy, no doubt, requires both aspects, if only because most of us, in different circumstances and on different issues, will sometimes feel drawn to one aspect, and sometimes to the other. The tension between them should play itself out through healthy democratic conflict regulated by strong democratic institutions. Yet it will not do to ignore or discount the tensions, because they can reflect a real antagonism. From the radical perspective, authoritarian democracy can be elitist and repressive. From the authoritarian vantage, radical democracy can be totalitarian.

A similar tension exists within Chinese dissident movements. Dissent in closed societies sometimes seems to be cloned from the power structure. The Chinese regime has constantly spoken of the need for persons both red and expert, and in practice it has at different times valued one side or the other of this dialectical unity over its opposite. Dissent against the regime or its policies can also be fitted into a red-or-expert pattern. Red dissent, related to radical democracy, demands greater mass participation in decision making. It is directed against the bureaucratic structures dominating the regime and looks for the democratization of political power. Expert dissent is less opposed to institutional power as such. It calls instead for depolitization, for the withdrawal of political power from many areas of personal and professional life, and for the regulation of political power by law. Both the Red and Expert lines, in their dissident forms, subvert the power structure of the regime. Both, in their establishment or coopted form, bolster a system of repressive power, although in different ways. The Expert line can rationalize the power and privilege of a technocratic intellectual "new class." The Red line can be openly totalitarian. Thus, the announcement of the short-lived Shanghai commune of early 1967 reads: "Party, governmental, financial, and literary authority have returned directly to the hands of the proletarian revolutionary faction. The people of Shanghai have been liberated a second time and have become the direct masters of their own soil."[4] This is democratic, but it implies no principled limitations on political power. In the most articulate and compelling early statements of Expert dissent--those directed against radical Maoism by the Party intellectuals of the "capitalist road" period of the early 1960s-- there is ample indication that people ought to be left alone to live in peace and be happy in their work. There is little, if anything, to show they should participate decisively in the making of political decisions.

It is easy enough to say that the Red and Expert lines of dissent are complementary. This, in fact, becomes increasingly apparent as time goes on. At the same time, however, there are deep historical divisions between them. At its mass level the Cultural Revolution can be seen as the mobilizing of Red dissent by one segment of the rulers against another segment which had been using Expert dissent for its own purposes. The experts perhaps remain easily persuaded that the Reds are identified with violent, nihilistic chaos. The Teng Hsiao-p'ing (Deng Xiaoping) regime has shown itself inclined to indulge most Expert dissent-- until that dissent begins to verge upon democracy--and the Reds can easily see the Experts as sell-outs, persons who, like the bandits in Water Margin, have accepted the imperial amnesty.

In spite of the antagonism, the substantive differences between the two lines have almost vanished. The Reds now realize that participation can take place only in the context of laws and institutions, while the Experts appear to know that in present circumstances power cannot be limited unless there is some popular control over its exercise. In effect, the dissent along both lines has converged toward classical, standard, garden-variety liberal democracy. The Li I-che wall poster of 1973 and 1974 represents a kind of coming of age of Red Guard radicalism. In the Cultural Revolution itself some Red Guard groups moved beyond denunciations of cow devils and snake spirits and capitalist roaders to call for free elections by the whole people. The Li I-che poster also conceives of democracy in terms of elections (rather than, say, merely in terms of themselves or people like themselves holding power), but goes on to argue that democracy can function only within a stable framework of law.[5] The April 5, 1976, incident, in which workers, functionaries, and students in Peking and a few other cities protested the dishonoring of the memory of Chou en-lai (Zhou enlai), the purge of Teng Hsiao-p'ing, and radical obscurantism generally, shows a new sort of Expert dissent. The participants were more the type one identifies as victims of Cultural Revolution radicalism than representatives of it--many were educated technicians with, I am told, persons in the civil and military agencies responsible for missile development being particularly fierce--and the featured slogans of the demonstration were more for modernization than democracy. The demonstration demanded not participation, but depoliticization, asserting, say, the autonomy of scientific and technical truth from politics and demanding the opportunity to do one's work without political interference. Yet the demonstration and protest was Red in style. The Reds and Experts were learning from each other.

The Li I-che poster and the April 5 demonstrations were in fact directed against the same target--the radical establishment at the top of the party, particularly the Gang of Four. To generalize, both were directed against Maoist totalitarianism. Despite the intellectual convergence of the two lines, however, the movements they represent have continued parallel rather than linked.

Red and Expert dissent have persisted into the post-Mao period, although the Reds haved remained more pristinely dissident. The democracy movement of 1978 and 1979, taken as a whole probably, and certainly in its radical extreme, is a continuation of Red dissent. The radicalism by that time was divorced from any particularly leftist content--the radicals in the democracy movement were those who wanted democracy pure and simple, whether or not it was socialist (that question, presumably, being one of those to be decided through the democratic process). The most famous of the democracy movement radicals was Wei Ching-sheng (Wei Jingsheng), and while it is probably not accurate to picture him as a Maoist, more than traces of Maoism adhere to his style of thought. Human rights are not absolute and eternal, but are shaped in the process of politcal struggle. All persons are equal--which means that no person's values or desires have any greater intrinsic worth than those of anyone else. The struggle over whose desires should prevail goes on forever. Marxism is wrong-headed and inhuman precisely because it postulates an end to human history. Democracy is a good form of government not for its own sake, but because it provides a regulating framework for the struggle through which human rights take shape.[6]

The expert line was most vocal in 1980 (the year keng-shen in the sixty-year cyclical reckoning, so the proposals are sometimes called the keng-shen reforms). Those who proposed the reforms were close to the centers of power, so it is dubious that they should be considered dissidents. The reforms themselves, however, had they been adopted, would have led to a truly radical reorganization of the system along democratic lines. The People's Daily, echoing a statement by Teng Hsiao-p'ing at a closed party meeting, said that socialism today is construed to mean that everything--science, the economy, culture--can exist if only subordinate to some adminstrative organization. This is said to be a "post-Leninist mutation," but it is a mutation characteristic of all Leninist systems.[7] This would seem to be in effect a tacit repudiation of Leninism, at least as it is universally practiced. Other essays in the official press criticize the shibboleth of monolithic leadership: what is needed is greater plurality. Other essays praise the American system of separation of powers and checks and balances as a way to prevent arbitrary rule. Concrete proposals included the strict separation of the functions of party and state, with the party allowed to operate only within the sphere permitted by the laws of the state. The powers of the National People's Congress should be increased and elections should become more competitive. The economy should be decentralized, with firms allowed more autonomy, and greater use made of the market to allocate resources. Factories should be managed in a democratic fashion. Labor unions should become more democratic as well, and similar democratically run institutions should be established among peasants. There should be greater freedom of the press. There were even proposals to decentralize power and set up a system of checks and balances within the Party itself.[8]

Both the democratic movement and the keng-shen reform movement served as political instruments of persons not necessarily committed to their aims. The democratic movement was used with mixed success by Teng Hsiao-p'ing against the non-radical left, the "whateverists," headed by Hua Kuo-feng. The keng-shen reforms were directed more against the "restorationists," the old Chou En-lai allies inside the economic bureaucracies who allegedly think everything would be fine if China would simply return to the way things were before the 1958 Great Leap Forward. The democratic movement was suppressed in the Spring of 1979, when its use backfired and Teng's enemies came to be able to accuse him of fomenting disorder. The keng-shen reforms were effectively shut down at the end of 1980, with the trial of the Gang of Four and the retrenchments in economic and cultural policy. Talk of reform has revived in 1982 and 1983, and attenuated versions of some of the keng-shen proposals have even been adopted. The emphasis is now less on limiting arbitrary power, however, than on increasing efficiency.

The democratic movement's proposals for law and democracy and human rights were rather abstract. The keng-shen proposals flesh them out with concrete designs for institutional development. Yet those outside the ruling circles who favor the reforms were unable to push for their adoption. Their only power base is the good will and sense of expediency of a faction or two among the rulers. Their natural mass base is in the democratic movement, but it is doubtful they could consolidate this base even were China less of a police state than it remains.

To return to culture, it would seem that democracy develops, if it develops at all, under conditions in which social forces are strong in themselves and autonomous from the state. A country becomes democratic when such forces can express themselves through a legislature strong enough to control the executive, and that legislature, in its turn, becomes responsible to substantial segments of the general population. These conditions existed potentially in Western Europe, although it is only in England that they led more or less "naturally" in a democratic direction--and then, only after centuries of spectacular political violence.

China, of course, had no legislature in traditional times. Nor did it have a strong autonomous social order. China has always had individuals willing to oppose arbitrary or immoral uses of political power. But the strongest social units have not been abstract categorical estates--nobility, peasantry, or the like-- but personalistic primary groups, particularly families. In traditional times the social structure was itself partly a creature of the state. This does not mean that Chinese society was subordinate to the state--the state was very much limited by the ethos of the examination class which was, almost certainly, itself an expression of the conventional ethical notions of the people as a whole. But entry into the social elite was by way of the examination system, and the examination system was a product of the state. Modern China is not traditional China. But the modernization process, while at various times weakening the Chinese state, has not done much to strengthen society against the state.

The People's Republic has often emphasized "class struggle," and indeed it appears that certain social groupings do at times have a strong sense of identity and of "class" interest. These groupings are identified not so much by occupation or relationship to the means of production; they are an artifact, rather, of the policies of the regime. In the Cultural Revolution the bitterest "class struggle" was within the Red Guard movement: between Red Guards of "good" class backgrounds and those whose class background was "not good." The not-good background students in the universities and academic middle schools tended to be children of non-Party cadres.[9] It seems unlikely there was any intrinsic difference between the two groups--in fact, in many cases even the social background of the parents was probably very much the same. The groups were distinct only because the regime had chosen to identify them and to treat them as distinct. Similarly, the old

210

class enemies used to be: landlords, rich peasants, counterrevo-
lutionaries, rightists, and "bad elements." The landlord and rich
peasant categories ceased to have any meaning by the early 1950s,
and the other terms refer to political opinion or to personal
behavior, not to economic function. Yet until the end of 1978
these constituted a pariah class in China. The social structure,
as in traditional China, remained a creature of the political
system. This social weakness (which a generation of totalitarian
rule has only intensified) means there is little leverage against
the rulers. Opposition movements tend to fragment along personalistic lines.

The democratic movement, especially, illustrates this. During
that period the human rights agitation in Peking was carried out
by students and young workers. At the same time there was economic agitation by peasants who had come to the capital to shang-
fang, "petition the superior" for redress of grievances. The two
groups were able to coordinate their activities somewhat, but only
to a limited degree and in a clumsy fashion. The human rights
activists were divided into two tendencies, the "abolitionists"
like Wei Ching-sheng who wanted a complete transformation of the
Chinese system and the more moderate "socialist democrats."[10]
Each of these tendencies was itself divided into numerous small
factions.

Fragmentation means isolation. The abolitionists or radical
democrats may be especially isolated. Kjeld Brodsgaard asserts
that dissent in the democratic movement is "rooted not in the
intellectuals (as in 1957), nor in the students (as in 1967), but
rather, in the working class."[11] But the democracy movement was
not a workers' movement in the sense, say, that the Polish Solidarity is. It did not articulate the particular interests of
workers nor did it mobilize great numbers of factory workers. To
the extent that the movement did articulate the particular interest of any social segment, it was that of youth. Participants
report that older workers would understand and sympathize with the
movement, but would themselves remain passive: they, after all,
had families, seniority, and their place in society--and also a
sense that in the end the movement was not going to bring about
basic changes anyway. Many of the activists did, to be sure, hold
jobs in factories. It is probably at least as relevant that many
of them were former Red Guards. Brodsgaard reports that the 1979
situation was the reverse of that of the Cultural Revolution.
During the Cultural Revolution bad class-background Red Guards
tended to be the most radical, while Red Guards of "red" back-

ground tended to suppport the establishment. In 1979 the reds were radical--Wei Ching-sheng, for example, is the son of a low-ranking communist official, and he had belonged to a Red Guard group consisting largely of cadres' children--while the socialist democrats tended to be former radical Red Guards.[12] One reason for this is, perhaps that under the new conditions the children of "bourgeois intellectuals" can, more easily than the reds, see themselves being recruited into the emerging technocracy. For them, cooptation now seems both possible and not entirely dishonorable.[13]

The democracy movement was not a workers' movement, but neither, of course, was it a movement of the grown children of communist officials. Most of the persons in that category, according to the stereotypes, have become apolitical hedonists. Others, no doubt, try to make their way as best they can given conditions as they are, with attitudes ranging all along the spectrum from cynicism to idealism. In effect, the democracy movement grew out of certain social conditions, but it should probably not be considered a social movement. It was a set of the activities of particular individuals having particular opinions, "aggregating" into factions based upon friendship or some other personal relationship.

The regime does what it can to increase the isolation of the radical democrats. Chinese society perhaps inclines toward prudishness, and the regime rather consciously attempts to link unconventional political opinion with unconventional personal behavior. A 1982 bestseller portrays three college girls, each of a different type. One has overcome the adverse environment of the past decade, and more, and has her head together. The second one has become disillusioned with the world and has, unfortunately, fallen into Christianity. The third is sexually promiscuous. It turns out she was also a political activist and connects her personal immorality with the liberation of thought. The novel apparently accepts this connection as a matter of course.[14] If this kind of impression gains currency it would only serve to alienate the ordinary person from democratic activism. From the point of view of liberalization as a political movement, the Li Shuang affair, involving the arrest of an avant-guarde artist for her liason with a French diplomat, is tactically unfortunate.

What is probably more serious, the regime attempts to link the democratic movement with chaos and violence. The official line has now apparently become that the democracy movement was the last gasp of the Cultural Revolution. One of the regime's more hard-line spokesmen (who is currently in disgrace, although not directly for voicing the opinions quoted here) asserts:

> There's one kind of person, a small minority, who thinks our party has already changed its nature, that it has no hope, that it must be overthrown, that there must be a change of dynasty. Or they might say we should be like America and have a two-party system, one party in power and one party out, taking turns running the government. This is the theory of the remnant forces of the "Gang of Four," including Chiang Ch'ing and Chang Ch'un-ch'iao and that ilk who are locked in jail.[15]

It is interesting to think that the Gang of Four are converts to liberal democracy. It is also interesting, from the outside, to see the fear a revolutionary one-party dictatorship has for the revolutionary implications of liberal democracy. Concretely, however, from the inside the image this talk of a "new revolution" or a change of dynasty conjures up is not of a new dawn of freedom, but of Red Guard violence and anarchy. This should help isolate the democratic movement from the intellectuals, who may have the most directly to gain from further liberalization, but also have the most to lose from chaos. This antipathy will be reinforced if those democrats who do not fall into passivity react to frustration by becoming re-radicalized, returning, say, to a version of Maoism--although this time, one assumes, it will be an impotent Maoism.

The intellectuals, except for some creative writers, may now have things much their own way and may feel no pressing need for immediate further liberalization. Their position, however, remains precarious. The dominant faction in the regime protects them, but other factions among the rulers are clearly hostile and jealous. Should the current rulers decide to turn against them in order to conciliate factional rivals, the intellectuals will have no way to defend themselves. The radical democrats are isolated from the intellectual reformers, but this also means the intellectual reformers are isolated from the radical democrats. If it comes to that, the rulers themselves may be isolated. The current ruling group--the "reform faction"--probably does have, in the abstract, a genuine commitment to far-reaching structural reform, particularly if the reforms will weaken their rivals without giving them too much ammunition at the same time. The desired reforms would have more to do with depoliticization than with democratization. The logic of the keng-shen reforms, however, is that depoliticization beyond a certain point requires democratization. The rulers are afraid to democratize, and those in society who would benefit most directly from it are too weak to push them into it. By failing to democratize, the regime nourishes its own crisis of legitimacy.

Notes

1. Richard H. Solomon, Mao's Revolution and the Chinese Political Culture (University of California Press, 1971), p. 524.

2. Solomon, p. 44.

3. Compare Wolfgang Bauer, China and the Quest for Happiness (New York, 1976).

4. Wen Hui Pao, February 5 1967.

5. Li I-che, "On Socialist Democracy and Legality," Chung-kung Yen-chiu, November 1975, pp. 117-131.

6. Wei Ching-shen, "More on the Fifth Modernization," T'an-so, March, 1979.

7. Pao T'ung, "A Few Thoughts on Opposing Bureaucratism," Jen-min Jih-lao, October 30, 1980.

8. Liao Kai-lung, "The 'Ken-shen Reform' Program in China," Ch'i-shih Nien-tai, March, 1981.

9. Jonathan Unger, Education Under Mao: Class and Competition in Canton Schools, 1960-1980 (Columbia University Press, 1982).

10. Kjeld Erik Brodsgaard, "The Democracy Movement in China, 1978-1979; Opposition Movements, Wall Poster Campaigns, and Underground Journals," Asian Survey, Vol. XXI, No. 7 (July 1981), pp. 747-774, pp. 768-773.

11. Brodsgaard, p. 774.

12. Brodsgaard, pp. 768-769.

13. Compare Maria Hirszowicz, The Bureaucratic Leviathan: A Study in the Sociology of Communism (Oxford, 1980), pp. 188-192.

14. See the discussion of this novel in Hsin Hua Wen-chai, September 1982, pp. 171-175.

15. Wang Jen-chung, "Unite Thought, Earnestly Rectify Party Style," Hung Ch'i, March 1, 1982, pp. 1-13, p2.

Gastil remarked that the saying Moody quoted, "Confucianist in office, Daoist out of office," betrays a kind of individualism that the conferees generally denied. **Grieder** said "individuality" was the word Professor de Bary used because individualism has so many connotations that are reminiscent of the American frontier. But there is certainly a strong tradition of individualism, individuality or expression of self.

Gastil said that he was interested in the possibility of holding values above the state. If a Chinese relapses into Daoism and goes off to the mountains he is putting individual values ahead of the state. **Grieder** and **Sullivan** thought he was putting them outside the state, which is a very different thing. He is saying, "To hell with the state, I'm going to get up to the mountain."

Dreyer was delighted that Moody had come back to this saying. It had struck her that one important indicator of democratization might be if the Chinese communists were to provide for a right of withdrawal, an honorable withdrawal for the discredited, out-of-office official. Now if one is out of office he is totally pilloried and discredited, and movements are begun against him. It can actually be said that the Gang of Four was nicer to Deng Xiaoping than he was to them; Deng was allowed a sort of exile. **Sullivan** added that Deng had many protectors, particularly in the army. **Dreyer** noted that all of these protectors have since been purged, and that the Gang of Four still have sympathizers who might have protected them in exile had Deng allowed it.

Moody thought that one of the first geng sheng (keng-shen) reforms (ca. 1980) was to diffuse power within the party. That would really be a break with Leninism. They had established the absurd advisors committee for the old Party leaders. It was not much but it might be progress of a sort.

Sullivan thought a tenure system that involves giving up position at retirement must have some honor attached to it. Secondly, there is the problem of an economic base. The press admits that one of the problems with getting people to voluntarily retire is the perception that power brings influence, such as the ability to place your son in the right school, bring your relatives to the city, and the other amenities. To make a retirement system work, the government will have to go beyond moral requests and provide both symbolic and real resources so that people will give up power. Sullivan did not think the advisory commission was the most critical thing. Zhang Wentian was purged by Mao and kept around for a long time. **Dreyer** agreed there were such instances. Wei Guoqing's last appearance since he was purged was at a performance of the Singapore Children's Choir.

Seymour found Moody's paper had many useful insights. He was, however, disturbed by the idea that totalitarianism is modern. It is coincidental with our times, but we need a more useful concept of modernization than that which happens to be contemporary. If we call both totalitarianism and constitutional democracy "modern," the only thing left out is right-wing dictatorship. Are we going to say that totalitarianism is more modern than right-wing dictatorship? If not, if dictatorships such as Taiwan are "modern," then everything is modern, so it is not very useful to talk about modernization.

There were problems with Moody's two types of democracy-- authoritarian and radical. "Authoritarian democracy" had Seymour worried, because it is a term like "democratic centralism" that takes two opposites and puts them together. As to radical democracy, democracy can be considered the most radical idea to come along in human history; if this is the case, then it is redundant to say "radical democracy." Radical or "red" democracy is a metaphor within a metaphor, and we get tangled up in it because red originally meant political left (and that came from a color), but then when we take red in this sense and use it as a label for a type of democrat in China, it leads Moody to say that the red line can be openly totalitarian. Seymour understood the point, there is a relationship between the red guards and that kind of democracy--the democracy wall types are the radicals in this sense. But the very reason Moody needed heavy quotation marks about this usage is that the democracy wall people were also absolutely opposed to totalitarianism.

Seymour saw the recent situation developing differently than Moody described it. Moody linked the April 5, 1976, pro-Zhou Enlai demonstration with the democracy of the experts. He may be right or he may have been misled by the labels, because the real democrats, the democracy wall democrats, look back to April 5 just as much as do the reformers within the Party. There may be an interesting analogy between the April 5 movement and the May 4 movement (in 1919). The May 4 movement went off in different directions, communist and liberal democratic. This may have happened after the April 5th movement. Perhaps it started as one movement and went in two directions.

Seymour could have misunderstood, but he thought the democratic dissidents needed more favorable treatment. There were comments that seemed to be slights. For instance, Moody wrote about how abstract they were. It is true that their most interesting essays are philosophical, but many were quite concrete. Of course the specific ones are less profound. Seymour had tried in his book, The Fifth Modernization, to produce a representative sample. For example, while no purpose would have been served in putting in a long piece about interference in the mail, he had included a couple of paragraphs just to show there were concrete issues. Questions of law and of ethnic minorities are also raised. Wei Jingsheng's long piece about Qincheng prison was also pretty specific.

Moody said that he would be prepared to defend the proposition that liberalism and totalitarianism have common roots. He did not wish to imply that "modern" was simply what is going on now. There is a mode of reasoning that can be called modern no matter when it comes up--the Sophists and Legalists were modern. The essay that impressed him most on totalitarianism was Hannah Arendt's. To the nineteenth century propositions that everything is permitted and there is no god, one adds the twentieth century proposition that everything is possible. These are basic to both, and totalitarianism becomes a version of liberalism. Right-wing authoritarian dictatorships form a residual category. Some may be "post-totalitarian." Taiwan is hard to place, but it is modern. This suggests that "modern" fits a variety of political forms.

Sullivan thought the usual interpretation is that we associate totalitarianism with modernization because modern societies produce the capacity for total control. **Seymour** countered that Qinshi Huangdi in the third century B.C. did a pretty good job at setting up a totalitarian state. **Moody** would call that modern. **Sullivan** said that his impression was that Qinshi Huangdi did not control the system all that well.

Dreyer supported Sullivan's definition. Qinshi Huangdi (the Qin emperor) was undoubtedly cruel and reasonably effective. Yet, because of the lack of development of communications and modern techniques, he could not have been a totalitarian. **Sullivan**

suggested that was why he was assassinated. **Seymour** added that the Emperor was able to mobilize vast numbers of people to build the roads and the Great Wall, and so on. Of course, he didn't have the means to be totalitarian in the modern sense. **Gastil** said that certainly small units did. There was Calvin's Geneva, and the city of Münster was taken over by totalitarian Anabaptists.

Kintner raised the question of the fundamental attitude of the Chinese toward the sanctity of the individual, which is critical for human rights. Without individuals having any true significance and without human rights, democracy becomes very inadequate. He wished to recall a wartime experience. He was commander of Porkchop Hill in Korea for quite a few months and went through many battles. It was interesting to see how the Chinese operated. When they wanted to attack a main point they always had a diversionary attack. When we made a diversionary attack, we always made a lot of noise, smoke. But the Chinese would simply send a whole company, and they would all be killed. They did it quite frequently. It seemed that the human being was treated as absolutely nothing. In their last battle, in which they took Porkchop, just two weeks before the armistice, they threw in two divisions against a little over a regiment on our side. We had pill boxes with machines guns. To get in they used the tactic of sending a man up with a grenade at night time. Sometimes it would take twenty-five to fifty men to get a grenade through the slot, and then they would get in. At this point the Chinese were trying to prove in these last six months of the war that they had not lost the war. They were the ones doing the attacking, we were the defenders. So they could have done it any way they wanted. Yet human life was treated like dirt. You would see these young bodies stacked up in the morning after some of these battles, and one wondered how they did it. We thought they were doped for a while, but they were not. This use of life seemed fundamentally different. In our military, when we give an order, we tell our men they have a fighting chance. But they gave orders that had no chance whatsoever. Kintner wanted those who knew Chinese history and culture to comment on this issue. Is there contempt of life, particularly among those at the bottom of the heap where it does not make a great deal of difference whether they live or die?

Grieder said that this was a point often raised. Obviously from one point of view it seems totally anomalous, the expression of a totally barbaric culture. To a certain extent the Japanese fought this way in the Second World War. (**Dreyer** added the Russians, but **Kintner** thought they were slightly better.) In a crunch the Germans did it at Stalingrad. Grieder did not have military experience, but he wondered if at some point a kind of mythic capacity took over. He did not know to what extent this phenomenon can be generalized as a basis for understanding the social instincts of the people. **Gastil** thought perhaps the contempt for life was in the officers who sent them.

Sullivan recalled Westmoreland's statement in the film **Hearts and Minds**. He described the Vietnamese as Kintner had the Chinese, but then the film makers, in a somewhat manipulative way, showed the mother of a Vietnamese killed in the war sitting next to a grave crying as any mother cries when her son has been killed. **Dreyer** said this was one of the things that so vexed her in listening to one of John Fairbanks' lectures. He would say, "Everyone says the Chinese have contempt for human life, but here is a picture of a lady crying because her child has just been killed." These are two totally different things--the government's contempt for the lives of its citizens and the mother's feeling for her child.

Sullivan thought that the example surely demonstrated that at least some people in the government have contempt for life. The people who put Wei Jingsheng in prison for fifteen years do. But these things become very complex. MacArthur had more concern for his soldiers than Patton. Patton threw units in, and his losses were enormous. He wondered what kind of concern for life Americans showed when we fire-bombed Dresden or Tokyo. This did not prove that we were barbarians; we must examine the context. **Gastil** thought the lives of other people was a different issue. It mattered whose lives, and when. But it seemed to him that in the First World War both sides sent waves of soldiers into machine guns very much like the Chinese.

Dreyer thought the answer might be in the rationalizations in the mind of the person sending the soldiers in. He may justify losing man after man trying to lob grenades into a bunker by thinking that this is saving 50,000 lives somewhere else. There are always excuses in the mind. **Gastil** wondered if at the time the officer was not just responding reflexively.

Zhu pointed out the comparative advantages for the Chinese. The Chinese had just people while the United States had advanced weapons. Mao has a sentence--the most important weapon is the people. **Grieder** agreed that given this situation the Chinese were perhaps more willing to consider raw manpower as a military weapon.

Gastil thought it would be interesting to find how these ideas developed. Throwing away lives was one thing the American Indians, for example, never did. They never sent people in waves. When they had to lose large numbers of soldiers, they left. This is one reason they turned the country over to the white people. So throwing away the lives of soldiers is not really primitive, it comes with a degree of civilization.

Smith thought the response stemmed from a very intensive internal propaganda that the Chinese with their submachine guns and grenades are perhaps superior to these Xiao Ye bing, little gentlemen, cosseted soldiers on the American side. "We can prevail because of our courage. We are better than they are." **Sullivan** also remarked on the context. Here was a country just two years out of civil war, with an ill-equipped army taking on the victor of World War II. We had overwhelmed Germany and Japan, and now we were taking on a force that two years before had just emerged from a difficult civil war. Then there was General MacArthur going up to the Yalu. He did not think that Kintner's example said anything in general.

Smith added that in some of the earlier engagements in Korea, the Chinese had deliberately thrown in ex-Kuomintang troops to get them ground up. If they took a few miles in the process so much the better. **Zhu** also reminded us that MacArthur had done the same thing in the Pacific. To take isolated islands in the Pacific he lost many men.

In response **Kintner** agreed, "we are all barbarians," but he was addressing the question of the transfer of democracy to China. In what he had read and experienced, it seemed the sanctity of the individual was less. This may retard the ability of China to move toward democracy because it is a key to how people look at the individual. In totalitarian society the individual is a tool of the state. Unless a society recognizes inalienable individual rights it may not be able to have a democracy.

Moody said that in Confucian thinking a high value is placed on the person, but not the individual. The individual is a historical construct, a disembodied thing in his own skin unconnected to any social relationship except those he voluntarily chooses. The person exists only in a social network, as son or daughter, father or mother, subject or ruler. Whether this creates a mindset especially adapted to communism is a question. In Marxism there is also the idea there is no such thing as the individual. The individual is an artifact of the social class which belongs to the collectivist orientation. So there is conceivably a connection, but they are very different ideas.

Returning to Kintner's question **Dreyer** pointed out that according to Confucianism you ought to take care of yourself because your body is a gift from your parents. Therefore, you must protect it or they will be insulted by your mutilated body. **Smith** noted that each role has its duty, and the duty of a soldier is to be willing to die. **Zhu** added that there are priorities, and one must sacrifice the parent's interest if the good of the state is at risk. Yet this is not to be done lightly.

Grieder brought up a subcondition of Confucian thought that had not yet been paid attention to. He had consciously ignored it because it has been so romanticized and abused by being patronized. But there is in the Chinese political tradition a strong insistence on the primacy of people, at least at the level of rhetoric. The people first, and the prince second. Because the ideal and the real so seldom coincide in China (any more than anywhere else), there was a long tradition of active and sometimes extremely biting political criticism that emphasized this discrepancy between what was supposed to be and what was. The only justification for government and its first responsibility is its ability to create a moral environment that will make life tolerable for the people. It was not that the people should participate or be involved, but that any government that neglected as its first concern their welfare was ipso facto illegitimate. Many Chinese in the twentieth century, and Westerners, seized on this as a proof the Chinese were the democrats of Asia, the John Locke's, all they need is kerosene, literacy, or whatever. This was greatly romanticized. Still if there is anything that is hopeful for a conference like this, it would be in this tradition.

Gastil proposed that unless the people are individualized, personified, or separated from the group they can be talked about endlessly without being taken seriously. However, **Sullivan** thought that democracy can exist in an environment in which individualism as we define it does not exist. There is an incredible force for conformity in Japanese society. It is in many ways one of the most conformist societies in history. Consider the role of Japanese women, as well as the prejudice against left-handedness, and the treatment of its few ethnic minorities. De Tocqueville said the problem with the United States was conformity in thought. There is a broad range of social values that can exist in a democracy. This is why Sullivan liked what Moody had to say at

221

the beginning of this paper.   The problem of the Solomon-Pye
emphasis on political culture is that it says, in effect, that
there is a certain personality type or national character that is
more supportive of democracy. He believed that Taiwan has all the
prerequisites for democracy; if a democracy were set up tomorrow,
Taiwan would be as able to run its own affairs as any place else.
The same is true of Hong Kong and Singapore. However, **Gastil**
added that the only one that really had a chance--Singapore--has
not established a democracy.   **Sullivan** did not think this was
because of cultural factors, but other reasons.

Returning to Moody's paper, **Dreyer** said that J. L. Talmon wrote
long ago that liberalism and totalitarianism both arose from
Rousseau, and of the same tradition. **Moody** replied that "totalitarian democracy," or "conservative democracy," might be better
terms for his category. **Grieder** said "dirigiste democracy" was
what Giovanni Sartori called it. **Moody** said that in this system
the expert wanted to depoliticize the system. There is not necessarily a demand for mass participation, although the keng sheng
reforms do talk about it. But you cannot depoliticize without
also democratizing. If the state is separated from running
things, and lets the people do what they want, the people are
going to want to put demands on the state.

Sullivan said that the notion of limiting state power is
favored by scientific and similar groups. They don't want interference in their research; for example, they do not want the state
to define what is the correct theory of genetics or physics.
There should be areas of autonomy. **Gastil** said it is not only the
technocratic approach, it is also the Confucian sage. The claim
is to both technical and moral status.

Sullivan asked Moody to tell him why he thought Japan and India
were comparatively less hospitable to democracy than China. **Moody**
answered that he shared the cliche about the Chinese being individualistic, the idea that the people are the root of the state.
Compared to Japan, he found a greater diversity and openness of
cultural groups. He would also contrast the guanxi which emphasizes "connections" and relationships in a less hierarchical sense
than the patron-client system to the Japanese patron-client system
where the groups are very closed in on themselves and people have
set status--the hierarchy is everything. The Chinese have agreed
since time immemorial on the innate equality of people; and thus
there is no caste system as in India, although there are social
levels that are respected. So the Chinese seem closer to the
standard idea of democratic political culture.

   Sullivan replied that Hu Hanmin, one of the earlier democrats
Grieder alluded to, made the same claim that the Chinese political
culture was favorable for democracy.   **Hu** said that one reason
China could have a democracy was that, like the United States, it
lacked an aristocracy.   Hu also contrasted the unified culture and
the agreement on fundamental principles in China with the diversity of India.   **Grieder** added that there was also no social confrontation or slavery.   But **Dreyer** added that we should not over-
emphasize China's "unified culture," because often the greatest
disputes take place over the smallest differences.

Obstacles to the Formation of Dissident Organizations in China

Liang Heng

Since the Communist Party attained power in 1949, it has functioned as a one-party dictatorship. For thirty years, even though struggles for political power and divergences from ideology have frequently occurred, no opposition faction ever became institutionalized. Outside the party, such groups as the National People's Conference, the Communist Youth League, the labor unions, the Women's Federation, and the Young Pioneers are all controlled by the Party. Though there are a few noncommunist political parties, they exist in name only. As for the people, the peasants, workers, students, cadres, commercial employees, soldiers, and intellectuals are all controlled by their own units, which are in turn directly controlled by level after level of party organization. Dissident ideas have been expressed from time to time, but in contemporary times China has had no sustained dissident organization: no political force or group which is independent of the Communist Party of China, and also critical of it. (In practice, the Party and government are one under the Chinese political system.) This paper presents a few of the reasons for this, including strong political control, Mao's hatred of intellectuals, cultural factors such as the inertia of the peasants, and the limitations stemming from the social values of the intellectuals. These factors, of course, are only partial answers to a complex question.

Strong Political Control.

For thousands of years, China has been a centralized society with an imperial power at the top. The unification of territory and culture was the basic standard by which to measure the greatness of an emperor, and this unification could only be realized through a strong political dictatorship. The unified system established by the Qin and Han dynasties became the main line of development for the Chinese political system. In every dynasty in which imperial power was strong, social relationships were simple, and the politcal structure was relatively stable. Except for the roles of governor and governed, there were no other political roles. In other words, there was no balanced strength. But despite the social and political structure, there were still some elements in society that could mitigate social problems. The gentry, for example, could play a role by helping magistrates with local administration.

In modern society, the Communist Party has adopted this system, but without many of the benign aspects of feudal dictatorship. The modern system reflects, on the one hand, a historical inheritance, and on the other, the influence of Leninism. Lenin emphasized the establishment of a party organization which was secret, disciplined, and effective. This organization was to be controlled by a few members of the party elite. Theoretically, these members of the elite were representatives of the interests of the whole proletariat. This totalitarian theory became the basis for the construction of a centralized socialist nation.

When the Communist Party of China established its political system, there were additional reasons for it to prefer dictatorship. When it came to power the economy was extremely poor and the country was undeveloped; the kind of industrial and commercial classes that need a pluralistic system to develop and protect themselves did not exist. Under such conditions, it was relatively easy for the Communist Party to enlarge and strengthen a unified dictatorship. The dictatorship was also able to consolidate its power through a highly organized, one-party system. Compared with the insurrectionary armies of peasant rebels in the past, the Party had a much greater ability to control the country.

Mao's Hatred of Intellectuals.

In China, even though it is difficult for a dissident organization to appear, there are people within and outside the Party who are displeased with the government. Most of them are intellectuals, but Chinese intellectuals have traditionally played the role in practical political life of spokesmen for the ordinary people. Obviously, this role should make them active in alleviating social contradictions. In Western countries this role is often played by the large middle class, but in agrarian China it has been played by a few intellectuals with only a weak position in Chinese economic life.

Unfortunately, the autocratic tendencies of the communist system were enhanced by Mao Zedong's personal hatred of intellectuals. Taken together Mao's culture and personal attitudes led him to aggressively deny intellectuals their traditional role. In his desire to strengthen his power, he particularly could not tolerate their dissenting voices.

Mao's educational background was in feudal China. When he was young, he became very familiar with the Confucian Class Book, studied the Yu Pi Tong Jian (Collection of Imperial Decrees) on his own, and liked Han Yu's articles. When he was older, he continued to study the unofficial history. These works were reflected in his politics. Moreover, he had a peasant's feeling of inferiority and obstinacy. He hated modern civilization and the intellectuals who disseminated it. From his jealousy of some early revolutionaries with good education to the rectification movement in Yanan, to the Cultural Revolution, his policies expressd his hatred and fear of intellectuals.

Some believe that now that Mao is dead the function of intellectuals in practical political life will become greater, and it may become possible for effective dissident organizations to emerge. But how can the intellectuals discharge their responsibilities in a country which is ruled without law? It will remain true that social groups that are not important in national economic life are weak in national political life. In China the group with the preponderant influence on the economy is the peasantry, not the intellectuals or businessmen.

The Peasant's Inertia.

Chinese culture is agrarian and its development has been very slow. For thousands of years the Chinese peasants have been accustomed to stable production without much economic or social exchange. Their goal has remained a self-sufficient and self-satisfied life. Essentially inert, they have played a passive role in cultural development. The main characteristics of the peasants are selfishness, self-abasement, and complacency. Their views are frequently narrow and limited. Except for a desire to

227

maintain present conditions, they are little interested in social or political questions.

Confucian tradition emphasizes the value of "energetic work," but Confucianism is the culture of the literati and officials. The ideologies of ordinary people are primarily Taoism and Buddhism. These negative philosophies run very deep in the peasants and are expressed naturally in their actions. The fatalism of Buddhism not only strengthens the sense of inferiority of the peasants, but also weakens their sense of self. It is no wonder that the Chinese peasants have unusual tolerance for political and economic oppression. The inactivity preached by Taoism is also consistent with the peasant's tendency to be satisfied with his present situation. If, for example, an emperor gave them some minor charity, or if the government adopted a policy that was beneficial to them, they felt satisfied and thankful, but gave no thought to wanting more. Taoism also gave them their belief in the power of gods and ghosts. If their conditions became worse, the leaders of uprisings used religion to incite them. Through historical experience we see that the Chinese peasants participated in major revoluionary upheavals almost blindly--and this includes their participation in Mao's revolution.

As we know, a passive group, even though its economic position may be important, cannot play an active role. After many years, if the economy promotes prosperity and if education is popularized in the countryside, the peasants may come to want to influence the Party and government through participation in political life. But then, those that play this role and that begin, for example, to form opposition factions will no longer be considered peasants. They will have developed into agricultural capitalists or joined the industrial and commercial classes.

The Intellectual's Social Values.

The revolutionary role of Chinese intellectuals has historically been limited by the tradition that they "will not treat the ruler as their enemy." In the past those who were considered truly upright were not the people who wanted to help disloyal officials overturn the emperor, but those who frankly criticized the emperor's faults. If their criticisms were not adopted, they complained that they were not understood, and perhaps turned to drink or committed suicide. Today this recourse has disappeared, but the intellectuals still do at times criticize the Party and speak for the ordinary people. During the Hundred Flowers Movement of 1957, for example, intellectuals helped the Party criticize itself. As in the past, they did not want to treat the Party as their enemy, although Mao doubted their intentions. Some hated the policies and actions of the Party, yet they took no physical action to oppose it.

The restraints on Chinese intellectuals were not only because of the power of the emperor, but also because they themselves advocated and protected the feudal system. Like the peasants, they treated the emperor as the Son of Heaven, and saw everything he did as representing the command of Heaven. When the country had a crisis, the literati and officials desired to strengthen the system and realize the ideal of benevolent government. This was why they criticized the emperor even at the risk of their own lives. From this perspective, the Chinese intellectual's social values were very conservative. They lacked an active desire for social change.

Today most Chinese intellectuals of the middle and older generations not only have accepted the negative aspects of the traditional culture but have also adopted a little Marxism and been educated in Leninism and Maoism. The quality of modern intellectuals has declined. The realities of Chinese life and their private suffering in the Cultural Revolution made them hate the Chairman and his policies. But when they had a chance to criticize the system after his death, their criticisms were shallow and almost naive. They continued to believe that although Mao had his faults, real Marxism could help China. They have not performed their role of speaking for the people. They have not seriously analyzed the main reasons the Chinese situation is so poor and have not tried to explain which parts of Marxism are consistent with Chinese culture, and whether these parts are beneficial for the society as a whole. They continue to agree with the Party that a pure Marxism could manage all China's problems.

Thus, even if Chinese intellectuals were given a greater opportunity to criticize, the criticism of most older intellectuals would remain within narrow limits. Their thought has already been predetermined by the society in which they live. They have accepted its values and are left with little independent or creative spirit. It is impossible for them to break away from the dogma that has guided their thought.

However, younger intellectuals are still capable of change and, if given the chance, would make much more basic criticisms. Their

educational background is weaker than that of the older generations, but in some ways this is their good fortune. Because they
are young their thought is less traditional; they are full of
vitality, see more clearly, and are more enterprising. They could
play the role of speaking for the people today.

It remains true that it is impossible for even this group to
form a stable dissident organization. The Party controls the
media and only it decides who can write and publish. So the
thoughts and opinions of the younger intellectuals are known to
very few. Since transportation is undeveloped and there are few
telephones, it is difficult to exchange ideas even within this
group, and it is very easy for the government to destroy people
with dissenting opinions. The Democracy Wall movement has quickly
disappeared. Now it is difficult for us to judge to what extent
these young intellectuals will be able to perform their critical
function. However, if they can adopt the rational element in
Chinese traditional culture and learn more of Western democratic
thought, it is possible that they will find a way to make a
greater contribution to the development of China than that of the
older generation that in its time was denied this role by the
severity of political oppression.

COMMENTS AND DISCUSSION

After his paper **Liang** added that the older generation of intellectuals still has very conservative values, very different from
his generation. The Confucian tradition was very useful to the
communists. It emphasized state first, then family, then person,
everyone is to serve the state. But the cultural revolution has
caused the younger generation to reject such "feudal-communist"
thought.

Gastil asked if Liang thought his father was actually influenced
more by traditional reading than by communist reading. **Liang**
answered that he was, and this was characteristic of intellectuals
of his generation. He was also influenced by his previous
experience.

Huang noted that Liang criticized the intellectuals for their
conservatism, which upheld party authority. Seymour criticized
the intellectuals for their elitism. He had the uncomfortable
impression that we are all feeling the trunk of the elephant. We
need to understand the intellectual better for he will play a
crucial part in the next few decades in China and Taiwan. We will
need to look at this again.

When we talk about individualism, the assumption is that Americans are very individualistic, and that unless the Chinese are as
individualistic, they cannot have democracy. This needs to be
examined. Democracy in Taiwan and in China is going to be quite
different than what we know in the United States or Japan. We
need to develop a broader view and bridge the gap.

Smith wished to reenforce what Huang had said. He had lived in
Japan at various times for over thirty years. It had seemed to
him that there was no reason Japanese democracy should work, yet
by all the normal standards of human rights it had. It is interesting to note that communism as it has evolved in China over
fifty years is also quite distinct from communism as it has developed in any other country. Democracy in China would be at least
equally transformed.

Zhu questioned Liang's statement that the Chinese do not have an organized dissident movement. It depended on what period is being considered. During the past thirty years, this is true; yet after 1978 there were some weak dissident organizations. In the future it depends on what crises there are. If the communist party loses control, there could be a real dissident movement. In Poland before the crisis arose with Solidarity there was little information on a dissident organization in Poland.

The first reason we do not have a strong dissident movement is the attitude and strength of the communist party, as Liang said. But we cannot blame the lack of a movement in the future on Mao, because Mao is already dead. He also questioned the idea of intellectual conservatism. At many times in Chinese history the intellectuals have been quite aggressive when they find something wrong with the system. Most early communists were intellectuals.

Sullivan asked Liang which of the four obstacles to dissident organization he had mentioned was the most important, the most difficult to change, and why. **Liang** replied that, first, he was speaking of "organization," and this was not what Zhu was talking about. For example, even though he was a leader he did not think his group was really a "dissident organization." They were just young friends together. They discussed the political situation and decided they should do something. So they wrote their posters (dazibao) and held demonstrations. Some students set up their elections committee. But not an organization. An organization should have members and a definite program; they never reached this point.

Zhu replied that they did not have a chance to do it. They did organize a publication. But after that, they were put in jail. If they had not been, the movement would have gone further. The real obstacle was the government. The dissidents wanted to do something.

Liang also suggested that another weakness was the fact that in China the intellectuals' economic position was not important. The government can ignore them. Solidarity really bothers the government, because it represents the workers. **Zhu** thought that while intellectuals may not be important in the Chinese economy, the dissidents must have an important impact or the government would not put them in jail. Under present conditions with an unstable economic situation, if they criticized government and organized small groups, this could mean real trouble for the government. This is why, when they start to develop a nationwide organization, the government puts them all in jail.

Smith made two observations. First, there was a house they take visitors to in Shanghai where a group of Chinese intellectuals got together and then took a boat ride; on the ride they formed the Chinese Communist party. This indicated to him that for good or bad, Chinese intellectuals can accomplish quite a lot when they organize themselves in a disciplined way.

Second, he found it curious that he did not recall any point in the discussion of changes in the communist system where there was explicit reference to workers, which are supposed to be basic to communist theory. There has developed since 1949 a large and widely dispersed group of workers and technicians in basic industry and increasingly in high technology fields such as computers. The workers are mostly junior high graduates or at least have fairly good educations. Yet as far as he knew they had no political expression beyond their workplace. Potentially they could be a factor. The intellectuals could find a base here much more responsive than the traditional peasants or villagers.

Zhu added that most activists in the democracy movement were actually not intellectuals, but workers. **Liang** said that at the end of his paper he had mentioned the "young generation"; most were actually young workers along with some students, not really intellectuals. We should also remember that in China high school students are intellectuals. However, since only high party officials have telephones and the government controls the media, it is difficult for young workers and others to come together and share ideas. It is easy for the police to arrest them. Information does not get around. I went to hear Wang Xizhe (leftist dissident writer) in my home town, Changsha, in Hunan, and found that people did not know who Wang was.

Grieder pointed out that this seemed to be what Liang meant by an organization. It was not so much an ability to organize action as to operate a communications network that enlarges the group's sense of solidarity. **Sullivan** suggested this was the function of the Democracy Wall. **Liang** added that there were today some underground groups but not really organizations. **Moody** thought that although intellectuals do not have much to do with economic life, they have everything to do with political life. This might be the situation on Taiwan as well. The opposition groups there seem to be basically intellectuals talking with and relating to other intellectuals. The Democracy Wall people were workers in the sense of how they made their living, but they were not a workers' movement. In Eastern Europe dissident movements have prospered when the intellectuals connect with the workers or peasants, with "real people." This is a connection that has not been made in China since the time when the communists were themselves dissidents. One reason the regime is set up the way it is, is to prevent such connections.

Democracy and Chinese Political Culture

Lucian W. Pye

The relationship of traditional cultures to democracy is an elusive matter that raises profound questions which seem to be beyond our ability to answer satisfactorily. Since democracies have emerged out of a variety of traditions, culture cannot be the determining factor. Yet, on the other hand, it is hard to identify any other factor more critical than culture. My colleague Myron Weiner has noted that the rare democracies of the Third World appear to have nothing in common--some are economically successful while others remain stagnatingly poor, some have huge populations while others are small, manageable entities--except for the cultural fact that all of them were at one time British colonies, taught in the Westminister way.[1] (But, of course, not all former British colonies are now democracies.) The importance of cultural considerations in democracy was substantiated nearly two decades ago in the classic study by Almond and Berba who discovered that what they call the "civic culture" constituted the basis of Western democracies.[2]

Thus, as we try to foresee the prospects for democracy among the heirs of the Confucian tradition, we need to keep alive a modicum of hope even as we realistically weigh the difficulties. We can take heart from the way in which Confucian Japan has become so stoutly democratic, but we must also respect the massive obstacles which that cultural tradition has raised against the ethos of responsible popular government.[3] With respect to the People's Republic of China (PRC) there are not only the burdens of a long tradition of centralized, imperial authority, but also their more recent conversion to the tenets of Marxism-Leninism-Maoism which, for all of its populist rhetoric, remains the dogma of totalitarianism.[4] As for the Chinese in Taiwan, their problem is that their authoritarian tradition has been reinforced by a permanent state of martial law and its accompanying siege mentality.[5]

It is true that pressures for change are at work on both sides of the Taiwan straits. Peking has discovered that on opening the door for technological modernization other winds of change will enter their hertofore hermetically sealed society. They are discovering that ideas about democracy are part and parcel of the world culture of modernization.[6] Sending people abroad to pick up skills has meant that some have been captivated by other ideas that could become the yeast for a modest degree of intellectual ferment. So far, however, these currents, including even the bold move to establish such a movement as China Spring, are pathetic in comparison to the lively and liberating intellectual life that awakened young Chinese in the 1920s and 30s.[7] The authorities of today in Peking are, of course, infinitely more efficient than the Kuomintang ever was when it comes to thought control.[8]

Pressures are also building up in Taiwan for greater freedom. For two decades the central focus of competition between the leaders in Taiwan and those on the mainland was in the economic and welfare realms, but now Taiwan has clearly won that competition. As the people in Taiwan have come to participate in all phases of modern life, they have become increasingly ready to try their hands at political participation.[9] Moreover, the competition with the mainland is certain to focus more and more on questions of liberty and democratic decision-making. In order to counter the enticement of Peking for peaceful reunification, the ROC leadership will have to accentuate the differences between the two societies in life styles, including, above all, political participation and electoral politics.[10]

In spite of these encouraging trends toward possible democratic development, the obstacles continue to loom large, and one should not minimize the prospects for continuity in the two political cultures. In both governments there are strong institutional forces that stubbornly resist liberalization. There are not only well entrenched bureaucracies, which instinctively strive to preserve their monopolies in decision-making, but there are also a variety of secret police and other institutions of repression which are well staffed with energetic professionals who have their careers to protect.[11]

Neither government confronts enough significant international pressure to become more democratic. Indeed, the American foreign policy emphasis on spreading democracy, which bulked large during the Japanese Occupation era and contributed to shaping Korean political development was oddly muted in Asia in the 1970s. President Carter's human rights policy was largely negated in Asia because of the U. S. government's and the American people's enthusiasm for China.[12] Americans, in rediscovering the realities of China, were quick to put a positive gloss on just about everything they saw there, even when many totalitarian actions should have been repugnant to them. The fact that many Americans, and especially government officials, could find so much good in China has meant that the human rights issue was severely compromised in Asia. Indeed, since every government in the region has a better record than the regime in Peking, it would mean going beyond the bounds of hypocrisy allowable even in diplomacy for American officials to criticize any Asian government on human rights violations.[13]

If we step back from the immediate situation and ask more basic questions about Chinese political culture, it becomes apparent that in Confucian culture there are two fundamental obstacles to the development of democracy. The first is that Confucianism, behind all its humanistic values and its extolling of moderation and the golden mean, is a quintessential authoritarian culture.[14] Confucian authoritarianism does not take the form of legitimizing brutal repression or vicious rulers. Instead, the spirit of authoritarianism in the Confucian world is elitist and one of expecting authority to be able to solve all manner of problems. It is a culture that demands deference to authority and treats any criticism of authority as totally unacceptable. Rulers should be good and virtuous, as should their subjects. Let each have his or her separate roles, and clearly officials must rule and subjects obey. Any confusion over who should be doing what becomes a source of anxiety.[15]

The second major obstacle to democratic development in Confucian culture has been the stress on the collectivity rather than on the individual. Chinese political culture assumes that all individuals are members of some larger group to which they must yield their identities. In the past, of course, it was the family and the clan that provided the basis of the collective identity. Now it is the danwei, or small group, in the PRC.[16] The danwei governs nearly every facet of life: decisions about marriage and divorce must pass its review; it determines when parents will be allowed to have a child; it governs employment and residence decisions; it looks into the political and social standards of each member; it allocates ration cards and coupons; it acknowledges no rights of privacy or individuality. In short, the danwei has become the modernized, all-enveloping "family" that treats all Chinese as its "children."

The combination of a deferential authority and collective responsibility has produced a system of control in China that is not that of cat and mouse, of cops and robbers, or of the all-seeing police and the lonely individual. Rather, it is a world of pressures for conformity in which everyone keeps an eye on everyone else. The principle of collective responsbility produces a reward system in which it is to everyone's advantage to report on the misdeeds of others.[17]

The problem of bringing democracy into such a political culture is that it involves more than just institutional changes and policy shifts. Basic attitudes, deeply instilled in the child-rearing process, make it second nature to want to have competent, self-assured authority and identification with a collectivity. To be one's own is frightening. Self-realization becomes merely the comfort of conformity.

Those who rise to positions of power have every right to expect that they will be honored by others who will defer to their superior status. Consequently, they can be extraordinarily thin-skinned even to hints of criticism, and challenges may trigger an outpouring of aggression. This is true even among the elite, for the leadership is supposed to uphold consensus and avoid factional strife. Since leaders should be disinterested in power, the result is a politics of stealth. Issues must be debated in elliptical fashion, through the use of code words and analogies. Secrecy prevails; decisions can only be publicly presented for ritualized rubber-stamping.[18]

We could go on listing the innumerable obstacles to democratic practices, but rather, let us go directly to the question of where should we look for hope. Here again we may identify two major sources: the growth of a rule of law, and the flow of international communications.

Traditionally, the Confucianists have praised rule by upright men and castigated rule by law as being impersonal, harsh, lacking in human understanding, and generally frightening--always suggesting, of course, that the object of such impersonal terror would be the common man, when in fact they must have had themselves more in mind. And for themselves they obviously preferred tolerance for human errors to strict regulations.[19] Under Communism, as under Confucianism, law could be dispensed with because of the supremacy of ideology.

Now, however, ideology in the PRC is in disarray, and the impetus exists for some degree of law, if for no other reason than the need for international commerce.[20] The pride Chinese officials seem to take in their inchoate legal system may be no more than hypocrisy, but as hypocrisy is the homage that vice pays to virtue, it can be a powerful force for progress. When the Chinese were forced to operate within a Communist system of regulations, they demonstrated that they could adapt to a society based on law. The big question is whether the erosion of ideology is going to lead to the spread of hypocrisy and cynicism. The significance of the difference was stated by Georges Bernanos, "Democracies cannot dispense with hypocrisy any more than dictatorship can with cynicsm."[21]

The impact of international communication means that Chinese society will be increasingly exposed to the values of freedom which are still a part of the world culture of modernity. The Chinese believe that they are superior people, but they are perplexed because of their difficulties with modernization. They therefore long for recognition and praise. They are gradually learning that many of the ecstatic compliments of the early visitors were superficial, and that now more critical evaluations will be coming.

As China breaks out of its isolation, its leaders will feel increasing pressures to bring the country more into line with the progressive world. As they seek to improve their country they will inevitably come face to face with the issues of liberty. The process will be slow, for China is only beginning a gradual move toward liberalization from a far more repressive condition than when the May Fourth Movement and the early idealist Communist confronted only the ineffectual rule of warlords.[22] We should keep in mind that even where conditions have been conducive to competitive politics and where there have been reasonably sizeable Chinese populations, the Chinese have tended to excel in other fields than politics. Hong Kong remains extraordinarily apolitical and Singapore has been unable or unwilling to maintain an effective opposition. For all of its great strengths in producing civil populations, the Confucian heritage has not been helpful in nurturing democratic politicians and activist citizens.

Notes

1. Presentation to the Joint Harvard–M.I.T. Faculty Seminar on Political Development, Winter 1982.

2. The original Civic Culture by Gabriel A. Almond and Sidney Verba was published by the Princeton University Press in 1963 and created lively debates as to whether the syndrome of attitudes they identified as basic to democracy might not be too close to the Anglo-American state of democracy. In response to the debate over their work the authors, in combination with country specialists and general political theorists, reanalyzed the work in a new book, The Civic Culture Revisited (Boston: Little, Brown, 1980).

3. Enthusiasts of Japanese ways in industry have looked increasingly far back into the origins of Japan's success. Some have found the beginning of the story not just with the Meiji Restoration but in the Tokagawa era, and some have gone to even earlier times. In many respects this is a revisionist version of the essence of the Pacific War, for it seems to leave out the philosophy behind Japanese imperialism. To recapture the nature of Japanese politics prior to the American occupation it is helpful to reread books which stressed the Japanese Confucian tradition, such as Robert Karl Reischauer (the brother of Professor Edwin Reischauer), Japan: Government-Politics (New York: Ronald Press, 1939).

4. It is hard to select the candidates for the best treatment of the proposition that Confucianism softened the ground for Communism, as it did for mainland China, half of Korea, and half of Vietnam. One of the best kept secrets of Asian studies is that it took a total American war effort to save Japan for democracy, a limited but wearing war effort to keep half of Korea on the democratic side, incalculable efforts to save a remnant of China on Taiwan, and, sad to admit, we failed to save any part of Confucian Vietnam. We are, however, doing right by some Vietnamese refugees.

5. An interesting example of Chinese orderliness is that when Harold Lasswell was teaching in Peking in 1935, he drafted his classic statement about the "garrison state." In retrospect, this may have been his reaction to the stifling effect of normal Confucian ways and not his response to the realities of totalitarianism to which his theories were soon to be associated.

6. The crisis over tennis player Hu Na's request for asylum has been made into a legalistic matter by the U.S. government and by the Chinese into an issue of sincerity between "friends," and, consequently, the key point that a nineteen-year-old craved autonomy and independence was dismissed by all.

7. One of the most fascinating, but ambivalent, books on modern Chinese intellectual life is Jonathan D. Spence, The Gate of Heavenly Peace (New York: Viking, 1981) which on the one hand dramatizes the vitality of the modernist Chinese thinkers of the twenties and thirties, but, on the other hand, barely makes clear that once the Communists came to power, intellectuals were smothered. For less ideologically involved people his story graphically dramatizes how far China's thinkers were to be put into a strait jacket under Communism.

8. The first generation of Western correspondents in the PRC—Fox Butterfield, Richard Bernstein, and David Bonavia—have written more factually damaging but less passionately critical works than the earlier anti-Kuomintang correspondents— Theodore White, Jack Belden, and Harold Isaacs. Unquestionably the earlier correspondents had greater freedom and more overt informants than those who now report

from a society they can barely penetrate.

9. The perverseness of the anti-liberal authorities in Taiwan was revealed in their ludicrous detention of J. Bruce Jacobs, one of the few Western scholars prepared to make a career of studying Taiwan. The head of the American Institute of Taiwan, Charles T. Cross, was able to gain the release of Professor Jacobs by spelling out to Taiwan authorities the absurdity of their welcoming to the island a conference of American scholars who would be staying at the Grand Hotel where Mr. Jacobs was being detained, thereby providing him with access to articulate spokesmen for his side of the story.

10. Whereas all the "smoke" of Peking's ire is about U.S. arms sales to Taiwan, the real issue is whether the solution of Honk Kong's future will make more or less reasonable the idea of a peaceful reunification of Taiwan and the mainland.

11. Odd as it may seem, Peking officials, including the topmost, like to whisper gleefully into American ears that Deng Xiaoping could be easily toppled by his surrounding enemies if he is pressured even slightly by American demands. Similarly on Taiwan, appeals for caution are routinely raised in the name of protecting the most rational officials. It never seems to occur to the Chinese that if their leadership is, in fact, in such dire straits it ought to be willing to pay a high price for help. Instead, they seem to believe that they are playing a strong card by trumpeting weakness.

12. In the divisive contest between Zbigniew Brzezinski and Cyrus Vance over China policy during the Carter administration, it is strange that the Vance forces could only come up with the lame argument that Washington should not offend Moscow by befriending Peking, and ignore the more telling point that Washington was offending all of the free countries of Asia by applauding totalitarian China.

13. One among many reasons why Ambassador Richard Walker has had success in liberating arrested opposition leaders in South Korea is that there is now less hypocrisy about the PRC, and hence Washington's concerns for democracy seem more convincing.

14. In John K. Fairbank's first edition of his classic book, The United States and China (Cambridge: Harvard University Press, 1955) he entitled his chapter describing traditional Chinese government "The Authoritarian Tradition," an accurate and appropriate characterization which unfortunately was in later editions toned down to "The Political Tradition," although the content remained the same.

15. In the voluminous literature on confucianism the work of Arthur F. Wright stands out, especially his edited book, The Confucian Persuasion (Stanford: Stanford University Press, 1960).

16. The best academic work on the danwei is Martin Whyte, Small Groups and Political Rituals in China (Berkeley: University of California Press, 1974). The most up-to-date description is in Richard Bernstein, From the Center of the Earth (Boston: Little, Brown, 1982).

17. The way these pressures of conformity have operated to destroy even the resilient Chinese family has been most dramatically told in Liang Heng and Judith Shapiro, Son of Revolution (Boston: Little, Brown, 1982).

18. For an excellent analysis of how inner elite debates take place see: Merle Goldman, China's Intellectuals; Advise and Dissent (Cambridge: Harvard University Press, 1981).

19. For the best description of the paralysis of the Chinese bureaucracy because every official favored ritual and propriety over law and policy see, Ray Huang, 1587: A Year of No Significance (New Haven; Yale University Press, 1981).

20. Former Harvard professor, Jerold Cohen, has been instrumental in helping China devise a new commercial code, and he has been cautiously optimistic about the possible spread of a rule of law in the PRC.

21. Nous autres Francais (We French).

22. Harold Isaacs, who constantly described the crude repressions of the Kuomintang in the 1930s, now finds it troublesome that people overlook the even more total repression in today's China. See his review of One Day in China: May 21, 1936, translated, edited and introduced by Sherman Cochran and Andrew C. K. Hsieh, with the assistance of Janice Cochran (New Haven: Yale University Press, 1983) in the New York Review of Books, forthcoming in May.

COMMENTS AND DISCUSSION

After summarizing the paper **Gastil** recalled Pye's contention that neither Taiwan nor the PRC confronted significant international pressure to become democratic. This implied that if they had more international pressure they might be more likely to become democratic. This is an interesting hypothesis. Some have suggested it is not true, that reaction to international pressure might have a negative result. Equally significant was Pye's point that because recent United States administrations have been unwilling to criticize the human rights performance of the People's Republic, they cannot credibly criticize the performance of other East Asian states such as South Korea, Taiwan, or the Philippines. He is saying here we should be more critical; he also suggests the communists will now expect more criticism from the West. This seems to contradict other papers and comments by the conferees.

Gastil also questioned Pye's claim that all Chinese see themselves as members of a larger group to which they must yield their identity: Self-realization becomes the comfort of conformity. This just does not fit with the idea of Daoist retreat. Surely the retreat is not the comfort of conformity; it is surely not throwing your identity away for the group.

Grieder pointed out it was all very well to say, and probably quite true, that much of the early reporting on recent China--the Roger Garside-John Fraser phase of reporting in the late 1970s-- was favorable. Now we are coming to realize the real situation. But just because reporting is now more negative does not mean it is any less superficial than before.

Smith thought that Pye's mention of the danwei should be developed further. He refers to it incorrectly as a small group. The danwei that really counts is often large. **Dreyer** asked if it was not usually translated "work unit." **Smith** agreed, but danwei as used in Chinese might sometimes refer to a large group--an entire enterprise, for example, or a province or a city would be one's danwei. One of the most important developments in Communist China has been the development of the danwei as a kind of universal form of party, social, and political organization. It cuts across from the former commune right across to large industrial, commercial, or military units. In cities it used to be they would ask where one is from, but now they say, "Shema danwei?" It is not just a bureaucratic question. It is how a person is placed. It has tremendous implications. Deng Xiaoping has every day to deal with many independent danwei that are comparable to interest groups. Strong interest groups are a new thing in China. Now there are these very strongly entrenched groups. The lobbying efforts of cities and provinces have been stepped up enormously.

The discussion then turned to an analysis of what danwei really signified. **Smith** gave as a synonym the military term "outfit": this could mean, for example, the marines, a particular battalion, or a company, depending on the context. He saw danwei as more a psychological identification than a formal term.

Dreyer added that the level one chooses to identify oneself with depended on what the person chose to be a part of. It also depends on to whom one is speaking. If both parties are in the air force, for example, the answer would be much more specific.

Seymour pointed out that in China everything is in one great tree with units within units, all coming together at the top. Depending on to whom one is talking, one refers to the leaf or the twig or the branch.

However, Seymour also saw it as a quite formal term. **Grieder** added that realistically, if a person is stopped on the street by a Chinese policeman, one of the first things he asks is what your danwei is. The policeman means the person's immediate occupational group. **Liang** mentioned three formal aspects. First, salaries are received from one's **danwei**. Your hukou, or residence permit, is in your danwei. If you want to go to Peking or Shanghai, you must get certification from your danwei. In the village, danwei refers to the brigade or team, but for those like his grandmother who receive no salary, the danwei is less clear.

Gastil found it hard to mesh this discussion of danwei with the idea of a pressure group.

Smith agreed that from the individual point of view the danwei was your occupational group. The model for this as the communist system evolved was probably military, the outfit, rather than anything pre-existing in Chinese civil society. But from the Deng Xiaoping point of view, there is another set of danwei which involves differential use of resources by different units in the society. The whole air force can be a danwei, and in this sense the whole air force is an organized pressure group with its own identity and relative power. In this sense China becomes a pluralistic system. It is difficult for Deng Xiaoping to really give an order and be sure it will be done. He has to use his guanxi (connections), too.

Smith continued, that by the bureaucratic rule where your file is is your danwei. It may in the case of peasants be very rudimentary. Also if the person was to do anything outside this unit, they would have to get permission.

Grieder suggested that evidently one could use the term danwei to explicitly describe a particular level or unit, but also use it metaphorically. **Smith** agreed and said it was often used metaphorically.

Sullivan doubted this, and also suggested that not all danwei appear on charts; and some that are do not function as real danwei. **Smith** added that local elections were generally below the level of a full danwei. For example, a worker in a factory, his face-to-face group of co-workers is the unit for election, but the whole factory is his danwei. (**Landman** doubted this.)

Kintner wondered if Smith agreed with Pye that the danwei was an obstacle to democracy because of the psychological pressure on the individual. **Smith** thought it worked both ways. The danwei was required to provide service for the individual; it was also a mechanism for social control.

Moody thought Pye's citation of Martin Whyte's book about small groups was misleading because danwei is not a normal translation of small group. The small group would be something else. It is the **xiaozu** in which criticism and self-criticism takes place.

Smith thought the xiaozu is now largely of party significance. In most enterprises it is pretty much a sham. **Liang** said it was mostly to collect people together for political studies. We read People's Daily, the party magazine, and sleep.

Turning to another topic, **Sullivan** remarked that Pye's picture of the political culture was very different from Moody's. He had always been surprised that Pye and others who consider themselves very anti-Marxist often make a deterministic analysis, not economic in their case, but cultural. Specific cultures are linked to specific political systems so that culture becomes the base and politics the superstructure. This is just a little too tight. The way Moody began his paper was much more comforting. There are many things in Japanese culture that are in Chinese culture. They are both very authoritarian. Yet Japan did not become a democracy simply because it was imposed on them. What happened in the 1930s was more a copy of European fascism than traditional Japan. You have to look at the thirties in the context of the international system. If international politics had been radically different in the 1930s, the Japanese pattern of development would have been different, too. (See the writings of Berger and others on Japanese political parties at that time.) Read Scalapino's book on party politics in the 1950s and 1960s: although Japan probably had more authoritarian characteristics than it does now, it still supported a democratic system. He described the patron-client relation as fairly tight. Entire neighborhoods voted as one just to meet the needs of the patron.

What seems a more challenging task is to show the way a variety of cultures can end up with democracy--coincidental with it, neither causing it nor opposing it. Cultures are not irrelevant, the tie is just not that tight.

As a final point, Pye's statement on page 237 that Confucian culture demands deference to authority and treats any criticism of authority as totally unacceptable, is simply untrue. We can look at the evolution of the imperial censorate to see that criticism was actually built into the bureaucratic system--again much more tightly and in different ways than in the West. If one reads much of the anthropological work on Chinese families, one will see many exceptions. **Dreyer** seconded Sullivan's remarks. If anyone had any doubts he or she should read Ray Huang's book, 1587 A Year of No Significance. Not only does Huang talk about censors being extremely critical, but about the situation created when the Emperor expressed his desire to make his third son the heir instead of the first-born. This was legally possible, but the officials grumbled about it so much that he was unable to do it. One feels very sorry for the Emperor being set upon by these people throughout the year telling him what to do and what not to do. Other high officials were also thrown out of office by the same forces.

Sullivan noted that Professor Bartlett, who is at Harvard this year doing work on the Qing, finds the same thing, even Qian Long and Han Shi on any number of occasions tried to force certain things through but were blocked.

Grieder suggested that political opposition and bureaucratic obstructionism are different things. Things ground to a halt in 1587 because the Emperor was being frustrated in his choice of an heir. His way of getting back was not to do anything. When he did nothing, nothing could be done. The bureaucracy could not end run the Emperor.

Moody said it was characteristic of the structure of government. Under Confucianism the ruler in fact was supposed to solicit criticism. The other side of this is that there was no institutional protection for the critics. The job of the censorate was primarily to check the behavior of other lower-ranking officials. But part of their responsibility was to defy the emperor to his face when he was wrong. Of course, the censor was taking dreadful risks in doing so. There was no personal immunity to jailing, torture, and execution. (**Sullivan** added that the censor could also be executed for failing to criticize.) **Moody** thought it was a moralistic idea on both sides, which Pye brings out. Politics was incorporated into morals, so the emperor was supposed to be good and to listen to criticism, yet there was no absolute check.

Kintner wondered what might be the philosophical basis for the communist criticism of Confucius; in many ways it seems he should be quite useful to them.

Moody answered that to him Confucianism teaches that there are certain things that just cannot be done by rulers or anybody. There are limits on power. There is order. The communists see this as a feudal notion supporting the role of the exploiting classes.

Dreyer said that on the surface it appeared as though Confucianism might help. During the more radical phases of the cultural revolution the people were told it was the peasants who create, and there is no role for the entrepreneur and businessman, which Confucius would have totally agreed with. But the opposition to Confucius is too deep-seated; it is the legacy of what happened in the nineteenth century, which was very real in the minds of people like Mao and Chu De. The view was that China had fallen on very bad times. It was being humiliated by the West and not able to cope with various internal barbarians. Many decided Confucianism was at fault. It was sitting like a mountain oppressing the Chinese people. We are now talking of the 1910s and 1920s, the period of the May 4th Movement. The family system seemed very oppressive. It was something the people wanted to get rid of. At this point, twenty or thirty years after the communist revolution, it is almost impossible to resuscitate Confucius, despite the ways in which he might help.

Liang disagreed. Among the masses, Daoism and Buddhism are stronger traditionally than Confucionsism. Confucianism is the intellectuals' literary culture. The numbers who believed in it were always very few. Daoism and Buddhism have greatly helped the communists--peasants believe in fate, and wuwei, "no action is action'' (Daoism). Chairman Mao said himself in his book, Investigation Into the Peasant Movement in Hunan, that the Revolution cannot depend on the peasants. It depends on the liu mang (vagabonds), their black society. Whenever the peasants rebelled it was not the peasants themselves but the "black society," some gentry, that led them to rebel.

Dreyer agreed, but pointed out that the people who led the May 4th Movement were outspoken in their opposition to Confucianism. The novels of Ba Jin rail against Confucius. We should also remember Mao's criticism of the Eight-Legged Essays, and the oppressive family system that forced women into arranged marriages at a very young age. These were criticisms of Confucianism.

Pluralism in the People's Republic of China: The Interaction between Beijing and the Minorities

June Teufel Dreyer

Background.

China's fifty-five officially recognized ethnic minorities comprise a scant 6.7 percent of the population of the People's Republic of China (PRC). Only fifteen have populations exceeding one million, and relatively few minorities have educational levels or living standards comparable to that of the country's majority group, the Han Chinese. Yet the Chinese Communist Party (CCP) and government have devoted efforts and resources to the minorities in a manner disproportionate to their share of the population. The factors underlying this concern with what PRC media refer to as "the nationalities question" may be subsumed under the headings strategic, demographic, economic, and propagandistic.

Strategic: Most of the PRC's minorities live near the country's land borders, which frequently divide ethnic groups arbitrarily. There is considerable dispute over the precise location of these borders, and each side has attempted to manipulate cross-border tensions to its own advantage, particularly when the border demarcation is contested by a country hostile to the PRC. The PRC's ability to do this successfully is heavily dependent on the loyalty of its own minority population.

Demographic: Despite their rather small numbers, minorities inhabit a rather large proportion of China's land mass, estimated at between fifty to sixty percent of the total. While this figure is misleading in that it includes areas which are unsuitable for human habitation, other areas have been deemed capable of absorbing emigrants from Han China's more densely populated areas.

Economic: Areas traditionally inhabited by minority groups include several that are rich in natural resources, including fossil fuels, precious metals, and timber. In addition, eighty percent of the PRC's meat, milk, and wool-producing animals come from nationalities areas. The proper exploitation of these resources could significantly help the success of China's modernization program.

Progadanda: The CCP has maintained that its particular interpretation of Communist ideology has applicability for other, non-Chinese states. The existence of prosperous, content, non-Han ethnic groups bettering their lives according to the Chinese variant of socialism would be an important argument in favor of the PRC's claims.

Several reasons conspired to produce a policy of relative leniency in the treatment of minority groups. First, Marxist ideology holds that nationality differences and antagonisms are the result of class exploitation in previous social orders, and will gradually wither out of existence under the new order. Second, the CCP had come to power basically through its victories in Han areas. Very few minority group members were CCP members, and the Party was well aware of its ignorance of the customs and habits of many minority groups, and of the apprehension and hostility with which many of these groups viewed the communist government. And third, the CCP was very much influenced by the Soviet model of nationalities policy. During the high point of Sino-Soviet friendship in the early 1950s, the USSR sent advisers to guide the PRC in many aspects of state building, including devising policies for the minority nationalities. These advisers were themselves heavily influenced by Soviet policies, which had been developed in a country where minorities totalled nearly half of the population, and in which many minorities enjoyed a standard of living and educational levels that equalled or even exceeded that of the dominant ethnic group. While the reality of Stalin's policies toward minorities was frequently cruel, the theory of these policies was decidedly tolerant of ethnic minorities. It was the theory rather than the reality that Soviet advisers imparted to their Chinese hosts.

Thus influenced by an ideology that envisioned a largely effortless withering away of ethnic antagonisms, a concern that ignorance might lead the Party to commit blunders in minorities areas that would be detrimental to Party goals, and presented with a ready-made socialist model of nationalities policy, it is scarcely surprising that the CCP opted for a basically pluralistic policy which allowed considerable flexibility in its dealings with ethnic minorities.

The most obvious example of this pluralism is the granting of autonomous status to areas in which minority groups are concentrated. The largest of these designated autonomous regions had an administrative status equal to that of provinces. Areas where there were smaller concentrations of minorities were able to form autonomous counties or prefectures. The areas granted autonomous status were to conduct government business in the language of the host minority, and were required to have a certain minimum percentage of minority group members in the organs of government. The leaders of certain minority groups, including the governments of Xinjiang and Tibet, were able to make special arrangements safeguarding their positions even before these regions had formally been accorded autonomous status.

While there were no provisions made for financial autonomy in the original scheme, amendments allowing for a somewhat more flexible use of funds in minority areas were added later. In fact, the central government has generally underwritten the budgets of minority areas; there has been a net capital transfer from China's wealthier provinces into the minorities areas. In extreme cases, such as Tibet, this can involve over seventy-five percent of the area's budget.

Whether or not minority group members lived in autonomous areas, they were given the right to be educated in their own languages, promised government help in developing these languages, and given exemptions from certain provisions of the marriage law, permission to slaughter animals on certain festival days, and other privileges in recognition of what the official media referred to as minorities' "special characteristics."

Relevance of Minorities Policy to the Encouragement of Democracy in the PRC.

It has been argued that the special privileges and dispensations granted to minorities, and in particular the autonomous area system, may provide a conduit for the liberalization of China as a whole. The theory is also frequently advanced that the autonomous area system can provide an administrative model for the incorporation of Taiwan into the PRC.

While these possibilities are intriguing, my personal opinion is that neither is very likely. Special exemptions given minorities in recognition of their special characteristics could not be generalized to large groups of people without jeopardizing the government's social and economic programs. Allowing early marriage and exempting all Chinese from the restrictions of the birth control campaign, for example, would clearly wreak havoc with Beijing's development plans. Similarly, permitting lavish holiday celebrations involving the loss of several days work in field or factory, and the consumption of unnecessarily large quantities of scarce foodstuffs would not be feasible for the population as a whole.

Minorities can be granted privileges only because they represent a rather small proportion of the population, yet one whose anger and resentments might cause more trouble for the government's strategic, demographic, economic, and propaganda goals than the cost of the relatively small privileges and exemptions they have been granted. Minorities that are annoyed at restrictions against large families may accuse the host government of genocidal motives; those prohibited the use of their language and practice of their religion will protest against what they regard as forced assimilation. They are likely to retaliate by seeking support from external powers and international organizations, by acts of violence against Han Chinese immigrants in their areas, and by sabotaging agricultural and industrial production.

In effect, then, the PRC government's policies attempt to "buy off" the minority nationalities. However, given the virtually certain continuation of overpopulation and economic scarcities in the PRC, there is little chance that these policies can be extended to the population as a whole.

The autonomous area system presents a more plausible framework for the liberalization of China. Nonetheless, as they have functioned in the past and present, the autonomous areas do not serve their avowed purpose of making minorities "masters in their own homes." Their leaders are chosen in Beijing and removed from Beijing. They are not responsible to constituencies in the areas they theoretically represent, nor do they usually speak for the interests of these areas at the central government level.

The state constitution adopted in December 1982,[1] arguably the most liberal China has had, provides that the administrative head of an autonomous region, prefecture, or county shall be a citizen of the nationality, or one of the nationalities, exercising regional autonomy in the area concerned. This is a stipulation not contained in any previous state constitution, and may be considered an advance for minority nationalities. Yet it should be noted that the real power in China lies not in the government, but in the Party. And the Party constitution adopted in September 1982[2] is silent on the matter of representation of minorities in the higher echelons of administration, as have been all previous Party constitutions. At present, none of the First Party Secretaries of the five autonomous regions is a member of the host nationality. All except Tibet have had First Party Secretaries of minority nationalities at various times in the past, but each has been of a sort likely to be described as an "Uncle Tom"--a long-time party stalwart with little connection with the language and customs of his forebears.

The 1982 state constitution also gives autonomous areas the power to enact regulations on autonomy and specific regulations in light of the political, economic, and cultural characteristics of the nationality or nationalities concerned. However, these regulations must be submitted to the Standing Committee of the National People's Congress--a body in which the enacting nationality will inevitably be greatly outnumbered--before the regulations can go into effect. So far, the Chinese press has reported modifications of national laws being passed by Xinjiang[3] and Tibet.[4] These are quite innocuous: Xinjiang has legislated a supplement to the national marriage law allowing a slightly lower minimum age for marriage and exemption from birth control regulations. Both are to apply only to minority peoples within the region.

In Tibet, the People's Congress has passed three bills, the first modifying the national marriage law, the second changing the law governing election of deputies to local people's congresses, and the third amending the PRC's laws on trial procedure. The marriage law supplement is similar to Xinjiang's, the election law allows for a deputy to be elected for a smaller number of people than in Han China, in recognition of Tibet's large area and sparse population, and the trial law stipulates that courts must have at least one judge of local nationality on the bench. All of these simply formalize practices that were already common, and both Xinjiang's and Tibet's legislation was passed before the constitution gave them the formal right to do so. Whether Beijing's recently introduced policy on curbing births in minority areas[5] will nullify Xinjiang's and Tibet's laws on exemptions from birth control remains to be seen.

The 1982 constitution contains no right to self-determination. It does give autonomous areas the power to administer their own finances. However, with the majority of the areas' budgets being provided from Beijing, it is doubtful that there is much local initiative exercised in the allocation of funds. In several instances, including the Karamai oil fields in Xinjiang and the Hulusitai coal mines of Inner Mongolia, potentially very lucrative installations are under central government rather than regional control.

Moreover, rights granted by the constitution are not necessarily rights that can be exercised. For example, the provisions for bilingualism in the deliberations of government and the work of the courts are often ignored on the grounds that they are expensive and time-consuming. During the Hundred Flowers campaign of 1956-57 minorities complained that they had "many rights in theory but few in practice" and that the autonomous area system was a farce that was "as useful as ears on a basket." These charges were made during a time when policy toward minorities was quite tolerant and allowed a relatively high degree of pluralism. During periods of ideological extremism, most notably the Great Leap Forward and the Cultural Revolution, policies were radically assimilationist, and there was far more repression of minorities' languages and cultures. During the Cultural Revolution, radicals demanded the abolition of the autonomous area system, arguing that it encouraged "national splittism" and the perpetuation of differences among ethnic groups. The fact that their efforts failed to bring about the demise of the autonomous area system does not preclude a group with similar opinions from raising the issue successfully at some future time.

The Relevance of the Autonomous Area System to Taiwan.

It is frequently suggested that the autonomous area system might be a means to solve the issue of the reunification of China. The most frequent parallel mentioned by Western media is between Taiwan and Tibet, and the PRC has for years made a point of beaming news about Tibet to Taiwan. A common theme of these broadcasts was how Tibetans, despite differences between their social system and that of Han China, were benefiting from the provisions of the autonomous area system and from the benign help of the Party to progress toward prosperity.

Apart from the general problems of lack of autonomy associated with the autonomous area system which were discussed above, Tibet is a particularly poor example with which to entice Taiwan. After its tiny, ill-equipped army was defeated by a PRC force, the theocratic government of Tibet entered into negotiations with China. Under threat of further invasion, the Tibetans finally signed, in 1951, an agreement which appeared to provide numerous guarantees for the area.[6] In return for surrendering control of its foreign relations to the PRC and agreeing to have its military absorbed into the People's Liberatin Army (PLA), Tibetans were assured that the existing political system would not be altered, that the established status, functions, and powers of the Dalai and Panchen lamas would remain unchanged, and that there would be freedom of religion and no change in the income of the monastaries.

An uneasy period then followed in which the PRC authorities, convinced they were acting in the name of progress and national unity, tried to circumvent and undermine the 1951 agreement. At the same time, the local government of Tibet, equally convinced that the PRC authorities' intentions were malevolent and subversive, maneuvered to block their reforms. Tempers rose, and in March 1959, there was an armed uprising against Chinese rule.

The PRC put down the revolt without undue difficulty and instituted sweeping reforms in Tibet's economic, political, and social structure, in contravention of the 1951 agreement. The PRC's argument that the rebellion in effect invalidated the 1951 agreement and relieved the Chinese government of any obligations incurred thereunder has a certain plausibility. However, one can easily imagine another scenario, in which revolt is provoked by the central government with the explicit intent of invalidating a treaty it no longer wished to be bound by.

It is less easy to accept what happened in the mid-1970's, when the Chinese government insisted that Tibetans plant wheat rather than the barley that they prefer to eat.[7] The region's autonomous status and the wishes of its inhabitants notwithstanding, wheat was planted. The result was ecological disaster: initially good yields fell sharply as the soil became depleted of essential nutrients.[8] Near-starvation conditions prevailed for several years. The PRC government later rescinded its directives on wheat-growing and instituted compensatory policies.[9] However, the constitution provides no guarantees that residents of autonomous areas will be able to forestall the implementation of other unwanted or inappropriate policies.

Perhaps because of the PRC government's realization that its record in Tibet is unlikely to appeal to many residents of Taiwan, the PRC no longer seems to regard Tibet as a model for the incorporation of the island. It has thus devised another arrangement, the special administrative region. According to article 31 of the 1982 state constitution, the state may establish these regions "when necessary." Official spokespersons made it clear that the new arrangements were enacted for the express purpose of incorporating Taiwan, Hong Kong, and Macao into the PRC. How the special admnistrative regions would actually be administered appears to depend mainly on the will of the central government. Broadcasts beamed from Beijing to Taiwan have indicated that Taiwan's current socioeconomic systems, its way of life, and its economic and cultural relations with other countries will remain unchanged. The island has also been promised approximately one hundred delegates to the National People's Congress.[10]

However, it is only "after the country is reunified [that] the systems to be instituted on Taiwan shall be prescribed in the light of its specific conditions."[11] The nature of what systems these would be will depend heavily on the central government's interpretation of the term "specific conditions." Article 64 of the 1982 constitution provides that statutes and resolutions are adopted by a majority vote of more than one-half of the deputies to the National People's Congress; it would clearly be impossible for Taiwan's one hundred-odd delegates to prevent the over three-thousand-member National People's Congress from passing amendments modifying its economic and social status. Alternatively, the PRC could simply adopt a new constitution, as it has done several times in the past,[12] deleting any provisions for special administrative regions.

In an ironic twist of the previous practice of regarding Tibet as a model for the incorporation of Taiwan into the PRC, representatives of the Dalai Lama petitioned Beijing to allow Tibet the same treatment as Taiwan. The Chinese government's reply stressed that since Tibet had been liberated for over thirty years and had carried out various socialist reforms, the provisions being made for Taiwan were inapplicable to it.[13] This aroused suspicions that the PRC saw its provisions for a special status for Taiwan as transitory, and that the PRC's promises to Taiwan in 1981-1982 meant little more than had the strikingly similar promises it made to Tibet in 1951-1952.[14]

Evolution Toward Greater Pluralism?---An Assessment.

Thus it would seem that neither the autonomous area system nor the special administrative regions presently provides a means of introducing genuine pluralism into the PRC's governing system. The rights that are given to each are heavily circumsbribed, and may be taken away if they are exercised more vigorously than suits the central government, or if Party policy should change. It is conceivable that, as the acute ideological phase of the Chinese revolution passes and the country's political and economic systems become more routinized, the autonomous areas and--if they actually come into being--the special administrative regions, will evolve in the direction of certain rights and freedoms being habitually accorded to their inhabitants. Their leaders would then be in a position to make demands on the central government, giving rise to a situation which, if not precisely democratic, would at least involve competing centers of power and diminish the ability of the Beijing government to force inappropriate and unwanted policy decision on its subordinate units.

Such evolution would almost certainly have to take place within the context of an overall liberalization of the Chinese communist system. There is little evidence that this is taking place. After an initial period of liberalization in 1978, restrictions have been gradually reintroduced, including the closing of Democracy Wall and the deletion of the so-called "Four Freedoms" from the Constitution--the rights to "speak out freely, air views freely, hold great debates, and write big-character posters."

Many of the critics of the Party and government who emerged during the brief period of liberalization have been imprisoned. A few continue to be active, working at great peril to themselves, their families, and their friends. But non seems to have taken up the cause of the minorities, not even to the modest extent that Russian dissidents have expressed sympathy for the oppressed ethnic groups of the Soviet Union. One reason may be the relatively smaller number of minority peoples in China as opposed to the USSR. A second may be the fact that most of the PRC's dissidents, or at least those who come to Westerners' attention, tend to live in major urban areas while most minorities live in remote frontier areas. With many injustices to protest, it is understandable that the dissidents choose those issues that are nearest to them.

These first two reasons could easily change, as public opinion "discovers" the cause of the minorities. A third reason, however, will not change, and is likely to permanently impede the development of Han sympathy for the cause of minorities. It is that in the areas where minorities and Han live in close proximity, they must compete for scarce land and other resources. Given the resistance to China's recent draconian birth control campaign, which might best be described as "too much and too late," there are apt to be still more people competing for finite amounts of land and other resources in the future. There were demonstrations in Inner Mongolia in late 1981 in protest against Han immigration, with the central government eventually agreeing that the autonomous region could accept no more newcomers.[15]

In other instances, the government's decision has not been so easy, since a solution with justice for all is elusive. As a case in point, in 1980 a Han Chinese soldier shot and killed a Uygur civilian who was trespassing on PLA land. Uygurs, who would doubtless argue that the land had been stolen from them in the first place, rioted in protest. The Beijing government appealed for calm and, to show its good intentions, announced that the soldier would be tried for murder. At this point, the army revolted, seizing a local Party headquarters.[16]

One can imagine other, similar scenarios occurring in the future, with Han Chinese tending to side with Han and minorities with minorities. Interestingly, when, also in 1980, there was fighting in another part of Xinjiang between Uygurs and young Han Chinese who had emigrated from Shanghai, there were sympathy riots in several areas in Xinjiang in support of the Uygurs,[17] and in Shanghai in support of the emigrants.[18] Under the conditions of scarcity that are likely to characterize the forseeable future, it is unlikely that Chinese public opinion will espouse the cause of minority rights. In fact, minorities may come to be regarded as nuisances to be moved aside in the name of economic progress.

Nor can one easily imagine the government granting meaningful additional rights to minorities in the future. Ethnic minorities in many parts of the world, including China, have argued that they should be granted the right to self-determination. In the PRC, many groups would probably choose not to exercise it. Indeed, given the large number of Han immigrants that have entered most minority areas except Tibet[19] since 1949, the host nationality is likely to be outvoted by the Han.[20]

But those who did choose to exercise their rights to self-determination could cause considerable problems for the Beijing government. The secession of relatively small numbers of people in isolated pockets of China would produce economically unviable units, unless the inhabitants devised ways to survive that involved permitting practices forbidden under the laws of the PRC. The Beijing government would surely not wish to tolerate this situation. Nor, in light of China's precarious financial condition, could it tolerate the loss of areas with potentially lucrative natural resources. The loss of larger areas such as Tibet and Xinjiang, where pressure for separatism would surely be strong, could not be permitted for strategic reasons.

The issue of self-determination aside, the government will also be unlikely to permit any meaningful degree of self-government to minority areas, feeling that local leaders might use it to establish contacts with outside powers. The specter of Tibetans colluding with India in support of the latter's claims on the Sino-Indian border, or Xinjiang's more than six-million Turkic Muslims establishing independent contacts with the Soviet Union or the international Islamic movement is reason enough to deny further rights to these areas. Minorities who were granted greater ability to govern their own areas might also seek to deny the use of valuable local resources to the Chinese central government, or use the control of these resources as a bargaining chip to gain still further concessions from the central government. Clearly this is not a situation the central government would wish to encourage.

As to what role the United States might play in encouraging the development of more liberal minorities' policies in China, the options are limited. Few governments appreciate foreign interference in their internal affairs, and the Chinese government is more sensitive than most on this issue.[21] The Chinese would doubtless point out that they are in no need of advice from a country whose attempts to solve its own minorities problems have fallen as short of success as have those of the United States. This should not intimidate the United States to the extent of not speaking out against major violations of human rights in China, but we should remember that the PRC has legitimate security and other concerns about foreign subversion in these areas. Strident American attempts to change Chinese policy toward minorities areas may convince the PRC government that the United States is a party to these subversive activities. This may lead to increased restrictions on minorities, thus working against the ends our policies aim at achieving.

The United States should recognize the value of the demonstration effect that its own domestic human rights policies may have on Chinese who come to know this country through recently opened channels of communication. It should strive to improve its own practice of democracy, to point up as sharply as possible the contrast between reality and the charges Chinese progaganda have made against the human rights record of the United States.

These suggestions aside, Americans must recognize that, despite their genuine desire to encourage pluralism in the PRC, the ability of the United States to influence the Chinese situation is limited. In the final analysis, democracy in China must be developed by the Chinese.

Notes

1. Text in Beijing Review(BR) 25.52(27 Dec 1982): 10–29.

2. Text in BR 25.38 (20 Sept 1982): 8–21.

3. U.S. Department of Commerce, Foreign Broadcast Information Service: China (FBIS-CHI), 17 Dec 1980, p. T/5.

4. FBIS-CHI, 30 Oct 1981, pp. Q/1–Q/2.

5. Christopher Wren, "China Cuts Births of Its Minorities," The New York Times, 10 Feb. 1983, p. 4.

6. The text of this agreement may be found in Tibet: 1950–1967, Hong Kong, Union Research Institute, 1968, pp. 19–23.

7. "How Can Winter Wheat Planted on the Tibetan Plateau Provide a High Yield?" New China News Agency (NCNA) Beijing, 4 June 1974 in FBIS-CHI, 10 June 1974, pp. J/3–J/5.

8. Lhasa Radio, 29 Nov 1979 in FBIS-CHI, 4 Dec 1979, pp. Q/2–Q/4; see also David Bonavia, "Mistakes on The Roof of the World," Far Eastern Economic Review, 8 Aug 1980, pp. 15–16.

9. "New Economic Policy for Tibet," BR 23.27 (7 July 1980), p. 4.

10. Liu Wei, "Random Talk," 24 Jan 1983 in FBIS-CHI, 26 Jan 83, pp. U/1–U/3.

11. Liu Wei, pp. U/1–U/3.

12. China has had one proto-constitution, the "General Program," plus four state constitutions and the same number of Party constitutions since 1949.

13. "Policy Toward Dalai Lama," BR 25.46 (15 Nov. 1982):3.

14. See the prepared statement of Dr. Hungdah Chiu to the U. S. House of Representatives, Committee on Foreign Relations, Subcommittee on Asian and Pacific Affairs, Hearing on Sino-American Relations Eleven Years After the Shanghai Communique, 28 Feb. 1983.

15. Beijing, China Daily, 8 Oct. 1981, p. 3.

16. Several different accounts of this incident have appeared in print. See for example Hong Kong, Cheng Ming, 1 July 1981, in U. S. Department of Commerce, Joint Publications Research Service (JPRS) 78873 (1 Sept 1981), p. 24.

17. Cheng Ming, 1 May 1981 in JPRS 78505 (14 July 1981), pp. 106–113; Cheng Ming, 1 June 1981 in JPRS 78576 (22 July 1981), pp. 66–77.

18. Hong Kong, South China Morning Post, 4 April 1981, p. 5.

19. Tibet's forbidding climate and precarious food/population balance are the major deterrents to large-scale Han immigration, not the Beijing government's concern for the area's ethnic or cultural integrity.

20. One can imagine certain scenarios in which portions of the Han population might vote with ethnic minorities for secession, with the understanding that they play a leading part in the post-independence phase of the new state, or, if they are unwilling immigrants, with the understanding that they be allowed to return to their native places. None of these would appeal to the Beijing government.

21. The PRC media, not practicing what they preach about noninterference, frequently rail out against the "inhuman" treatment of Blacks, Hispanics, and Indians in the United States.

To her paper **Dreyer** added that at the relatively open twelfth session of the Fourth Party Conference only a few minority complaints were heard. One example was by a Mongol delegate who criticized the placing of a coal mine in the Mongol area.

She also pointed out that many of the so-called nationality leaders were actually very far removed from their people. Some such as Seypidin and Ulanhu speak their national languages little, if at all.

In answer to a question on the historical claim of China to Tibet, Dreyer replied that Tibet is said to be a part of China at various periods in history. Those periods center around the Qing dynasty (Manchu) and Yuan (Mongol). The Tibetans say they never belonged to China, but that they had specific agreements with Qing and Yuan emperors who were not Chinese. She did not want to take sides on this question. **Seymour** said that the other side was that at other times Chinese dynasties, for example the Tang, recognized Tibet as independent. **Grieder** and **Smith** questioned whether this meant tributary or equal.

Dreyer added that during the Tang period the Tibetans marched into the Chinese capital and took it over. Then they were more than equal. This gave the Chinese a marvelous idea: to send a Tang dynasty princess to Tibet to convert the Tibetans to Buddhism. However, the Tibetans claim it was a Nepalese princess that did the converting. At any rate the Tibetans were never as warlike again. Dreyer said she had carefully followed the democracy movement's proclamations and found none referring to the nationalities. **Seymour** replied that one of the nineteen points in the famous declaration on the Democracy Wall was about the national minorities; considering the population ratio, one out of nineteen was not too bad. He also noted that Wei Jingsheng's girlfriend is Tibetan (although Wei has not written on this subject). **Dreyer** said she had seen little literature in the movement supporting minorities. Protests in Inner Mongolia did lead in late

1981 to government agreement to send no more immigrants--although
the Mongolians were already outnumbered about five to one.

In answer to a question, **Dreyer** said that the Soviet Turkic
areas were less Russified than the equivalent areas in China were
Sinified. The standard of living on the Soviet side also is much
higher than in China, perhaps even higher than in European Russia.
Zhu thought the standard of living in Xinjiang and other areas was
much higher than in other areas of rural China.

Liang agreed that the dissidents had mentioned in their articles almost nothing about the minorities. Wei Jingsheng's girlfriend is Tibetan, as Seymour mentioned. Her father was a high
party leader in Beijing. He was then placed in the Qincheng jail
as a result of political struggles. That was why Wei Jingsheng's
article mentioned the jail.

There are some minority dissidents, especialy from religious
groups, for example, the Hui (Muslims of the Chinese race). While
he was in Yunnan province for a month, he met the Hui people in
Kunming. They see themselves as religious dissidents. For minorities, religion is a weapon against communist thought. Their
leaders do not hate the Han Chinese; they hate the government
because the communist government destroyed their religion. So
this is why they want to build their organization.

Zhu thought that before the Cultural Revolution Chinese government policies toward minority peoples were not too bad. Little
was heard of these problems. There were problems within the
minority groups themselves. In Xinjiang and Inner Mongolia he
thought the government had been helpful. Zhu asked if the government had seriously attacked religion before the cultural revolution. **Dreyer** answered that it was heavily attacked during the
Great Leap Forward. **Liang** added that before the cultural revolution, the religious leaders who disliked the communist party were
sent to Qincheng jail. **Moody** and **Dreyer** mentioned several Muslim
rebellions in the 1950s.

Gastil wondered if dissidents were to emphasize, as they have
for example in the Soviet Union, the problems of minority areas,
such as Tibet or Xinjiang, would this hurt the cause of the dissidents with the Chinese people as a whole? If the dissidents
started talking about the rights of such minorities to self-
determination what would be the effect? Would it diminish their
audience?

Landman guessed it would; she had found considerable disdain,
if not contempt, towards the minorities among the Han. If the Han
dissidents were to express support for the minorities, they could

turn off quite a few people. She also thought it worked the other way. Minorities who are fighting for their culture or religion are also not going to unite with the Han because of the hostility.

Seymour felt that for foreigners to take up the cause of the ethnic minorities was particularly sensitive. He had often been accused of attempting to divide China. But Chinese dissidents might not be quite so open to criticism on this ground. **Gastil** added that the United States recently cancelled its Radio Liberty program to the Uygur people of Central Asia, for budgetary reasons, and conflicting priorities. **Dreyer** said that it is claimed the Uygurs can readily understand other Turkic languages. **Smith** said the program was specifically aimed at the Soviet Union, not China.

Gastil pointed out that in fact there are many more Uygurs in China, and they must have heard it. He did not believe we had ever had a Tibetan program. His question was whether Dreyer's paper implied that we should not broadcast in such minority languages.

Dreyer said it depended on the broadcast. If VOA news were simply translated into Tibetan, this would be no problem. But if we broadcast a special program about self-determination with suggestions to rebel, this would be very unfortunate. She didn't think the very fact of broadcasting in a minority language would be a problem.

Smith noted that we have to distinguish the large, distinct geographically separate minorities like the Mongolian and Tibetans and the Uygurs from the Hui, Zhuang, Li, and the others who are mixed in with the Chinese and generally speak Chinese. These highly acculturated groups are only beginning to develop an ethnic consciousness. They want to be themselves. This is noted in places like Hainan where there is geographic separation as well. Secondly, the Han Chinese presence is very important anywhere, especially in the cities, such as Hohhot (capital of Inner Mongolia), or some of those in Xinjiang where they have come not to be farmers, but for industrial jobs. Many of the xiafang youth have stayed for these jobs. This leads to real conflict over who is to run the city, and who gets into the universities. For example, there is a protected Mongol quota at the University of Inner Mongolia. Many Han think this is a raw deal, but it is a different problem than that in the countryside. Dreyer said that the conflict at Inner Mongolia University two years ago sounded like it could have been a story about the City University of New York. **Zhu** said, though, that the basic interest of those in Xinjiang from Shanghai is to go back to Shanghai.

Seymour spoke of the varying degrees of appreciation of themselves as separate nationalities among members of ethnic groups. When he was riding a Xinjiang-bound train in October 1982, he struck up a conversation with a Uygur about her sense of nationhood. She was obviously somewhat sinified, and wore Chinese dress. However, she put on a Uygur costume when she learned of his interest. Xinjiang is a purely Chinese term meaning "New Frontier." When he had asked her what she called it in Uygur, she said, after a pause, that it was the same. So if she did not know any Uygur name for her "country," it cannot be her country in a psychological sense.

Since this was also a conference about Taiwan, **Seymour** thought there should be at least a brief mention of the Kao-shan Tzu or mountain people of Taiwan. They are discriminated against. This is one of the few areas where the communist policies on human rights are better than Taiwan's. At least Seymour likes what the communists say better than what the nationalists say. He had never heard such bigotry as he heard even from high officials in Taipei. He was lectured on this subject by the Minister of Justice once when he raised the issue. These were the attitudes of the ruling mainlanders on Taiwan. Taiwanese attitudes may be better; however, his friends may not be typical, particularly the Presbyterians who are notable for their sympathy with the mountain people. On the treatment of Native Taiwanese as a "minority" on Taiwan, the official line is that there is no such thing as a Taiwanese, we are all Chinese. The mountain people are seen differently.

Democratization on Taiwan

Mab Huang

By friends and foe alike, Taiwan has been given high marks for successfully managing its economic development in the past three decades. A war-torn and predominantly agricultural community at the end of World War II, Taiwan has become a highly industrialized and urban society by the early 1980s. As government spokesmen liked to point out, apparently having in mind the People's Republic of China and other Asian nations, the economic development strategy chosen had been effective and "prudent." A peaceful land reform program in the early 1950s provided the basis for the initial industrialization effort. Two decades later, the government had already shifted from its emphasis on promotion of export goods to that of building capital-intensive industries. By the early 1980s, Taiwan was moving rapidly into knowledge-intensive, high-technology industries. Diplomatic setbacks and oil crisis in the early 1970s adversely affected the economic performance of Taiwan, yet the island has managed to survive and prosper. For thirty years the growth of the GNP has been impressive. An economist estimated that by 1972, the GNP soared to more than five times its initial level, and per capita GNP was 182 percent higher than in 1952. Another economist suggested that in real terms (constant prices of 1971) Taiwan's GNP increased by seven hundred percent between 1952 and 1978, at an average annual rate of 8.4 percent, and a per capita annual rate of more than five percent. An American bank estimated that Taiwan's per capita GNP in 1981 was 2,559 U.S. dollars, almost ten times that of the People's Republic of China. Plainly, Taiwan was an affluent society.

Equally noteworthy is the degree of equality in the distribution of goods and services that Taiwan has been able to achieve. Through the decades of rapid economic growth, the low income

267

groups enjoyed an accelerated rate of absolute as well as relative improvement. According to a survey, in 1964 the top twenty percent of Taiwan's households on the family income ladder accounted for 41.1 percent of all family incomes. This ratio declined to 38.7 percent in 1970 and then to 37.5 percent in 1975. Given this economic achievement, Taiwan's society went through a profound and far-reaching transformation. Ancient cities became large and sophisticated urban centers; new cities and towns emerged. Compulsory and free education was extended from six to nine years, and schools and universities were built to meet the needs of a more complex society. Hospitals and clinics dotted the island, providing a fairly high level of public health care. Transportation was easy and efficient throughout the island. Attitudes on family and marriage began to change, giving more support to individuality and personal choice. All in all, Taiwan was fast becoming a modern society.

Against this background, it could have been anticipated that politics would have developed in parallel with that of the economy and society, especially in such areas as civil liberties, rule of law, and degree of political participation. Moreover, Taiwan's close links with the United States, including defense aid and trade, should have reinforced such a democratic trend. In a rough sense, the experience of the European nations and the United States in the eighteenth and nineteenth centuries suggests such a scenario. Economic growth and industrialization contributed to the rise of the bourgeoisie, which in turn demanded and secured democratic rule. Liberal political thought in our time, as it by necessity drew on the historical developments of Europe and America, tended to hold the position that economic changes would ultimately make for democratic rule in Asia, Latin America, and Africa.

But it was not to be so for Taiwan. Politics on Taiwan moved ever so slowly to accommodate the emerging social forces. The Nationalist Party has been unyielding in its monopoly of power, maintaining its control of the army, secret police, and the government bureaucracy. Though more Taiwanese politicians were recruited into the Party hierarchy, the mainlander Chinese were plainly in command. Freedom of the press was severely curtailed; local elections were regularly manipulated; and the spectre of an effective opposition party provoked such anger and nervousness in the ruling party that it reacted with violence. Secret surveillance, intimidation, and selective persecution of political opponents became an integral part of the political process. In a word, Taiwan remained an authoritarian single-party system in spite of its amazing economic progress and social change.

How can we account for this discordance between economic development and democratic rule? What powerful obstacles led to retardation in the political arena? Is the liberal political theory absolutely wrong? What is the prospect for democratization in the near future? And finally, what can the United States government and outside organizations do to help to come to grips with these issues, aiming at a clarification of the entanglement? Only when issues are presented clearly can effective actions and policy recommendations be developed.

II.

Traditional China reached great height in the art of government, with a sophisticated and articulated political culture which met the needs of the political community for many centuries, but the lingering influence of that political culture has been detrimental to democratic rule in China and Taiwan in our time. The deep-seated idea of an enlightened elite governing in the name of the people for the well-being of the whole nation, the contempt of the rule of law, the pressure for conformity, and denial of individual freedoms and rights contradict the basic tenets of democracy and can be easily used to bolster authoritarian or dictatorial doctrines and practices. Both the Nationalist and the Communist parties have been guilty of resorting to the traditional political culture for support. By comparison, the influence of the past has been weaker in Taiwan, given the rapid economic and social changes, yet its hold is still tenacious, affecting both rulers and the ruled.

A more serious obstacle to democratic rule on Taiwan, no doubt, has been the desire of the Nationalist Party to monopolize power, and its obsession with a life and death struggle with the Chinese Communist Party. The experience of defeat in the hands of the Communists on mainland China apparently had not persuaded the Nationalist leaders to approach politics from a different perspective. They were still wedded to the self-image of a revolutionary party fighting against an evil, shrewd, and ruthless enemy. The government of the Republic of China still presented itself as the sole legitimate government of all parts of China. Thus, in the early 1980s, the island was still governed under martial law adopted to help suppress a Communist rebellion thirty years before. Any challenge was likely to be condemned as inspired or led by the Chinese Communists, or both, no matter how unlikely this seemed to observers in the international community. It is true that by the seventies, the Formosan Independence Movement was more and more recognized as a distinct threat to the Nationalist rule, yet it was very loosely defined. Never was a serious effort made to analyze the motivation, sources of support, and strategies of the opposition forces. A more discriminating attitude would have persuaded the Nationalist leaders that support for both the Chinese Communists and the separatist movement in the island was limited, and that the ruling Party and government were not faced with imminent violent destruction. Moreover, a more realist approach would have distinguished those political dissidents who were committed to an independence movement from those who urged basic structural reforms. It was precisely because of such an indiscriminating and arbitrary policy towards the dissidents that many critics of the Nationalist Party were driven to a more radical position, and ultimately into the separatist camp. This was particularly true of the Taiwanese community in the United States.

Dictated by political doctrines and burdened by traditional authoritarian and bureaucratic style, the political institutions and processes on Taiwan simply could not keep pace with the economic and social changes. They were slow, arbitrary, and stagnant. The National Assembly and the Legislative Yuan had not faced a genuine and comprehensive re-election in thirty years; the courts were subject to political interference as well as being notorious for their weakness for bribery; the mass media were tightly controlled; and local elections were regularly manipulated.

Yet by all accounts, the most calamitous development was the expansion of power by the military and secret police agencies. Not only did they exercise more and more power, they were arrogant and arbitrary, creating a climate of fear and mistrust. Under such circumstances, it took great courage to challenge the authorities and to profess and work for democratic rule.

Finally, not much of a claim can be made by the American government for having helped democratize the politics of Taiwan. Indeed, the Nationalist Party had always desired to present itself in a good light to the American government and people, and this concern has at times saved the victims of political persecution from even harsher treatments. But clearly the Nationalist leaders have not been deterred from moving against their opponents when in their judgment the stakes were high. Through the decades, the government of the United States has never seriously and openly

criticized the Nationalist Party for political persecution; economic aid has not been used to put pressure on the Nationalist
leaders to proceed with democratic reforms. On the contrary, as
an American official has proudly stated, the success of aid to
Taiwan has been precisely due to a deliberate policy of self-
restraint, of not using aid as a leverage for democratic change.

III.

   Despite the stringent political control, democracy on Taiwan
inched on. Contemporary liberal thinkers were not completely
mistaken. Economic and social changes had brought about a new
middle class which in turn demanded freedom of speech, rule of
law, and greater political participation. By the early 1970s, a
new breed of politicians had entered the political arena. They
were young, usually in their early thirties, talented, well-
educated, and hard-working. They were impatient with the Nationalist monopoly of power and angry with its high-handed methods of
governing. They were the driving force of democratization on
Taiwan.
   This uphill struggle for democracy was complicated and agoni-
zing. Many times in the past thirty years, it reached a crescendo
before it was again pushed back. In the late 1950s, Lei Chen, a
prominent Nationalist leader, moved to organize an opposition
party with the support of many famous intellectuals and Taiwanese
politicians, businessmen, and community leaders. To the degree
that Lei had been a supporter of Chiang Kai-shek in mainland
China, his conversion to democracy and his challenge to Chiang was
a continuation of Chinese politics on Taiwan; yet to the degree
that he chose to cooperate with Taiwanese politicians and community leaders, he opened up a new vista. Unfortunately, he was not
tolerated. On a trumped-up charge of providing sanctuary for a
Communist agent, he was sentenced to ten years imprisonment. His
journal, **Free China Fortnightly**, was closed down, and the embryonic opposition party did not see the light of the day. In his
last years, he gave his moral support to the opposition movement
and was held in reverence by the opposition politicians of the
younger generation for his contribution to, and sacrifice for, the
noble cause of democracy on Taiwan.
   Through the decade of the sixties, the Nationalist Party was in
firm control. While the economy was making great strides, political dissent was effectively suppressed. It was not until the

early 1970s when the ruling Party and government were confronted with diplomatic setbacks that demands for democratic reforms were heard again. A group of university professors and students began to gather around the **Ta-hseuh Magazine** and agitated for basic structural change. For a short time, they gained significant support from the professional class and the youth. However, internal disputes and pressures from the National Party succeeded in defeating them. They soon faltered and disintegrated. Nevertheless, they had served a useful purpose. The intellectual ferment for political reforms provided a training ground for many young men who later assumed an important part in the political arena.

Since then, the pace of politics began to quicken. The new breed of politicians discovered as if by instinct that the most effective channel for their advancement was through election--both to local positions and a limited number of positions in the National Assembly and Legislative Yuan. It was only during election campaigns that they could effectively display their talents, present their political position, and criticize the Nationalist Party and government. To gain votes they learned to use propaganda and campaign techniques with imagination and skill against the government-sponsored candidates. In a span of ten years, the opposition movement must have published dozens of journals. When the government banned a particular journal for "speaking out against the national policy" or "confusing the public," as it was routinely done, the opposition would respond by issuing a new magazine. In a sense, the mass of readers of these opposition journals constituted the grass roots support of the political movement. Moreover, to better assist one another, the opposition politicians built a network of relationships. In a few short years, an opposition party in reality, if not in name, was rapidly coming into existence.

The Nationalist Party was slow in adapting itself to the new situation. It clung to the idea that it must win overwhelmingly in the elections, even if it required fraud and manipulation. But this policy backfired. The prestige and status of the Nationalist Party declined perceptibly, inviting even more serious challenge in subsequent elections. Thus, election campaigns were always a time of tension and confrontation between the Nationalist and the opposition movement.

The year 1977 marked the coming of age of the opposition. In November of that year in Chungli, in connection with the heated campaign of Hsu Hsin-liang for the position of magistrate of Taoyuan Hsien, an estimated ten thousand angry citizens rioted against the police, claiming that the government had attempted to rig the election. The meaning of such an act of open contempt of the authorities was not lost on the opposition. They acted more boldly and pushed on with their effort to establish an opposition party. The vehicle they chose this time was a new magazine called **Formosa**, which soon reached 100,000 in circulation and extended its network through the island. Encouraged by President Carter's human rights policy, they sponsored many political and human rights rallies, drawing ever larger crowds. The Nationalist Party was put on the defensive, yet it was not prepared to make substantial concessions. It reacted with cajolery, selective persecution, and ostentatious displays of force. A situation of precarious stalemate prevailed, but the battle lines were clearly drawn. The Nationalist Party controlled the army, the secret police, and the government, while the opposition enjoyed substantial backing of the population. It was a highly explosive and dangerous situation.

The impasse could not be maintained for long. On December 10, 1979, the opposition movement held a large demonstration in Kaohsiung to commemorate the thirty-first anniversary of the Universal Declaration of Human Rights. The negotiations with the authorities for permission to hold the demonstration had been long and inconclusive. There was no doubt that the opposition leaders intended to have a peaceful rally. However, when the demonstrators were met with riot troops backed up by anti-riot armored vehicles, a clash ensued. On December 12, most opposition leaders returned to Taipei and held a press conference. Their account was not given credence by the government-controlled mass media. Early next morning, the secret police agents began to round up the opposition, and in less than two days, more than one hundred thirty opposition politicians were arrested, including the eight well-known leaders of the movement.

Partly to pacify the outcry of human rights organizations in the international community, the Kaohsiung Eight were put on trial by the military court in March 1980. They received prison terms ranging from twelve years to life. Second echelon opposition leaders were tried and convicted later.

The Kaohsiung Incident and the massive arrest of the opposition leaders dealt the democratic reform movement a severe blow. Yet, the ruling Party has not been able to destroy the opposition, nor has it succeeded in reconciling with them. Many young men and women have risen to take the place of their jailed leaders, and the struggle goes on.

IV.

For the past three years, the attention of the Nationalist Party and the Taiwanese people has turned to the peace offensive initiated in Peking to incorporate Taiwan into China through negotiation. The post-Mao leadership in Peking has made several direct appeals to Chiang Ching-kuo, saying in so many words that he was getting old and should think of his position in history. Patriotism, they argued, should dictate his actions, and he could in good conscience only choose unification through negotiations. By putting great pressure on Chiang to compromise, the Chinese Communists inadvertently posed the issue of political succession on Taiwan more sharply than it had been permitted in the island. Speculation on Chiang's political heir became fashionable. An opposition journal several months ago openly discussed the issue, going so far as to rank the leading candidates. Succession to Chiang, it was widely recognized, must affect the future of Taiwan. Would Taiwan be absorbed by China in the near future? What would happen when Chiang is incapable of exercising power or when he dies? Would the Party and government bureaucracies manage to maintain control? Or was a coalition of civilian and military leaders likely to emerge? Or is a military dictatorship in the South Korean mold possible? And what is the prospect for democratic rule? Taiwan appears to be at a parting of the ways.

To begin with, there is little chance that the peace offensive by Peking will succeed in bringing political unification quickly. Chiang Ching-kuo has so far refused to negotiate, partly because he would not betray his father, partly because he saw no gains in compromise provided he could still count on the support of the United States. Moreover, it could be argued, even if he chose to negotiate, he may not have the support of the people. The majority of the population clearly would not want to live under communism; the opposition movement was uniformly hostile to negotiation; and the influential Presbyterian Church certainly entertained separatist ambitions. Under these circumstances, for Chiang to decide to negotiate could very well disrupt the society and risk his control. In his old age, Chiang Ching-kuo can be expected to play safe.

274

If it is assumed that Chiang is incapable of exercising power or that he dies in the next five years, two scenarios are more likely than the others. First, it is likely that a coalition of civilian and military leaders would work together to insure a smooth transfer of power. In this contingency, Taiwanese politicians in the Party hierarchy and government would share power and status, and concessions would have to be made to the opposition movement. An optimistic forecast would anticipate the release from jail of the Kaohsiung Eight and many other leaders. Of course, the military and secret police apparatus would still exercise substantial power, thus putting a brake on the extent of democratic reforms. Nevertheless, this scenario augurs well for democratization on Taiwan. As to relations with China, political unification would not be a priority, but some arrangements regarding trade, travel, and postal services between Taiwan and China are conceivable.

An alternative but less likely scenario suggests that the military and the secret police would make a grab for power. They would make the move if they judge that no compromise with the opposition is possible, and that the civilian leadership could not be trusted with governing the nation with a firm hand. This turn of events would, of course, lead to wholesale denial of civil and political rights and suppression of the opposition. It would portend political instability and economic downturn. Ironically, as the situation becomes untenable, it is not unthinkable that the military dictatorship would approach the Communists and seek to merge with China. In that contingency, the rationale of nationalism and patriotism would be resorted to, not without a degree of anti-Americanism.

V.

Taiwan cannot survive in isolation. As long as the American government is committed to implement the Taiwan Relations Act, to preserve and enhance "the human rights of all the people on Taiwan," and to sell arms for Taiwan's defense, the American government and outside private organizations (such as Freedom House, Amnesty International, the Society for the Protection of East Asians' Human Rights, and the Chinese Human Rights Society) could have some impact on the future of Taiwan. If the above analysis of the probable development in Taiwan is correct, the first priority is to encourage and support a smooth transition of political power and to prevent a military dictatorship. Many concrete measures could be taken; many of which the American government could do better than the private organizations, and vice versa.

1. The American government should convey to the Nationalist leaders on Taiwan its commitment to civilian rule on the island, and it should warn against the rise of a military dictatorship. It should make clear that a coalition with the military playing a role would be tolerable, but that the United States would be prepared to withhold support, including trade and sale of weapons, if the military grabs power.

2. The American government should convey to the Nationalist leaders on Taiwan its concern for democratic reforms, including a free press, an independent judicial system, and fair elections. In particular, the authorities on Taiwan should be urged to release all opposition leaders within a specified period of time and permit their re-entry into politics.

3. Private organizations in the United States and abroad should publicize and speak out against political persecution and human rights violations on Taiwan. They should urge a free press, an independent judicial system, and fair elections.

4. Private organizations in the United States and abroad should act in concert to initiate a campaign to release the Kaohsiung Eight. (Preferably in the fall of 1983, for a period of three months, culminating on December 10.) They should mobilize worldwide opinion and seek support from as many governments as possible. During the campaign, concrete measures should be taken to give aid and comfort to the political prisoners and their families.

COMMENTS AND DISCUSSION

After Huang's presentation **Zhu** wished to know what could be done by the people in Taiwan to help democratize Taiwan, and what the people in Taiwan thought about unification. As a mainlander he wished to ask four questions:

1. What is the relation of the Taiwan independence movement to the democracy movement?
2. What can be done by the people in Taiwan to help democratize the system?
3. What is the real reason the government does not want to negotiate with the Mainland?
4. What do the people in Taiwan think about reunification?

Huang replied that for many years the Formosan independence movement had its headquarters in Japan. Later on they moved to this country. They believe Taiwan should be independent and are prepared to use violence. They have no interest in the Chinese community. Hsu Hsin-liang's group, the Formosan magazine group that was headquartered in San Francisco, has in the past year tended more and more toward a socialist position in support of violent revolution. Kuo Yu-Hsin was very well known in Taiwan, having been elected many times. His "League for Supporting Democracy in Taiwan" has a very close link with the Tang-Wai, the independents in Taiwan. Tang-Wai is a very broad loose group in Taiwan with substantial support in the society. It is the most important group. A few leaders in the Tang-Wai may have special sympathy with the independence movement of a separatist kind. Most of them desire to share power with the mainlanders. However, although Tang-Wai has a few mainlanders in their camp, there is the danger that they may become more separatist and thus polarize the society.

Zhu asked if the government gave the people of Taiwan democracy, would they get independence? **Huang** said that so far they seem willing to share power. Their position is just that unification is a low priority.

Gastil asked what do the people of Taiwan really want? **Kintner** replied that he had discussed this matter several times with former Taiwanese officials. Their view is that for the time-being Taiwan has to stick with the present arrangement because what is left of their international position depends on the treaties made with the Republic of China. Over time (ten to twenty years), the trend will be toward independence. This opinion seems especially common in the "heir apparent" generation, those forty-five to fifty years old.

Liao said that it is his impression that in an election held tomorrow, most would vote for independence. There were various reasons. First, the Taiwanese people want to be separate from the People's Republic of China, and secondly, from the Nationalist government. They also think that being separate would be better because the PRC is economically more backward, and could not guarantee whatever freedoms they do have.

Smith said that from the point of view of the mainland Chinese on Taiwan the problem realistically is what do you do with all those people. If reunification meant free movement among provinces, the problems of adjustment and absorption would be enormous. China still has not come to terms with Shanghai after thirty years; the average standard of living in Shanghai remains two to three times that in other cities. The disparity with Taiwan is even greater, both economically and culturally. The enlightened on the mainland who are willing to talk about Hong Kong are looking toward a fairly permissive and loose association. They ask us how we manage Puerto Rico and hope to use that analogy. **Sullivan** said they should keep in mind that in Puerto Rico's case there is a plebiscite about every ten years. **Smith** replied they were not thinking of an exact model. But they would like the sovereignty question resolved. Much of their resentment against the United States is that they see us as blocking the resolution of the sovereignty question. **Dreyer** thought these choices of models suggested a frightening naivete about the situation. (For example, U.S. subsidies to Puerto Rico could not be duplicated.)

In answer to the question, "If an election were held tomorrow?", Dreyer said a great deal would depend on the voters' perception of what their real choices were. The PRC has said time and again, "If you move toward the Soviet Union or declare independence, we are going to invade." (**Liao** noted he had said "ideally.") In the real world people are going to be very worried. Most people she knew would not want an election just for this reason. One authority on the situation sees gradual evolution as the best solution, with the KMT becoming mostly Taiwanese in membership, and power being distributed in proportion to the percentage of the population in each group. He can give a number of examples of this evolution.

Grieder wondered if we see the evolution as the transformation of a largely exogenous dictatorship into a largely indigenous one-party dictatorship, where have we gotten in terms of the goals of this conference? Was the Taiwanization of one-party rule an acceptable destination? **Dreyer** said she had given the Gastil-Seymour paper to a former Deputy Chief of Mission of the U.S. Embassy in Taipei. He felt that most Taiwanese were not looking for a democratic society; he thought they wanted the type of system they already have, but staffed by Taiwanese.

Huang disagreed. Given the power of the Tang-Wai, it was too late to talk about the majority of the people there being satisfied with a Taiwanese nationalist dictatorship.

Gastil wondered if the problem isn't that the exogenous ruling group knows it would lose out if democracy were accepted. If so, with the passage of time and mixture of groups this would be overcome. **Huang** saw the problem also in the continuing image of the KMT as a revolutionary party.

Sullivan said that one of the problems he had always had with the argument that dictatorship is what the people want is that, if it is what the people want, why is it necessary to have such elaborate control mechanisms? The argument is that tough controls are only meant for the few who would disrupt the system. He thought this just a rationalization. They just simply do not want to put at risk their power and perks in an open and free political contest. He argued the situation on Taiwan was going to be evolutionary as long as the current government did not become more oppressive. As long as they liberalize gradually, giving in here and there--and this should be encouraged and applauded--the possibilities of democratization are substantial. As the old leaders die or retire, the KMT could become a less oppressive one-party dictatorship. The important change that is going to shape the future is what happens when the KMT is no longer synonymous with the Chiang family or with retaking the mainland. Sullivan had been on Taiwan before the old man died and had returned afterwards. Two things struck him. First, the outpouring of feeling for the death of Chiang was not all manipulated, nor was it restricted to mainlanders. But some of his Taiwanese neighbors certainly were not overwhelmed with grief. The other point is that Chiang Ching-kuo did make a real attempt to reduce propaganda on retaking the mainland and to cut public references on the connections between political power and the Chiang family. So there can be an evolution.

Dreyer is right on their fears of an election. What is most likely to happen is de facto independence. They won't declare it. Taiwan has proven it can exist without a definite status.

Moody thought that by every practical measure Taiwan was already independent. This creates the impossible situation. His impression is that perhaps eighty percent of the mass membership of the KMT is now Taiwanese. The leadership is not. It is to the advantage of local personalities to belong to the party. The problem with the government is that it is totally deprived of any kind of dignity. It cannot see itself as just the government of Taiwan, and the PRC is unwilling to grant it separate status. In 1979 they started saying, "Why can't we have the German solution?" Maybe they could have gotten it earlier. The United States has been willing to make every possible concession to the PRC on the grounds it really does not commit us. But it also deprives us of any moral or legal standing against Beijing. It is increasingly difficult to go on lecturing Taiwan's leaders about "military dictatorship" when we have progressively lost the leverage we once had on the situation. What incentive is left for the government to listen to the United States?

Gastil wondered if the dignity problem would be resolved by Taiwanization. One way to achieve dignity for a Taiwanese is to take over the state and run it as a Taiwanese state.

Moody said that if that were done, it would create serious problems in relation to China. In the abstract the world would jump at the chance of recognizing an independent Taiwan. But it cannot be done smoothly now without a loss of face all around.

Dreyer added that in 1978 it became obvious that the Carter administration was moving toward complete recognition of the PRC and abrogation of the 1954 security treaty. At this point a small group of influential Republicans who saw themselves as close friends of "Free China"--people with specially close relations with Chiang Ching-kuo--went to Taipei and urged a formal declaration of independence. They said they had the votes in the Senate to back up Taiwan, and at that time the United States and Taiwan still had a security treaty. But they were told by the Nationalist leaders that they simply could not do it (and **Moody** agreed they could not).

Seymour recalled that people who say that it does not really matter if a country is a democracy often give Taiwan as an example. The economy is said to be so great, and there would only be trouble if they were a democracy. But Seymour thought this discussion suggested what a high price people paid for not having a democracy. The reason why the Chiang family has been able to present itself as the government of all of China and Mongolia is that nobody in Taiwan could get up and say, "The Emperor wears no clothes." The few who did were dragged right off to long sentences in jail, even life terms. The legitimacy of a small group rested on the myth. Yet the interests of the people of the island as a whole would have been better served by claiming nationhood while they still had a generally recognized government. They have now lost their best opportunity, maybe the only one. So much depends on the United States. We have now gone ninety-nine percent of the way toward saying that the PRC is the official government of Taiwan. Seymour did not know why. There was almost nothing Richard Nixon did he approved of, but the original Shanghai communique had left the door open in a very clever manner. It said, "The United States recognizes that the Chinese on both sides of the Straits acknowledge that there is only one China, and Taiwan is part of that China. The United States does not challenge this view." (Unfortunately the Chinese text was a little less tricky.) But ever since this, we have moved closer to Beijing's view. What was to stop us? After all, the government in Taiwan was saying the same thing. If the Taiwanese people had enjoyed freedom of speech, the government of Taiwan could not have behaved in such a counterproductive manner, and the official break with the United States could have been avoided.

Huang thought that conveying to the government on Taiwan the United States position that we will not support a military dictatorship should not make for a serious problem of dignity. It depended on how it was said. It need not make the government lose face with the people. Huang also questioned Seymour's assumption that, if the government of Taiwan had the foresight a few years ago to declare independence, it would have been better. That is true in regard to preserving the high living standard and the relative freedom of Taiwan. But with the present relationship, what happens on Taiwan could have an impact on China. If Taiwan was independent, it would not have this impact. So he was prepared to defend democracy on Taiwan while preserving Taiwan's potential influence on China in democracy and human rights. He saw it in a broader framework.

Seymour doubted Huang's hope that the tail could be made to wag the dog. So he could not see compromising Taiwan's evolution in this hope.

Zhu wondered what was the relation between the people in Taiwan getting independence and getting democracy. He also did not see a very strong influence on the mainland from Taiwan. For over thirty years both sides have established totally different social structures, ideologies, and life styles.

Gastil asked the Chinese students at the conference, "If Taiwan has a full-fledged democracy similar to Japan's, would you be talking about it, and comparing mainland China to it in your writing?" **Sullivan** also wanted to know how fervent was the Chinese desire to get back Taiwan because "it is ours?"

Liang and **Zhu** replied that in the PRC the older people do not care. Only when Deng Xiaoping gets close to dying does he talk of Taiwan. So ordinary people pay no attention. The older generation had a strong feeling against the Chiang Kai-shek government; today most young people dream of Taiwan's material luxuries, color television, and so forth, they do not see it in terms of democracy, but rather like Hong Kong. Intellectuals and scholars think that the Taiwan situation is much better than that of the PRC, but they do not think it can be a model for the PRC. The PRC is so big. No matter how advanced Taiwan is, it is only one province. Today it is impossible for the communist party to negotiate with Taiwan. Taiwan should keep to itself and resolve its own problems.

Liao added that no democracy movement can be separated from parochial interests. If there is a genuine referendum in Taiwan, then the people will choose independence, or whatever they want. The two movements are not different.

Huang reflected that the discussants were approaching the question from many directions. Seymour apparently felt that for democracy and human rights in Taiwan, independent status would be preferable to the current ambiguity.

Seymour interjected to say that he was earlier talking about lost opportunities, and not the present. Now, because we have recognized Beijing as the government of China, we cannot legally do anything.

Zhu thought that we could not have done differently, because the United States had wanted good relations with China. **Seymour**

reminded us that relations in the past between the United States and China were bad anyway. Ten years ago most countries in the world recognized the Taipei government, and there was a United States-Taiwan treaty. Taipei could have renounced its claims to the mainland and made the transition. As to Taiwan independence and its present relation to China, his position was that the people there should make the decision. It should not be up to a small elite or outsiders.

Dreyer asked Huang about his disappointment that Chiang Ching-kuo said he would refuse to negotiate because it would be a betrayal of his father. She wondered how much Huang thought this was the only reason Chiang would not negotiate. **Huang** agreed this was not the only reason. He was just pointing out this was poor statesmanship.

Smith reminded us of Willy Brandt's negotiations with the Russians and Lee Kuan Yew's negotiations over the status of Singapore. In both cases these were really tough dilemmas. There seemed to be no solutions, and the principals on both sides were acting quite autocratically. Yet decisions were reached, and the problems worked out. It is not the detailed discussion, but political decisions at the highest level that are critical.

Sullivan asked if anybody here believed that the PRC would launch an offensive attack against Taiwan. **Zhu** said they would if it became independent. The position of the Chinese leaders would be similar to that of the British leaders in the Falkland crisis. If they did not act there would be a governmental crisis.

Huang questioned the sophistication of the view that the Taiwan experience was not very important because it is only one province, and that ordinary people in China do not care about Taiwan. The question is not the size of the provinces or the millions of people. Of course, the ordinary people have not cared much about Taiwan, but in the last year or two there has been quite a bit of discussion about Taiwan; they know it has been doing well in economic progress. There is a desire to negotiate with the authorities on Taiwan to incorporate it into China. The Pandora's box has been opened. You cannot close it again. To say Taiwan will not have an impact on China cannot be right. Then Liao suggests democracy and independence are inseparable issues. Taiwan might become independent, if the people eventually vote for it. But before that point, many different positions will be developed. It is likely we will end up with some complicated negotiations and compromises that cannot be anticipated at this time.

Grieder suggested that Liang's point was not that the relationship to Taiwan would have no impact, but that Taiwan as a model was inappropriate, because geographically and historically, and because of its size and economic infrastructure, it was not generalizable to China. This is a perfectly valid point.

Gastil raised two points. He noted the sentence on page 270, "Finally not much claim can be made for the American government having helped democratize Taiwan." This brought up the question Lucian Pye and others had raised, that we should have done and should be doing more to support democracy in these countries. Gastil wanted to see what people specifically thought of that later. Secondly, several conferees had claimed earlier that if Taiwan became a democracy it would function without great trouble as a democracy. This implies a democratic potential within one concept of the influence of Chinese political culture on Chinese political behavior.

Communications Within
and With China

Norris Smith

Since the death of Mao in 1976 and the repudiation of his most conspicuous adherents, a great deal has changed in China. In particular, the persistence of the old has become apparent. The durability of familiar, traditional values is evident, although 1983 is obviously a long way from 1949 or 1969, or even 1979.

I will focus on a few areas of great importance to the political and literary China, the China of the word, as well as to the China of ordinary life: internal communication and the mass media, education, and culture.

Then I will touch on communication between China and the outside world. This relates to the question of the possibilities for outsiders like ourselves to influence the evolution of democracy, or indeed any other aspect of the evolution of Chinese political life.

Before 1949 (or 1935, or 1925, depending on the analysis) education and mass communication in China were limited both in quality and quantity. The only exceptions were a few cities along the coast and along the main rivers, where both education and mass media were influenced by Western, modern (or Japanese-modern, which at that time amounted to roughly the same thing) examples. The people reached by these new forms were few, but were in time immensely influential on politics and on other expressions of the mind and spirit. Traditional Confucian-style education remained in some places, but had lost confidence and legitimacy.

Universities expanded greatly after 1949. Although they were split into narrow specialties on the Russian pattern, the quantity of graduates was increased many times without too much reduction in quality. In the sciences, some real advances were made. Newspapers were dull and repetitive, but there were many more of them, reaching a much larger proportion of the population. Radio became an almost universal medium, and films were not far behind. Basic education was not yet universal, but the proportion of young people offered at least the rudiments of education increased greatly across the countryside. The output of secondary schools also grew sharply. It is important to remember that in China a graduate of a senior high school is, in attitudes and prejudices, an intellectual.

The promising growths of the 1950s and early 1960s were chilled, shriveled, and uprooted during the dozen turbulent years up to 1976. A whole generation lost the opportunity for education, or pursued it under conditions of the utmost rigor and difficulty. Tens of thousands of talented young people were deprived of the chance to develop their creativity in even the circumscribed framework of a Chinese conservatory or academy of the arts.

People of learning, conviction, and ideas were badgered, humiliated, chastened, and punished--punished physically, punished by being separated from their work, or both. What has really happened since 1976? It is difficult to say with much confidence. The present Chinese leadership, like most other political experimenters, has discovered the difficulty of swimming and staying dry at the same time. They could very likely decide to get out of the stream, dry off, and go back to the bad old ways.

This will be made less probable by one general fact that has particular impact upon the communications media. A Chinese regime, and a Communist one at that, has admitted that it was wrong. It was wrong not just by committing minor errors of symbol or ceremony, to be made right by chastising a few misled officials (although that, also, was done) and changing the name of the reign. Error was admitted on numerous major matters: agricultural policy, basic economic strategy, policies toward intellectuals, and many others. It has not only admitted error, but downright falsehood, including imaginary statistics, favored models of success that turn out to have been specious fakes, and more.

Hypocrisy and self-righteousness have flourished for thousands of years in China. No prudent person would predict that either has been banished. The recent modest but highly significant experiment with truth in politics simply erects a barrier to a recurrence of old bad habits--perhaps a low barrier, but visible.

The leadership that succeeded Mao has also experimented with truth in the news media, and it has committed itself to quality in education. Neither Joseph Pulitzer nor Ed Murrow would find much to admire in the Chinese mass media today, but the media are a great deal less stultified and a great deal more informative than they were not long ago.

Pulitzer, indeed, might begin to feel at home. Chinese newspapers and even to some extent Chinese television news have introduced an extraordinary innovation: telling about local events that interest people, in at least a fairly interesting way, right after or soon after the event takes place. Even Murrow might approve, with reservations, the investigative reporting that Chinese newspapers relish so proudly, rooting out errors and injustices brought to light through their voluminous exchanges of letters with readers.

A commitment has been made to mass television. In the larger cities, and increasingly in smaller cities, ownership of television sets ranges from twenty to over fifty percent of households. Sets are appearing in the countryside. The creation of a mass audience is making China's television establishment somewhat the hostage of that audience. The decision to increase sharply the production of television sets was made in part to absorb restless purchasing power, in part to provide circuses as well as bread so that ordinary Chinese (mostly urban) would feel that someone was doing something on their behalf. Having taken this initial step, however, Chinese television managers are realizing that it will not work unless they provide fresh and reasonably interesting, entertaining programs.

As in other countries, sports and aiming a camera at established art forms such as the Peking opera can fill the gap for a while. But thirty-five hours of programs a week is a great deal, and seventy is, in practical terms, about four times as much-- variety must be added as well as quantity.

No one should underestimate the capability of any television system, capitalist or otherwise, to underestimate the quality of its audience, bore its viewers, or treat them as a captive parish locked into pews while sermons drone on. But, again, the Chinese leadership has embarked on something that cannot be turned back without paying a penalty in disgruntlement and a sense of betrayal. These are not intolerable political risks for a government that wants something--like political conformity or the appearance of it--very badly. Nevertheless, these are not risks to be taken lightly.

Unless China's luck is extraordinarily bad once again, education has a less doubtful outlook. Quality and competition, executed with the intention of honesty and fairness, have been restored. Some teachers and politicians mourn the passing of the egalitarianism, the idealistic reverence for dirty fingernails, the skepticism toward academic hot air that prevailed during the 1960s. On the whole, however, the change seems popular.

Chinese education is not a seamless marvel of consistency and unprejudiced dedication to quality. A Chinese campus has many similarities to the kind of prebendal system described by Anthony Trollope. Getting ahead, obtaining a living or a curacy, depends about as much on one's personal or family pull or connections with the dean as on one's brilliance or doctrinal purity.

Comparatively, however, the present system is an enormous improvement in fairness, perceived fairness, academic quality, and response to China's need for trained minds over the Chinese educational system in 1969, 1964, or even in 1935. This has involved repairing the damages of the Cultural Revolution period and continuing along familiar tracks. Since 1978, however, the Chinese leadership has added to its educational system a further resource, almost an additional layer, which is potentially of great significance and considerable political risk.

Chinese students have gone abroad before in the past hundred years. Usually, however, this was a short-lived experiment, an effort to either remove or pacify trouble-making young intellectuals, the result of influence by foreign institutions and foreign money, a reflection of weakness and indecision at the center of authority, or all the above. During the Tang and Yuan dynasties, for different reasons and under different kinds of leadership, China was curious and receptive toward the world outside.

Since then, especially since the profound uncertainty of the Qing about the proper response to the challenge posed by European guns and European ideas, it has been unusual for a Chinese administration established solidly in office to take deliberate steps to send its best scholars and most promising young people to study and to update their academic skills outside China. It has required exceptional political courage and a realistic recognition of the internationality of knowledge--and China's deficiency in many key aspects of science--for the China of the word to permit its most capable manipulators of the word to search out new words abroad--and bring them back.

Earlier experiments of this sort have not lasted long. The results of exposure to unfamiliar knowledge are never as neat, as predictable, or as controllable as is claimed by proponents of such schemes. Those who were doubtful from the outset, and those who think the whole enterprise was oversold and is too costly will point complacent fingers and shrug their shoulders in dismay when the inevitable happens--some participant in the exchange does something that can be portrayed as wicked or traitorous.

How about culture in China since 1976? In some areas, it has flourished remarkably. The stupidities of the Cultural Revolution period included paranoia about the long-established Chinese practice of commenting (or appearing to comment) on present politics by showing historical politics on stage. In addition to a general hostility about anything old or written by anyone else (an attitude much like that of the producer who said that Shakespeare would be given a bad table by the maitre d' at Elaine's), this bottled up or removed all the life from traditional art forms. This was true even of drama, which in China is sung and danced as well as spoken and has many local forms different from the Peking version most familiar outside China.

The traditional drama and some other arts of the past have been among the aspects of Chinese life that have shown the most remarkable resilience. They are enormously popular and exploited by modern media like radio and television to fill air time and keep listeners reasonably contented. Top political figures still grit their teeth and look pained when certain historical passages with political pointedness show up on the stage. But they smile and chuckle fifteen minutes later when it is the turn of Lao Wang, seated in the middle of the row of honor, to stare fixedly into space and wish he had chosen instead to spend that evening giving prizes at a youth soccer festival.

The vigor of the past has not been matched by originality or tolerance of experimentation in newer cultural forms. This has received much attention abroad, and I will not attempt to describe its varied and indeed tedious detail. Forms such as the modern spoken drama, the film, and to some extent the novel are now the established arenas for interaction between the political process and the processes of creation. Chinese cultural commissars and political managers are every bit as much Chinese of the word as writers and film directors. A large, informed audience of Chinese of the word who do not participate personally in this interaction nevertheless watch it closely--for indications of political currents as much as out of concern for artistic quality.

Here, the best outside parallel is not just a Trollopian, Victorian England, but the interplay among patrons, talent, and impresarios in the Vienna of the late Austro-Hungarian Empire. Or, for that matter, Shakespeare's London. He and his players had to worry a great deal about royal censorship and the need to attract noble patrons--for protection as well as financial patronage.

Is a Hamlet, or a Moby Dick or Dead Souls about to appear on a Chinese stage or in Chinese bookstores? It is difficult to find evidence of this. Chinese readers are having the chance to read Eugene O'Neill, John Updike, and Herman Wouk in translation. Arthur Miller has now joined Brecht, Carmen, and the Merchant of Venice on Chinese stages. This is also important, with enormous potential long-term significance--something not tolerated during the worst years of the 1960s.

What can be expected from manuscripts which lie locked in drawers or are passed quietly from hand to hand? I can say little more than that the Chinese are determined and capable people. During the worst of the Decade of Disruption, an extraordinary amount of work was done in the sciences and even in the social sciences and humanities despite official discouragement and outright persecution. Much of this later came to light and was published. There are grounds to hope that creative work of the same originality and dedication is being carried forward despite the cultural conformity which still prevails.

Parenthetically, it is important to remind oneself that political shackles on culture are not a specifically Communist phenomenon in China. It has a long history: Confucianism and Legalism combined are worse than either by itself. Even in a society as pluralistic as Singapore, the China of the word remains moralistic, wringing its hands at pop culture and behavior which is considered unseemly. The rigors in China today are less severe than in many periods over the centuries.

But we are here today for a characteristically American purpose, not just to talk about something but to decide, if we can, what to do about it.

The short answer is: not much, beyond what is being done already. If there was ever a strong candidate for **wu-wei**, for action through inaction, this is it.

The American relationship with China has been unusual, even unique--not only since 1949, but ever since Yankee ship-captains first began to gratify their investors by bringing back to Boston gifts of porcelain, tea, and silk from China.

Over the years, China and the United States have each tended to see in the other only what was looked for. In optical terms, it has been a matter of looking into mirrors rather than observing through telescopes. Hands extended in friendship one moment have

290

been withdrawn out of outraged goodwill or waved angrily in admonition. Nevertheless, the U.S.-China relationship is one of exceptional intensity and sustained power, despite (or because of) its tendency toward sharp emotional oscillations.

For most of my adult life, I have been a professional propagandist. To maintain his humility, every propagandist should keep a stuffed paper tiger on his desk. Few targets of vituperation have ever been subjected to the comprehensive scorn, condemnation, and villification that China discharged tirelessly at the United States for over twenty years. When it was all done, most Chinese retained, at the minimum, a respect for the United States--perhaps a qualified and even grudging respect, but very rarely the contempt and dislike that propagandists of the 1950s and 1960s hoped to achieve. Many Chinese have a high opinion of the United States, sometimes an opinion elevated to an embarassing and even dangerously unrealistic height.

The United States is admired for material excellence, high-quality education, and general well-being. There is also a broad awareness in China that the United States remains a land of opportunity for individuals, especially for the educated. Many Chinese, not by any means dissidents or disaffected intellectuals, have compared their political system unfavorably with some aspect of the American system--as they understand it. There are many things about the United States that few Chinese are able to understand. These include our muddled and costly health-care delivery system, what many Chinese perceive as a shocking lack of concern for the elderly, and real separation of powers in a federal system that exists in reality as well as on paper. Nevertheless, in a very general and often fuzzy way, the America of Washington, Lincoln, Franklin Roosevelt, and Nixon retains deep emotional symbolic resonance in China.

The respect with which Americans are considered in China today brings with it a heavy responsibility, and it can easily be misunderstood. It does not bring with it a license to preach. The Chinese retain a sensitivity, perhaps even extreme hypersensitivity, to anything that looks or sounds like an attempt at outside interference. This is not imposed or false, but grows out of strong feelings stirred by a century of national disgrace. It relates to recent as well as earlier events, as bureaucrats in the Japanese Ministry of Education discovered when they decided to make a few small adjustments in the history of the Second World

War. It is not simply a political position adopted by the official China, but permeates the personal China of bus-riders and peasants as well.

A final paradox. A deliberate, concerned attempt to transmit the values and processes of democracy to China today would tend to have adverse effects roughly proportional to the scale and explicitness of such efforts. It might appeal to many Chinese, including those deeply dissatisfied with the works of Communism in China as well as those who have reasonably informed aspirations toward democracy--or, more realistically, toward some of the principles and processes which we associate with democracy. But, if perceived as intrusion, the adverse reaction is likely to be broad and determined, from Chinese sympathetic toward ideas as well as Chinese who reject them or are unable to understand them. Since 1978, changes in economic and to some extent political policies have brought palpable benefits to the China of ordinary life, even though the Chinese of the word may retain many complaints.

It is arguable that the ordinary Chinese has more of a real stake in the political system than has been the case for a long time. This is, in any event, the purpose of the present leadership. When persistent, shared values are also considered, it provides a total picture that a sensible outsider should attempt to amend only with extreme caution.

The United States is doing the right things. They are providing a low-keyed and sincere welcome to the Chinese interest in reducing the gap between Chinese and Western levels of technology. Americans respond with their usual warmth to individual Chinese that visit this country. We make an active but not overbearing response to Chinese interest in technical support for China's developing economy. Through the Voice of America, the Chinese translation of **Scientific American** magazine, and many other channels, we provide Chinese audiences with news and facts they are interested in, some explanations about the United States, other non-deliberate representations of what democracy can mean and what democratic ideas can accomplish, with a minimum of didactic and boring reiteration. (After all, the Chinese get plenty of that in their own media, and that is one reason they look to foreign sources.)

Above all, the communication between the United States and China, and for that matter the communication of other Western democracies (and Japan) with China is diverse, including many contradictory views, from unofficial sources of all kinds as well as from different parts of governments. This is in itself an important means for communicating the meaning of democracy to the Chinese.

During the past five years, the information media, education, and even the cultural establishment have expanded greatly in China and have in many important respects improved qualitatively as well. Thus ideas from abroad are accessible and can percolate. More important, it makes it easier for Chinese to come to their own conclusions about democracy and other outside ideas. It makes it easier for Chinese to develop their own solutions and attempt their own changes in political and social life, on the level of the China of ordinary life as well as the China of the word.

Whatever happens, it must take place in China and be done by Chinese. The durability of traditional values and patterns in China after Mao demonstrate the irrelevance of models based on experience outside China, in Communist countries and others. The exceptional symbolic significance and emotional appeal to China of the United States and the principles it embodies are resources that must be applied with restraint, good taste, and common sense.

Smith added to his discussion of television that the essential universality of radio should also be mentioned. The government has either broadcast radio or wired systems reaching into almost all villages. Of course, it controls what goes out over it, and the programming is not particularly imaginative or entertaining. When people are exposed to information, they become inoculated. They end up being convinced of the opposite of what you try to indoctrinate them with. This may have transformed the potential political role of the peasantry. Now that they have been woven into the communication structure, the whole population can respond everywhere to events--positively or negatively. **Sullivan** added that this is what Daniel Lerner was talking about as an aspect of modernization.

Smith added that there are hundreds of higher educational institutions, but perhaps only about twenty comprehensive universities. The percentage of college-educated people in China is, it is true, very low. There are now about three and a half million university students. By 1985-1990 the government is aiming at having ten million a year graduating; this will include the graduates of many rather low-level technical schools on the Soviet model.

There has also been an explosion in scholarly publishing. There is so much the Chinese themselves find it hard to keep up. For example, to find out about the educational system just three or four years ago, it was necessary to do a lot of interviews, cross check, and so on. Now most information is available in authoritative and reasonably accurate form, often even in English. The Chinese can now know a lot more about their society. Beijing now has a telephone book; Moscow still does not. There has been an important movement of material from neibu availability (restricted) to public print. Information is generally becoming more available. These concrete specifics need to be tracked. For example, if the high-level cadres could increase the access for

295

their children into higher education, if there was a change from the current four-to-five percent of backdoor entry to the twenty-to-thirty percent it could readily become, this would have tremendous impact not only on the educational system but on people's perception of the long-term fairness of the whole system, which in turn could have consequential political effects. This would be disruptive, because one reason people put up with the present system is the feeling it is reasonably honest. If one does not pass a test, he can feel the people who passed got better scores; as is also true on Taiwan where there is a feeling the examination system is generally run fairly. Such trends need to be tracked. Another is creative writing which continues to be very drab.

Sullivan asked whether it was simply that the people who are already literate and already in the cities, the Chinese of the word as Smith called them, are having more access to a greater variety of communications, or is it that the people without the word were being brought in. **Smith** thought the people were being brought in. Certainly it was not yet anything like Taiwan or Japan, but radio and even television are reaching out into rural areas. It is still largely a potential.

Gastil believed we should distinguish between intellectuals and those who are literate and involved, that is, are interested in these issues but may have any kind of job, even be a farmer. It makes a difference, because the intellectual class has a class interest it wants to defend, while this other group is not a class. **Sullivan** said he was not talking about intellectuals, but about people in the cities with education (xiaoxi, "people in the know").

Smith noted that China was a terribly inconsistent country. There are many policies which are totally contradictory, and there are tremendous geographical differences. One of the most important distinctions in communications is between those regularly given access to Reference News and other internal publications, and those who do not have access. A wide circle now have access. Reference News is printed in more copies than the People's Daily.

Gastil asked if anyone could get access to the internal reference news. **Smith** replied it depended on where one was. At a university, yes, and in some enterprises like hotels. Those who regularly have access number about ten million. **Seymour** said there were many more who obtained access through those who regularly received it. **Smith** added that those who got this information received a great deal of undigested information, including news from Taiwan and Hong Kong.

296

Landman said that although there is a lot more published material in existence, it cannot be overemphasized that what is published and what is distributed is not the same. She had been in a
city 450 miles from Beijing (in Henan Province) where it took the
Peoples Daily three or four days just to arrive. Other publications simply never do arrive. While, the publications are not
expensive by our standards, they are difficult to buy for the
average Chinese, because they represent a considerable expen-
diture. Moreover, the worker in the fields simply has no time to
sit and read. She objected to the bias that the only people who
count are the intellectuals in the city. Eighty percent of the
population is not there.

Smith agreed, but pointed out that there are twenty-to-fifty
million in larger cities who had an opportunity that did not exist
just a few years ago.

Grieder said that qualitatively and quantitatively there was a
difference in the information imparted to the fifteen million who
may have had access and the sixty-to-seventy million that might
not easily have access. It seemed to him there was a qualitative
change. **Sullivan** thought the qualitative change was quite dramatic. He used to have the hardest time reading material from the
People's Republic--it was so boring and ridiculous. But the last
two or three years, especially 1979-81, was much more interesting.

Liang said that according to his experience most city people
have a chance to read newspapers. Often it is free because the
danwei pays for the workers. Every week there are two afternoons
for political study. The workers spend most of this time reading
the newspapers or magazines that are provided.

Seymour said that during his trip to northwest China he visited
Dunhuang in Gansu, a little town in the middle of the desert near
the Xinjiang border. The day he arrived was also the day that
television arrived (by cable). People were all gathered around
little open shops watching television.

Smith declared that it would be disastrous for the Voice of
America to slant the news; our reputation of fairness had been
earned over a period of years. If we lose this by lecturing, we
will be losing a great deal. **Grieder** agreed we could blow our
reputation very quickly. **Smith** said there had been a great deal
of informal polling of the Chinese as to why they listen to the
Voice. The response generally is, "The Voice gives us information
that is timely, balanced, and accurate, such as we do not get in

our own media." **Liang** added that unlike the Taiwan radio that attacks the system all the time, the Voice is very relaxed in its discussions.

Gastil asked what it was timely and accurate about. He thought there was an in-between ground. Many people, for example dissidents from Yugoslavia, are outraged that our radios seldom if ever mention human rights problems in Yugoslavia. Outside broadcasts can by mentioning sensitive topics, even if quite neutrally, serve a different function than by avoiding these topics. **Smith** said VOA mentions problems in China because it has to stay up with the nightly news.

Gastil wondered if it covered Chinese dissidents, for example. **Smith** thought it would when they were sufficiently newsworthy. He assumed the Voice had reported the recent hijacking to South Korea, and whatever facts were available. He was sure this was listened to in China with great interest. **Landman** said one of the things the Chinese she knew found most attractive was that news about their own country was carried by the Voice before their own press carried it.

Kintner found Smith's paper and remarks very interesting, especially since he had been involved in this field for many years, going back to the Psychology Strategy Board in 1951. Smith's conclusions were essentially that we should be very, very careful about doing anything. The purpose of this conference was to see what we can do. Kintner had thought communications was the area in which we could do something, yet Smith's suggestions were not positive. He wondered if Smith was, in fact, suggesting that we be very wary about using this instrument.

Smith replied that he thought we were using the instrument now in the most effective way we could. He noted that the VOA plans to spend an extra twenty million dollars for a transmitter in Sri Lanka, so we could reach Chinese audiences better. He was in favor of a reasonable increase in scholarship opportunities for Chinese students in the United States. There were other things of this kind. But in terms of sailing in with both fists, the general American way, saying, "Since we want to influence democracy in China, let's talk with them about democracy all day long," this would be a mistake.

Kintner wondered if there was anything from the experience of Radio Liberty and Radio Free Europe that would be applicable to China. **Smith** had concluded after long consideration that such efforts should not be initiated in Asia. **Sullivan** thought the difference was the Soviet control of Eastern Europe.

Smith said that in China there had been no jamming for a very long time. He was concerned that, if we take a Radio Liberty or Radio Marti approach, Beijing would begin jamming, and we would lose credibility.

Kintner asked what Smith thought of Taiwan's broadcasts. **Smith** said they were ignored. They had no audience. **Seymour** added that technically the reception was excellent. **Grieder** remembered that even when he was living in Taiwan, a long time back, the people in Taiwan were listening to the mainland--but not for political commentary. **Smith** added that immediately after the 1981 offers to Taiwan, the Chinese were listening to Taiwan Radio to get the full flavor of the response, if there was one. So they listened for a while, and when nothing much happened they dropped it. Otherwise, they were not much interested.

Liang said he supported Smith's opinion--"No action is action"--because he thought the Chinese people had strong national feelings. The dissidents need help and support, but they do not want the American government to ask the Chinese people to do anything. In order to support democracy in China he thought the best way was for the American government to keep a good relationship with the Chinese government. The open policies, such as sending students to this country and sending American teachers and scholars to China on cultural exchanges, were very important. Of course, the relationship to the mainland depends on the Russian relationship to China and Taiwan's relationship to America. The United States should support Taiwan no matter what its government, but its support should be very subtle, because for China's future the relationship to the PRC is more important.

Gastil asked if cultural exchange was so important, what would the discussants be willing to sacrifice for it? How would they react when students who come here begin claiming asylum? **Liang** thought very few would. Most students want to go back. A few want to stay here, because they have a bad background--for example, he might be on the police's list. When the children of high party leaders go back, they will go into important positions in the government, such as the propaganda bureau or the Peoples Daily. Perhaps they will still believe in Marxism and want to contribute to socialism, but they will at least know what is happening in America. They are getting new experiences.

Gastil suggested it might only take a few cases to destroy cultural exchange. To what extent should we be willing to force these people onto the planes? **Seymour** thought it would never come to forcing people onto planes, unless they had actually committed criminal actions in American terms. The U.S. government can handle these things delicately or clumsily--the Hu Na case was handled terribly clumsily. The INS (Immigration and Naturalization Service) can stall forever, and often does. For some reason there was pressure to act in the Hu Na case. Seymour had many friends in greater danger of being persecuted if they were sent back home than Hu Na. They have not gotten asylum, the cases are just delayed again and again. The only difference between granting asylum and delaying is that the former is a slap in the face to the foreign country involved.

Gastil asked if they were confident that the Chinese government would be willing to keep cultural exchange going as long as there was no slap in the face. **Smith** was not confident, but thought it would. The exchanges were a very important resource for the Chinese; they want to get trained people back. What they have cut off are exchanges they can do without, like American movies. **Seymour** mentioned that they had just taken a big contract with AMC, which was much more important.

Grieder said there was an acerbic exchange in the New York **Times** the other morning quoting Deng Xiaoping taking issue with Reagan's view that China needs the United States more than they need us. Deng Xiaoping said that the United States should not bet on it. But in a limited sense Reagan may be right. **Seymour** was not sure our government would be able to act shrewdly, but he hoped it could. There was a built-in incentive on the Chinese side that should be sensibly taken advantage of.

Zhu said that very few Chinese students in America studied the social sciences, but they were very important for China's future, especially in regard to democracy. There had been no contact with the outside for so long. Ninety percent of the students who study in the United States study the natural sciences, but when they return in three or four years they will get a very good job, and in ten years they will have influence. They will be quite different from people who did not get a chance to go abroad.

Liang gave the example of Dr. Wang Bingzhang, the leader of **China** Spring. If he had gone back to China he could have gotten a very good job. The Chinese Embassy in Canada told him that he could easily be made a party member, director of an institute, and later get a higher job. Yet he finally decided to stay and lead his movement. He agrees with Zhu most of those who go back will get important jobs.

Landman thought we were interested in more than the people who study and go back and get into big positions. She said that when

Americans go to China we do not only influence people at the top. It is very important that a more or less ordinary person might learn and see a little bit about America, about which they have so many misconceptions. **Liang** thought that such people are only important in the West. But in China the high party leaders control everything. If we have some friends in the high positions, this is what is important. **Landman** countered that when **Liang**'s wife-to-be (Judy Shapiro) went to Changsha and others to Henan, they were not only influencing the provincial Party secretaries.

Liang agreed that his wife brought many books, and they were all borrowed by students. That had been **Landman**'s point; it was important, and those students were not necessarily going to be leaders. **Zhu** pointed out that many of the students now in the United States will go back to teach in colleges or universities. They will have considerable influence in this way.

Huang thought we should face the fact that many more Chinese students will choose to stay in this country than Liang and Zhu had optimistically assumed. If we draw on the experience of Taiwan, in the past thirty years 63,000 came to study here and 7,000 returned. How many return to the PRC will depend on the situation in China, on the "four modernizations," on the degree the society becomes more open, and other considerations. It is true that when Taiwan does well more do return.

Kintner who had been on the Board of Foreign Scholarships in East Asia, the Fulbright Program, noted that one of the biggest problems had been the unwillingness of Asian scholars from all over to go back to Asia. Even though they were sent by their own governments, they had one lifetime to lead, and they wanted to enjoy the benefits of their education as much as possible. Kintner also noted that at the University of Pennsylvania and similar institutions there were students from Hong Kong and Taiwan, as well as mainland China. They did get together and talk. He wanted to ask the Chinese students at the conference what the impact was of a Chinese scholar from the mainland studying with these other groups, as far as the development of attitudes was concerned. **Zhu** said they had good relations. **Liao** said his experience was that hostility was greatly reduced. They have disagreements, but on basic issues there are no fundamental differences. He certainly hoped there would not be a war between the two states. All hope there will be democracy. Some from the PRC might have strong nationalist sentiments and say we must become a unified country. But this does not really matter.

Grieder said he shared Huang's skepticism on the return rate, although the cases of Taiwan and the mainland were quite different. In large part this is because there is a limited vocational opportunity in Taiwan for the specializations picked up in the United States. It is a walk-on-two-legs situation. If vocational opportunity actually develops on the mainland for people who go back, the incentive will be greater. He did not know how to assess ideological incentives.

Zhu reminded us that half of the students were sponsored by the government. This meant they had to go back, for if they fail to return they will run big risks, especially for their families still in China. So most people will go back.

Gastil concluded that several of the papers and discussants had suggested that in the case of Taiwan we should be doing more. In other words, we should preach to Taiwan, but not to the PRC. He wondered if this was really what they believed.

Seymour would accept this proposition, yet he thought we needed to maintain a single standard under whatever American administration. When the Beijing government does something that violates human rights standards, this should be pointed out in the normal course of news reporting. If they lock up a nonviolent dissident, this should be pointed out as a violation of their official standards. At the same time he agreed with Smith and Liang there was not a great deal we can do to support democracy directly in the PRC, and, if we do the wrong things, it is apt to be counter-productive. But in the case of Taiwan, there was a great deal that we could and should do.

One reason we do not do more to criticize Taiwan's record is poor reporting by the media. Seymour disagreed with Bernstein's statement that Taiwan was relatively so democratic we should not be discussing it at the same conference--yet this view is widely held. One reason the situation in Taiwan is not adequately reported is that the journalists who go there are three-day wonders. The New York Times reported the so-called 'Kaohsiung Trial.'' It was not a trial--the trial had taken place earlier behind closed doors--but the government had called it a trial, so the Times called it a trial. There are no regular American reporters in Taipei he knew of, and, of course, the government screens who comes and who does not. Seymour cannot obtain a visa. This is symptomatic of the way the government controls information. If one cannot go there, he cannot report very authoritatively. American papers depend primarily on stringers who are there for other reasons: they may be married to a Taiwanese or engaged in

another business. They naturally indulge in heavy self-censorship. The KMT is brilliant in manipulating the coverage. The
result of inaccurate perception is that little is done to improve
the situation. The would-be opposition is in prison. The United
States could and should do something about it.

Huang distinguished between preaching and political maneuver.
In his paper he wrote primarily of political maneuver. He would
never say that we should not do anything about the PRC. Smith had
said we should not lecture, but he was not saying we should be
passive. Our opportunities, governmental or private, will
increase. He agreed with Seymour that we should be talking about
human rights violations in China and conveying our position. The
human rights society Huang had set up with his friends in 1974 has
been doing this for almost ten years. It might be good for the
Voice of America to report more about human rights groups or
cultural exchange groups, but we should be very careful.

Seymour said we should apply political and economic pressure to
Taiwan. When they come asking us for A, B, C, and D, we should
answer, "Well, how many political prisoners do you have?" **Gastil**
wondered why we couldn't say the same to the PRC. **Seymour** said
that in a sense Deng Xiaoping was right; they did not need us that
badly.

Liang said that, "No action is action," does not mean doing
nothing. But if the Voice of America starts reporting about
dissident groups, then the Chinese government will not allow
people to listen. Today the government allows people to listen to
the Voice, because it has little political content. Giving more
fellowships to scholars in the PRC is also action. On the other
hand, American newspapers, radio, and television are private.
They should discuss human rights issues, because they are not
government. For example, in the Liu Qing case, the Washington
Post reported it, but the **New York Times** did not. There should be
more reporting of this kind.

Seymour said that over the years the Times had reported a great
deal about human rights violations in the PRC (although not in
Taiwan). Even before they had their own reporters in Beijing,
they used to carry John Fraser's pieces from the **Toronto Globe and
Mail**.

Moody said that if the U.S. government was going to support
democracy in either case, the government would have to make a link
with what the general foreign policy was. What bothered him about
Seymour's approach to Taiwan was that it was highly confrontatio-
nal. We have so distanced ourselves from Taiwan that we have also

to a large extent forfeited the right to lecture them. Of course we did this for foreign policy reasons. In the United States government there has been a tendency to overestimate the delicacy of our relation to mainland China--as Pye intimated in his paper. The Chinese know this tendency full well and take advantage of it. If the relationship is not founded on objective interests on both sides, Moody thought it was not much of a relationship anyway. If the Chinese turn to the Russians just out of irritation, then our relations were not that important anyhow. The PRC is approaching Moscow now, and there are good objective reasons why it should. Since today they do not have to worry about the United States, under President Reagan, they can afford to moderate their own position and thereby reduce the extent to which they are tied to the United States. He concluded that in relation to both Taiwan and the mainland there was a good deal of room for give and take, but the United States could take a somewhat firmer position with both.

Smith said that the Voice of America actually gave a lot of coverage to the Chinese community in this country, including coverage of scholars and visitors. The question of coverage of exile or dissident groups in this country is a tougher one. We have confronted it in regard to Afghanistan and decided to go ahead and push the coverage of freedom fighters that are brought here, and so forth. Whether or not this is right is another question. **Grieder** thought Afghanistan a less ambiguous situation.

Smith said that in the end he went back to the CBS or NBC rules: if a group makes legitimate full-scale news, then cover it. Certainly the nongovernmental media will cover it. We could, for example, put Fox Butterfield and Richard Bernstein on the Voice of America talk shows, and they could talk about dissidents. **Liang** recalled that last month the Voice interviewed him and his friends, and his family in China heard it. Of course, they were not talking about communism; they were describing American culture, education, and so on.

Grieder wondered if the Chinese government would not perceive the New York Times as an organ of the U.S. government. **Smith** said some would, but many would not. It was worth making the extra effort. In regard to Taiwan it is the same way. If there is a tendency for the government to lean over backwards to avoid irritating the PRC, the tendency is even stronger in regard to Taiwan.

Dreyer remained uncomfortable with Seymour's double standard. What about all the people in the Chinese communist "gulag," in Qinghai province, people who for minor peccadilloes are sentenced to five years of labor? She did not think it was fair to criticize one and not the other; this is what it came down to.

Seymour replied that it did not come down to that. He was simply agreeing with the statement of everyone who had spoken earlier that there was not a great deal we can do to make the PRC democratic. He thought we should do anything we can, we should maintain a single standard, but we should not be under the illusion that anything we do will make the PRC democratic.

Sullivan agreed with Smith that the current administration's idea to promote democracy is too heavy-handed and preachy. Another problem he saw with their approach was that it was not so much an effort to promote democracy as a way to attack communism. In the hearing on the democracy project Congressman Solarz asked Secretary of State Shultz, "Are you going to bring people over from South Korea to promote democracy there?" Shultz stumbled and really could not answer.

Sullivan agreed that in Taiwan we could expect more, because they are not as obnoxious a government as that in the PRC. **Dreyer** said, "Not so obnoxious, so therefore we can preach more?" **Sullivan** thought we could since we had sold them military weapons, given them aid, and signed treaties with them. **Gastil** wondered if there wasn't the same danger of a negative reaction by Taiwan's leaders as by the communists. **Sullivan** did not see as much. We have more right to apply pressure, and we have more contacts. We can tell them that this is not the way to run a civilized society, that they should know better.

Liao thought there were ways to influence the Taiwanese government. However, in the past several years Taiwanese have begun to feel they are no longer secure. Both the people and the government want to get more weapons from the United States or Europe. Their fear is shown in the outflow of capital, in the movement of the rich to the States. If the U.S. government puts pressure on the Taiwanese government, the impression will be created that, "You don't sell me weapons I need, and yet you put pressure on." This is likely to polarize Taiwanese society. It will be perceived that the U.S. government is actually backing one political faction. For example, it is the sense on Taiwan that the U.S. Government or some Americans are backing Tang-Wai.

Sullivan asked if Liao thought that by not selling the weapons we were losing our instrument of leverage. **Liao** said that weapons symbolize a long-term commitment to Taiwan's security. Without security what is the point of democracy? If we cannot defend ourselves, after one year of democracy we might disappear. **Zhu**

wondered, however, if the United States agreed to sell advanced weapons, what would be the reaction from the mainland. The communists might counter by moving more of their forces to the Formosa Straits opposite Taiwan.

Liao agreed this was a problem, but the feeling was this way in Taiwan. There is a feeling that there is no longer a long-term American commitment to its security. He suggested that Freedom House or a similar organization should invite Taiwanese opposition leaders and moderate KMT people to come to the United States to hold a conference with American scholars to discuss the year's achievements in democratization. If possible it should be done every year. If Americans did not want to see a military dictatorship in Taiwan, the United States should endorse, in this way or some other, the opposition and the liberal faction in the KMT. **Sullivan** asked if the moderate KMT people would attend such a conference. **Liao** thought they would as long as it was a diverse group.

Gastil wondered about an American group endorsing the opposition. If there is a conference with people from a wide variety of parties this is one thing, but if we seem to endorse a particular group, this is quite another. **Liao** said he was not suggesting endorsing any particular group or leader. Rather, hold a conference and then select participants that fit our goals.

Seymour pointed out that one element that should be represented is in prison, so they could not come. Would Liao, he wondered, include overseas Taiwanese in this country, such as the Taidu (T'ai-tu) people? **Liao** said he would. **Seymour** thought this would get other attendees in trouble. **Sullivan** felt the KMT people would not show up.

Another conference topic that an organization like Freedom House might consider, **Smith** suggested, was the future political evolution of China—he would not use a term like democracy. People could be invited from the mainland, and probably Taiwan, to discuss their future without foreigners getting in the way. The discussion would be very cautious, but there would be some very useful talk in the corridors. It might be worth trying.

Liao gave some examples of similar efforts. At the annual meeting of the Association for Asian Studies there had been a panel on the problem of unification. There were participants from both Taiwan and China. This was possible because the conference was sponsored by the American association. There was also a conference at St. Johns University two years ago to which representatives from China and Taiwan were invited. Liao concluded such conferences were quite possible. **Liang** noted that Chinese students here often hold small group discussions on China's future.

Gastil recalled that someone had said ninety percent of the Chinese students in the United States were in the natural sciences or related technologies, and this is true of students from other parts of the world, too. The United States has never had any way to give such students education either in democracy or the United States' political system. There is nothing on the campuses directed toward this objective. Unless the student takes political science or a similar course, he can spend several years here and learn nothing about the democratic system. Gastil had found that many Iranian students spent most of their time with other Iranians, and they barely spoke English even after four years. About all they had gained was their specialty. **Smith** disagreed. He thought just the evening news gave them enough.

Liang said this was why he felt the scholars from China needed a magazine. He and his friends hope to publish essays and information of particular interest to this group. He agreed that they could just watch news for four years and learn very little.

Sullivan asked Landman whether she had gotten a very good idea from her two-to-three years in China about how the system worked, even though it was a closed system. **Landman** said she had, but added that she had taken many courses on China before she had gone. **Liao** pointed out that most Chinese students know nothing about the United States before they come.

Landman still felt that it would be difficult to stay in the United States for four years without knowing about our system. **Smith** had talked with many Chinese students when they returned. Their knowledge was fragmentary, but they had very strong positive reactions about many aspects of American life. When added together they would be seen to have learned about democracy. Smith added that he would not underestimate all of the activities on American campuses which in an informal way serve this function.

What would be the difference, **Landman** asked, between having an organized course on the American way of life for Chinese students who come to the United States, and Chinese "political study?" It would be seen, **Sullivan** thought, in the way missionaries are seen as imposing ideas. It would be much better to tell these students what courses are available to all students in these fields and let them take what they want. If a course is set up for foreign students, it is going to be propaganda.

Gastil said he was talking about something completely voluntary. We have that now, **Sullivan** suggested. Some students do not have an interest in politics. We should not force it down their throats. This is what we criticize others for.

In many countries, **Gastil** pointed out, the average student who later goes into politics either has an engineering or a medical degree. These are the people who may eventually become prime ministers. **Sullivan** thought Kwame Nkrumah received a degree in history and political science, and then became a dictator. **Moody** added Ghotbzadeh.

Sullivan said he opposed heavy-handed methods. Their absence in the United States is what makes us different from the Soviet Union and Taiwan. Taiwan's propaganda is so obvious that it is ineffective. The principle of our system is the right to make a choice. If you want to vote you can; if you don't, you don't have to.

Zhu said he was from the mainland, studying social science. He was going back to China to teach. He will teach social science, not just what he learned about American society. What was important was to learn to apply to China modern methodology and analysis.

Seymour thought Gastil had pointed to a real need. He did not think a course should be offered, but perhaps a fairly regular discussion group might be organized for foreign students. He thought many students coming from China might be embarrassed talking about American politics with American students or professors; they are afraid to ask apparently stupid questions. They might be less hesitant, for example, at a brown-bag lunch attended mostly by foreign students. Not "political study," but genuine discussion.

We should avoid the attitude that "We are going to mold you," **Sullivan** repeated. Such a program will get the students who will be contacted anyway. The others will stay away. Of course, as long as it was low level and nongovernmental, through institutions such as the International Houses, it would be fine. He agreed with Zhu that we are trying to instill through social science a methodology, not values; this is why he had taken the line on culture he did. If China develops a democracy, it will be in a unique way, as was Japan's, and it will have uniquely Chinese characteristics. **Gastil** argued it would, but it would also have many values taken from Western culture.

Sullivan thought we should let them find these values. One does not have to go very far in this country to know there is freedom of the press and freedom of speech.

Moving to another subject, it seemed to be generally assumed by the group, **Gastil** recalled, that if Taiwan became a democracy tomorrow it would be able to make the system work. He asked if everyone agreed with this.

Huang agreed in a very broad sense. **Sullivan** agreed, but emphasized that democracy in Taiwan would look very different. Democracy in either of the "two Chinas" would place more emphasis on the leader, the executive would be stronger, perhaps more on the French model. It would be unitary, not federal. Like the French President, the leader would be able to push through his budget without parliamentary approval, and he would have the power to dissolve parliament once a year. There would be factionalism, but not the same as Japan's. There would be more limitation on individual rights than we are used to, and greater concern with internal security. It would have something close to the Official Secrets Act of Great Britain. The independent court system would not take hold, mainly because they borrowed so much of their legal system from the Germans. There would be a strong national- istic strain. He added that a mainland democracy would be less likely to be cheek-and-jowl with the United States mainly because an authoritarian state is more able to switch its allegiance. **Gastil** noted that he posited many restrictions. **Sullivan** said restrictions would go even further than what is seen in England, particularly in areas the Chinese consider "vulgar" or "insincere." **Smith** thought he was describing Singapore. Others disagreed. The selection of the executive, said **Sullivan**, would probably be in several steps. Many government positions would be beyond direct public control. There would be no initiative or recall. Yet it would be a democracy with periodic elections that all sectors would agree should be overturned or postponed only in extreme emergencies.

Would it be, asked **Gastil**, essentially as democratic as Japan? **Sullivan** saw Taiwan's "democracy" being analogous to that of Japan in the late fifties. **Moody** thought this possible, but doubted there was cohesion in the government or opposition. The main thing that holds the KMT together is probably the access to power. There are many in the KMT who ideologically could as easily be Tang-Wai. The Tang-Wai itself has many positions. Liberalization would not solve this highly fractionated situation. So, for a democracy to work, it might have to be a highly authoritarian democracy.

Taiwan "democracy" sounded more and more like Taiwan today to **Gastil**. **Sullivan** objected that the people in power today have no basic institutional accountability to the population at large. The picture he paints would represent a significant change. "They could be thrown out?", **Gastil** asked. They could, **Sullivan** replied, but once in power they would not operate under a separation of power. There would not be as free-wheeling a press, individuals will be more restricted as in fact they are in many democracies. People would not be arbitrarily thrown in jail, there would be freedom to organize, so it would not be like Taiwan today. He disagreed with the fear Taiwan would become an inevitably factionalized and fractionized political system. The society has the necessary cohesion.

Huang said the argument that the Tang-Wai would be so fractionated it could not rule is one the KMT has long been promoting. When Yü Teng-fa was about to get everybody together he was jailed. When others moved toward an opposition party, they were suppressed. The argument was greatly exaggerated. If the Tang-Wai had power, they would learn to compromise. As to the type of democracy, he agreed generally but could not be as definite as Sullivan.

The political developments would be hard to forecast, **Liao** thought. First, political parties must be organized. After forming the parties to run an election, the election will cause more splitting. But then coalitions might form for later elections.

Liang hoped Taiwan would protect its image. If democracy improved steadily there, then the mainland could learn from Taiwan. **Seymour** agreed that in theory the mainland could learn a good deal from Taiwan, but basic changes would depend on what happened in the PRC itself. As to democracy in Taiwan, Seymour said that after the death or retirement of Chiang Ching-kuo, there will be instability and anything might happen. It would accomplish a great deal if martial law were lifted. There was now a dual legal system, and the civil system was not that bad. If the military were kept out of the system, the secret police were restricted, and the party reduced its interference, then movement in the democratic direction would be greatly facilitated. The form democracy would take was hard to estimate. Taiwan was under Japan for fifty years, and especially the older people remember this. There is a tendency to look to Japan as much as there was a tendency on the mainland not to look to Japan. Anything could happen.

The bureaucracy would be important, **Sullivan** concluded, more like that in Japan and France, more protected and self-perpetuating. He agreed that elimination of martial law would be a good first step.

Summary and Conclusions*

The conference attempted to put in perspective some assumptions about the possibilities for democratic evolution in mainland China and Taiwan. There are obviously many reasons to doubt that there will be a rapid movement toward stable democracy in either land. The obstacles that are generally cited are real, including poverty and a relatively low educational level on the mainland, the long history of authoritarian government (often called political culture), and, for the mainland, the sheer size of the country and its population. However, in the short-term the overriding reason that rapid change is improbable is the strength of the control apparatus in both countries and the unlikelihood that the leadership of either country will risk the liberalizations that would inevitably accompany democratic evolution. They simply have too much to lose.

The political and philosophical history of China has in many ways left a difficult legacy. Religion and religious institutions did not reach the stage of development found in other civilizations. This is an important reason China has never developed the concept of limited government with its accompanying pluralistic assumptions. Chinese governments have historically been absolute in theory, and the claims of the state have gone largely unchallenged. It is significant that in Tibet, in Muslim areas, and on Taiwan dissent is organized to a significant extent around religious institutions that are not traditionally a part of Chinese civilization. The acceptance of the concept of limited government is basic to democracy. Democracy as we know it is also based on the idea of individual autonomy as expressed in the terminology of individual rights. The group or society, whether

---

*This is the author's personal summarization of the conference proceedings and does not necessarily reflect the views of the other participants.

extended family, village or state, has often been given primacy in China: while democracy is not impossible in societies giving more weight to group interests than our own, appeals to the primacy of the state over the individual have been used almost universally as a means to deny basic human rights.

Traditionally, Chinese society has been split between a small, literate elite adhering to an autocratic, elitist Confucian tradition and a large peasant population more influenced by Buddhist, Daoist, and folk beliefs. The power of the elite has to a degree been built on the passive, fatalistic, and other-worldly content of peasant beliefs. As China modernizes both communists and noncommunists debate the role of the peasant and the definition of democracy against this background. It is hard for elitists of either group to view the peasant majority as a positive force in development or to see democracy as more than the transfer of power from a stultifying bureaucracy to a modernizing, technological elite.

To a degree the concept of democracy in the Chinese context can be built on the traditional concept of the government and bureaucracy as the servants of the interests of the people as a whole. When they no longer served this function the "Mandate of Heaven" was withdrawn--usually through the instrumentality of revolt by the elite. In practice this traditional view expressed more of a pious hope than reality. This tradition has also served to support a highly elitist view of politics that assumes that a small educated minority should and must rule over the uneducated "masses." This approach is easily assimilated into the communist belief in the leadership role of the "vanguard party." In its ideological roots the Kuomintang that rules on Taiwan accepts the same assumptions in this regard as the Chinese Communist Party. Technological modernists within the latter party appear to be engaged in yet another adaptation to ensure the continuity of elite rule. Several of the conferees noted that one problem with the Chinese dissident movement, at least as it has periodically expressed itself on the mainland, is its absorption in intellectual causes and lack of connection with the interests of the peasants that make up eighty percent of the population. Among the Chinese in our group there was a hope that the coming of democracy to China would not affect the elite role of the intellectuals.

It is often argued and was argued in this group that the requirements of development inevitably lead to large-scale planning and a degree of control over the economy and population growth that is not consonant with democracy.

Both the argument from the necessities of development and arguments from the nature of the political culture suffered in the group's opinion from comparison with counterexamples. Countries such as India and Japan certainly have traditions that hold little promise of receptivity to liberal traditions. Both are traditionally more hierarchical than China, and certainly India's caste system is spectacularly "anti-democratic" in a psychological sense. We also need hardly mention the overwhelming problems of development that India faces. Yet India and Japan are today much more democratic than either Taiwan or the People's Republic of China.

The general feeling of the group about the limited effect of Chinese culture on the possibilities of the future evolution of its politics was reflected in the feeling of most participants that democracy could be operated by the Taiwanese should they be able to overcome the present authoritarian rule. There was also considerable agreement on the nature of democracy should it come to Taiwan--and later to the mainland. In either area democracy would have many of the attributes that we associate with Japanese democracy, although it would be characteristically Chinese. The key to its claim to political and civil democracy would be the periodic and fair election of national leaders. Beyond this, however, there would be more constraints on expression and less separation of powers among the branches of government than Americans are used to.

The group as a whole, and particularly those of Chinese background or citizenship, felt that the primary obstacles to democracy were authoritarian controls themselves. For example, on the one hand the Nationalists in Taiwan have developed a mythology that they rule all China. This has persisted as serious policy only because those who objected were punished: the dogma could not be questioned. Now they, and therefore the land they rule, are trapped in the myth. To abandon it would be to lose all legitimacy, and open democracy would lead rapidly, in the opinion of most of the group, to the replacement of the mainland elite now ruling Taiwan.

Even more critical is the position of the elite now ruling China. Its legitimacy rests primarily on its control over the communist ideology. Yet now in a practical sense the communist elite seems to have abandoned many of its key tenets. Its leaders understand that in many ways the more liberal West represents the "modern" political-economic system, and that mythology will no longer do. Of course, in a general sense most Chinese probably

adhere to "socialism," but this is far from the intense belief
that brought the communists to power. Yet even if those at the
top were willing to risk democracy, millions of lower-level party
officials, particularly in the security services, would be most
loathe to do so. Anyone who tried to carry liberalization very
far at the top would probably be replaced by his lieutenants.

An alternative path to change would be through the growth of
popular dissidence on the "Solidarity" model, only here without an
equivalent threat of Soviet intervention. But it was generally
felt that a Solidarity-type situation could not develop in China
because of the much more severe repression, particularly on the
mainland. Free trade unions for example exist in neither land.
There is some opposition on Taiwan. Although it operates under
severe constraints, and is not allowed to organize formally into a
political party, its representatives are elected to a few positions in assemblies at local, regional, and national levels. In
the People's Republic no opposition of any kind is generally
permitted, although for short periods dissident views have been
publicly expressed.

The implications of the group's analysis for American policy or
for groups such as Freedom House were warmly debated. However, a
consensus was reached on the main issues.

It was generally felt that Taiwan had reached a point where
movement to democracy could be expected to move rapidly under
favorable conditions. A large degree of economic freedom had been
obtained, the population was educated and knowledgeable about the
world. There was a relatively large group of people willing to
struggle to bring about more freedom. The role of the United
States as the main protector of Taiwan also placed it and its
people in a particularly favorable position to influence this
evolution. Without appearing to dictate change we could nevertheless make a connection between the scale and reliability of our
aid and international support and progress in such areas as human
rights and democratic evolution. Private groups could support
this policy through holding conferences that implicitly show a
degree of American support for those most interested in liberalization. In so far as possible we should stay neutral on the
eventual relation of Taiwan to the mainland, realizing that a
democratic Taiwan would probably be dominated by Taiwanese not
committed to the concept of one China.

America's role in influencing the evolution of the People's
Republic must on the other hand be a much more modest one. Until
now our most important influence has come through the Chinese

language broadcasts of the Voice of America. The commitment of these broadcasts and of other Western media to a high standard of objectivity has had a strong positive effect on a Chinese population that only now, and to a limited extent, is emerging from an overpowering experience with a totally controlled and narrowly propagandistic national communications system. All felt that this approach should be continued and strengthened, and that it should not be watered down by broadcasts of a more propagandistic nature. It was also felt that the exchange of students that is now occurring on an unprecedented scale was extremely important. We are training an important segment of the next generation of Chinese leaders, and for the first time they will have a real understanding of the West. Beyond activities of this sort it was felt that there was little we could do. For the sake of consistency, and to demonstrate the reality of our values, we should protest both publicly and privately violations of human rights in the PRC. Our failure to criticize the human rights record of either China consistently was felt by some to have damaged the effectiveness of our human rights effort in all of Asia. We should make known our interest in dissidents, and when appropriate include news about them in our media (and thereby reduce the news blackout that characterizes most dissident activity in China itself). But we have little economic or political leverage, and too overt an effort to force change in China would be likely to be counterproductive; it could even antagonize many of the liberalizing youth that are both highly nationalistic and in the forefront of the struggle for change.

Although the conferees were not primarily activists, and were believers in evolutionary change rather than revolutionary, most participants did see hope for an expansion of freedom. This was particularly true of Taiwan, and some felt that democracy on Taiwan would have at least a limited effect on the evolution of the Chinese mainland. Change in the PRC would come slowly, and with the change of generations, and in response to changing economic conditions. Growing economic freedoms, if allowed to continue, would have an increasing impact in political and cultural areas. There would, of course, be setbacks, but the group doubted that there would be a return to the anarchical tyranny of the Cultural Revolution.

PART IV

Country Summaries

Introduction

The following country descriptions summarize the evidence that lies behind our ratings for each country. They first bring together for each country most of the tabular material of Part I. Then, political rights are considered in terms of the extent to which a country is ruled by a government elected by the majority at the national level, the division of power among levels of government, and the possible denial of self-determination to major subnationalities, if any. While decentralization and the denial of group rights are deemphasized in our rating system, these questions should not be ignored. The summaries also contain consideration of civil liberties, especially as these include freedom of the media and other forms of political expression, freedom from political imprisonment, torture, and other forms of government reprisal, and freedom from interference in nonpublic group or personal life. Equality of access to politically relevant expression is also considered. Economic conditions and organization are also considered in their relation to freedom. In some cases the summaries will touch on the relative degree of freedom from oppression outside of the government arena, for example, through slavery, labor bosses, capitalist exploitation, or private terrorism: this area of analysis is little developed at present.

At the beginning of each summary statement the country is characterized by the forms of its economy and polity. The meanings of the terms used in this classification may be found in Part I, "The Relation of Political-Economic Systems to Freedom," and its accompanying Table 6. The classification is highly simplified, but it serves our concern with the developmental forms and biases that affect political controls. As in Table 6 the terms **inclusive** and **noninclusive** are used to distinguish between societies in which the economic activities of most people are organized in accordance with the dominant system and those dual societies in which they remain largely outside. The system should be assumed to be inclusive unless otherwise indicated.

Each state is categorized according to the political positions of the national or ethnic groups it contains. Since the modern political form is the "nation-state," it is not surprising that many states have a relatively homogeneous population. The overwhelming majority in these states belong to roughly the same ethnic group; people from this group naturally form the dominant group in the state. In relatively homogeneous states there is no large subnationality (that is, with more than one million people or twenty percent of the population) residing in a defined territory within the country: Austria, Costa Rica, Somalia, and West Germany are good examples. States in this category may be ethnically diverse (for example, Cuba or Colombia), but there are no sharp ethnic lines between major groups. These states should be distinguished from **ethnically complex states**, such as Guyana or Singapore, that have several ethnic groups, but no major group that has its historic homeland in a particular part of the country. Complex states may have large minorities that have suffered social, political, or economic discrimination in the recent past, but today the governments of such states treat all peoples as equals as a matter of policy. In this regard complex states are distinguishable from **ethnic states with major nonterritorial subnationalities**, for the governments of such states have a deliberate policy of giving preference to the dominant ethnic group at the expense of other major groups. Examples are Burundi or China (Taiwan).

Another large category of states is labeled **ethnic states with (a) major territorial subnationalities(y)**. As in the homogeneous states there is a definite ruling people (or Staatsvolk) residing on its historic national territory within the state. But the state also incorporates other territories with other historic peoples that are now either without a state, or the state dominated by their people lies beyond the new border. As explained in **Freedom in the World 1978** (pp. 180-218), to be considered a subnationality a territorial minority must have enough cohesion and publicity that their right to nationhood is acknowledged in some quarters. Often recent events have forged a quasi-unity among quite distinct groups--as among the peoples of Southern Sudan. Typical countries in this category are Burma and the USSR. **Ethnic states with major potential territorial subnationalities** fall into a closely related category. In such states--for example, Ecuador of Bolivia--many individuals in pre-national ethnic groups have merged, with little overt hostility, with the dominant ethnic strain. The assimilation process has gone on for centuries. Yet in these countries the new consciousness that accompanies the diffusion of nationalistic ideas through education may reverse the process of assimilation in the future, especially where the potential subnationality has preserved a more or less definable territorial base.

There are a few truly multinational states in which ethnic groups with territorial bases coexist in one state without an established ruling people of Staatsvolk. In such states the several "nations" each have autonomous political rights, although these do not in law generally include the right to secession. India and Nigeria are examples. One **trinational** and a few binational states complete the categories of those states in which several "nations" coexist.

The distinction between truly multinational states and ethnic states with territorial subnationalities may be made by comparing two major states that lie close to the margin between the categories--the ethnic Russian USSR and multinational India. In the USSR, Russian is in every way the dominant language. By contrast, in India Hindi speakers have not achieved dominance. English remains a unifying lingua franca, the languages of the several states have not been forced to change their script to accord with Hindi forms, and Hindi itself is not the distinctive language of a "ruling people"--it is a nationalized version of the popular language of a portion of the population of northern India. (The pre-British ruling class used a closely related language with Arabic, Persian, and Turkish infusions; it was generally written in Persian-Arabic script.) Unlike Russians in the non-Russian Soviet Republics, Hindi speakers from northern India do not have a special standing in their own eyes or those of other Indians. Calcutta, Bombay, and Madras are non-Hindi speaking cities, and their pride in their identities and cultures is an important aspect of Indian culture. By contrast, many Soviet Republics are dominated by Russian speakers, a situation developing even in Kiev, the largest non-Russian city.

Finally, transethnic heterogeneous states, primarily in Africa, are those in which independence found a large number of ethnically distinct peoples grouped more or less artificially within one political framework. The usual solution was for those taking over the reins of government to adopt the colonial approach of formally treating all local peoples as equal, but with the new objective of integrating all equally into a new national framework (and new national identity) as and when this would be possible. Rulers of states such as Senegal of Zaire may come from relatively small tribes, and it is in their interest to deemphasize tribalism. In some cases the tribes are so scattered and localistic that there is no short-term likelihood of secession resulting from tribalism. However, in other cases portions of the country have histories of separate nationhood making the transethnic solution hard to implement. In a few countries recent events have placed certain ethnic groups in opposition to one another or to ruling circles in such a way that the transethnic state remains only the formal principle of rule, replaced in practice by an ethnic hierarchy, as in Congo, Sierra Leone, or Ghana.

The descriptive paragraphs for political and civil rights are largely self-explanatory. Subnationalities are generally discussed under a subheading for political rights, although the subject has obvious civil liberties aspects. Discussion of the existence or nonexistence of political parties may be arbitrarily placed in one or the other section. These paragraphs only touch on a few relevant issues, especially in the civil liberties discussion. An issue may be omitted for lack of information, because it does not seem important for the country addressed, or because a particular condition can be inferred from the general statement of a pattern. It should be noted that we have tried where possible to incorporate the distinction between a broad definition of political prisoners (including those detained for violent political crimes) and a narrow definition that includes those arrested only for nonviolent actions--often labeled "prisoners of conscience." Obviously we are primarily concerned with the latter.

Under civil liberties there is often a sentence or two on the economy. However, this is primarily a survey of politically relevant freedoms and not economic freedoms. In addition our view of economic freedom depends less on the economic system than the way in which it is adopted and maintained. (See Lindsay Wright, in Freedom in the World 1982, pp. 51-90, and her article pp. 73-96 in this volume.)

At the end of each country summary we have included an overall comparative statement that places the country's ratings in relation to those of others. Countries chosen for comparison are often neighboring or similar ones, but juxtaposing very different countries is also necessary for tying together the system.

The following summaries take little account of the oppressions that occur within the social units of a society, such as family and religious groups, or that reflect variations in the nonpolitical aspects of culture. In particular, the reader will note few references in the following summaries to the relative freedom of women. This may be a serious gap in the Survey, but with limited resources we felt that it was better to omit this range of issues than to only tangentially include it. We suspect that including the freedom of women would not affect the ratings a great deal. Democracies today have almost universally opened political and civic participation to women on at least a formal basis of equality, while most nondemocratic societies that deny these equal rights to women also deny effective participation to most men. In such societies granting equal rights has limited meaning. There is little gain for political and most civil rights when women are granted equal participation in a totalitarian society. However, it is hoped that future annuals will be able to look specifically at denials of freedom to women, as well as other examples of rank disparity in the treatment of social groups, classes, races, or religions.

AFGHANISTAN

Economy: noninclusive socialist   **Political Rights:** 7
Polity: communist one-party   **Civil Liberties:** 7
Population: 14,000,000   **Status of Freedom:** not free

An ethnic state with major territorial subnationalities.

Political Rights. Afghanistan is now ruled by a communist party under the tutelage and direct control of the Soviet Union. The rule of this very small party has no electoral or traditional legitimization. Soviet forces control the major cities but their control is contested by a variety of resistance movements throughout the country. Subnationalities: The largest minority is the Tajik (thirty percent), the dominant people of the cities and the western part of the country. Essentially lowland Persians, their language remains the lingua franca of the country. The Persian speaking Hazaras constitute five to ten percent of the population. Another ten percent belong to Uzbek and other Turkish groups in the north.

Civil Liberties. The media are primarily government owned and under rigid control. Antigovernment organization or expression is forbidden. Conversation is guarded and travel is restricted. In a condition of civil war and foreign occupation, political imprisonment, torture and execution are common, in addition to war deaths and massacres. Resources have been diverted to the Soviet Union as payment for its military "assistance." The modern sectors of the economy are controlled; much of the agricultural economy has been destroyed. the objectives of the state are totalitarian; their achievement is limited by the continuing struggle for control.

Comparatively: Afghanistan is as free as Mongolia, less free than Iran.

ALBANIA

Economy: socialist   **Political Rights:** 7
Polity: communist one-party   **Civil Liberties:** 7
Population: 2,900,000   **Status of Freedom:** not free

A relatively homogeneous population

Political Rights. Albania has been a communist dictatorship under essentially one-man rule since 1944. While there are a number of elected bodies, including an assembly, the parallel government of the communist party (4.5 percent of the people) is decisive at all levels; elections offer only one list of candidates. Candidates are officially designated by the Democratic Front, to which all Albanians are supposed to belong. In recent years extensive purges within the party have apparently been designed to maintain the power of the top leaders.

Civil Liberties. Press, radio, and television are completely under government or party control, and communication with the outside world is minimal. Media are characterized by incessant propaganda, and open expression of opinion in private conversation is rare. Political imprisonment is common; torture is frequently reported. All religious institutions were abolished in 1967; religion is outlawed; priests are regularly imprisoned. Apparently there are no private organizations independent of government or party. Economic disparities are comparatively small: all people must work one month of each year in factories or on farms, and there are no private cars. Attempting to leave the state is a major crime. Private economic choice is minimal.

Comparatively: Albania is as free as Cambodia, less free than Yugoslavia.

ALGERIA

Economy: socialist
Polity: socialist one-party
Population: 20,700,000

Political Rights: 6
Civil Liberties: 6
Status of Freedom: not free

An ethnic state with a potential subnationality

Political Rights. Algeria has combined military dictatorship with one-party socialist rule. Elections at both local and national levels are managed by the party; they allow little opposition to the system, although individual representatives and specific policies may be criticized. However, the pragmatic, puritanical, military rulers are probably supported by a fairly broad consensus. Subnationalities: fifteen to twenty percent of the people are Berbers which have demonstrated a desire for enhanced self-determination.

Civil Liberties. The media are governmental means for active indoctrination; opposition expression is controlled and foreign publications are closely watched. Private conversation appears relatively open. Although not fully independent, the regular judiciary has established a rule of law in some areas. Prisoners of conscience are detained for short periods, but no long-term political prisoners are now held. Appeals from the decisions of special courts for state security and economic crimes are not allowed. Land reform has transformed former French plantations into collectives. Although government goals are clearly socialist, small farms and businesses have been encouraged recently. Travel is generally free. Eighty percent of the people are illiterate; many are still very poor, but extremes of wealth have been reduced. Unions have slight freedom. Islam's continued strength provides a counterweight to governmental absolutism. There is freedom of religious worship.

Comparatively: Algeria is as free as Tanzania, freer than Iraq, less free than Morocco.

ANGOLA

Economy: noninclusive socialist
Polity: socialist one-party
Population: 7,600,000

Political Rights: 7
Civil Liberties: 7
Status of Freedom: not free

A transethnic heterogeneous state with major subnationalities

Political Rights. Angola is ruled by a very small communist-style socialist party in which military commanders may wield considerable power. The ruling party has relied heavily on Soviet equipment and Cuban troops to dominate the civil war and to stay in power. There is an elected parliament but essentially no choice in the elections. Subnationalities: The party is not tribalist, but is opposed by groups relying on particular tribes or regions--especially in Cabinda, the northeast, and the south-central areas. The UNITA movement among the Ovinbundu people actively controls much of the south and east of the country.

Civil Liberties. The nation remains in a state of war, with power arbitrarily exercised, particularly in the countryside. The media in controlled areas are government owned and do not deviate from its line. Political imprisonment and execution are common; repression of religious activity is reported. Travel is tightly restricted. Private medical care has been abolished, as has much private property--especially in the modern sectors. Strikes are prohibited and unions tightly controlled. Agricultural production is held down by peasant opposition to socialization and lack of markets.

Comparatively: Angola is as free as Ethiopia, less free than Zambia.

ANTIGUA AND BARBUDA

Economy: capitalist
Polity: centralized multiparty
Population: 79,000

Political Rights: 2
Civil Liberties: 3
Status of Freedom: free

A relatively homogeneous population

Political Rights. Antigua is a parliamentary democracy with an elected house and appointed senate. The secessionist island of Barbuda has achieved special rights to limited self-government.

Civil Liberties. Newspapers are published by opposing political parties, but an opposition paper was forced to close in 1982. Radio is government and private and reports fairly. There is freedom of organization and demonstration. Unions are free and have the right to strike. The rule of law is guaranteed in the British manner.

Comparatively: Antigua and Barbuda is as free as Jamaica, freer than Malta, less free than Dominica.

ARGENTINA

Economy: capitalist-statist
Polity: centralized multiparty
(military influence)
Population: 29,100,000

Political Rights: 3
Civil Liberties: 3

Status of Freedom: partly free

A relatively homogeneous population

Political Rights. By the time this book is published a parliamentary system should be reestablished in Argentina after a strongly contested multiparty election. The military retains a veto through its ever-present threat to return again.

Civil Liberties. Private newspapers and both private and government broadcasting stations operate. In the recent past censorship of media and private expression occurred informally through the threat of terrorist attacks from radical leftist or rightist groups, with the latter apparently supported by elements of the military and police. Today political parties organize dissent, and public demonstrations are frequent. The universities have been closely controlled. Courts have considerable independence, but arbitrary arrest, torture, and execution have occurred at least until recently. The church and trade unions play a strong political role. Human rights organizations are active. For non-Catholics religious freedom is curtailed. The economy includes a large government sector. The civilian government comes to power in a time of extreme inflation.

Comparatively: Argentina is as free as Honduras, freer than Uruguay, less free than Bolivia.

AUSTRALIA

Economy: capitalist
Polity: decentralized multiparty
Population: 15,300,000

Political Rights: 1
Civil Liberties: 1
Status of Freedom: free

A relatively homogeneous population with small aboriginal groups

Political Rights. Australia is a federal parliamentary democracy with strong powers retained by its component states. With equal representation from each state, the Senate provides a counterbalance to the nationally representative House of Representatives. The British appointed Governor General retains some power in constitutional deadlocks. Trade unions (separately and through the Labour Party) and foreign investors have great economic weight. The states have separate parliaments and premiers, but appointed governors. There are recurrent attempts to improve the condition and degree of self-determination of the aborigines.

Civil Liberties. All the newspapers and most radio and television stations are privately owned. The Australian Broadcasting Commission operates government radio and television stations on a basis similar to BBC. Although Australia lacks many formal guarantees of civil liberties, the degree of protection of these liberties in the common law is similar to that in Britain and

Canada. Freedom of assembly is generally respected, although it varies by region. Freedom of choice in education, travel, occupation, property, and private association are perhaps as complete as anywhere in the world. Relatively low taxes enhance this freedom.

Comparatively: Australia is as free as the United Kingdom, freer than Italy.

AUSTRIA

Economy: mixed capitalist
Polity: centralized multiparty
Population: 7,600,000

Political Rights: 1
Civil Liberties: 1
Status of Freedom: free

A relatively homogeneous population

Political Rights. Austria's parliamentary system has a directly elected lower house and an upper (and less powerful) house elected by the provincial assemblies. The president is directly elected, but the chancellor (representing the majority party in parliament) is the center of political power. The two major parties have alternated control since the 1950s but the government often seeks broad consensus. The referendum is used on rare occasions. Provincial legislatures and governors are elective. **Subnationalities:** Fifty thousand Slovenes in the southern part of the country have rights to their own schools.

Civil Liberties. The press in Austria is free and varied; radio and television are under a state-owned corporation that by law is supposed to be free of political control. Its geographical position and constitutionally defined neutral status places its media and government in a position analogous to Finland, but the Soviets have put less pressure on Austria to conform to Soviet wishes than on Finland. The rule of law is secure, and there are no political prisoners. Banks and heavy industry are largely nationalized.

Comparatively: Austria is as free as Belgium, freer than Greece.

331

BAHAMAS

Economy: capitalist-statist
Polity: centralized multiparty
Population: 200,000

Political Rights: 2
Civil Liberties: 2
Status of Freedom: free

A relatively homogeneous population

Political Rights. The Bahamas have a parliamentary system with a largely ceremonial British Governor General. The House is elective and the senate appointed. The ruling party has a large majority, but there is an opposition in parliament. Government power is maintained in part by discrimination in favor of supporters and control over the broadcast media. There has not been a change in government since independence. Most islands are administered by centrally appointed commissioners. There is no army.

Civil Liberties. There are independent newspapers and no censorship. Radio and television are government owned and not free of government influence. Labor and business organization are free; there is a right to strike. A program of Bahamianization is being promoted in several sectors of the economy. Rights of travel, occupation, education, and religion are secure. Corruption is widely alleged.

Comparatively: Bahamas is as free as Fiji, freer than Honduras, less free than Barbados.

BAHRAIN

Economy: capitalist-statist
Polity: traditional nonparty
Population: 400,000

Political Rights: 5
Civil Liberties: 5
Status of Freedom: partly free

The citizenry is relatively homogeneous

Political Rights. Bahrain is a traditional shaikhdom with a modernized administration. Direct access to the ruler is encouraged. At present the legislature is dissolved, but powerful merchant and religious families place a check on royal power. There are local councils. Subnationalities: The primary ethnic problem has been the struggle between the Iranians who once ruled and the Arabs who now rule; in part this is reflected in the opposition of the Sunni and majority Shi'a Muslim sects.

Civil Liberties. The largely private press seldom criticizes government policy. Radio and television are government owned. There is considerable freedom of expression in private, but informers are feared. Rights to assembly and demonstration are limited. The legal and educational systems are a mixture of traditional Islamic and British. Short-term arrest is used to discourage dissent, and there are long-term political prisoners. In security cases involving violence fair and quick trials are delayed and torture occurs. Rights to travel, property, and religious choice are secured. There is a record of disturbances by worker groups, and union organization is restricted. Many free social services are provided. Citizenship is very hard to obtain; there is antipathy to foreign workers (but unlike neighboring shaikhdoms most people in the country are citizens).

Comparatively: Bahrain is as free as China (Taiwan), freer than Saudi Arabia, less free than India.

BANGLADESH

Economy: noninclusive capitalist-statist

Polity: military nonparty

Population: 96,500,000

Political Rights: 6

Civil Liberties: 5

Status of Freedom: partly free

An ethnically and religiously complex state

Political Rights. Bangladesh alternates between military and parliamentary rule. In 1982 military rule with some popular support was reintroduced, but its continuation erodes that support. Political parties still exist but are inactive. Local government is being strengthened. Subnationalities: Fighting with minor tribal groups along the border continues as attempts to resettle 500,000 Chittagong tribesmen on new lands are resisted. The Bihari minority suffers discrimination.

Civil Liberties. The press is private, government, and party. The papers are not censored, but there is pervasive self-censorship through both government support and pressure. Radio and television are government controlled, but are not actively used for mobilization. In a violent context there have been recurrent executions and imprisonments, and considerable brutality. Political imprisonment continues to occur, but there are now few prisoners of conscience. Many trials have been before military

333

courts. The civilian courts can decide against the government. In spite of considerable communal antipathy, religious freedom exists. Travel is generally unrestricted. Although they do not have the right to strike, labor unions are active and strikes occur. Over half of the rural population are laborers or tenant farmers; some illegal land confiscation by local groups has been reported. Corruption remains a major problem.

Comparatively: Bangladesh is as free as Poland, freer than Burma, less free than Malaysia.

B A R B A D O S

Economy: mixed capitalist
Polity: centralized multiparty
Population: 300,000

Political Rights: 1
Civil Liberties: 1
Status of Freedom: free

A relatively homogeneous population

Political Rights. Barbados is governed by a parliamentary system, with a ceremonial British Governor General. Elections have been fair and well-administered. Power alternates between the two major parties. Public opinion has a direct and powerful effect on policy. Local governments are also elected.

Civil Liberties. Newspapers are private and free of government control. Both the private and government radio stations are largely free; the only television station is organized on the BBC model. There is an independent judiciary, and general freedom from arbitrary government action. Travel, residence, and religion are free. Although both major parties rely on the support of labor, private property is fully accepted.

Comparatively: Barbados is as free as the United Kingdom, freer than Jamaica.

B E L G I U M

Economy: capitalist
Polity: decentralized multiparty
Population: 9,900,000

Political Rights: 1
Civil Liberties: 1
Status of Freedom: free

A binational state

Political Rights. Belgium is a constitutional monarchy with a bicameral parliament. Elections lead to coalition governments, generally of the center. Linguistic divisions have produced considerable instability. Subnationalities: The rise of nationalism among the two major peoples--Flemish and Walloon--has led to increasing transfer of control over cultural affairs to the communal groups. However, provincial governors are appointed by the national government.

Civil Liberties. Newspapers are free and uncensored. Radio and television are government owned, but independent boards are responsible for programming. The full spectrum of private rights is respected; voting is compulsory. Property rights, worker rights, and religious freedom are guaranteed.

Comparatively: Belgium is as free as Switzerland, freer than France.

B E L I Z E

Economy: capitalist
Polity: centralized multiparty
Population: 160,000

Political Rights: 1
Civil Liberties: 2
Status of Freedom: free

An ethnically complex state

Political Rights. Belize is a parliamentary democracy with an elected house and appointed senate. Elections are competitive and fair. Competitive local elections are also a part of the system.

Civil Liberties. The press is free and varied. Radio is government controlled but presents opposition viewpoints. Organization and assembly are guaranteed, as is the rule of law, although there have been restrictions on assembly in emergencies. The opposition is well-organized. Private cooperatives have been formed in several agricultural industries. Unions are independent; strikes have been used to gain benefits.

Comparatively: Belize is as free as Trinidad and Tobago, freer than Honduras, less free than Costa Rica.

BENIN

Economy: noninclusive socialist
Polity: socialist one-party
   (military dominated)
Population: 3,700,000

Political Rights: 7
Civil Liberties: 6

Status of Freedom: not free

A transethnic heterogeneous state

Political Rights. Benin is a military dictatorship buttressed by a one-party organization. Regional and tribal loyalties may be stronger than national. Elections are single-list, with no opposition. Local assemblies are closely controlled.

Civil Liberties. All media are rigidly censored; most are owned by the government. Opposition is not tolerated; criticism of the government often leads to a few days of reeducation in military camps. There are long-term political prisoners, and the rule of law is very weak. Detainees are mistreated. Private schools have been closed. Although there is general freedom of religion, some sects have been forbidden. Independent labor unions are banned. Permission to leave the country is closely controlled. Economically, the government's interventions have been in cash crops and external trade, and industries have been nationalized; control over the largely subsistence and small entrepreneur economy remains incomplete. Widespread corruption aggravates already large income disparities.

Comparatively: Benin is as free as Togo, freer than Angola, less free than Upper Volta.

BHUTAN

Economy: preindustrial
Polity: traditional nonparty
Population: 1,400,000

Political Rights: 5
Civil Liberties: 5
Status of Freedom: partly free

An ethnic state with a significant subnationality

Political Rights. Bhutan is a hereditary monarchy in which the king rules with the aid of a council and an indirectly elected National Assembly. There are no legal political parties and the Assembly does little more than approve government actions. Villages are traditionally ruled by their own headmen, but districts are directly ruled from the center. The Buddhist hierarchy is still very important in the affairs of the country. In foreign policy Bhutan's dependence on India has been partially renounced; it is still dependent for defense. Subnationalities: The main political party operates outside the country, agitating in favor of the Nepalese minority (about twenty-five percent) that is restricted to one part of the country, and in favor of a more modern political system.

Civil Liberties. The only paper is the government weekly. There is no broadcasting service. Outside media are freely available. There are few if any prisoners of conscience. No organized opposition exists within the country. The legal structure exhibits a mixture of traditional and British forms. There is religious freedom and freedom to travel. Traditional agriculture, crafts, and trade dominate the economy.

Comparatively: Bhutan is as free as Ivory coast, freer than Bangladesh, less free than Nepal.

B O L I V I A

Economy: noninclusive capitalist-statist

Polity: military nonparty

Population: 5,900,000

Political Rights: 2

Civil Liberties: 3

Status of Freedom: free

An ethnic state with major potential subnationalities

Political Rights. In 1982 Bolivia returned to parliamentary democracy. Temporarily the traditional power of the military and security services was greatly reduced, although not yet eliminated. Provincial and local government is controlled from the center. Subnationalities: Over sixty percent of the people are Indians speaking Aymara or Quechua; these languages have been given official status alongside Spanish. The Indian peoples remain, however, more potential than actual subnationalities. The Spanish speaking minority still controls the political process.

Civil Liberties. The press and most radio stations are private and are now largely free. In mid-1982 all restrictions on political and union activity were officially removed and a complete amnesty announced. But fear remains in the presence of private security forces. The Catholic Church retains a powerful and critical role. The people are overwhelmingly post-land-reform,

337

subsistence agriculturists. The major mines and much of industry are nationalized; the workers have a generous social welfare program, given the country's poverty.

Comparatively: Bolivia is as free as India, freer than Guyana, less free than Venezuela.

BOTSWANA

Economy: noninclusive capitalist
Polity: decentralized multiparty
Population: 900,000

Political Rights: 2
Civil Liberties: 3
Status of Freedom: free

A relatively homogeneous population

Political Rights. The republican system of Botswana combines traditional and modern principles. The assembly is elected for a fixed term and appoints the president who rules. There is also an advisory House of Chiefs. Nine districts, led either by chiefs or elected leaders, have independent power of taxation, as well as traditional control over land and agriculture. Elections continue to be won overwhelmingly by the ruling party as they were before independence, yet there are opposition members in parliament and local governments. There is economic and political pressure from both black African and white neighbors. **Subnationalities:** The country is divided among several major tribes belonging to the Batswana people, as well as minor peoples on the margins. The latter include a few hundred relatively wealthy white farmers.

Civil Liberties. The radio and the main daily paper are government owned; a private newspaper began in 1982. There is no censorship, and opposition party and foreign publications offer alternative views. Rights of assembly, religion, and travel are respected but regulated. Passport controls may be restrictive. Prisoners of conscience are not held. Unions are independent, but under pressure. In the modern society civil liberties appear to be guaranteed, but most people continue to live under traditional rules.

Comparatively: Botswana is as free as Nigeria, freer than Gambia, less free than Barbados.

B R A Z I L

Economy: capitalist-statist
Polity: decentralized multiparty
(military dominated)
Population: 131,300,000

Political Rights: 3
Civil Liberties: 3

Status of Freedom: partly free

A complex but relatively homogeneous population with many very small, territorial subnationalities

Political Rights. Brazil is currently governed by a president elected by the military and a popularly elected but weak assembly. Party activity is increasingly competitive--only the Communist Party remains banned--but illiterates may not vote. There are independently organized elected governments at both state and local levels. **Subnationalities:** The many small Indian groups of the interior are under both private and governmental pressure on their lands, culture, and even lives.

Civil Liberties. The media are private, except for a few broadcasting stations. The powerful and critical press is now free of overt censorship; however, government control of most industry, and thus advertising, limits freedom to criticize government. Radio and television practice limited self-censorship. There is a general right of assembly and organization, and few if any prisoners of conscience. Private violence against criminals, suspected communists, peasants, and Indians continues outside the law; police brutality remains common. Opposition voices are regularly heard--including parliamentarians, journalists, and church officials. Union organization is powerful and strikes are widespread, though sometimes repressed. There is considerable large-scale government industry, but rights to property, religious freedom, travel, and education of one's choice are generally respected. Growth policy has favored modern and relatively wealthy sectors.

Comparatively: Brazil is as free as Argentina, freer than Uruguay, less free than Colombia.

B U L G A R I A

Economy: socialist
Polity: communist one-party
Population: 8,900,000

Political Rights: 7
Civil Liberties: 7
Status of Freedom: not free

A relatively homogeneous population

Political Rights. Bulgaria is governed by its Communist Party, although the facade of a parallel government and two-party system is maintained. The same man has essentially ruled over the system since 1954; elections at both national and local levels have little meaning. Both economically and politically the country is subservient to the Soviet Union. Subnationalities: Muslim minorities numbering about one million are discriminated against.

Civil Liberties. All media are under absolute control by the government or its Party branches. Citizens have few if any rights against the state. There are hundreds or thousands of prisoners of conscience, many living under severe conditions. Brutality and torture are common. Those accused of opposition to the system may also be banished to villages, denied their occupations, or confined in psychiatric hospitals. Believers are subject to discrimination. Citizens have little choice of occupation or residence, and it is very difficult to leave the country legally. Political loyalty is required to secure many social benefits. The most common political crimes are illegally trying to leave the country, criticism of the government, and illegal contacts with foreigners.

Comparatively: Bulgaria is as free as Mongolia, less free than Hungary.

BURMA

Economy: noninclusive mixed socialist

Polity: socialist one-party (military dominated)

Population: 37,900,000

Political Rights: 7

Civil Liberties: 7

Status of Freedom: not free

An ethnic state with major territorial subnationalities

Political Rights. Burma is governed by a small military elite as a one-party socialist state. The government's dependence on the army makes its strengths and weaknesses more those of a military dictatorship than those of a communist regime. Elections are held at both national and local levels: the Party chooses the slate of candidates. Subnationalities: The government represents essentially the Burmese people that live in the heartland of the country. The Burmese are surrounded by millions of non-Burmese living in continuing disaffection or active revolt. Among the minorities on the periphery are the Karens, Shan, Kachins, Mon, and Chin.

Civil Liberties. All media are government owned, with alternative opinions expressed obliquely if at all; both domestic and foreign publications are censored. The media are expected to actively promote government policy. Organized dissent is forbidden; even private expression is dangerous. Prisoners of conscience have been common and torture reported. However, few ethnic Burmans now seem to be detained for reasons of conscience. The regular court structure has been replaced by "people's courts." Racial discrimination has been incorporated in government policy. Emigration or even travel outside the country is very difficult. Although the eventual goal of the government is complete socialization, areas of private enterprise remain, subject to control by government marketing monopolies.

Comparatively: Burma is as free as Cambodia, less free than Bangladesh.

BURUNDI

Economy: noninclusive mixed capitalist

Polity: socialist one-party (military dominated)

Population: 4,500,000

Political Rights: 6

Civil Liberties: 6

Status of Freedom: not free

An ethnic state with a major, nonterritorial subnationality

Political Rights. Burundi is ruled by a self-appointed military president with the assistance of a Party Central Committee and Politburo. The assembly election in 1982 allowed only the narrowest choice of pre-selected candidates from the one party. Subnationalities: The rulers continue to be from the Tutsi ethnic group (fifteen percent) that has traditionally ruled; their dominance was reinforced by a massacre of Hutus (eighty-five percent) after an attempted revolt in the early 1970s.

Civil Liberties. The media are all government controlled and closely censored, as are often the foreign media. Lack of freedom of political speech or assembly is accompanied by political imprisonment and reports of brutality. Under current conditions there

341

is little guarantee of individual rights, particularly for the Hutu majority. However, in recent years the exclusion of the Hutu from public services, the Party, and other advantages has been relaxed. There are no independent unions, but short wildcat strikes have been reported. Religion is closely regulated, especially in the areas of education and missionary activity. Traditional group and individual rights persist on the village level: Burundi is not a highly structured modern society. Travel is relatively unrestricted. Although officially socialist, private or traditional economic forms predominate.

Comparatively: Burundi is as free as Cameroon, freer than Somalia, less free than Kenya.

CAMBODIA

Economy: noninclusive socialist   **Political Rights:** 7
Polity: communist one-party   **Civil Liberties:** 7
Population: 6,000,000   **Status of Freedom:** not free

A relatively homogeneous population

Political Rights. Cambodia is divided between the remnants of the Pol Pot tyranny and the less tyrannical, imposed Vietnamese regime. The people have little part in either regime.

Civil Liberties. The media continue to be completely controlled in both areas; outside publications are rigorously controlled. Political execution has been a common function of government. Reeducation for war captives is again practiced by the new government. There is no rule of law; private freedoms are not guaranteed. Cambodians continue to be one of the world's most tyrannized peoples. At least temporarily much of economic life has been decollectivized.

Comparatively: Cambodia is as free as Ethiopia, less free than Thailand.

CAMEROON

Economy: noninclusive capitalist **Political Rights:** 6
Polity: nationalist one-party   **Civil Liberties:** 6
Population: 9,100,000   **Status of Freedom:** not free

A transethnic heterogeneous state with a major subnationality

Political Rights. Cameroon is a one-party state ruled by the same party since independence in 1960. The government has steadily centralized power. Referendums and other elections have little meaning; voters are given no alternatives, although a legislative candidate is occasionally rejected. Provincial governors are appointed by the central government. An attempt has been made to incorporate all elements in a government of broad consensus. Subnationalities: The most significant opposition has come from those opposing centralization. Politics is largely a struggle of regional and tribal factions.

Civil Liberties. The largely government-owned media are closely controlled; censorship and self-censorship are common; works of critical authors are prohibited, even university lectures are subject to censorship. Freedom of speech, assembly, and union organization are limited, while freedom of occupation, education, and property are respected. Prisoners of conscience are detained without trial and may be ill-treated. Allegations have been made of torture and village massacres. Internal travel and religious choice are relatively free; foreign travel may be difficult. Labor and business organizations are closely controlled. Although still relatively short on capital, private enterprise is encouraged wherever possible.

Comparatively: Cameroon is as free as Gabon, freer than Niger, less free than Upper Volta.

CANADA

Economy: capitalist
Polity: decentralized multiparty
Population: 24,900,000

Political Rights: 1
Civil Liberties: 1
Status of Freedom: free

A binational state

Political Rights. Canada is a parliamentary democracy with alternation of rule between leading parties. The provinces have their own democratic institutions with a higher degree of autonomy than the American states. Subnationalities: In an attempt to prevent the breakup of Canada, the government has moved toward granting French linguistic equality; French has become the official language in Quebec. In addition, Quebec has been allowed to opt out of some national programs and maintains its own representatives abroad.

Civil Liberties. The media are free, although there is a government-related radio and television network. The full range of civil liberties is generally respected. In Quebec rights to choose English education and language have been infringed. There has been evidence of the invasion of privacy by Canadian security forces in recent years, much as in the United States. Many judicial and legal structures have been borrowed from the United Kingdom or the United States, with consequent advantages and disadvantages. Some provinces limit employment opportunities for nonresidents.

Comparatively: Canada is as free as the United States of America, freer than Italy.

CAPE VERDE

Economy: noninclusive socialist   **Political Rights:** 6
Polity: socialist one-party   **Civil Liberties:** 6
Population: 400,000   **Status of Freedom:** not free

An ethnically complex state

Political Rights. The ruling party is small and tightly organized. Elections allow no choice, but abstention and negative votes are allowed.

Civil Liberties. The media are government owned; all are closely controlled to serve party purposes. Prisoners of conscience are frequently detained for short periods; rights to organize opposition, assembly, or political expression are not respected. The judiciary is weak. The Islands' plantation agriculture has been largely nationalized, but drought and endemic unemployment continue to lead to emigration. Most professions, fishing, farming, and small enterprises are private. Religion is relatively free, although under political pressure; labor unions are government controlled. Travel is relatively free.

Comparatively: Cape Verde is as free as Tanzania, freer than Ethiopia, less free than Ivory Coast.

CENTRAL AFRICAN REPUBLIC

Economy: noninclusive
    capitalist-statist
Polity: military nonparty
Population: 2,500,000

Political Rights: 7

Civil Liberties: 5
Status of Freedom: not free

A transethnic heterogeneous state

Political Rights. The Central African Republic is currently a military dictatorship without representative institutions. Prefects are appointed by the central government in the French style. Heavily dependent on French economic and military aid, France has influenced or determined recent changes of government, and French forces are still present.

Civil Liberties. All media are government controlled, but there are periods of free expression and assembly. There are prisoners of conscience. Religious freedom is generally respected. Union activity was suspended following the September 1981 coup. The judiciary is not independent. Movement is occasionally hampered by highway security checks. Most economic activity is private with limited government involvement. Corruption is particularly widespread.

Comparatively: Central African Republic is as free as Algeria, freer than Togo, less free than Kenya.

CHAD

Economy: noninclusive capitalist
Polity: military decentralized
Population: 4,700,000

Political Rights: 7
Civil Liberties: 6
Status of Freedom: not free

A transitional collection of semi-autonomous ethnic groups

Political Rights. Central government has been reestablished except in the far north where Libyan interference continues. The victorious leader rules with the more or less willing cooperation of other groups. **Subnationalities:** Ethnic struggle pits the southern negroes (principally the Christian and animist Sara tribe) against a variety of northern Muslim groups (principally nomadic Arabs). Political factionalism is only partly ethnic.

Civil Liberties. Media are largely government controlled. In recent years many have been killed or imprisoned without due process, but the return of organized government to most of the country has allowed some relaxation. Labor and business organizations exist with some independence. Religion is relatively free. Not an ideological area, traditional law is still influential. The economy is predominantly subsistence agriculture with little protection of property rights.

Comparatively: Chad is apparently as free as Malawi, freer than Ethiopia, less free than Tanzania.

C H I L E

Economy: capitalist	**Political Rights:** 6
Polity: military nonparty	**Civil Liberties:** 5
Population: 11,500,000	**Status of Freedom:** partly free

A relatively homogeneous population

Political Rights. Chile is a military dictatorship. Although a 1980 plebiscite confirming government policy allowed an opposition vote of thirty percent, all power is concentrated at the center; there are no elective positions. An appointive Council of State is supposed to represent most sectors of society.

Civil Liberties. All media have both public and private outlets; newspapers are primarily private. The media, although censored and often threatened with closure, express a considerable range of opinion, occasionally including direct criticism of government policy. Limited party activity is tacitly allowed, and human rights organizations operate under pressure. Students, church leaders, and former political leaders regularly express dissent, sometimes massively and in the face of violent government repression. While one can win against the government, the courts are under government pressure. Prisoners of conscience are still commonly taken for short periods, torture occurs; political expulsions and internal exile continue. The right to travel is generally respected. Unions are restricted but have some rights, including a limited right to strike and organize at plant levels. Many nationalized enterprises have been resold to private investors, with government intervention in the economy now being limited to copper and petroleum.

Comparatively: Chile is as free as Nicaragua, freer than Czechoslovakia, less free than Peru.

C H I N A (Mainland)

Economy: socialist
Polity: communist one-party
Population: 1,023,300,000

Political Rights: 6
Civil Liberties: 6
Status of Freedom: not free

An ethnic state with peripheral subnationalities

Political Rights. China is a one-party communist state under the collective leadership of the Politburo. A National People's Congress is indirectly elected within party guidelines, but does not function as a competitive parliament. National policy struggles are obscured by secrecy; choices are sharply limited. There has been competition in a very few local elections. Subnationalities: There are several subordinated peripheral peoples such as the Tibetans, Uighurs, and Mongols. These are granted a very limited degree of separate cultural life. Amounting to not more than five percent of the population, non-chinese ethnic groups have tended to be diluted and obscured by Chinese settlement or sinification.

Civil Liberties. The mass media remain closely controlled tools for mobilizing the population. While the underground and wall-poster literature of 1978-79 has been suppressed, there is limited non-political cultural freedom. Although there is movement toward "socialist legality" on the Soviet model, court cases are often decided in political terms. There are unknown thousands of political prisoners, including those in labor-reform camps; the government has forced millions to live indefinitely in undesirable areas. Political executions are still reported. Millions of Chinese have been systematically discriminated against because of "bad class background," but such discrimination has recently been curtailed. Political-social controls at work are pervasive.

Compared to other communist states popular opinions and pressures play a considerable role. Recurrent poster campaigns, demonstrations, and evidence of private conversation shows that pervasive factionalism has allowed elements of freedom and consensus into the system; recurrent repression, including imprisonment, equally shows the government's determination to keep dissent from becoming a threat to the system or its current leaders. Rights to travel and emigration are limited, as are religious freedoms. Rights to marry and have children are perhaps more limited than in any other country in the world. Economic pressures have forced some, not wholly successful, rationalization of economic policy, including renunciation of guaranteed employment for youth. Introduction of private sector incentives has greatly increased freedom for small enterpreneurs and farmers. Small local strikes and slowdowns have been reported concerning wage increases and worker demands for greater control over choice of employment. Inequality derives from differences in political position rather than direct income.

Comparatively. China (Mainland) is as free as Algeria, freer than Mongolia, less free than China (Taiwan).

C H I N A (Taiwan)

Economy: capitalist-statist

Polity: centralized dominant-party

Population: 18,900,000

Political Rights: 5

Civil Liberties: 5

Status of Freedom: partly free

A quasi-ethnic state with a majority nonterritorial subnationality

Political Rights. Taiwan is ruled by a single party organized according to a communist model (although anticommunist ideologically). There is a parliament to which representatives from Taiwan are elected in fairly free elections; a few members oppose the regime but no effective opposition party is tolerated. Most parliamentarians are still persons elected in 1947 as representatives of districts in China where elections could not be held subsequently because of communist control. Late 1980 elections allowed some opposition success. The indirect presidential election is pro forma, but the election of a Taiwanese to the vice-presidency in 1978 was significant. Important local and regional positions are elective, including those in the provincial assembly that are held by Taiwanese. Subnationalities: The people are eighty-six percent native Taiwanese (speaking two Chinese dialects); opposition movements in favor of transferring control from the mainland immigrants to the Taiwanese are repressed.

Civil Liberties. The media include government or party organs, but are mostly in private hands. Newspapers and magazines are subject to censorship or suspension, and practice self-censorship. Television is one-sided. Rights to assembly are limited, but are sporadically granted. There are several hundred political prisoners, including prominent leaders of the moderate opposition. Union activity is restricted; strikes are forbidden. Other apolitical groups are free to organize. Private rights to property, education, and religion are generally respected; there is no right to travel to the mainland.

Comparatively: China (Taiwan) is as free as South Korea, freer than Burma, less free than Malaysia.

C O L O M B I A

Economy: capitalist
Polity: centralized multiparty
Population: 27,700,000

Political Rights: 2
Civil Liberties: 3
Status of Freedom: free

A relatively homogeneous population with scattered minorities

Political Rights. Colombia is a constitutional democracy. The president is directly elected, as are both houses of the legislature. The opposition won the 1982 presidential election in which participation rose to over fifty percent. Members of the two principal parties are included in the government and the list of departmental governors. Both of the leading parties have well-defined factions; among the minor parties several are involved in revolutionary activity. The provinces are directly administered by the national government. The military is alleged to be only partly under government control.

Civil Liberties. The press is private, with some papers under party control, and quite free. Radio and television include both government and private stations. All media have been limited in their freedom to report subversive activity. Personal rights are generally respected; courts are relatively strong and independent. Riots and guerrilla activity have led to periodic states of siege in which these rights are limited. Assemblies are often banned for fear of riots. In these conditions the security forces have infringed personal rights violently, especially those of leftist unions, peasants, and Amerindians in rural areas. Many persons are rounded up in antiguerrilla or antiterrorist campaigns, and may be tortured or killed. However, opponents are not given prison sentences simply for the nonviolent expression of political opinion, and the government and courts have attempted to control abuses. Human rights organizations are active. The government encourages private enterprise where possible; union activity and strikes for economic goals are legal.

Comparatively: Colombia is as free as India, freer than Brazil, less free than Venezuela.

C O M O R O S

Economy: noninclusive capitalist
Polity: decentralized nonparty
Population: 350,000

Political Rights: 4
Civil Liberties: 4
Status of Freedom: partly free

A relatively homogeneous population

Political Rights. The present Comoran leader returned to power with the aid of mercenaries in 1978, and they continue to protect him. Subsequently the voters have at least formally approved the new presidential system. The majority probably support the new system--the previous ruler had become very oppressive and the new president was prime minister in the past. There is only one party but independents contest elections. Elections may be manipulated. Each island has an elected governor and council. (The island of Mayotte is formally a part of the Comoros, but it has chosen to be a French dependency.)

Civil Liberties. Radio is government owned. There is no press, but some outside publications are available. There are few if any prisoners of conscience. Pressure is reported against the opposition, but public criticism is allowed. There is a new emphasis on Islamic customs. The largely plantation economy has led to severe landlessness and concentrated wealth; emigration to the mainland for employment is very common. There have been no strikes.

Comparatively: Comoros appears to be as free as Senegal, freer than Kenya, less free than Mauritius.

C O N G O

Economy: noninclusive mixed socialist	**Political Rights:** 7
Polity: socialist one-party (military dominated)	**Civil Liberties:** 6
Population: 1,700,000	**Status of Freedom:** not free

A formally transethnic heterogeneous state

Political Rights. Congo is a military dictatorship with a very small ruling party. One-party elections allow no opposition, but criticism is aired in parliament.

Civil Liberties. The press and all publications are heavily censored. Radio is government owned. Criticism may lead to imprisonment, yet there is some private discussion and limited dissent. Executions and imprisonment of political opponents have occurred, but conditions have improved. The only union is state sponsored; strikes are illegal. Religious groups are limited but generally free. There is little judicial protection; passports are difficult to obtain. At the local and small entrepreneur level private property is generally respected; most large-scale commerce and industry are either nationalized or controlled by expatriates. Literacy is high for the region.

Comparatively: Congo is as free as Iraq, freer than Mozambique, less free than Cameroon.

C O S T A   R I C A

Economy: capitalist	**Political Rights:** 1
Polity: centralized multiparty	**Civil Liberties:** 1
Population: 2,400,000	**Status of Freedom:** free

A relatively homogeneous population

Political Rights. A parliamentary democracy, Costa Rica has a directly elected president and several important parties. No parties are prohibited. This structure is supplemented by an independent tribunal for overseeing elections. Elections are fair; rule alternates between parties. Provinces are under the direction of the central government.

Civil Liberties. The media are notably free, private, and varied; they serve a society ninety percent literate. The courts are fair, and private rights, such as those to movement, occupation, education, religion, and union organization, are respected.

Comparatively: Costa Rica is as free as Ireland, freer than Colombia.

C U B A

Economy: socialist   **Political Rights:** 6
Polity: communist one-party   **Civil Liberties:** 6
Population: 9,800,000   **Status of Freedom:** not free

A complex but relatively homogeneous population

Political Rights. Cuba is a one-party communist state on the Soviet model. Real power lies, however, more in the person of Fidel Castro and in the Russian leaders upon whom he depends than is the case in other noncontiguous states adopting this model. Popular election at the municipal level is closely supervised. Provincial and national assemblies are elected by municipalities but can be recalled by popular vote. The whole system is largely a show: political opponents are excluded from nomination by law, many others are simply disqualified by Party fiat; no debate is allowed on major issues; once elected the assemblies do not oppose Party decisions.

Civil Liberties. The media are state controlled and publish only as the state directs. Thousands of political prisoners have been released in recent years, mostly into exile. Torture has been reported in the past, but hundreds who have refused to recant continue to be held in difficult conditions, and new arrests are frequent. There are hundreds of thousands of others who are formally discriminated against as opponents of the system. There is freedom to criticize policy administration though the press and the institutions of "popular democracy," but writing or speaking against the system, even in private is severely repressed. There are reports of psychiatric institutions also being used to incarcerate. Freedom to choose work, education, or residence is greatly restricted; new laws force people to work harder. It is generally illegal to leave Cuba, but some have been forced to leave. The practice of religion is discouraged by the government.

Comparatively: Cuba is as free as Guatemala, freer than Czechoslovakia, less free than El Salvador.

C Y P R U S

Economy: capitalist
Polity: decentralized multiparty
Population: 650,000

Political Rights: (G) 1, (T) 4
Civil Liberties: (G) 2, (T) 3
Status of Freedom: (G) free
(T) partly free

A binational state

Political Rights. At present Cyprus is one state only in theory. Both the Greek and Turkish sectors are parliamentary democracies, although the Turkish sector is in effect a protectorate of Turkey. Elections have seemed reasonably fair in both sectors, but in the violent atmosphere pressure has been applied to all nonconforming groups or individuals. Greek Cypriots in the North are denied voting rights. Nationalities: Greeks and Turks now live almost exclusively in their own sectors. Eighty percent of the population is Greek, sixty percent of the land is in the Greek sector.

Civil Liberties. The newspapers are free and varied in both sectors, with the constraints mentioned above. Radio and television are under the respective governments or semigovernmental bodies. The usual rights of free peoples are respected in each sector, including occupation, labor organization, and religion, although somewhat more circumscribed in the Turkish sector. Because of communal strife and invasion, property has often been taken from members of one group by force (or abandoned from fear of force) and given to the other. Under these conditions rights to choose one's sector of residence or to travel between sectors have been greatly restricted.

C Z E C H O S L O V A K I A

Economy: socialist
Polity: communist one-party
Population: 15,400,000

Political Rights: 7
Civil Liberties: 6
Status of Freedom: not free

A binational state

Political Rights. Czechoslovakia is a Soviet style, one-party communist state, reinforced by the presence of Soviet troops. Elections are noncompetitive and there is essentially no legislative debate. **Subnationalities:** The division of the state into separate Czech and Slovak socialist republics has only slight meaning since the Czechoslovak Communist Party continues to rule the country (and under the guidance of the Soviet Communist Party). Although less numerous and poorer than the Czech people, the Slovaks are granted their rightful share of power within this framework.

Civil Liberties. Media are government or Party owned and rigidly censored. However, some relatively free private and literary expression occurs. Freedoms of assembly, organization, and association are denied. Heavy pressures are placed on religious activities, especially through holding ministerial incomes at a very low level and curtailing religious education. There are a number of prisoners of conscience; exclusion of individuals from their chosen occupations and short detentions are more common sanctions. The beating of political suspects is common, and psychiatric detention is employed. Successful defense in political cases is possible, but lawyers may be arrested for overzealous defense. Human rights groups are persecuted. Travel to the West and emigration are restricted. Independent trade unions and strikes are forbidden. Rights to choice of occupation and to private property are restricted.

Comparatively: Czechoslovakia is as free as Romania, freer than Bulgaria, less free than Poland.

DENMARK

Economy: mixed capitalist
Polity: centralized multiparty
Population: 5,100,000

Political Rights: 1
Civil Liberties: 1
Status of Freedom: free

A relatively homogeneous population

Political Rights. Denmark is a constitutional monarchy with a unicameral parliament. Elections are fair. Since a wide variety of parties achieve success, resulting governments are based on coalitions. Districts have governors appointed from the center and elected councils; local officials are under local control.

Civil Liberties. The press is free (and more conservative politically than the electorate). Radio and television are government owned but relatively free. Labor unions are powerful both socially and politically. All other rights are guaranteed. The very high tax level constitutes more than usual constraint on private property in a capitalist state, but has provided a fairly equitable distribution of social benefits. Religion is free but state supported.

Comparatively: Denmark is as free as Norway, freer than Finland.

DJIBOUTI

Economy: noninclusive capitalist   **Political Rights:** 5
Polity: nationalist one-party   **Civil Liberties:** 6
Population: 300,000   **Status of Freedom:** not free

A binational state with subordination

Political Rights. Djibouti is formally a parliamentary democracy under French protection. Only one party is allowed, and in recent elections there has been little if any choice. Although all ethnic groups are carefully included in the single party lists, one group is clearly dominant. A large French garrison continues to play a role.

Civil Liberties. The media are government owned and controlled and there is no right of assembly. There are prisoners of conscience and torture. Unions are under a degree of government control, but there is a right to strike. There is extreme poverty and the market economy is still dominated by French interests.

Comparatively: Djibouti appears to be as free as North Yemen, freer than Somalia, less free than Sudan.

DOMINICA

Economy: capitalist   **Political Rights:** 2
Polity: centralized multiparty   **Civil Liberties:** 2
Population: 100,000   **Status of Freedom:** free

A relatively homogeneous population with a minority enclave

Political Rights. Dominica is a parliamentary democracy with competing political parties. An opposition party came to power in highly competitive 1980 elections. There have been several violent attempts to overthrow the government, and the military has subsequently been disbanded. The rights of the native Caribs may not be fully respected.

Civil Liberties. The press is private and the radio public. The press is generally free and critical and the radio presents alternative views. Rights of assembly and organization are guaranteed. There is rule of law and no prisoners of conscience. States of emergency have recurrently limited rights to a small extent. Personal rights to travel, residence, and property are secured, as are the union rights of workers.

Comparatively: Dominica is as free as Nauru, freer than Guyana, less free than Barbados.

D O M I N I C A N   R E P U B L I C

Economy: capitalist
Polity: centralized multiparty
Population: 6,200,000

Political Rights: 1
Civil Liberties: 2
Status of Freedom: free

A complex but relatively homogeneous population

Political Rights. The Dominican Republic is a presidential democracy on the American model. Elections are free and competitive. Military influence is greatly reduced. Provinces are under national control, municipalities under local.

Civil Liberties. The media are generally privately owned, free, and diverse. Communist materials are restricted. Broadcasting is highly varied, but subject to government review. Public expression is generally free; the spokesmen of a wide range of parties quite openly express their opinions. There are no prisoners of conscience. The courts appear relatively independent and human rights groups are active. Labor unions operate under moderate constraints. Travel overseas is sometimes restricted. State-owned lands are slowly being redistributed.

Comparatively: Dominican Republic is as free as Trinidad and Tobago, freer than Colombia, less free than Barbados.

ECUADOR

Economy: noninclusive capitalist   **Political Rights:** 2
Polity: centralized multiparty   **Civil Liberties:** 2
Population: 8,800,000   **Status of Freedom:** free

An ethnic state with a potential subnationality

Political Rights. Ecuador is governed by an elected president
and parliament. There have been minor restrictions on party
activity and nominations. Provinces and municipalities are
directly administered, but there are elected local and provincial
councils. Subnationalities: Forty percent of the population is
Indian, most of whom speak Quechua. This population at present
does not form a conscious subnationality in a distinct homeland.

Civil Liberties. Newspapers are under private or party control
and quite outspoken; there is no censorship. Radio and television
are mostly under private control. There are no long-term prisoners
of conscience, but persons are detained for criticizing government
officials. Human rights organizations are active. The court
system is not strongly independent, and imprisonment for belief
may occur. Land reform has been hampered by resistance from
landed elites. Although there are state firms, particularly in
major industries, Ecuador is essentially a capitalist and traditional state.

Comparatively: Ecuador is as free as Mauritius, freer than
Colombia, less free than Venezuela.

EGYPT

Economy: mixed socialist   **Political Rights:** 5
Polity: centralized   **Civil Liberties:** 5
      dominant-party
Population: 45,851,000   **Status of Freedom:** partly free

A relatively homogeneous population with a communal religious
minority

Political Rights. Egypt is a controlled democracy. Within
limits political parties may organize: communist and religious
extremist parties are forbidden. Referendums receive unlikely
ninety-eight and ninety-nine percent approvals. The ruling party

won ninety percent of parliamentary seats in the 1979 election, but other parties achieved representation. **Subnationalities:** Several million Coptic Christians live a distinct communal life.

Civil Liberties. The Egyptian press is mostly government owned. Radio and television are under governmental control. All media are governmental means for active indoctrination, but opposition journals are allowed to appear sporadically; a fairly broad range of literary publications has recently developed. There is limited freedom of assembly. severe riot laws and a variety of laws restricting dissent have led to large-scale imprisonment or banning from political or other organizational activity. Many prisoners of conscience have been held in the last few years, but very seldom for long periods. Women's rights have improved. In both agriculture and industry considerable diversity and choice exists within a mixed socialist framework. Unions have developed some independence from the government, but there is no right to strike. The predominance of state corporations contributes to the acquiescence of unions in official policy. Travel and other private rights are generally free.

Comparatively. Egypt is as free as Kenya, freer than Algeria, less free than Nigeria.

EL SALVADOR

Economy: capitalist
Polity: centralized multiparty (military dominated)
Population: 5,000,000 (unknown)

Political Rights: 4
Civil Liberties: 5
Status of Freedom: partly free

A relatively homogeneous population

Political Rights. El Salvador is ruled by an elected parliament and interim president (chosen in effect by parliament, the army, and foreign supporters). The 1982 election was reasonably fair but some groups did not participate. Extra-legal forces often determine outcomes. In the countryside a bloody struggle between government and guerrilla forces continues.

Civil Liberties. Newspapers and radio are largely in private hands. The media are under strong pressures from all sides and are generally self-censored. Legal and illegal opposition papers and broadcasts appear. The rule of law is weak; assassination common. Atrocities have been committed by both sides in the

conflict, probably frequently without the authorization of leaders. The judiciary is ineffective in political cases. Human
rights organizations have been active. The Catholic Church
remains a force. Although still a heavily agricultural country,
rural people are to a large extent involved in the wage and market
economy. Banking and foreign trade of export crops have been
nationalized; land reform has had limited success.

Comparatively: El Salvador is as free as Morocco, freer than
Guatemala, less free than Mexico.

EQUATORIAL GUINEA

Economy: noninclusive capitalist-statist	**Political Rights:** 7
Polity: military nonparty	**Civil Liberties:** 6
Population: 340,000	**Status of Freedom:** not free

An ethnic state with a territorial minority

Political Rights. Equatorial Guinea is a military dictatorship. The coup that replaced the former dictator was popular, but
the population as a whole played and plays little part. A
several-hundred-man Moroccan bodyguard protects the incumbent at
Spanish expense.

Civil Liberties. The media are very limited, largely government owned, and do not report opposition viewpoints. The rule of
law is tenuous; there are political prisoners, but perhaps none of
conscience. Compulsory recruitment for the plantations occurs.
Opposition parties are not tolerated. Religious freedom was
reestablished in 1979, and private property is recognized. Plantation and subsistence farming is still recovering from near destruction under the previous government.

Comparatively: Equatorial Guinea appears to be as free as
Congo, freer than Somalia, less free than Tanzania.

ETHIOPIA

Economy: noninclusive socialist	**Political Rights:** 7
Polity: military nonparty	**Civil Liberties:** 7
Population: 31,300,000	**Status of Freedom:** not free

An ethnic state with major territorial subnationalities

Political Rights. Ethiopia is ruled by a military committee that has successively slaughtered the leaders of the ancien regime and many of its own leaders. A spectrum of mass organizations has been established on the model of a one-party socialist state. Locally elected village councils are the primary effort to mobilize the people. Subnationalities: The heartland of Ethiopia is occupied by the traditionally dominant Amhara and acculturated portions of the diffuse Galla people. In the late nineteenth century Ethiopian rulers united what had been warring fragments of a former empire in this heartland, and proceeded to incorporate some entirely new areas. At this time the Somali of the south came under Ethiopian rule; Eritrea was incorporated as the result of a UN decision in 1952. Today Ethiopia is crosscut by linguistic and religious conflicts: most important is separatism due to historic allegiances to ancient provinces (especially Tigre), to different experiences (Eritrea), and to the population of a foreign nation (Somalia).

Civil Liberties. The media are controlled, serving the mobilization needs of the government. Individual rights as we know them are unprotected under conditions of despotism and anarchy. Political imprisonment, forced confession, execution, disappearance, and torture are common. There are no rights to assembly. Many thousands have been killed aside from those dying in civil war. Education is totally controlled. What independence there was under the Ethiopian monarchy has been largely lost, but the land reform benefited many. Choice of residence and workplace is often made by the government; there have been reports of forced transport to state farms. Religious groups have been persecuted, and there is limited religious freedom. Peasant and worker organizations are closely controlled. Travel outside the country is strictly controlled; hostages or guarantors are often required before exit. The words and actions of the regime indicate little respect for private rights in property. The economy is under increasing government control through nationalizations, state-sponsored peasant cooperatives, and the regulation of business licenses.

Comparatively: Ethiopia is as free as Cambodia, less free than Sudan.

FIJI

Economy: noninclusive capitalist
Polity: centralized multiparty
Population: 700,000

Political Rights: 2
Civil Liberties: 2
Status of Freedom: free

A binational state

Political Rights. Fiji has a complex political structure designed to protect the interests of both the original Fiji people and the Indian people, who now form a slight majority. The Lower House is directly elected on the basis of both communal and national rolls. The Upper House is indirectly elected by a variety of electors (including the council of chiefs, the prime minister, and the opposition leader). Local government is organized both by the central government and by a Fijian administration headed by the council of chiefs. Although the opposition has ruled only briefly since independence, the 1982 general election illustrated the vitality of the election process, albeit with some unfair practices.

Civil Liberties. The press is free and private (but government positions must sometimes be published); government radio is under a separate and independent commission. Freedom to assemble is not impeded. The full protection of the rule of law is supplemented by an ombudsman to investigate complaints against the government. Some rights to property may have been sacrificed to guarantee special rights of inalienability of land granted the Fijians. Strong unions have full rights. Religion, travel, and other personal rights are secured. The nation may be about evenly divided between a subsistence economy, based on agriculture and fishing, and a modern market economy.

Comparatively: Fiji is as free as Papua New Guinea, freer than Tonga, less free than New Zealand.

FINLAND

Economy: mixed capitalist
Polity: centralized multiparty
Population: 4,800,000

Political Rights: 2
Civil Liberties: 2
Status of Freedom: free

An ethnic state with a small territorial subnationality

Political Rights. Finland has a parliamentary system with a strong, directly elected president. Since there are a large number of relatively strong parties, government is almost always by coalition. Elections have resulted in shifts in coalition membership. By treaty foreign policy cannot be anti-Soviet, but the 1982 presidential election indicated a weakening of a more general Soviet veto on the political process. The provinces have centrally appointed governors. Subnationalities: The rural Swedish minority (seven percent) has its own political party and strong cultural ties to Sweden. The Swedish-speaking Aland Islands have local autonomy and other special rights.

Civil Liberties. The press is private, diverse, and uncensored. Most of the radio service is government controlled, but there is an important commercial television station. The government network has been manipulated at times. Discussion in the media is controlled by a political consensus that criticism of the Soviet Union should be circumspect. There is a complete rule of law, and private rights are secured.

Comparatively: Finland is as free as Mauritius, freer than Spain, less free than Sweden.

F R A N C E

Economy: capitalist-statist
Polity: centralized multiparty
Population: 54,604,000

Political Rights: 1
Civil Liberties: 2
Status of Freedom: free

An ethnic state with major territorial subnationalities

Political Rights. France is a parliamentary democracy. However, the directly elected president is more powerful than the premier and assembly. There is also a constitutional council that oversees elections and passes on the constitutionality of assembly or executive actions on the model of the United States Supreme Court. Regional and local power has recently been greatly increased. Subnationalities: Territorial subnationalities continue to have limited rights as ethnic units. At present the Alsatian minority seems well satisfied, but there is a demand for greater autonomy among many Bretons, Corsicans, and Basques. New regional governments help to meet their demands.

Civil Liberties. The French press is free, although there is government involvement in financing and the registration of journalists. Press laws restrict freedom more than in other Western states. Criticism of the president and top officials may be muted by government threats and court actions. The news agency is private; radio and television are divided among a variety of theoretically independent companies under indirect government control. In spite of recent changes there is still an authoritarian attitude in government-citizen relations, publications may be banned at the behest of foreign governments, and arrest without explanation still occurs, particularly of members of subnationalities. Police brutality is commonly alleged. Information and organization about conscientious objection is restricted. France is, of course, under the rule of law, and rights to occupation, residence, religion, and property are secured. Both through extensive social programs and the creation of state enterprises France is quite far from a pure capitalist form.

Comparatively: France is as free as West Germany, freer than India, less free than the United Kingdom.

G A B O N

Economy: noninclusive capitalist
Polity: nationalist one-party
Population: 1,200,000

Political Rights: 6
Civil Liberties: 6
Status of Freedom: not free

A transethnic heterogeneous state

Political Rights. Gabon is a moderate dictatorship operating in the guise of a one-party state, with controlled elections characteristic of this form. Candidates must be party approved but there may be limited competition. Major cities have elected local governments; provinces are administered from the center.

Civil Liberties. All media are government controlled, and few legitimate opposition voices are raised, and journalists may be arrested for expression. Some critical items appear in local or available foreign media. There are prisoners of conscience and mistreatment. There is no right of political assembly; only one labor union is sanctioned. The authoritarian government generally does not care to interfere in private lives, and respects religious freedom, private property, and the right to travel. The government is taking a more active role in the economy and is gradually replacing foreign managers with Gabonese.

Comparatively: Gabon is as free as Jordan, freer than Angola, less free than Ghana.

GAMBIA

Economy: noninclusive capitalist **Political Rights:** 3
Polity: dominant party **Civil Liberties:** 4
Population: 600,000 **Status of Freedom:** partly free

A transethnic heterogeneous state

Political Rights. This is a parliamentary democracy in which the same party and leader have been in power since independence in 1965; they always win with substantial electoral margins. In a recent election the opposition candidate campaigned from prison. There is local, mostly traditional autonomy, but not regional self-rule. The state is now in confederation with Senegal, and the system is protected by Senegalese troops.

Civil Liberties. The private and public newspapers and radio stations are generally free, but are subject to self-censorship. Although opposition leaders have been jailed following a major insurrection, the independent judiciary maintains the rule of law. Labor unions operate within limits. The agricultural economy remains traditionally organized and is largely dependent on peanuts, the export of which is a state monopoly. Internal travel is limited by document checkpoints.

Comparatively: Gambia is as free as Malaysia, freer than Senegal, less free than Botswana.

GERMANY, EAST

Economy: socialist **Political Rights:** 7
Polity: communist one-party **Civil Liberties:** 7
Population: 16,700,000 **Status of Freedom:** not free

A relatively homogeneous population

Political Rights. East Germany is in practice a one-party communist dictatorship. No electoral competition is allowed that involves policy questions; all citizens are compelled to vote for a government-selected list of candidates. In addition, the presence of Soviet troops and direction from the Communist Party of the Soviet Union significantly reduces the sovereignty (or group freedom) of the East Germans.

Civil Liberties. Media are government-owned means of indoctrination. Dissidents are repressed by imprisonment and exclusion; the publication or importation of materials with opposing views is forbidden. One may be arrested for private criticism of the system, but complaints about policy implementation occur in all the media. Among the thousands of prisoners of conscience, the most common offense is trying to leave the country illegally (or in some cases even seeking permission to leave), or propaganda against the state. Prisoners of conscience may be severely beaten or otherwise harmed. Political reeducation may be a condition of release. The average person is not allowed freedom of occupation or residence. Once defined as an enemy of the state, a person may be barred from his occupation and his children denied higher education. Particularly revealing has been the use of the "buying out scheme" by which West Germany has been able intermittently to obtain the release of prisoners in the East through cash payments and delivering goods such as bananas and coffee. There is considerable religious freedom, with the Catholic and Protestant hierarchies possessing some independence. Freedom exists within the family, although there is no right to privacy or the inviolability of the home, mail, or telephone. Agriculture is highly collectivized and virtually all industry is state controlled. Membership in unions, production cooperatives, and other associations is compulsory.

Comparatively: East Germany is as free as Bulgaria, less free than Poland.

GERMANY, WEST

Economy: capitalist   **Political Rights:** 1
Polity: decentralized multiparty **Civil Liberties:** 2
Population: 61,543,000   **Status of Freedom:** free

A relatively homogeneous population

Political Rights. West Germany is a parliamentary democracy with an indirectly elected and largely ceremonial president. Both major parties have ruled since the war. The weak Senate is elected by the assemblies of the constituent states and loyally defends states' rights. Successive national governments have been based on changing party balances in the powerful lower house. The states have their own elected assemblies; they control education, internal security, and culture.

Civil Liberties. The papers are independent and free, with little governmental interference. Radio and television are organized in public corporations under the usually neutral direction of the state governments. Generally the rule of law has been carefully observed, and the full spectrum of private freedoms is available. In recent years jobs have been denied to some individuals with radical leftist connections; terrorist activities have led to tighter security regulations, invasions of privacy, and less acceptance of nonconformity. Arrests have been made for handling or producing inflammatory literature, for neo-Nazi propaganda, or for calling in question the courts or electoral system. Government participation in the economy is largely regulatory; in addition, complex social programs and mandated worker participation in management have limited certain private freedoms while possibly expanding others.

Comparatively: West Germany is as free as France, freer than Finland, less free than the United States of America.

GHANA

Economy: mixed socialist
Polity: military nonparty
Population: 13,900,000

Political Rights: 6
Civil Liberties: 5
Status of Freedom: not free

A transethnic heterogeneous state with subnationalities

Political Rights. A small military faction rules with the support of radical organizations. On the local level traditional sources of power still exist. Local councils are elected, but under close government supervision. Subnationalities: The country is composed of a variety of peoples, with those in the South most self-conscious. The latter are the descendants of a number of traditional kingdoms, of which the Ashanti are the most important. A north-south, Muslim-Christian opposition exists but is weakly developed, because of the numerical and economic weakness and incomplete hold of Islam in the north. In the south and center of the country a sense of Akan identity is developing among the Ashanti, Fanti, and others; since they include forty-five percent of the people, this amounts to strengthening the ethnic core of the nation. The one million Ewe in the southeast (a people divided between Ghana and Togo) play a major role in the new revolutionary government.

Civil Liberties. Radio and television and most of the press are government owned. All are under close government scrutiny. Private opinion is restrained. There have been hundreds of political arrests and political trials; many professionals have been murdered, apparently for "revolutionary" reasons. There has been a great deal of government control in some areas of the economy--especially in cocoa production, on which the economy depends, and in modern capital intensive industry. The assets of many businesses have been frozen. Some groups, including the strong women's marketing associations, have resisted government attempts to impose price ceilings on all goods. Labor unions are controlled. Like Senegal, Ghana has a relatively highly developed industry and its agriculture is dependent on world markets. There is religious freedom; travel is controlled.

Comparatively: Ghana is as free as North Yemen, freer than Niger, less free than Ivory Coast.

G R E E C E

Economy: capitalist-statist
Polity: centralized multiparty
Population: 9,900,000

Political Rights: 1
Civil Liberties: 2
Status of Freedom: free

A relatively homogeneous state

Political Rights. Greece is a parliamentary democracy with a theoretically strong, but indirectly elected, president. The stabilization of free institutions is proceeding rapidly; recent elections have been competitive and open to the full spectrum of parties. Provincial administration is centrally controlled; there is local self-government.

Civil Liberties. Newspapers are private and the judiciary is independent. Broadcast media are government owned and controlled, but opposition opinions are frequently aired. There are no known prisoners of conscience. Because of the recent revolutionary situation all views are not freely expressed (a situation similar to that in post-fascist Portugal). One can be imprisoned for insulting the authorities or religion. The courts are not entirely independent. Union activity is under government influence, particularly in the dominant public sector. Private rights are respected.

Comparatively: Greece is as free as France, freer than Finland, less free than Netherlands.

GRENADA

Economy: mixed socialist	**Political Rights:** 7
Polity: centralized dominant-party	**Civil Liberties:** 6
Population: 118,000	**Status of Freedom:** not free

A relatively homogeneous population

Political Rights. In 1979 a major opposition party came to power by force. The change was initially popular, but the new leaders increasingly monopolized power. After a bloody coup massive foreign intervention left the political system barely operative as this went to press. The final outcome hopefully will be the return of constitutionalism and freedom. There is no local government.

Civil Liberties. The news media had become government controlled with the elimination of nongovernmental or opposition media. Journalists and many others were arbitrarily arrested. Opposition assemblies were regularly broken up and opposition political leaders had been detained indefinitely on vague charges. State-sponsored cooperatives were being formed, though the private economy remained.

Comparatively: Grenada was as free as Guinea, freer than Ethiopia, less free than Panama.

GUATEMALA

Economy: noninclusive capitalist	**Political Rights:** 6
Polity: military nonparty	**Civil Liberties:** 6
Population: 7,900,000	**Status of Freedom:** not free

An ethnic state with a major potential territorial subnationality

Political Rights. Until the 1982 coup Guatemala was formally a constitutional democracy on the American model, but election results were often altered in favor of a preselected candidate. Recent military leaders have continued to promise a return to democracy. The provinces are centrally administered. Military and other security forces maintain decisive extra-constitutional power at all levels. Subnationalities: Various groups of Mayan and other Indians make up half the population; they do not yet have a subnationalist sense of unity, but are involved both forcibly and voluntarily in guerrilla activity.

Civil Liberties. The press and a large portion of radio and television are privately controlled. The press is generally free, but self-censorship has been common, because of the threat of torture and murder by political opponents. Following the 1982 coup a state of siege led to direct control of the press and suspension of unions. The struggle against rural guerrillas has led to frequent attacks on recalcitrant peasants or Indians by security forces. Thousands have sought refuge internally and in border areas. Torture and kidnapping are practiced by both sides in the conflict. The judiciary is under both leftist and governmental pressure in political or subversive cases and has become relatively ineffective in these areas. Unions have been intimidated; political parties are active on a limited basis. Searches without warrants have been widespread; property rights have not been secure. Fear of attack inhibits domestic travel, but other private rights seem fairly well respected.

Comparatively: Guatemala is as free as Cuba, freer than Haiti, less free than Nicaragua.

GUINEA

Economy: noninclusive socialist
Polity: socialist one-party
Population: 5,400,000

Political Rights: 7
Civil Liberties: 7
Status of Freedom: not free

A formally transethnic heterogeneous state

Political Rights. Guinea is a one-party socialist dictatorship. Elections for president and parliament are uncontested.
The party controls all levels of government. Power is concentrated in one tribal group.

Civil Liberties. All media are government or party owned and
closely controlled. Ideological purity is demanded in all areas
except religion. Political imprisonment, torture, and execution
are now uncommon, but hundreds or thousands may have died in
detention. Everyone must participate in guided political activity. Few private rights, such as those to organize unions,
develop property, or choose one's education are recognized. Private lawyers are not permitted. Industry is heavily nationalized
and private farmers, who provide most produce, are denied credit.
A pervasive black market circumvents the state distribution system. Seasonal migration within the country and across the border
is unrestricted. There is no legal sanctity of the home.

Comparatively: Guinea is as free as Ethiopia, less free than
Zambia.

GUINEA-BISSAU

Economy: noninclusive socialist   **Political Rights:** 7
Polity: socialist one-party   **Civil Liberties:** 6
     (military dominated)
Population: 800,000   **Status of Freedom:** not free

A transethnic heterogeneous state

Political Rights. Guinea-Bissau is administered by one party;
all other parties are illegal. Local economic control under party
guidance is emphasized.

Civil Liberties. The media are government controlled; criticism of the system is forbidden. There are prisoners of conscience. Union activity is government directed. Land ownership
is public or communal. The small industrial sector remains mixed,
but the continuing economic crisis has virtually halted all private sector activity. An additional block to further decollecti-
vization is the Soviet and Cuban presence. Religion is relatively
free, as are travel and other aspects of private life.

Comparatively: Guinea-Bissau is as free as Mozambique, freer
than Guinea, less free than Senegal.

G U Y A N A

Economy: mixed socialist
Polity: centralized multiparty
Population: 900,000

Political Rights: 5
Civil Liberties: 5
Status of Freedom: partly free

An ethnically complex state

Political Rights. Guyana is a parliamentary democracy with a strong executive and an increasingly dominant ruling party. In recent elections the government has been responsibly charged with irregularities that resulted in its victory. The 1980 parliamentary elections were criticized by both foreign and local observers for lack of adequate controls. Opposition parties are denied equal access to the media, and their supporters are discriminated against in employment. Administration is generally centralized but there are some elected local officials.

Civil Liberties. Radio is now government owned. Several opposition newspapers have been nationalized; the opposition press has been nearly forced out of existence. However, a variety of foreign news media are still available. There is a right of assembly, but harassment occurs. There is an operating human rights organization. All private schools have been nationalized recently, and the government has interfered with university appointments. It is possible to win against the government in court; there are no prisoners of conscience, though torture of convicts may be practiced. Art and music are under considerable government control. Unions are free but under increasing pressure. The private sector is stagnating under official intimidation and extensive state control of productive property, although a black market thrives. The opposition is terrorized by armed gangs and the police; the general public suffers under increasingly arbitrary and severe controls. Political patronage is extensive and some social benefits are allocated on a preferential basis. Internal exile has been used against political opponents.

Comparatively: Guyana is as free as Indonesia, freer than Nicaragua, less free than Colombia.

HAITI

Economy: noninclusive capitalist
Polity: dominant party
Population: 5,700,000

Political Rights: 7
Civil Liberties: 6
Status of Freedom: not free

A relatively homogeneous population

Political Rights. Haiti is a dictatorship with an ephemeral ruling party. Elections allow little if any opposition. Small parties have been organized, but effectively neutralized.

Civil Liberties. The media are both private and public. Censorship is legal for all media, including films and theatre; attempts at independence in journalism are frequently repressed. Rights of assembly and organization are restricted, but a private human rights organization has been active. A government sponsored militia has suppressed opposition; political murders, imprisonment without trial, exile, and torture have characterized the system intermittently. An acceptable rule of law has been in abeyance during a prolonged "state of siege"; property has been seized indiscriminately by security forces. Many people attempt to flee the country illegally every year; several dozen opponents have been forcibly expelled. Union activity is restricted. Corruption seriously infringes rights to political equality.

Comparatively: Haiti is as free as Benin, freer than Guinea, less free than Panama.

HONDURAS

Economy: noninclusive capitalist
Polity: centralized multiparty
Population: 4,100,000

Political Rights: 3
Civil Liberties: 3
Status of Freedom: partly free

A relatively homogeneous population

Political Rights. The government is a parliamentary democracy with an elected president. Military leaders have retained and recently extended their influence over the political system. Provincial government is centrally administered; local government is elected.

Civil Liberties. The media are largely private and free of prior censorship. Human rights organizations are active. Militant peasant organizations are quite active, and the struggle of peasants for land often leads to violence. The spreading of guerrilla war from neighboring countries has led to represssions of refugees and others. Most private rights are respected--in so far as government power reaches. Labor unions have suffered oppression, but are relatively strong, especially in plantation areas. There is freedom of religion and movement.

Comparatively: Honduras is as free as Malta, freer than Panama, less free than Venezuela.

HUNGARY

Economy: socialist
Polity: communist one-party
Population: 10,700,000

Political Rights: 6
Civil Liberties: 5
Status of Freedom: not free

A relatively homogeneous population

Political Rights. Hungary is ruled as a one-party communist dictatorship. Although there is an elective national assembly as well as local assemblies, all candidates must be approved by the party, and the decisions of the politburo are decisive. Within this framework recent elections have allowed little or no choice among candidates. The group rights of the Hungarian people are diminished by the government's official acceptance of the right of the Soviet government to interfere in the domestic affairs of Hungary by force.

Civil Liberties. Media are under government or party control. Basic criticism of top leaders, communism, human rights performance, or the Soviet presence is inadmissable, but some criticism is allowed; this is expressed through papers, plays, books, the importation of foreign publications or listening to foreign broadcasts. Informally organized dissident groups are allowed to exist. Individuals are regularly detained for reasons of conscience, though usually for short periods. Control over religious affairs is more relaxed than in most communist states. Although private rights are not guaranteed, in practice there is considerable private property, and permisson to travel into and out of the country is easier to obtain than in most of Eastern Europe. The border with Austria is esentially open. Unions are Party directed and have no right to strike; however, workers have gained some control over enterprise management and operations.

Comparatively: Hungary is as free as North Yemen, freer than Czechoslovakia, less free than Egypt.

I C E L A N D

Economy: capitalist
Polity: centralized multiparty
Population: 230,000

Political Rights: 1
Civil Liberties: 1
Status of Freedom: free

A relatively homogeneous population

Political Rights. Iceland is governed by a parliamentary democracy. Recent years have seen important shifts in voter sentiment, resulting successively in right and left-wing coalitions. Although a small country, Iceland pursues an independent foreign policy. Provinces are ruled by central government appointees.

Civil Liberties. The press is private or party and free of censorship. Radio and television are state owned, but supervised by a state board representing major parties and interests. There are no political prisoners and the judiciary is independent. Private rights are respected; few are poor or illiterate.

Comparatively: Iceland is as free as Norway, freer than Portugal.

I N D I A

Economy: noninclusive
           capitalist-statist
Polity: decentralized multiparty
Population: 730,000,000

Political Rights: 2
Civil Liberties: 3
Status of Freedom: free

A multinational and complex state

Political Rights. India is a parliamentary democracy in which the opposition has an opportunity to rule. 1982-83 saw a resurgence of opposition strength on a regional basis. The strong powers retained by the component states have been compromised in recent years by the central government's frequent imposition of direct rule. Calling immediate state elections where the opposition continues to rule after a national change of government is a practice compromising the federal system.

Subnationalities.   India contains a diverse collection of mostly territorially distinct peoples united by historical experience and the predominance of Hinduism.   India's dominant peoples are those of the north central area that speak as a first language either the official language, Hindi (Hindustani), or a very closely related dialect of Sanskrit origin.   The other major subnational peoples of India may be divided into several groups: (1) peoples with separate states that are linguistically and historically only marginally distinct from the dominant Hindi speakers (for example, the Marathi, Gujerati, or Oriya); (2) peoples with separate states that are of Sanskrit background linguistically, but have a relatively strong sense of separate identity (for example, Bengalis or Kashmiris); (3) peoples with separate states that are linguistically and to some extent racially quite distinct (for example, Telegu or Malayalam); and (4) peoples that were not originally granted states of their own, and often still do not have them. These peoples, such as the Santali, Bhuti-Lepcha, or Mizo, may be survivors of India's pre-Aryan peoples.   With the partial exception of the last group, the Indian federal system accords a fair amount of democratic rights to all peoples.   Several peoples from groups (2), (3), and (4) have shown through legal (especially votes) and illegal means a strong desire by a significant part of the population for independence or greater autonomy (notably Kashmiris, Nagas, and Mizos). This accounting leaves out many nonterritorial religious and caste minorities, although here again the system has granted relatively broad rights to such groups to reasonable self-determination. Nevertheless, India faces today a serious problem of Sikh unrest in the Punjab.

Civil Liberties. The Indian press is strong and independent. Radio and television are government controlled in this largely illiterate country and they serve government interests.   There is freedom of organization and assembly, but there have been illegal arrests, questionable killings, and reports of torture by the police, which have often been out of control. The judiciary is generally responsive, fair, and independent. The problem of extreme trial delay has recently been addressed. The frequent approach to anarchy in Indian society offers many examples of both freedom and repression.   There are few if any prisoners of conscience, but there are hundreds imprisoned for real or "proposed" political violence, and demonstrations often lead to fatalities and large-scale jailings.   Due to the centralized political structure there is a great deal of regional variation in the operation of the security laws. Kashmir has especially repressive security policies in relation to the press and political detention; Sikkim is treated as an Indian colony and the same might be said for some other border areas. Assam is necessarily under stricter supervision. Indians enjoy freedom to travel, to worship as they please, and to organize for mutual benefit, especially in unions and cooperatives. Lack of education, extreme poverty, and surviving traditional controls certainly reduce the meaning of such liberties for large numbers of Indians.

Comparatively: India is as free as Nigeria, freer than Malaysia, less free than Japan.

INDONESIA

Economy: noninclusive capitalist-statist

Polity: centralized dominant-party (military dominated)

Population: 160,932,000

Political Rights: 5

Civil Liberties: 5

Status of Freedom: partly free

A transethnic complex state with active and potential subnationalities

Political Rights. Indonesia is a controlled parliamentary democracy under miltary direction. Recent parliamentary elections allowed some competition but severely restricted opposition campaigning and organization. The number and character of opposition parties are carefully controlled, parties must refrain from criticizing one another, candidates of both government and opposition require government approval, and the opposition is not allowed to organize in rural areas. In any event parliament does not have a great deal of power. Regional and local government is under central control. Local assemblies are elected.

Subnationalities: Indonesia includes a variety of ethnic groups and is divided by crosscutting island identities. Although the island of Java is numerically dominant, the national language is not Javanese, and most groups or islands do not appear to have strong subnational identifications. There is discrimination against Chinese culture. Both civilian and military elites generally attempt to maintain religious, ethnic, and regional balance, but government-sponsored settlement of Javanese on outer islands results in the destruction of minority cultures and the denial of self-determination. Groups demanding independence exist in Sulawesi, the Moluccas, Timor, West Irian, and northern Sumatra, and continue to mount revolts against the government.

Civil Liberties. Most newspapers are private. All are subject to fairly close government supervision; there is heavy self-censorship and censorship in some areas. Criticism of the system is muted by periodic suppressions. Radio and television are government controlled. Freedom of assembly is restricted, but citizens are not compelled to attend meetings. There continue to be prisoners of conscience, but most are now detained only for short periods. Thousands of released prisoners remain in a second-class status, especially in regard to residence and employment. In this area the army rather than the civilian judiciary is dominant. Torture has been infrequent recently; the army has been responsible for many thousands of unnecessary deaths in its suppression of revolt in, or conquest of, East Timor. Recently there have been many murders of nonpolitical criminals, apparently at the hands of "hit squads" allied to the security services. Union activity is closely regulated, but labor organization is widespread and strikes occur. Many people are not allowed to travel outside the country for political reasons. Movement, especially to the cities, is restricted; other private rights are generally respected. The Indonesian bureaucracy has an unenviable reputation for arbitrariness and corruption, practices that reduce the effective expression of human rights. There are many active human rights organizations. Much of industry and commercial agriculture is government owned; sharecropping and tenant farming are relatively common, particularly on Java.

Comparatively: Indonesia is as free as China (Taiwan), freer than Burma, less free than Singapore.

IRAN

Economy: noninclusive capitalist-statist	**Political Rights:** 6
Polity: quasi-dominant party	**Civil Liberties:** 6
Population: 42,500,000	**Status of Freedom:** not free

An ethnic state with major territorial subnationalities

Political Rights. Iran has competitive elections, but the direction of the nonelective, theocratic leadership narrowly defines the alternatives. Those who oppose the system in any way are generally eliminated from the system. Subnationalities: Among the most important non-Persian peoples are the Kurds, the Azerbaijani Turks, the Baluch, and a variety of other (primarily Turkish) tribes. Many of these have striven for independence in the recent past when the opportunity arose. The Kurds are in active revolt.

Civil Liberties. Newspapers are semi-private or factional, and all are closely controlled. The other media are largely government owned propaganda organs. The right of assembly is denied to those who do not approve of the new system. There are many prisoners of conscience and executions for political offenses, often nonviolent, have been frequent. Unions have been suppressed. Vigilante groups compete with the official security system; many private rights have become highly insecure, as the goal of the Islamic system is control over most aspects of life. This is especially so for the Bahais and other religious minorities. Legal emigration is quite difficult. Education is subject to religious restrictions; the freedom and equality of women is radically curtailed.

Comparatively: Iran is as free as Jordan, freer than Iraq, less free than Bangladesh.

I R A Q

Economy: noninclusive socialist   **Political Rights:** 6
Polity: socialist one-party   **Civil Liberties:** 7
      (military dominated)
Population: 14,500,000   **Status of Freedom:** not free

An ethnic state with a major territorial subnationality

Political Rights. Iraq is a one-party state under military leadership, with control in the hands of a small minority faction. Elections allow some choice of individuals, but all candidates are carefully selected and no policy choices are involved in the process. Resulting parliaments have little if any power. Provinces are governed from the center. Subnationalities: The Kurds have been repeatedly denied self-determination, most recently through reoccupation of their lands and an attempt to disperse them about the country.

Civil Rights. Newspapers are public or party and are closely controlled by the government; foreign and domestic books and movies are censored. Radio and television are government monopolies. The strident media are emphasized as governmental means for active indoctrination. Political imprisonment, brutality, and torture are common and execution frequent. Poisoning on release from prison is reported. The families of suspects are often imprisoned. Rights are largely de facto or those deriving from traditional religious law. Religious freedom or freedom to organize for any purpose is very limited. Education is intended to serve the party's purposes. Iraq has a dual economy with a large traditional sector. The government has taken over much of the modern petroleum-based economy; land reform is, however, now expanding private choice.

Comparatively: Iraq is as free as Czechoslovakia, freer than Somalia, less free than Iran.

IRELAND

Economy: capitalist
Polity: centralized multiparty
Population: 3,500,000

Political Rights: 1
Civil Liberties: 1
Status of Freedom: free

A relatively homogeneous population

Political Rights. Ireland is a parliamentary democracy that successively shifts national power among parties. The bicameral legislature has an appointive upper house with powers only of delay. Local government is not powerful, but is elective rather than appointive. Referendums are also used for national decisions.

Civil Liberties. The press is free and private, and radio and television are under an autonomous corporation. Strong censorship has always been exercized over both publishers and the press, but since this is for social rather than political content, it lies within that sphere of control permitted a majority in a free democracy. The rule of law is firmly established and private rights are guaranteed.

Comparatively: Ireland is as free as Canada, freer than France.

ISRAEL

Economy: mixed capitalist
Polity: centralized multiparty
Population: 4,000,000

Political Rights: 2
Civil Liberties: 2
Status of Freedom: free

An ethnic state with microterritorial subnationalities

Political Rights, Israel is governed under a parliamentary system. Recent elections have resulted in shifts of power among the many political parties. Provinces are ruled from the center, although there are important local elective offices in the cities. Subnationalities: National elections do not involve the Arabs in the occupied territories, but Arabs in Israel proper participate in Israeli elections as a minority grouping. Arabs both in Israel and the occupied territories must live in their homeland under the cultural and political domination of twentieth century immigrants.

Civil Liberties. Newspapers are private or party, and free of censorship except for restrictions relating to the always precarious national security. Radio and television are governmentally owned. In general the rule of law is observed, although Arabs in Israel are not accorded the full rights of citizens, and the orthodox Jewish faith holds a special position in the country's religious, customary, and legal life. Detentions, house arrest, and brutality have been reported against Arabs opposing Israel's Palestine policy. Because of the war, the socialist-cooperative ideology of its founders, and dependence on outside support, the role of private enterprise in the economy has been less than in most of Euro-America. Arabs are, in effect, not allowed to buy land from Jews, while Arab land has been expropriated for Jewish settlement. Unions are economically and politically powerful and control over twenty-five percent of industry. Freedom House's rating of Israel is based on its judgment of the situation in Israel proper aand not that in the occupied territories.

Comparatively: Israel is as free as Ecuador, freer than India, less free than France.

ITALY

Economy: capitalist-statist
Polity: centralized multiparty
Population: 56,300,000

Political Rights: 1
Civil Liberties: 2
Status of Freedom: free

A relatively homogeneous population with small territorial subnationalities

Political Rights. Italy is a bicameral parliamentary democracy. Elections are generally free. Since the 1940s governments have been dominated by the Christian Democrats, with coalitions shifting between dependence on minor parties of the left or right. Recently premiers have often been from these smaller parties. The fascist party is banned. Referendums are used to supplement parliamentary rule. Opposition parties gain local political power, but regional and local power are generally quite limited. Regional institutions are developing.

Civil Liberties. Italian newspapers are free and cover a broad spectrum. Radio and television are both public and private and provide unusually diverse programming. Laws against defamation of the government and foreign and ecclesiastical officials exert a slight limiting effect on the media. Freedom of speech is inhibited in some areas and for many individuals by the violence of extremist groups or criminal organizations. Since the bureaucracy does not respond promptly to citizen desires, it represents, as in many countries, an additional impediment to full expression of the rule of law. Detention may last for years without trial. Unions are strong and independent. Major industries are managed by the government, and the government has undertaken extensive reallocations of land.

Comparatively: Italy is as free as Greece, freer than Morocco, less free than the Netherlands.

IVORY COAST

Economy: noninclusive capitalist
Polity: nationalist one-party
Population: 8,900,000

Political Rights: 5
Civil Liberties: 5
Status of Freedom: partly free

A transethnic heterogeneous state

Political Rights. Ivory Coast is ruled by a one-party, capitalist dictatorship in which a variety of political elements have been integrated. Assembly elections have recently allowed choice of individuals, including nonparty, but not policies. Organized in the 1940s, the ruling party incorporates a variety of interests and forces. Provinces are ruled directly from the center. Contested mayoralty elections occur.

Civil Liberties. Although the legal press is party or government controlled, it presents a limited spectrum of opinion. Foreign publications are widely available. While opposition is discouraged, there is no ideological conformity. Radio and television are government controlled. Short-term imprisonment and conscription are used to control opposition. Travel and religion are generally free. Rights to strike or organize unions are quite limited. Economically the country depends on small private or traditional farms; in the modern sector private enterprise is encouraged.

Comparatively: Ivory Coast is as free as Sierra Leone, freer than Guinea, less free than Senegal.

JAMAICA

Economy: capitalist-statist
Polity: centralized multiparty
Population: 2,300,000

Political Rights: 2
Civil Liberties: 3
Status of Freedom: free

A relatively homogeneous population

Political Rights. Jamaica is a parliamentary democracy in which power changes from one party to another. However, political life is violent; the last election was accompanied by seven hundred deaths in the pre-election period. The general neutrality of the civil service, police, and army preserves the system. Regional or local administrations have little independent power, although there are elected parish councils.

Civil Liberties. The press is largely private; the broadcasting media largely public. Critical media are widely available to the public. Freedom of assembly and organization are generally respected. The judiciary and much of the bureaucracy retain independence, although the police and legal system have been accused of countenancing brutality and severe punishments. Some foreign companies have been nationalized, but the economy remains largely in private hands. Labor is both politically and economically powerful.

Comparatively: Jamaica is as free as Colombia, freer than Panama, less free than Dominica.

JAPAN

Economy: capitalist
Polity: centralized multiparty
Population: 119,205,000

Political Rights: 1
Civil Liberties: 1
Status of Freedom: free

A relatively homogeneous population

Political Rights. Japan is a bicameral, constitutional monarchy with a relatively weak upper house. The conservative-to-centrist Liberal Democratic Party ruled with solid majorities from independence in the early 1950s until the mid-1970s. Although the Liberal Democrats have lost considerable support in recent elections, through coalitions with independents they have maintained control at the national level and have recently showed increased strength at the local level. Concentrated business interests have played a strong role in maintaining Liberal Party hegemony through the use of their money, influence, and prestige. In addition, a weighting of representation in favor of rural areas tends to maintain the Liberal Party position. Opposition parties are fragmented. They have local control in some areas, but the power of local and regional assemblies and officials is limited. Democracy within the Liberal Party is increasing.

Civil Liberties. News media are generally private and free, although many radio and television stations are served by a public broadcasting corporation. Television is excellent and quite free. Courts of law are not as important in Japanese society as in Europe and America; both the courts and police appear to be relatively fair. Travel and change of residence are unrestricted. By tradition public expression and action are more restricted than in most modern democracies. Japanese style collectivism leads to strong social pressures, especially psychological pressures, in many spheres (unions, corporations, or religious-political groups, such as Soka Gakkai). Human rights organizations are very active.

Comparatively: Japan is as free as Australia, freer than France.

JORDAN

Economy: capitalist
Polity: traditional nonparty
Population: 3,600,000

Political Rights: 6
Civil Liberties: 6
Status of Freedom: not free

A relatively homogeneous population

Political Rights. Jordan is an absolute monarchy. There are no parties; parliament is dissolved. In 1978 an appointive National Consultative Council was established, but it has little power. Provinces are ruled from the center; elected local governments have limited autonomy. The king and his ministers are regularly petitioned by citizens.

Civil Liberties. Papers are mostly private but self-censored and occasionally suspended. Television and radio are government controlled. Free private conversation and mild public criticism are allowed. Under a continuing state of martial law normal legal guarantees for political suspects are suspended, and organized opposition is not permitted. There are prisoners of conscience and instances of torture. Labor has a limited right to organize and strike. Private rights such as those of property, travel, or religion appear to be respected. The government has partial control over many large corporations.

Comparatively: Jordan is as free as Cuba, freer than South Yemen, less free than Egypt.

KENYA

Economy: noninclusive capitalist **Political Rights:** 5
Polity: nationalist one-party **Civil Liberties:** 5
Population: 18,600,000 **Status of Freedom:** partly free

A formally transethnic heterogeneous state with active and potential subnationalities

Political Rights. Kenya is a one-party nationalist state in which the largest tribal group has a preponderance of political power. Election results often express popular dissatisfaction, but candidates avoid discussion of basic policy or the president. Selection of top party and national leaders is by consensus or acclamation. The administration is centralized, but elements of tribal and communal government continue at the periphery. Subnationalities: Comprising twenty percent of the population, the Kikuyu are the largest tribal group. In a very heterogeneous society, the Luo are the second most important subnationality.

Civil Liberties. The press is private, but essentially no criticism of major policies is allowed. Radio and television are under government control. Rights of assembly, organization, and demonstration are limited. The courts have considerable independence. Prisoners of conscience detained intermittently include university lecturers and writers. Defending them in court has now become itself dangerous. Unions are active but strikes are de facto illegal. Private rights are generally respected. Land is gradually coming under private rather than tribal control.

Comparatively: Kenya is as free as Ivory Coast, freer than Djibouti, less free than Gambia.

K I R I B A T I

Economy: noninclusive capitalist- **Political Rights:** 1
                statist
Polity: decentralized nonparty   **Civil Liberties:** 2
Population: 57,000   **Status of Freedom:** free

A relatively homogeneous population with a territorial subnationality

Political Rights. Although there are not formal parties, both the legislature and president are elected in a fully competitive system. Local government is significant.

Civil Liberties. The press is private; radio government owned. Public expression appears to be free and the rule of law guaranteed. The modern economy is dominated by investments from the now virtually depleted government-run phosphate industry. A free union operates, and most agriculture is small private subsistence; land cannot be alienated to non-natives.

Comparatively: Kiribati is as free as France, freer than Western Samoa, less free than Australia.

K O R E A, N O R T H

Economy: socialist   **Political Rights:** 7
Polity: communist one-party   **Civil Liberties:** 7
Population: 19,200,000   **Status of Freedom:** not free

A relatively homogeneous state

Political Rights. North Korea is a hard-line communist dicta-torship in which the organs and assemblies of government are merely a facade for party or individual rule. National elections allow no choice. The politburo is under one-man rule; the dicta-tor's son is the dictator's officially anointed successor. Military officers are very strong in top positions.

Civil Liberties. The media are all government controlled, with glorification of the leader a major responsibility. External publications are rigidly excluded and those who listen to foreign broadcasts severely punished. No individual thoughts are advanced publicly or privately. Individual rights are minimal. Everyone is given a security rating that determines future success. Oppo-nents are even kidnapped overseas. Rights to travel internally and externally are perhaps the most restricted in the world: tourism is unknown--even to communist countries. Social classes are politically defined in a rigidly controlled society. There are thousands of long-term prisoners of conscience; torture is reportedly common. There are also reeducation centers and inter-nal exile. There is no private business or agriculture.

Comparatively: North Korea is as free as Albania, less free than South Korea.

K O R E A ,   S O U T H

Economy: capitalist
Polity: centralized multiparty
Population: 41,366,000

Political Rights: 5
Civil Liberties: 6
Status of Freedom: partly free

A relatively homogeneous state

Political Rights. South Korea is under a military regime with the support of a partly free legislature. Recent elections of both president and assembly have given the opposition a restricted right to compete. There is no independent local government.

Civil Liberties. Although most newspapers are private, as well as many radio stations and one television station, they have been reorganized by government fiat. Freedom to express differing opinion has been repeatedly restricted only to reemerge, and the mobilization of public opinion by the opposition directly affects government policy. Because of government pressure, self-censorship is the rule. Special laws against criticizing the constitution, the government, or its policies have resulted in many prisoners of conscience and the use of torture. The courts have not been able to effectively protect the rights of political suspects or prisoners. Many political opponents have been denied travel permits, but freedom of internal and external travel is otherwise unabridged. There is religious freedom (but not freedom of religious groups to criticize the government). Human rights organizations are active, but have been under heavy pressure. Outside this arena, private rights have been generally respected. Rapid capitalistic economic growth has been combined with a relatively egalitarian income distribution. Government controls most heavy industry; other sectors are private. Union activity remains severely curtailed under the 1980 labor law.

Comparatively: South Korea is as free as Indonesia, freer than China (Mainland), less free than Thailand.

K U W A I T

Economy: mixed capitalist-statist **Political Rights:** 4
Polity: traditional nonparty   **Civil Liberties:** 4
Population: 1,600,000   **Status of Freedom:** partly free

The citizenry is relatively homogeneous

Political Rights. Kuwait is a constitutional and parliamentary monarchy with a limited franchise and concentration of power in the monarch. Citizens have access to the monarch. More than half the population are immigrants: their political, economic, and social rights are inferior to those of natives, and they very seldom achieve citizenship for themselves or their children.

Civil Liberties. Although the private press presents diverse opinions and ideological viewpoints, papers are subject to suspension for "spreading dissension," or for criticism of the monarch, Islam, or friendly foreign states. Radio and television are government controlled. Imported media are censored. Freedom of assembly is curtailed. Public critics may be detained, expelled, or have their passports confiscated. Formal political parties are not allowed. Private discussion is open, and few, if any, political prisoners are held. Private freedoms are respected, and independent unions operate. There is a wide variety of enabling government activity in fields such as education, housing, and medicine that is not based on reducing choice through taxation.

Comparatively: Kuwait is as free as Senegal, freer than Qatar, less free than Nepal.

L A O S

Economy: noninclusive socialist
Polity: communist one-party
Population: 3,600,000

Political Rights: 7
Civil Liberties: 7
Status of Freedom: not free

An ethnic state with active or potential subnationalities

Political Rights. Laos has established a traditional communist party dictatorship in which the party is superior to the external government at all levels. The government is subservient to the desires of the Vietnamese communist party, upon which the present leaders must depend. Vietnam continues to maintain five divisions in the country. There is continued resistance in rural areas, where many groups have been violently suppressed. Subnationalities: Pressure on the Hmong people has caused the majority of them to flee the country.

Civil Liberties. The media are all government controlled. There are many political prisoners; large numbers remain in reeducation camps. There are few accepted private rights, but there is relaxed opposition to traditional ways, particularly Buddhism. Collectivization has been halted since 1979 because of peasant resistance; most farmers continue to be small, individual owners. The limited industry is nationalized. Travel within and exit from the country is highly restricted.

Comparatively: Laos is as free as Mongolia, less free than China (Mainland).

L E B A N O N

Economy: capitalist
Polity: decentralized multiparty
Population: 2,600,000

Political Rights: 5
Civil Liberties: 4
Status of Freedom: partly free

A complex, multinational, microterritorial state

Political Rights. In theory Lebanon is a parliamentary democracy with a strong but indirectly elected president. In spite of

388

the calamities of the last few years the constitutional system still functions to varying degrees in some parts of the country. The parliament is elected, although the last general election was in 1972. Palestinians, local militias, Syrian, and Israeli forces have all but erased national sovereignty in much of the country. Subnationalities: Leading administrative and parliamentary officials are allocated among the several religious or communal groups by complicated formulas. These groups have for years existed semi-autonomously within the state, although their territories are often intermixed.

Civil Liberties. Renowned for its independence, the press still offers a highly diverse selection to an attentive audience. Most censorship is now self-imposed, reflecting the views of locally dominant military forces. Radio is government and party; television is part government and now officially uncensored. Widespread killing in recent years has inhibited the nationwide expression of most freedoms and tightened communal controls on individuals. In many areas the courts cannot function effectively, but within its power the government secures most private rights. Few if any prisoners of conscience are detained by the government. Unions are government-supervised and subsidized and generally avoid political activity. There is little government intervention in the predominantly service-oriented economy. There is an active human rights organization.

Comparatively: Lebanon is as free as Morocco, freer than Syria, less free than Cyprus.

L E S O T H O

Economy: noninclusive capitalist   **Political Rights:** 5
Polity: partially centralized   **Civil Liberties:** 5
     dominant party
Population: 1,400,000   **Status of Freedom:** partly free

A relatively homogeneous population

Political Rights. Lesotho is a constitutional monarchy essentially under the one-man rule of the leader of the ruling political party who suspended the constitution to avoid being defeated in 1970. Opposition parties as well as the king have been repressed, although members of opposition parties have been introduced into the government. Guerrilla activity continues. There is some local government, and the chiefs retain power at this level. Although there are frequent expressions of national independence, Lesotho remains under considerable South African economic and political pressure. Lesotho is populated almost exclusively by Basotho people, and the land has never been alienated. A large percentage of the male citizenry works in South Africa.

Civil Liberties. The media are government and church; criticism is muted. Opposition political activity or assembly is repressed, but not eliminated. Opponents are periodically detained. Paramilitary forces apparently are responsible for the deaths of several political opponents. The judiciary preserves considerable independence vis-a-vis the government. Limited union activity is permitted; some strikes have occurred. Most private rights are respected, but political opponents may be denied foreign travel.

Comparatively: Lesotho is as free as Indonesia, freer than South Africa, less free than Botswana.

L I B E R I A

Economy: noninclusive capitalist
Polity: military nonparty
Population: 2,100,000

Political Rights: 5
Civil Liberties: 5
Status of Freedom: partly free

A formally transethnic heterogeneous state

Political Rights. Liberia moved in 1983 from a military dictatorship toward a constitutional democracy. The new constitution has gone through a review process that included examination by an assembly of the representatives of most sectors. However, control has not been transferred to elected representatives. There is some traditional local government.

Civil Liberties. The press is private, exercises self-censorship, but represents a variety of positions. Radio and television are largely government controlled. Lack of legal protection continues to characterize the country, but execution and imprisonment for expression are now rare. Travel and other private rights are generally respected. Only blacks can become citizens. Religion is free. Union organization is partly free; illegal strikes have occurred, often without government interference. Most industry is government or foreign owned.

390

Comparatively: Liberia is as free as Ivory Coast, freer than Togo, less free than Senegal.

L I B Y A

Economy: mixed socialist **Political Rights:** 6
Polity: socialist quasi-one-party **Civil Liberties:** 6
      (military dominated)
Population: 3,300,000 **Status of Freedom:** not free

A relatively homogeneous state

Political Rights. Libya is a military dictatorship effectively under the control of one person. Although officially there is no party, the effort to mobilize and organize the entire population for state purposes follows the socialist one-party model. The place of a legislature is taken by the direct democracy of large congresses, but elections held at local levels reflect local interests and are relatively fair. Whatever the form, no opposition is allowed on the larger questions of society. Institutional self-management has been widely introduced in the schools, hospitals, and factories. Sometimes the system works well enough to provide a meaningful degree of decentralized self-determination.

Civil Liberties. The media are government-controlled means for active indoctrination. Political discussion at the local level is relatively open. There are many political prisoners; the use of military and people's courts for political cases suggests little respect for the rule of law, yet acquittals in political cases occur. All lawyers must work for the state. Torture and mistreatment are frequent; executions for crimes of conscience occur--even in foreign countries through assassination. Although ideologically socialist some of the press remains in private hands. Oil and oil-related industries are the major areas of government enterprise. Socialization tends to be announced at the top and imposed rather anarchically and sporadically at the bottom. Most private associations and trade organizations are being integrated into or replaced by state organizations. Employment is increasingly dependent on political loyalty. Respect for Islam provides some check on arbitrary government.

Comparatively: Libya is as free as Algeria, freer than Afghanistan, less free than Tunisia.

L U X E M B O U R G

Economy: capitalist
Polity: centralized multiparty
Population: 365,000

Political Rights: 1
Civil Liberties: 1
Status of Freedom: free

A relatively homogeneous state

Political Rights. Luxembourg is a constitutional monarchy on the Belgian model, in which the monarchy is somewhat more powerful than in the United Kingdom or Scandinavia. The legislature is bicameral with the appointive upper house having only a delaying function. Recent votes have resulted in important shifts in the nature of the dominant coalition.

Civil Liberties. The media are private and free. The rule of law is thoroughly accepted in both public and private realms. Rights of assembly, organization, travel, property, and religion are protected.

Comparatively: Luxembourg is as free as Iceland, freer than France.

M A D A G A S C A R

Economy: noninclusive mixed socialist
Polity: dominant party (military dominated)
Population: 9,500,000

Political Rights: 5

Civil Liberties: 6

Status of Freedom: partly free

A transethnic heterogeneous state

Political Rights. Madagascar is essentially a military dictatorship with a very weak legislature. Legislative elections have been restricted to candidates selected by the former political parties on the left grouped in a "national front"; resulting parliaments appear to play a very small part in government. The presidential election in late 1982 allowed vigorous opposition. Although the opposition candidate was later arrested, he subsequently won a seat in the 1983 parliamentary elections. Emphasis has been put on developing the autonomy of local Malagasy governmental institutions. The restriction of local elections to approved front candidates belies this emphasis, but contests are genuine. Although tribal rivalries are very important, all groups speak the same language.

Civil Liberties. There is a private press, but papers are carefully censored and may be suspended. Broadcasting is government controlled. Movie theatres have been nationalized. There is no right of assembly; still, election processes allow periods of intense criticism and vocal, organized opposition persists. There are few long-term prisoners of conscience; short-term political detentions are common, often combined with ill-treatment. The rule of law is weak, but political prisoners may be acquitted. Labor unions are not strong and most are party-affiliated. Religion is free and most private rights are respected. Public security is very weak. Overseas travel is restricted. While still encouraging private investment, most businesses and large farms are nationalized. Corruption is widespread.

Comparatively: Madagascar is as free as Philippines, freer than Mozambique, less free than Morocco.

MALAWI

Economy: noninclusive capitalist
Polity: nationalist one-party
Population: 6,800,000

Political Rights: 6
Civil Liberties: 7
Status of Freedom: not free

A transethnic heterogeneous state

Political Rights. Malawi is a one-man dictatorship with party and parliamentary forms. Elections allow some choice among individuals. Administration is centralized, but there are both traditional and modern local governments.

Civil Liberties. The press is private or religious but under strict government control, as is the government-owned radio service. Even private criticism of the administration remains dangerous. Foreign publications are carefully screened. The country has been notable for the persecution of political opponents, including execution and torture. There are prisoners of conscience, and even slight criticism can lead to severe penalties. Asians suffer discrimination. Corruption and economic inequality are characteristic. The comparatively limited interests of the government offer considerable scope for individual rights. There is some protection by law in the modernizerd sector. Small-scale subsistence farming is dominant, with much of the labor force employed in South Africa.

Comparatively: Malawi is as free as South Yemen, freer than Somalia, less free than Zambia.

M A L A Y S I A

Economy: capitalist **Political Rights:** 3
Polity: decentralized **Civil Liberties:** 4
   dominant-party
Population: 15,000,000 **Status of Freedom:** partly free

An ethnic state with major nonterritorial subnationalities

Political Rights. Malaysia is a parliamentary democracy with a weak, indirectly elected and appointed senate and a powerful lower house. The relatively powerless head of state is a monarch, rotating among the traditional monarchs of the constituent states. A multinational front has dominated electoral and parliamentary politics. By such devices as imprisonment or the banning of demonstrations, the opposition is not given an equal opportunity to compete in elections. The states of Malaysia have their own rulers, parliaments, and institutions, but it is doubtful if any state has the power to leave the federation. Elected local governments have limited power. Subnationalities: Political, economic, linguistic, and educational policies have favored the Malays (forty-four percent) over the Chinese (thirty-six percent), Indians (ten Percent) and others. Malays dominate the army. Traditionally the Chinese had been the wealthier and better educated people. Although there are Chinese in the ruling front, they are not allowed to question the policy of communal preference.

Civil Liberties The press is private and highly varied. However, nothing that might affect communal relations negatively can be printed, and editors are constrained by the need to renew their publishing licenses annually to follow government advice on many issues. Foreign journalists are closely controlled. Radio is mostly government owned, television entirely so. Academics are restrained from discussing sensitive issues, and journals may be banned for nonviolent political expression. There have been reports of an atmosphere of fear in both academic and opposition political circles, as well as widespread discrimination against non-Malays. An attempt to establish a private university for Chinese language students has been blocked. About three hundred political suspects are detained, generally on suspicion of communist activity. Some are clearly prisoners of conscience; several have held responsible political positions. Confessions are often extracted. Nevertheless, significant criticism appears in the media and in parliament. Unions are permitted to strike and have successfully opposed restrictive legislation. Although the government has begun to assume control of strategic sectors of the economy, economic activity is generally free, except for government favoritism to the Malays.

Comparatively: Malaysia is as free as Mexico, freer than Indonesia, less free than India.

MALDIVES

Economy: noninclusive capitalist Political Rights: 5
Polity: traditional nonparty Civil Liberties: 5
Population: 160,000 Status of Freedom: partly free

A relatively homogeneous population

Political Rights. The Maldives have a parliamentary government in which a president (elected by parliament and confirmed by the people) is predominant. The elected parliament has gained some fredom of discussion. Regional leaders are presidentially appointed, but there are elected councils. Both economic and political power are concentrated in the hands of a very small, wealthy elite. Islam places a check on absolutism.

Civil Liberties. Newspapers present some diversity of views but are under pressure to conform; the radio station is owned by the government. Foreign publications are received; political discussion is limited. Several persons have been arrested for their political associations since a coup attempt. Law is traditional Islamic law. No unions have been formed. Most of the people rely on a subsistence economy; the small elite has developed commercial fishing and tourism.

Comparatively: Maldives is as free as Qatar, freer than Seychelles, less free than Mauritius.

M A L I

Economy: noninclusive mixed
      socialist
Polity: nationalist one-party
      (military dominated)
Population: 7,300,000

Political Rights: 7

Civil Liberties: 6

Status of Freedom: not free

A transethnic heterogeneous state

Political Rights. Mali is a military dictatorship with a recently constructed political party to lend support. The regime appears to function without broad popular consensus. National elections allow no choice, though there is some at the local level. Subnationalities: Although the government is ostensibly transethnic, repression of northern peoples has been reported.

Civil Liberties. The media are nearly all government owned and closely controlled. Antigovernment demonstrations are forbidden. Private conversation is relatively free. There are prisoners of conscience and reeducation centers are brutal. Student protests are controlled by conscription and detention. Religion is free; unions are controlled; travelers must submit to frequent police checks. There have been reports of slavery and forced labor. Private economic rights in the modern sector are minimal, but collectivization has recently been deemphasized for subsistence agriculturists--the majority of the people. Corruption, particularly in the state enterprises, is widespread and costly.

Comparatively: Mali is as free as Benin, freer than Somalia, less free than Liberia.

M A L T A

Economy: mixed capitalist-statist
Polity: centralized multiparty
Population: 400,000

Political Rights: 2

Civil Liberties: 4

Status of Freedom: partly free

A relatively homogeneous population

Political Rights. Malta is a parliamentary democracy in which the governing party has become increasingly antidemocratic. The most recent election resulted in a government victory in spite of an opposition majority in the popular vote. Opposition response has been to boycott parliament.

Civil Liberties: The press is free, but foreign and domestic journalists are under government pressure. Radio and television are government controlled and partial. The government has tried to prevent the opposition use of Italian stations and to forbid criticism of the system to foreigners. Although the rule of law is generally accepted, the government is suspected of fomenting gang violence against its opponents. The government has concentrated a great deal of the economy in its hands in a manner that reduces freedom by reducing pluralism. The governing party and major union have been amalgamated; one union confederation remains independent but subdued.

Comparatively: Malta is as free as Brazil, freer than Turkey, less free than Cyprus(G).

MAURITANIA

Economy: noninclusive capitalist-statist	**Political Rights:** 7
Polity: military nonparty	**Civil Liberties:** 6
Population: 1,800,000	**Status of Freedom:** not free

An ethnic state with a major territorial subnationality

Political Rights. Mauritania has been ruled by a succession of military leaders without formal popular or traditional legitimation. Subnationalities: There is a subnational movement, in the non-Arab, southern part of the country.

Civil Liberties. The media are government owned and censored, but foreign publications and broadcasts are freely available. There are few if any long-term prisoners of conscience. Conversation is free; no ideology is imposed, but no opposition organizations or assemblies are allowed. Travel may be restricted for political reasons. Internal exile has been imposed on some former officials. Union activity is government controlled. There is religious freedom within the limits of an Islamic country. The government controls much of industry and mining, as well as wholesale trade, but there have been recent moves to reduce government involvement. The large rural sector remains under tribal or family control. Only in 1980 was there a move to abolish slavery.

Comparatively: Mauritania is as free as Romania, freer than Guinea, less free than Morocco.

397

MAURITIUS

Economy: capitalist
Polity: centralized multiparty
Population: 1,000,000

Political Rights: 2
Civil Liberties: 2
Status of Freedom: free

An ethnically complex state

Political Rights. Mauritius is a parliamentary democracy. Recent elections have shifted control from one party to another. A variety of different racial and religious communities are active in politics, although they are not territorially based. There are guarantees in the electoral system to make sure no major group is unrepresented in parliament. There are elected local governing bodies.

Civil Liberties The press is private or party and without censorship. Broadcasting is government owned, but opposition views are aired. Opposition parties campaign freely and rights are guaranteed under a rule of law. The labor union movement is quite strong, as are a variety of communal organizations. Strikes are common. There is religious and economic freedom; social services are financed through relatively high taxes.

Comparatively: Mauritius is as free as St. Lucia, freer than India, less free than France.

MEXICO

Economy: capitalist-statist
Polity: decentralized dominant-party
Population: 75,700,000

Political Rights: 3
Civil Liberties: 4
Status of Freedom: partly free

An ethnic state with potential subnationalities

Political Rights. Mexico is ruled by a governmental system formally modeled on that of the United States; in practice the president is much stronger and the legislative and judicial branches much weaker. The states have independent governors and legislatures, as do local municipalities. The ruling party has had a near monopoly of power on all levels since the 1920s. Political competition has been largely confined to factional struggles within the ruling party. However, in 1979 new parties participated, and the new election law gave twenty-five percent of the seats to minor parties by proportional representation; the resulting congress showed unusual independence. Further progress in opening the system to other parties was reflected in the 1982 elections. Voting and campaign irregularities have been common, particularly on the local level. The clergy are not allowed to participate in the political process. **Subnationalities:** There is a large Mayan area in Yucatan that has formerly been restive; there are also other smaller Indian areas.

Civil Liberties. The media are mostly private. Although they have operated under a variety of direct and indirect government controls (including take-overs), they are generally free of overt censorship but operate under government "guidance." Literature and the arts are free. The judicial system is not strong. However, decisions can go against the government; it is possible to win a judicial decision that a law is unconstitutional in a particular application. Religion is free. Widespread bribery and lack of control over the behavior of security forces greatly limits freedom, especially in rural areas. Disappearances occur, detention is prolonged, torture and brutality have been common. Private economic rights are respected; government ownership predominates in major industries. Access to land continues to be a problem despite reform efforts. Nearly all labor unions are associated with the ruling party. There is a right to strike. Some union and student activity has been repressed. Critical human rights organizations exist.

Comparatively: Mexico is as free as Malaysia, freer than Nicaragua, less free than Colombia.

MONGOLIA

Economy: socialist
Polity: communist one-party
Population: 1,800,000

Political Rights: 7
Civil Liberties: 7
Status of Freedom: not free

A relatively homogeneous population

Political Rights. A one-party communist dictatorship, for many years Mongolia has been firmly under the control of one man. Power is organized at all levels through the party apparatus. Those who oppose the government cannot run for office. Parliamentary elections offer no choice and result in 99.9% victories.

Mongolia has a subordinate relationship to the Soviet Union, which it depends on for defense against Chinese claims. It must use the USSR as an outlet for nearly all of its trade, and its finances are under close Soviet supervision.

Civil Liberties. All media are government controlled. Religion is restricted; Lamaism is nearly wiped out. Freedom of travel, residence, and other civil liberties are denied. Employment is assigned; workers committees are extensions of the party.

Comparatively. Mongolia is as free as Bulgaria, less free than the USSR.

M O R O C C O

Economy: noninclusive capitalist-statist

Polity: centralized multiparty

Population: 22,900,000

Political Rights: 4

Civil Liberties: 5

Status of Freedom: partly free

An ethnic state with active and potential subnationalities

Political Rights. Morocco is a constitutional monarchy in which the king has retained major executive powers. Recent elections at both local and national levels have been well contested in most localities. Most parties participated (including the communist); independents (largely supporters of the king) have been the major winners, but opposition leaders were included in subsequent governments. The results of 1980 referendums were more questionable. The autonomy of local and regional elected governments is limited. Subnationalities: Although people in the newly acquired land of the Western Sahara participate in the electoral process, it has an important resistance movement. In the rest of the country the large Berber minority is a subnationality whose self-expression is restricted.

Civil Liberties. Newspapers are private or party, and quite diverse. Recently there has been no formal censorship; there are other pressures, including the confiscation of particular issues or the closing of publications. Monarchical power must not be criticized. Broadcasting stations are under government control, although they have recently been opened to the parties for campaign statements. In the past the use of torture has been quite common and may continue; the rule of law has also been weakened by the frequent use of prolonged detention without trial. There are many political prisoners; some are prisoners of conscience. Private organizational activity is vigorous and includes student, party, business, farmer, and human rights groups. There are strong independent labor unions in all sectors; religious and other private rights are respected. State intervention in the economy is increasing, particularly in agriculture and foreign trade.

Comparatively: Morocco is as free as Guyana, freer than Algeria, less free than Spain.

M O Z A M B I Q U E

Economy: noninclusive socialist
Polity: socialist one-party
Population: 13,100,000

Political Rights: 7
Civil Liberties: 6
Status of Freedom: not free

A transethnic heterogeneous state

Political Rights. Mozambique is a one-party communist dictatorship in which all power resides in the "vanguard party." All candidates are selected by the party at all levels, but there is some popular control of selection at local levels. Regional administration is controlled from the center. Southerners and non-Africans dominate the government.

Civil Liberties. All media are rigidly controlled; however, discussion in party congresses and in other meetings can be quite critical. Rights of asssembly and foreign travel do not exist. There are no private lawyers. Secret police are powerful; thousands are in reeducation camps, and executions occur. Police brutality is common. Unions are prohibited. Pressure has been put on several religions, especially the Catholic clergy and Jehovah's Witnesses. Villagers are being forced into communes, leading to revolts in some areas. However, the socialization of private entrepreneurs has been partially reversed. The emigration of citizens is restricted, although seasonal movement of workers across borders is unrecorded. Pressure on religion has been relaxed recently.

Comparatively: Mozambique is as free as Iraq, freer than Somalia, less free than Tanzania.

N A U R U

Economy: mixed capitalist-
statist
Polity: traditional nonparty
Population: 9,100

Political Rights: 2
Civil Liberties: 2
Status of Freedom: free

An ethnically complex state

Political Rights. Nauru is a parliamentary democracy in which governments change by elective and parliamentary means. Realignments have led to occasional political instability. The country is under Australian influence.

Civil Liberties. The media are free of censorship but little developed. The island's major industry is controlled by the government under a complex system of royalties and profit-sharing. No taxes are levied; phosphate revenues finance a wide range of social services. The major cooperative and union are independent.

Comparatively: Nauru is as free as Fiji, freer than Maldives, less free than New Zealand.

N E P A L

Economy: noninclusive capitalist
Polity: traditional nonparty
Population: 15,800,000

Political Rights: 3
Civil Liberties: 4
Status of Freedom: partly free

An ethnic state with active and potential subnationalities

Political Rights. Nepal is a constitutional monarchy in which the king is dominant. A relatively free referendum held in 1980 rejected a move toward party government, but the new constitution opened the system to direct parliamentary elections. However, candidates must belong to certain "class" organizations, the king continues to appoint many members, and has essentially unchecked power to intervene. Subnationalities: There are a variety of different peoples, with only fifty percent of the people speaking Nepali as their first language. Hinduism is a unifying force for the majority. Historically powerful Hindu castes continue to dominate.

Civil Liberties. Principal newspapers are public; private journals carry criticism of the government but not the king. Some offending publications have been suspended in the recent past. Radio is government owned. Private contacts are relatively open. Political detention is common, sometimes probably for little more than expression of opinion. Political campaigning for a variety of different alternatives has recently been relatively open. Parties are banned as the result of the referendum, but human rights organizations function. Unions exist only informally, but their activity has been increasing. The judiciary is not independent. Religious proselytizing and conversion is prohibited, and the emigration of those with valuable skills or education is restricted. The population is nearly all engaged in traditional occupations; sharecropping and tenant farming is common. Illiteracy levels are very high.

Comparatively; Nepal is as free as Thailand, freer than Bhutan, less free than Mauritius.

N E T H E R L A N D S

Economy: mixed capitalist
Polity: centralized multiparty
Population: 14,400,000

Political Rights: 1
Civil Liberties: 1
Status of Freedom: free

A relatively homogeneous population

Political Rights. Netherlands is a constitutional monarchy in which nearly all the power is vested in a directly elected legislature. The results of elections have periodically transferred power to coalitions of the left and right. There is some diffusion of political power below this level, but not a great deal. The monarch retains more power than in the United Kingdom both through the activity of appointing governments in frequently stalemated situations, and through the advisory Council of State.

Civil Liberties. The press is free and private. Radio and television are provided by private associations under state ownership. A wide range of views is broadcast. The courts are independent, and the full spectrum of private rights guaranteed. The burden of exceptionally heavy taxes limits economic choice.

Comparatively: The Netherlands is as free as Belgium, freer than Portugal.

NEW ZEALAND

Economy: capitalist
Polity: centralized multiparty
Population: 3,200,000

Political Rights: 1
Civil Liberties: 1
Status of Freedom: free

A relatively homogeneous state with a native subnationality

Political Liberties. New Zealand is a parliamentary democracy in which power alternates between the two major parties. There is elected local government, but it is not independently powerful. Subnationalities: About eight percent of the population are Maori, the original inhabitants.

Civil Liberties. The press is private and free. Television and most radio stations are government owned, but without reducing their independence significantly. The rule of law and private rights are thoroughly respected. Since taxes (a direct restriction on choice) are not exceptionally high, and industry is not government owned, we label New Zealand capitalist. Others, emphasizing the government's highly developed social programs and penchant for controlling prices, wages, and credit, might place New Zealand further toward the socialist end of the economic spectrum.

Comparatively; New Zealand is as free as the United States, freer than France.

NICARAGUA

Economy: noninclusive mixed socialist
Polity: quasi-nonparty
Population: 2,800,000

Political Rights: 6
Civil Liberties: 5
Status of Freedom: partly free

A relatively homogeneous population

Political Rights. Government is in the hands of the Sandinista political-military movement and a governing junta installed by them. Although not elected, the new government initially had widespread popular backing. A few opposition members are still on the advisory Council of State, but are no longer represented in the governing junta. Subnationalities: Several thousand Miskito Indians have been forcibly resettled from the Atlantic Coast to the interior.

404

Civil Liberties. Newspapers and radio stations are private and diverse; private television is not allowed. There is pressure on dissident or radical journalists. A radio station and a paper have been closed. However, papers and private persons still vocally oppose the new system. No organizations representing previous Somoza movements are allowed to exist. Political activity by parties outside the Sandinista movement is closely restricted. There are thousands of political prisoners: most are former national guardsmen; a few more recent detainees are clearly prisoners of conscience. Neighborhood watch committees have been established. Killing and intimidation occur, especially in rural areas. Disappearances are comonly recorded. The independence of the judiciary is not well developed, but the government does not always win in the courts. Foreign travel is restricted for some political opponents. Unions are under pressure to join a new government-sponsored federation; strikes have been banned. A private human rights organization is active, but it has been intermittently harassed and oppressed. Some enterprises and farms have been nationalized; sixty percent of the economy remains private, though subject to occasional harassment.

Comparatively: Nicaragua is as free as Chile, freer than Cuba, less free than El Salvador.

N I G E R

Economy: noninclusive capitalist
Polity: military nonparty
Population: 6,100,000

Political Rights: 7
Civil Liberties: 6
Status of Freedom: not free

A transethnic heterogeneous state

Political Rights. Niger is a military dictatorship with no elected assembly or legal parties. A civilian "development assembly" has recently been appointed. All districts are administered from the center.

Civil Liberties. Niger's very limited media are government owned and operated, and are used to mobilize the population. Dissent is seldom tolerated, although ideological conformity is not demanded. There is little overt censorship, but also no barrier to censorship. A military court has taken the place of a suspended Supreme Court; a few political prisoners are held under severe conditions. Unions and religious organizations are relatively independent but nonpolitical. Foreign travel is relatively open; outside of politics the government does not regulate individual behavior. The economy is largely subsistence farming based on communal tenure; direct taxes on the poor have been abolished.

Comparatively. Niger is as free as Mali, freer than North Korea, less free than Liberia.

NIGERIA

Economy: noninclusive capitalist- **Political Rights:** 2
statist
Polity: decentralized multiparty **Civil Liberties:** 3
Population: 85,000,000 (Unknown) **Status of Freedom:** free

A multinational state

Political Rights. Nigeria is a multiparty democracy with an elected president and elected provincial governments. The many political parties include the full spectrum of acknowledged leaders. Five successive elections in 1983 confirmed and increased the ruling party's power, but were marked by violence and many irregularities. The results of at least the presidential election probably reflected the popular choice; court reviews of outcomes modified the results in the worst cases. Subnationalities: Nigeria is made up of a number of powerful subnational groupings. Speaking mainly Hausa, the people of the north are Muslim. The highly urbanized southwest is dominated by the Yoruba; and the east by the Ibo. Within each of these areas and along their borders there are other peoples, some of which are conscious of their identity and number more than one million persons. Strong loyalties to traditional political units--lineages or kingdoms--throughout the country further complicate the regional picture. With nineteen states (and twenty-nine more planned) and independent institutions below this level, the present rulers seem dedicated to taking into account the demands of this complexity in the new federal structure.

Civil Liberties. Traditionally, Nigeria's media have been some of the freest in Africa. Television and radio are now wholly federal or state owned, as are all but two of the major papers, in part as the result of a Nigerianization program. However, in spite of occasional suppressions, the media have considerable editorial independence. Political organization, assembly, and publication are now freely permitted. The universities, secondary schools, and the trade unions have been brought under close government control or reorganization in the last few years. Apparently the judiciary remains strong and independent, including, in Muslim areas, sharia courts. No prisoners of conscience are held; citizens can win in court against the government. However, police are often brutal, and military riot control has led to many deaths. There is freedomn of religion and travel, but rights of married women are quite restricted. The country is in the process of moving from a subsistence to industrial economy--largely on the basis of government-controlled oil and oil-related industry. Government intervention elsewhere in agriculture (cooperatives and plantations) and industry has been considerable. Since private business and industry are also encouraged, this is still far from a program of massive redistribution. General corruption in political and economic life has frequently diminished the rule of law. Freedom is respected in most other areas of life.

Comparatively: Nigeria is as free as India, freer than Senegal, less free than Portugal.

N O R W A Y

Economy: mixed capitalist
Polity: centralized multiparty
Population: 4,100,000

Political Rights: 1
Civil Liberties: 1
Status of Freedom: free

A relatively homogeneous population with a small Lapp minority

Political Rights. Norway is a centralized, constitutional monarchy. Labor remains the strongest party, but other parties have formed several governments since the mid-1960s. There is relatively little separation of powers. Regional governments have appointed governors, and cities and towns their own elected officials.

Civil Liberties. Newspapers are privately or party owned; radio and television are state monopolies, but are not used for propaganda. This is a pluralistic state with independent power in the churches and labor unions. Relatively strong family structures have also been preserved. Norway is capitalistic, yet the extremely high tax burden, perhaps the highest in the noncommunist world, the government's control over the new oil resource, and general reliance on centralized economic plans reduce the freedom of economic activity.

Comparatively: Norway is as free as the United Kingdom, freer than West Germany.

OMAN

Economy: noninclusive
      capitalist-statist
Polity: centralized nonparty
Population: 1,000,000

Political Rights: 6

Civil Liberties: 6

Status of Freedom: not free

An ethnic state with a territorial subnationality

Political Rights. Oman is an absolute monarchy with no political parties or elected assemblies. There is an appointed consultative assembly. Regional rule is by centrally appointed governors, but the remaining tribal structure at the local and regional level gives a measure of local autonomy. British influence remains strong. Subnationalities: The people of Dhofar constitute a small subnationality in periodic revolt.

Civil Liberties. Broadcasting is government owned; the daily papers are government owned, weeklies are subsidized. There is little or no criticism. Foreign publications are censored regularly. Although the preservation of traditional institutions provides a check on arbitrary action, the right to a fair trial is not guaranteed in political cases. Freedom of assembly is curtailed, and there are no independent unions. With all this there are few if any prisoners of conscience. There is freedom of travel; private property is respected. Proselytizing for non-Muslim faiths is illegal. The population is largely involved in subsistence agriculture.

Comparatively: Oman is as free as Algeria, freer than Saudi Arabia, less free than the United Arab Emirates.

PAKISTAN

Economy: noninclusive
      capitalist-statist
Polity: military nonparty
Population: 95,700,000

Political Rights: 7

Civil Liberties: 5

Status of Freedom: not free

A multinational state

Political Rights. Pakistan is under centralized military dictatorship. The political parties, religious leaders, and judiciary (and bar association) continue to be factors in the situation but consensus has progressively withered. The former prime minister was executed following a political trial. Political parties have been officially disbanded and promised elections put off indefinitely; local elections of limited significance have been held. Subnationalities: Millions of Pathans, Baluch, and Sindis have a long record of struggle for greater regional autonomy or independence. Provincial organization has sporadically offered a measure of self-determination, but at least the Baluch and Sindis continue to feel oppressed.

Civil Liberties. Newspapers are censored; the frequent detention of journalists and closing of papers lead to strict self-censorship. Radio and television are government controlled. For crime punishments are often severe; torture is alleged, and executions have been common. Thousands of members of the opposition have been imprisoned or flogged in the violent political climate. The officially dissolved parties retain considerable de facto organization. Rights of assembly are limited, as well as travel for political persons. Courts preserve some independence. Union activity is restricted but strikes and demonstrations occur. Emphasis on Islamic conservatism curtails private rights, especially freedom of religion and women's rights: religious minorities suffer discrimination. Private property is respected; some basic industries have been nationalized. Over half the rural population consists of sharecroppers and tenant farmers.

Comparatively: Pakistan is as free as Algeria, freer than the USSR, less free than Bangladesh.

PANAMA

Economy: capitalist-statist	**Political Rights:** 5
Polity: quasi-dominant party	**Civil Liberties:** 4
(military dominated)	
Population: 2,100,000	**Status of Freedom:** partly free

A relatively homogeneous population with small subnationalities

Political Rights. Panama is currently governed by an indirectly elected president. Assembly members are elected from very unequal districts, and assembly powers are very limited. The assembly elects in turn a smaller council with greater powers. In 1980 popular elections were held for a minority of council seats, and some opposition candidates were elected. The National Guard retains major political power. The provinces are administered by presidential appointees, with elected councils; there is considerable local power in Indian areas.

Civil Liberties. There are oppposition papers, and critical opposition positions are widely reported in all news media. Although criticism can lead to government sanctions, such as expulsion or suspension from journalism, the situation is now quite open. Political parties maintain their opposition role, and rights to organization and assembly are generally respected. The judiciary is not independent; the rule of law is weak in both political and nonpolitical areas. There are few if any prisoners of conscience. Labor unions are under some restrictions. There is freedom of religion, although foreign priests are not allowed. In general travel is free and private property respected. Major firms are state owned; land reform has been largely ineffective in reducing inequities in land ownership.

Comparatively: Panama is as free as Uruguay, freer than Nicaragua, less free than Colombia.

P A P U A   N E W   G U I N E A

Economy: noninclusive capitalist **Political Rights:** 2
Polity: decentralized multiparty **Civil Liberties:** 2
Population: 3,100,000 **Status of Freedom:** free

A transethnic heterogeneous state with many subnationalities

Political Rights. Papua New Guinea is an independent parliamentary democracy, although it remains partially dependent on Australia economically, technically, and militarily. Elections are fair and seats are divided among a number of major and minor parties. Since party allegiances are still fluid, there is considerable party-switching after elections. Because of its dispersed and tribal nature, local government is in some ways quite decentralized. Elected provincial governments with extensive powers have been established. Subnationalities: Development of provincial governments is meant to contain strong secessionist movements in Bougainville, Papua, and elsewhere.

Civil Liberties. The press is not highly developed but apparently free. Radio is government controlled but presents critical views; Australian stations are also received. There are no political prisoners. Rights to travel, organize, demonstrate, and practice religion are legally secured. The legal system adapted from Australia is operational, but a large proportion of the population lives in a preindustrial world with traditional controls, including violence, that limit freedom of speech, travel, occupation, and other private rights.

Comparatively: Papua New Guinea is as free as St. Vincent, freer than Vanuatu, less free than Australia.

P A R A G U A Y

Economy: noninclusive capitalist-statist

Political Rights: 5

Polity: centralized dominant-party (military dominated)

Civil Liberties: 5

Population: 3,500,000

Status of Freedom: partly free

A relatively homogeneous state with small Indian groups

Political Rights. Paraguay has been ruled as a modified dictatorship since 1954. In addition to an elected president there is a parliament that includes members of opposition parties. Presidential election results determine parliamentary representation. Elections are regularly held, but they have limited meaning: the ruling party receives about ninety percent of the vote, a result guaranteed by direct and indirect pressures on the media, massive government pressure on voters, especially in the countryside, interference with opposition party organization, and perhaps electoral fraud. The most important regional and local officials are appointed by the president. Subnationalities: The population represents a mixture of Indian (Guarani) and Spanish peoples; ninety percent continue to speak Guarani as well as Spanish. Several small tribes of primitive forest people are under heavy pressure from both the government and the public.

Civil Liberties. There is a private press, and a combination of private, government, and church radio and television. In spite of censorship and periodic suppression of publications, dissenting

411

opinion is expressed, especially by the church hierarchy and opposition newspapers. Opposition political organization continues, as do human rights organizations, but there is open discrimination in favor of members of the ruling party in education, government, business, and other areas. Imprisonment, torture, and execution of political opponents, particularly peasants, have been and to a limited extent still are an important part of a sociopolitical situation that includes general corruption and anarchy. Political opponents or dissident writers may also be refused passports or exiled. There are now few if any long-term prisoners of conscience, but the rule of law is very weak. Most unions are dominated by the ruling party. Beyond the subsistence sector, private economic rights are restricted by government intervention, control, and favoritism. A large proportion of peasants work their own land, partly as a result of government land reform.

Comparatively: Paraguay is as free as Indonesia, freer than Cuba, less free than Brazil.

PERU

Economy: noninclusive capitalist-statist	**Political Rights:** 2
Polity: centralized multiparty	**Civil Liberties:** 3
Population: 19,200,000	**Status of Freedom:** free

An ethnic state with a major potential territorial subnationality

Political Rights. Peru is ruled by an elected multiparty parliamentary system. Provincial administration is not independent, but local elections are significant. Subnationalities: Several million people speak Quechua in the highlands, and it is now an official language. There are other important Indian groups.

Civil Liberties. The media are largely private. Censorship has been abolished. Essentially all positions are freely expressed, but there is still the shadow of the military and the recent past. There is little if any imprisonment for conscience, but many are killed or imprisoned in the course of antiguerrilla and antiterrorist campaigns, and torture occurs. Periodic states of emergency reduce freedoms, especially in certain areas. Travel is not restrained, and rights to religion and occupation are

412

generally respected. Labor is independent and politically active; strikes are common. The public sector remains dominant, but private property has regained governmental acceptance.

Comparatively: Peru is as free as India, freer than Brazil, less free than Ecuador.

P H I L I P P I N E S

Economy: noninclusive
capitalist-statist
Polity: dominant party
Population: 52,800,000

Political Rights: 5

Civil Liberties: 5

Status of Freedom: partly free

A transethnic heterogeneous state with active and potential subnationalities

Political Rights. The Philippines is ruled as a plebiscitory family dictatorship with the aid of a largely docile assembly. The present ruler was elected in a fair election in the early 1970s, but more recent referendums and elections affirming his rule and his constitutional changes have not been conducted with open competition, free discussion, or acceptable voting procedures. Previously legitimate political parties exist, but they have little part to play in current poltical life. Assembly elections in 1978 were held with severely restricted opposition activity and were boycotted by the major parties. The results were subject to questionable tabulations. 1981 elections provided only token opposition. There is some decentralization of power to local assemblies. Many provincial and local officials are centrally appointed. **Subnationalities:** The Philippines includes a variety of different peoples of which the Tagalog speaking are the most important (although a minority). A portion of the Muslim (Moro) subnationality is in active revolt along the front of Christian-Muslim opposition. There are several major potential subnationalities that may request autonomy in the future on the basis of both territorial and linguistic identity.

Civil Liberties. Newspapers and broadcasting are largely private but under indirect government control. Certain topics are off-limits. Only minor opposition papers are allowed to exist, but diverse foreign publications are available. Access to radio and television for the opposition is restricted, as are rights of assembly. Nevertheless, there is considerable opposition political organization, and opposition leaders regularly hold public meetings. The courts have retained some independence, although it is much reduced. Hundreds of prisoners of conscience have been held; torture is used, but it is also sporadically condemned by the top levels of government and torturers have been punished. Unions have only limited independence, but strikes occur. Military actions against insurgents have led to many unnecessary arrests, killings, and destruction. Disappearances occur, as do private, progovernment killings. The Catholic Church still maintains its independence. The private economy is marginally capitalist, but rapid growth in government intervention, favoritism, and direct ownership of industries by government and government favorites brings the economy closer to capitalist-statist.

Comparatively: The Philippines is as free as Paraguay, freer than Burma, less free than Panama.

POLAND

Economy: mixed socialist

Polity: communist one-party (military dominated)

Population: 36,600,000

Political Rights: 6

Civil Liberties: 5

Status of Freedom: partly free

A relatively homogeneous population

Political Rights. Poland is a one-party communist and military dictatorship with noncompetitive, one-list elections. However, in recent years a few nonparty persons gained election to the assembly and some sessions have evidenced more than pro forma debate. There are elected councils at provincial levels. Although party and military hierarchies operating from the top down are the loci of power, the Catholic Church, academics, peasants, and workers must be considered by any government. The Soviet Union's claim to a right of interference and continual pressure diminishes Poland's independence.

Civil Liberties. The Polish newspapers are both private and government; broadcasting is government owned. Censorship is pervasive, but there have been anti-Marxist publications with limited circulations. There are prisoners of conscience, no formal rights of assembly or organization, nor concept of an independent judiciary. Short imprisonment, beating, and harassment are common means of restricting opposition. Under the "state of war" declared by the government in December, 1981, and recently rescinded in name, thousands were imprisoned. Although most have now been released, major figures remain in jail and the military regime remains in place. Illegal attempts to leave Poland have frequently led to arrest; while others have been forced into exile. Most agriculture and considerable commerce remain in private hands; industry is fully nationalized.

Comparatively: Poland is as free as South Africa, freer than Czechoslovakia, less free than Mexico.

PORTUGAL

Economy: mixed capitalist
Polity: centralized multiparty
Population: 9,900,000

Political Rights: 1
Civil Liberties: 2
Status of Freedom: free

A relatively homogeneous population

Political Rights. Portugal is a parliamentary democracy. Although the president was a general, the separate power of the military is now minimal. There is vigorous party competition over most of the spectrum (except the far right), and fair elections. Elections are competitive and power is shared by several groups. Provincial government is centrally directed.

Civil Liberties. In spite of government or party ownership of most major papers, journalism is now quite free. Radio and television are government owned, except for one Catholic station. They are both relatively free editorially. The government has restored the rule of law. There are few if any prisoners of conscience, yet one can be imprisoned for insult to the military or government. Long periods of detention without trial occur in isolated instances. Imprisonment for "fascist" organization or discussion was promulgated in 1978. The Catholic Church, unions, peasant organizations, and military services remain alternative institutions of power. Although there is a large nationalized sector, capitalism is the accepted form for much of the economy.

Comparatively: Portugal is as free as France, freer than Jamaica, less free than United Kingdom.

QATAR

Economy: mixed capitalist-statist **Political Rights:** 5
Polity: traditional nonparty   **Civil Liberties:** 5
Population: 300,000   **Status of Freedom:** partly free

A relatively homogeneous citizenry

Political Rights. Qatar is a traditional monarchy. The majority of the residents are recently arrived foreigners; of the native population perhaps one-fourth are members of the ruling family. Open receptions are regularly held for the public to present grievances. Consensus plays an important role in the system.

Civil Liberties. The media are public or subsidized private, and loyalist. Discussion is fairly open; foreign publications are controlled. Political parties are forbidden. This is a traditional state still responsive to Islamic and tribal laws that moderate the absolutism of government. The family government controls the nation's wealth through control over oil, but there are also independently powerful merchant and religious classes. There are no income taxes and many public services are free. There are no organized unions or strikes. The rights of women and religious minorities are quite limited: only native Muslim males have the full rights of citizens.

Comparatively: Qatar is as free as the United Arab Emirates, freer than Saudi Arabia, less free than Lebanon.

ROMANIA

Economy: socialist   **Political Rights:** 7
Polity: communist one-party   **Civil Liberties:** 6
Population: 22,700,000   **Status of Freedom:** not free

An ethnic state with territorial subnationalities

Political Rights. Romania is a now-traditional communist state. Assemblies at national and regional levels are subservient to the party hierarchy. Although the party is not large, all decisions are made by a small elite and especially the dictator. Elections involve only candidates chosen by the party; for some assembly positions the party may propose several candidates.

Soviet influence is relatively slight. Subnationalities: The
Magyar and German minorities are territorially based. If offered
self-determination one Magyar area would surely opt for rejoining
neighboring Hungary; many of the Germans evidently wish to migrate
to Germany, and many have. In Romania the cultural rights of both
groups are narrowly limited.

Civil Liberties. The media include only government or party
organs; self-censorship committees replace centralized censorship.
Private discussion is guarded. Dissenters are frequently imprisoned. Forced confessions, false charges, and psychiatric incar-
ceration are characteristic. Treatment may be brutal; physical
threats are common. Many arrests have been made for attempting to
leave the country or importing foreign literature (especially
bribes and material in minority languages). Contacts with foreigners must be reported if not given prior approval. Religious
and other personal freedoms are quite restricted. Outside travel
and emigration are not considered rights; potential emigrants may
suffer economic discrmination. Private museums have been closed.
Independent labor and management rights are essentially nonexis-
tent. Attempts to form a trade union in 1979 were crushed, as was
a major coal strike in 1981. Central planning is pervasive
throughout the highly nationalized economy.

Comparatively: Romania is as free as the USSR, freer than
Bulgaria, less free than Hungary.

R W A N D A

Economy: noninclusive mixed   **Political Rights:** 6
          socialist
Polity: nationalist one-party   **Civil Liberties:** 6
          (military dominated)
Population: 5,600,000   **Status of Freedom:** not free

An ethnic state with a minor nonterritorial subnationality

Political Rights. Rwanda is a military dictatorship with an
auxiliary party organization. Elections are not free and candidates are pre-selected. A legislature was elected on single-party
principles in 1981. Districts are administered by the central
government. However, everyone belongs to the party and party
elections and deliberations have some competitive and critical
aspects. There are elected local councils and officials. Subna-

tionalities: The former ruling people, the Tutsi, have been persecuted and heavily discriminated against, but the situation has improved.

Civil Liberties. The weak press is religious or governmental; radio is government owned. Only the mildest criticism is voiced. Political prisoners are held, and beating of prisoners and suspects may be common. The courts have some independence. Considerable religious freedom exists. Travel is restricted both within the country and across its borders. Labor unions are very weak. There are no great extremes of wealth. The government is socialist in intent, but missionary cooperatives dominate trade, and private business is active in the small nonsubsistence sector. Traditional ways of life rather than government orders regulate the lives of most.

Comparatively: Rwanda is as free as Tanzania, freer than Burundi, less free than Zambia.

ST. KITTS AND NEVIS

Economy: capitalist   **Political Rights:** 2
Polity: decentralized multiparty   **Civil Liberties:** 2
Population: 42,000   **Status of Freedom:** free

A relatively homogeneous state

Political Rights. St. Kitts and Nevis has a fully functioning parliamentary system in which the smaller Nevis has a relatively large share of power and internal self-government, and has a continuing option to secede.

Civil Liberties. The media are free, and there is a constitutional rule of law.

Comparatively: St. Kitts and Nevis is as free as St. Vincent, freer than Jamaica, less free than Barbados.

ST. LUCIA

Economy: capitalist   **Political Rights:** 2
Polity: centralized multiparty   **Civil Liberties:** 2
Population: 115,000   **Status of Freedom:** free

A relatively homogeneous state

Political Rights. This is a functioning parliamentary democracy in which power alternates between parties, most recently in
1982. There are elected local governments.

Civil Liberties. The media are largely private or party
controlled, and uncensored. Organization and assembly are free,
but harassment and violence accompany their expression. There are
strong business, labor, and religious organizations. Massive
strikes in part forced the resignation of the prime minister in
early 1982. Personal rights are secured.

Comparatively: St. Lucia is as free as Israel, freer than
Jamaica, less free than Barbados.

ST. VINCENT AND THE GRENADINES

Economy: capitalist   **Political Rights:** 2
Polity: centralized multiparty   **Civil Liberties:** 2
Population: 123,000   **Status of Freedom:** free

A relatively homogeneous state

Political Rights. St. Vincent is an operating multiparty
state. In a 1979 election the ruling party was returned to
office, winning eleven of thirteen seats with fifty-three percent
of the vote.

Civil Liberties. Weekly papers present a wide variety of
uncensored opinion, although there may be some government favoritism. Radio is government owned and has been accused of bias.
Foreign media are readily available. There is a full right to
assembly and organization; effective opposition to government
policies is easily organized and often successful. There is a
rule of law. Much of economic activity is based on agriculture.

Comparatively: St. Vincent is as free as Finland, freer than
Colombia, less free than Dominican Republic.

SAO TOME AND PRINCIPE

Economy: socialist   **Political Rights:** 7
Polity: socialist one-party   **Civil Liberties:** 7
Population: 85,000   **Status of Freedom:** not free

A relatively homogeneous population

Political Rights. Sao Tome and Principe are governed under strongman leadership by the revolutionary party that led the country to independence. There is an indirectly elected assembly. Popular dissatisfaction and factional struggles occasionally appear, but no public opposition is allowed. There are local elections. Angolan troops have been used to maintain the regime.

Civil Liberties. The media are government owned and controlled; opposition voices are not heard; there is no effective right of political assembly. Labor unions are not independent. The rule of law does not extend to poltical questions; there are few known political prisoners, but many opponents are in exile. There is little evidence of brutality or torture. The largely plantation agriculture has been socialized, as has most of the economy. Illiteracy is particularly high.

Comparatively: Sao Tome and Principe appear to be as free as Angola, less free than Comoros.

SAUDI ARABIA

Economy: capitalist-statist
Polity: traditional nonparty
Population: 10,400,000

Political Rights: 6
Civil Liberties: 7
Status of Freedom: not free

A relatively homogeneous population

Political Rights. Saudi Arabia is a traditional family monarchy ruling without representative assemblies. Political parties are prohibited. The right of petition is guaranteed, and religious leaders provide a check on arbitrary government. Regional government is by appointive officers; there are some local elective assemblies.

Civil Liberties. The press is both private and governmental; strict self-censorship is expected. Radio and television are mostly government owned, although ARAMCO also has stations. Private conversation is relatively free; there is no right of political assembly or political organization. Islamic law limits arbitrary government, but the rule of law is not fully institutionalized. There are political prisoners, and torture is reported; there may be prisoners of conscience. Citizens have no freedom of religion--all must be Muslims, and must observe Muslim rites. Strikes and unions are forbidden. Private rights in areas such as occupation or residence are generally respected, but marriage to a non-Muslim or non-Saudi is closely controlled. Women may not marry non-Muslims, and suffer other special disabilities, particularly in the right to travel. The economy is overwhelmingly dominated by petroleum or petroleum-related industry that is directly or indirectly under government control. The commercial and agricultural sectors are private.

Comparatively: Saudi Arabia is as free as Mauritania, freer than Ethiopia, less free than Bahrain.

SENEGAL

Economy: mixed capitalist
Polity: centralized
     dominant-party
Population: 6,100,000

Political Rights: 4
Civil Liberties: 4

Status of Freedom: partly free

A transethnic heterogeneous state

Political Rights. Although elections are fairly open and may represent opinions, one party continues to dominate elections and not without help from the government. Opposition parties are not allowed to form coalitions. Contested elections occur on the local level. Subnationalities: Ethnically eighty percent are Muslims; the Wolof people represent thirty-six percent of the population, including most of the elite, the urban population, and the more propserous farmers. However, regional loyalties, both within and outside of this linguistic grouping, seem to be at least as important as communal groupings in defining potential subnationalities. Rapid assimilation of rural migrants in the cities to Wolof culture has reduced the tendency toward ethnic cleavage, but a separatist movement in the far south has shown increasing activity.

Civil Liberties. The press is predominantly public; the independence of private publications is somewhat constrained, although opposition papers and journals appear. Radio and television are under an autonomous government body, but not fully impartial. There are at least some separatist prisoners of conscience. Unions have gained increasing independence. Religion, travel, occupation, and other private rights are respected. The government sometimes loses in the courts. Although much of the land

421

remains tribally owned, government-organized cooperatives, a
strong internal private market, and dependence on external markets
have transformed the preindustrial society. Many inefficient and
corrupt state and quasi-public enterprises are now being dis-
mantled.

Comparatively: Senegal is as free as Kuwait, freer than Ivory
Coast, less free than Gambia.

SEYCHELLES

Economy: mixed capitalist
Polity: socialist one-party
Population: 65,000

Political Rights: 6
Civil Liberties: 6
Status of Freedom: not free

A relatively homogeneous population

Political Rights. Seychelles is a one-party state allowing
little if any political competition for parliament but not president. The former ruling party is said to have "simply disappeared." Tanzanian troops continue to help maintain the
government in power. There is no local government.

Civil Liberties. There is no independent opinion press; radio
is government owned. No opposition in publication or even conversation is legal. Individuals have little judicial protection.
There is no right of political assembly, and the security services
have broad powers of arrest. Opposition party activities are
banned; people have frequently been arrested on political charges.
Critics are often urged to leave, exiled, or refused permission to
leave. Labor and government are interconnected. Private rights,
including private property, are generally respected. Religious
institutions maintain some independence and a monthly publication.
Quasi-government enterprises are being established; state monopolies control the marketing of all export crops. Government
services in this largely impoverished country are extensive.

Comparatively: Seychelles is as free as Tanzania, freer than
Somalia, less free than Maldives.

S I E R R A   L E O N E

Economy: noninclusive capitalist
Polity: socialist one-party
Population: 3,800,000

Political Rights: 5
Civil Liberties: 5
Status of Freedom: partly free

A formally transethnic heterogeneous state

Political Rights. Sierra Leone's one-party system has coopted
many members of the previous opposition. The 1982 competitive
one-party election was marked by widespread violence. There are
some elected and traditional local governments.

Civil Liberties. The press is private and governmental. Radio
is government controlled. There is occasional independence in the
press, but it is under heavy pressure; still there is considerable
freedom of private speech. The courts do not appear to be very
powerful or independent. Special emergency powers have sporadically given the government untrammeled powers of detention, censorship, restriction of assembly, and search. There may now be no
prisoners of conscience. Identity cards have recently been
required of all citizens. Labor unions are relatively independent, and travel is freely permitted. The largely subsistence
economy has an essentially capitalist modern sector. Corruption
is pervasive and costly.

Comparatively: Sierra Leone is as free as Sudan, freer than
Gabon, less free than Zimbabwe.

S I N G A P O R E

Economy: mixed capitalist
Polity: centralized
dominant-party
Population: 2,500,000

Political Rights: 4
Civil Liberties: 5

Status of Freedom: partly free

An ethnically complex state

Political Rights. Singapore is a parliamentary democracy in
which the ruling party traditionally won all legislative seats.
Economic and other pressures against all opposition groups
(exerted in part through control of the media) make elections very
unfair. Opposition leaders have been sentenced and bankrupted for

such crimes as defaming the prime minister during the campaign. The opposition still obtains thirty percent of the vote. In 1981 an opponent's victory in a by-election was regarded with great alarm, and court cases were soon launched against him. There is no local government.

Civil Liberties. The press is nominally free, but owners of shares with policy-making power must be officially approved--in some cases the government owns the shares. Broadcasting is largely a government monopoly. By closing papers and imprisoning editors and reporters, the press is kept under close control. University faculties are also under considerable pressure to conform. Most opposition is treated as a communist threat and, therefore, treasonable. Prisoners of conscience are held; in internal security cases the protection of the law is weak--prosecution's main task appears to be obtaining forced confessions of communist activity. Torture is alleged. Trade union freedom is inhibited by the close association of government and union. Private rights of religion, occupation, or property are generally observed, although a large and increasing percentage of manufacturing and service companies are government owned. Many youths have reportedly been forcibly drafted into construction brigades.

Comparatively: Singapore is as free as El Salvador, freer than Indonesia, less free than Malaysia.

SOLOMON ISLANDS

Economy: noninclusive capitalist   **Political Rights:** 2
Polity: decentralized multiparty   **Civil Liberties:** 2
Population: 300,000   **Status of Freedom:** free

A relatively homogeneous state with subnational strains

Political Rights. The Solomon Islands are a parliamentary democracy under the British monarch. Elections are intensely contested; party discipline is weak. There is some decentralization of power at the local level; further decentralization to the provincial level is planned.

Civil Liberties. Radio is government controlled; the very limited press is both government and private. There is no censorship. The rule of law is maintained in the British manner alongside traditional ideas of justice. Published incitement to inter-island conflict has led to banishment for several persons.

Union activity is free. The government is involved in major businesses. Most land is held communally but farmed individually.

Comparatively: The Solomon Islands are as free as Fiji freer than Vanuatu, less free than New Zealand.

SOMALIA

Economy: noninclusive mixed socialist

Polity: socialist one-party (military dominated)

Population: 5,300,000

Political Rights: 7

Civil Liberties: 7

Status of Freedom: not free

A relatively homogeneous state

Political Rights. The Somali Republic is under one-man military rule combining glorification of the ruler with one-party socialist legitimization. 1979 elections with ninety-nine percent approval allowed no choice, but even the assembly elected on this basis was suspended in 1980. Ethnically the state is homogeneous, although until the military coup in 1969 the six main clan groupings and their subdivisions were the major means of organizing loyalty and power. While politics is still understood in lineage terms, in its centralizing drive the government has tried to eliminate both tribal and religious power.

Civil Liberties. The media are under strict government control, private conversation is controlled, and those who do not follow the government are considered to be against it. There are many political prisoners, including prisoners of conscience. There have been jailings for strikes and executions of rebels. Travel is restricted. Some state farms and industries have been established beyond the dominant subsistence economy. A large black market circumvents official distribution channels; corruption is widespread in government and business.

Comparatively: Somalia is as free as Ethiopia, less free than Kenya.

S O U T H   A F R I C A

Economy: capitalist-statist
Polity: centralized multiparty
Population: 27,800,000

Political Rights: 5
Civil Liberties: 6
Status of Freedom: partly free

An ethnic state with major territorial and nonterritorial subnationalities

Political Rights. South Africa is a parliamentary democracy in which over eighty percent of the people have been excluded from participation in the national political process because of race. Recent constitutional changes add over ten percent more to the politically accepted population although the great majority black population remains excluded. For the white population elections appear fair and open. There is a limited scope for nonwhites to influence affairs within their own communities. Subnationalities: Most of the black majority is ascribed to a variety of "homelands" that they may or may not live in, although increasingly they have been forced to move to these limited areas. Several of these have become independent states in the eyes of South Africa but they have not received such recognition elsewhere. Except for Transkei we see these as dependent territories. Because of their close integration into South Africa politicaly and economically we treat these states as part of South Africa for most purposes. The dependent governments of these states are generally unpopular and tyrannical, although this seems not to be the case in Bophuthatswana. We feel that geographically and historically Transkei does have a reasonable claim to statehood, in spite of the reasons that may have brought it into being. It is in many ways comparable to Lesotho, Swaziland, or further afield states such as Bhutan or Mongolia. In the several homelands that have not yet separated from the country officially, black leaders have some power and support from their people. Most black political parties are banned, but operating political parties among Indians and people of mixed blood represent the interests of their peoples. Regionally, government within the white community includes both central government officials and elected councils.

Civil Liberties. The white South African press is private and quite outspoken, although pressures have been increasing, especially on reporters. Freedom for the nonwhite press is closely restricted. Broadcasting is under government control. The courts are independent on many issues, including apartheid, but have not

426

effectively controlled the security forces. There are political prisoners and torture--especially for black activists, who live in an atmosphere of terror. Nevertheless, black organizations regularly denounce the government's racial and economic policies, hold conferences, and issue statements. Private rights are generally respected for whites. Rights to labor organization have improved for blacks recently. Legal separation of the races remains, but has been relaxed in a number of ways. Rights to choice of residence and occupation are legally circumscribed for nonwhites. Hundreds of thousands are arrested or forcibly moved every year as a result of discriminatory laws and the government homelands policy. This includes large-scale deportations from one rural area to another. Human rights organizations are quite active in both white and black communities. Church organizations have become centers of opposition to apartheid.

Comparatively: South Africa is as free as Yugolsavia, freer than Tanzania, less free than Morocco.

S P A I N

Economy: capitalist
Polity: centralized multiparty
Population: 38,400,000

Political Rights: 1
Civil Liberties: 2
Status of Freedom: free

An ethnic state with major territorial subnationalities

Political Rights. Spain is a constitutional monarchy. 1982 elections were fair, resulting in a dramatic shift of control to the moderate left. For the time being military influence has been largely eliminated. Elected regional and local governments are of increasing importance. Subnationalities: The Basque and Catalan territorial subnationalities have had their rights greatly expanded in the last few years. The process has now been extended to Galicia and Andalusia and is being extended to other parts of the country.

Civil Liberties. The press is private and is now largely free. The television network and some radio stations are government owned. Television is controlled by an all-party committee. There are few prisoners of conscience; imprisonment still threatens those who insult the security services, the courts, the state, or the flag. Short detention periods are often used with little legal redress. Police brutality and torture are still alleged,

but offenders are punished. Criticism of the government and of
suspected human rights violators are quite freely expressed both
publicly and privately. Private freedoms are respected. Continued terrorism and reactions to terrorism affect some areas.
Union organization is free and independent.

Comparatively: Spain is as free as France, freer than Mexico,
less free than Norway.

S R I   L A N K A

Economy: mixed capitalist-statist **Political Rights:** 3
Polity: centralized multiparty   **Civil Liberties:** 4
Population: 15,600,000   **Status of Freedom:** partly free

An ethnic state with a major subnationality

Political Rights. Sri Lanka is a parliamentary democracy in
which opposition groups have been under increasing pressure. A
number of individuals have been barred from government for breach
of trust, and the main opposition party is close to being ruled
illegal. In late 1982 the government used its then current popularity to guarantee a six-year extension of its rule. The
referendum on this issue was held under a state of emergency
restricting opposition campaigning. Regional government is centrally controlled, but local government is by elected councils.
Subnationalities: Receiving a large vote in the most recent
election, the Tamil minority movement constitutes a serious secessionist tendency. There has been increasing private violence
against the Tamils, and the government has been increasingly
unable to protect them or even remain neutral.

Civil Liberties. The press has been strong, both private and
governmental. However, all journalists seem to be under increasing
governmental pressure. Broadcasting is under government control
and presents a relatively narrow range of views. Limited censorship has been applied to prevent violence at particular places and
times. The rule of law has been threatened by this communal
violence, as well as by the use and misuse of states of emergency
to detain political opponents. Courts remain independent of the
government; an important human rights movement supports their
independence. A few prisoners of conscience have been arrested,
at least for advocating Tamil independence; and torture and brutality is alleged. There is freedom of assembly but not demonstra-

tion. Private rights to movement, residence, religion, and occupation are respected. Strikes in public services are restricted, but unions are well-developed and politically influential. There has been extensive land reform; the state has nationalized a number of enterprises in this largely plantation economy. The system has done an excellent job in providing for basic nutrition, health, and educational needs within a democratic framework.

Comparatively: Sri Lanka is as free as Mexico, freer than Indonesia, less free than India.

S U D A N

Economy:	noninclusive mixed socialist	**Political Rights:**	5
Polity:	nationalist one-party (military dominated)	**Civil Liberties:**	5
Population:	20,600,000	**Status of Freedom:**	partly free

An ethnic state with major but highly diverse subnationalities

Political Rights. Sudan is a military dictatorship with a supportive single party and legislature. There has been a general reconciliation of the government and its noncommunist opposition. Anyone can join the governing party. Legislative elections allow the participation and frequent victory of individuals from de facto opposition groups. Several cabinet and party central committee members are also from these groups. There is considerable power "in the streets" and there has been a continuing devolution of power to the regions and provinces. Subnationalities: Southern separatism was conciliated by a separate assembly; a further subdivision into three regions satisfies the smaller tribes but has reignited the opposition of some, and guerrilla attacks and mutinies have accompanied the transition. The national government remains overwhelmingly northern, and southern politicians can be quickly jailed for verbal opposition to new arrangements. There are also major ethnic groups in the north for which regional arrangements are being developed.

Civil Liberties. The press is weak and nationalized. Radio and television are government controlled. The media have been used for active indoctrination, but criticism is also common in the parliament and press, and especially in private. The university campus maintains a tradition of independence, but the courts do not. There are many prisoners of conscience, reports of torture, and detention without trial. Religion is relatively free. Major political-religious groups maintain their organizations independent of government. Unions are relatively independent and strikes occur. Some force has been used to reduce urban migration. Sudan is socialist theoretically, but in business and agriculture the private sector has recently been supported by denationalizations. Bureaucratic corruption is costly.

Comparatively: Sudan is as free as Egypt, freer than Ethiopia, less free than Senegal.

SURINAME

Economy: noninclusive mixed socialist

Polity: military nonparty

Population: 350,000

Political Rights: 7

Civil Liberties: 6

Status of Freedom: not free

An ethnically complex state

Political Rights. Suriname is ruled by a military council without legitimization by elections or other means. Power shifts among factions of noncommissioned officers seem to have been replaced by the emergence of one dominant leader.

Civil Liberties. The press is under strong pressure. Political organization or assembly is forbidden. The leaders of all major opposition groups (of former political parties, unions, journalists, and academia) were executed without trial in late 1982. Prisoners of conscience have been detained and treated brutally. Courts and unions retain some independence. Houses are searched at will. The state is increasing its control over industry, but business groups continue to publicly express opposition to economic policy.

Comparatively: Suriname is as free as Haiti, freer than Albania, less free than Guyana.

SWAZILAND

Economy: noninclusive capitalist

Polity: traditional nonparty

Population: 600,000

Political Rights: 5

Civil Liberties: 5

Status of Freedom: partly free

A relatively homogeneous population

Political Rights. Swaziland is ruled by a king (or regent) with the aid of a council of tribal elders. Indirect elections for a part of an advisory legislature are held, but only one party is allowed. Local councils invite popular participation. South African political and economic influence is pervasive.

Civil Liberties. Private media exist alongside the dominant government media; little criticism is allowed; South African and other foreign media provide an alternative. Opposition leaders have been repeatedly detained, and partisan activity is forbidden. Criticism is common in parliament and other councils, but public assemblies are restricted, unions limited, emigration difficult. Religious, economic, and other private rights are maintained. The traditional way of life is continued, especially on the local level. Several thousand whites in the country and in neighboring Transvaal own the most productive land and business.

Comparatively: Swaziland is as free as Lesotho, freer than South Africa, less free than Botswana.

S W E D E N

Economy: mixed capitalist
Polity: centralized multiparty
Population: 8,300,000

Political Rights: 1
Civil Liberties: 1
Status of Freedom: free

A relatively homogeneous population

Political Rights. Sweden is a parliamentary democracy in which no party monopolizes power. Referendums are held. Although there are some representative institutions at regional and local levels, the system is relatively centralized. The tendency of modern bureaucracies to regard issues as technical rather than political has progressed further in Sweden than elsewhere.

Civil Liberties. The press is private or party; broadcasting is by state-licensed monopolies. Although free of censorship, the media are accused of presenting a rather narrow range of views. There is the rule of law. The defense of those accused by the government may not be as spirited as elsewhere, but, on the other hand, the ombudsman office gives special means of redress against administrative arbitrariness. Most private rights are respected.

431

State interference in family life is unusually strong, with many children unjustly taken from their parents. The national church has a special position. In many areas, such as housing, individual choice is restricted more than in other capitalist states--as it is of course by the very high tax load. Unions are a powerful part of the system. The state intervenes in the economy mainly through extensive business regulation rather than direct ownership.

Comparatively: Sweden is as free as Denmark, freer than West Germany.

SWITZERLAND

Economy: capitalist **Political Rights:** 1
Polity: decentralized multiparty **Civil Liberties:** 1
Population: 6,500,000 **Status of Freedom:** free

A trinational state

Political Rights. Switzerland is a parliamentary democracy in which all major parties are given a role in government determined by the size of the vote of each party. Parties that increase their vote above a certain level are invited to join the government, although such changes in party strength rarely occur. The lack of a decisive shift in power from one party to another in the last fifty years is a major limitation on the democratic effectiveness of the Swiss system. However, its dependence on the grand coalition style of government is a partial substitute, and the Swiss grant political rights in other ways that compensate for the lack of a transfer of power. Many issues are decided by the citizenry through national referendums or popular initiatives. After referendums, in keeping with the Swiss attitude even the losing side is given part of what it wants if its vote is sufficiently large. Subnationalities: The three major linguistic groups have separate areas under their partial control. Their regional and local elected governments have autonomous rights and determine directly much of the country's business. National governments try to balance the representatives of the primary religious and linguistic groups; this is accomplished in another way by the upper house that directly represents the cantons (regions) on an equal basis.

Civil Liberties. The high quality press is private and independent. Broadcasting is government operated, although with considerable independence of comparable West European systems. Unions are free but there are few strikes. The rule of law is strongly upheld; as in Germany it is against the law to question the intentions of judges. Private rights are thoroughly respected.

Comparatively: Switzerland is as free as the United States, freer than Italy.

S Y R I A

Economy: mixed socialist
Polity: centralized dominant-party (military dominated)
Population: 9,700,000

Political Rights: 6
Civil Liberties: 7
Status of Freedom: not free

A relatively homogeneous population

Political Rights. Syria is a military dictatorship assisted by an elected parliament. The election of the military president is largely pro forma; in assembly elections a variety of parties compete within the National Front, organized under the leadership of the governing party. The independence of these groups has progressively eroded. Because of its position in the army the Alawite minority (ten percent) has a very unequal share of national power. Provinces have little separate power, but local elections are contested.

Civil Liberties. The media are in the hands of government or party. Broadcasting services are government owned. The media are used as governmental means for active indoctrination. Nongovernmental political, employee, religious, and professional organizations continue to exist, although under great pressure. Thousands have been arrested and many executed. Other thousands have been killed in punitive expeditions. The courts are neither strongly independent nor effective in political cases where long-term detention without trial occurs. Political prisoners are often arrested following violence, but there are also prisoners of conscience. Political opponents may even be killed overseas. Torture has frequently been employed in interrogation. Religious freedom is restricted. Rights to choice of occupation or residence are generally respected; foreign travel and emigration are closely controlled for certain groups. Much of industry has been nationalized; the commercial sector remains private. Land reform has successfully expanded private ownership. There is no independent labor movement.

Comparatively: Syria is as free as Iraq, freer than Somalia, less free than Kuwait.

TANZANIA

Economy: noninclusive socialist
Polity: socialist one-party
Population: 20,500,000

Political Rights: 6
Civil Liberties: 6
Status of Freedom: not free

A transethnic heterogeneous nation in union with Zanzibar

Political Rights. Tanzania is a union of the paternalistic socialist mainland with the radical socialist Zanzibar. Although the governments are still not unified except in name, the single parties of each state have joined to form one all-Tanzanian party. Elections offer choice between individuals, but no issues are to be discussed in campaigns; all decisions come down from above, including the choice of candidates. The resulting parliament is not, however, simply a rubber stamp. Local government is an extension of party government. Subnationalities: Ethnically, the country is divided into a large number of peoples (none larger than thirteen percent); most are not yet at the subnational level. The use of English and Swahili as national languages enhances national unity. Since the two subnations (Zanzibar and Tanganyika) are in a voluntary union, there is no question of dominance of one over the other.

Civil Liberties. Civil liberties are subordinated to the goals of the socialist leadership. No contradiction of official policy is allowed to appear in the media, nearly all of which is government owned, or in educational institutions; private and limited criticism of implementation appears. The people learn only of those events the government wishes them to know. There is no right of assembly or organization. Millions of people have been forced into communal villages; people from the cities have been abruptly transported to the countryside; forced labor on the farms is still a problem. Thousands have been detained for political crimes. There are prisoners of conscience. Lack of respect for the independence of the judiciary and individual rights is especially apparent in Zanzibar. Union activity is government controlled. Neither labor nor capital have legally recognized rights--strikes are illegal. Most business and trade and much of agriculture are nationalized. Religion is free, at least on the mainland; overseas travel is restricted.

Comparatively: Tanzania is as free as Algeria, freer than Malawi, less free than Zambia.

THAILAND

Economy: noninclusive capitalist   **Political Rights:** 3
Polity: centralized multiparty   **Civil Liberties:** 4
        (military dominated)
Population: 50,800,000   **Status of Freedom:** partly free

An ethnic state with a major territorial subnationality

Political Rights. Thailand has a military-influenced, constitutional monarch. Both parties and parliament seem to be becoming more significant, but the record of repeated military interventions in recent years limits the freedom of civilian politicians. 1983 parliamentary elections were quite free but again held under the shadow of military threats. Provincial government is under national control; there are elected and traditional institutions at the local level. Subnationalities: There is a Muslim Malay community in the far south, and other small ethnic enclaves in the north.

Civil Liberties. The press is private, but periodic suppressions and warnings lead to self-censorship. Most broadcasting is government or military controlled. Some books are banned as subversive. There are few long-term prisoners of conscience, but many are periodically detained for communist activity. In rural areas arrest may be on vague charges and treatment brutal. Human rights organizations are active. Labor activity is relatively free; a ban on strikes was lifted in early 1981. Private rights to property, choice of religion, or residence are secure; foreign travel or emigration is not restricted. However, corruption limits the expression of all rights. Government enterprise is quite important in the basicallly capitalist modern economy.

Comparatively: Thailand is as free as Malaysia, freer than the Philippines, less free than India.

435

TOGO

Economy: noninclusive mixed
Polity: nationalist one-party
    (military dominated)
Population: 2,800,000

Political Rights: 7
Civil Liberties: 6

Status of Freedom: not free

A transethnic heterogeneous state

Politcal Rights. Togo is a military dictatorship ruled in the name of a one-party state. In this spirit there is a deliberate denial of the rights of separate branches of government, including a separate judiciary, or even of private groups. National elections allow little or no choice. But essentially everyone can join the party and there is some discussion in parliament and party organs. Below the national level only the cities have a semblance of self-government. **Subnationalities:** The southern Ewe are culturally dominant and the largest group (twenty percent), but militant northerners now rule.

Civil Liberties. No criticism of the government is allowed in the government or church media, and foreign publications may be confiscated. There is little guarantee of a rule of law; people have been imprisoned and beaten for offenses such as the distribution of leaflets or failure to wear a party badge. There are long-term prisoners of conscience. Jehovah's Witnesses are banned. There is occasional restriction of foreign travel. Union organization is closely regulated. In this largely subsistence economy the government is heavily involved in trade, production, and the provision of services. All wage earners must contribute to the ruling party.

Comparatively: Togo is as free as Haiti, freer than Ethiopia, less free than Cameroon.

TONGA

Economy: noninclusive capitalist
Polity: traditional nonparty
Population: 100,000

Political Rights: 5
Civil Liberties: 3

Status of Freedom: partly free

A relatively homogeneous population

Political Rights. Tonga is a constitutional monarchy in which the king and nobles retain power. Only a minority of the members of the legislative assembly are elected directly by the people; but the veto power of the assembly can be effectively expressed. Regional administration is centralized; there are some elected local officials.

Civil Liberties. The main paper is a government weekly; radio is under government control. Other foreign and local media are available. There is a rule of law, but the king's decision is still a very important part of the system. Private rights within the traditional Tonga context seem guaranteed.

Comparatively: Tonga is as free as Kuwait, freer than Seychelles, less free than Western Samoa.

T R A N S K E I

Economy: noninclusive capitalist
Polity: centralized
        dominant-party
Population: 2,400,000

Political Rights: 5
Civil Liberties: 6

Status of Freedom: partly free

A relatively homogeneous population

Political Rights. In form Transkei is a multiparty parliamentary democracy; in fact it is under the strong-man rule of a paramount chief supported by his party's majority. The meaning of recent elections has been largely nullified by governmental interference, including the jailing of opposition leaders. Chiefs and the balancing of tribal interests remain very important in the system, but beyond that there is little decentralization of power. South Africa has a great deal of de facto power over the state, particularly because of the large number of nationals that work in South Africa. However, Transkei is at least as independent as several Soviet satellites; it has had continuing public disputes with South Africa.

Civil Liberties. The press is private, but under strong government pressure. Broadcasting is government controlled. Many members of the opposition have been imprisoned; new retroactive laws render it illegal to criticize Transkei or its rulers. Freedom of organization is very limited, although an opposition party still exists. Private rights are respected within the limits of South African and Transkei custom. Capitalist and traditional economic rights are diminished by the necessity of a large portion of the labor force to work in South Africa.

Comparatively: Transkei is as free as Zambia, freer than Mozambique, less free than Swaziland.

TRINIDAD AND TOBAGO

Economy: capitalist-statist   **Political Rights:** 1
Polity: decentralized multiparty   **Civil Liberties:** 2
Population: 1,200,000   **Status of Freedom:** free

An ethnically complex state

Political Rights. Trinidad and Tobago is a parliamentary democracy in which one party has managed to retain power since 1956 (in part due to the division of the electorate among ethnic groups). However, there has been a decentralization of power and elections have been vigorously contested by a variety of parties. There is elected local government. Tobago has an elected regional government.

Civil Liberties. The private or party press is generally free of restriction; broadcasting is under both government and private control. Opposition is regularly voiced, although the government-owned television is said to favor the government. There is a full spectrum of private rights. Violence and communal feeling reduce the effectiveness of such rights for many, as does police violence. Many sectors of the economy are government owned. Human rights organizations are active. Labor is powerful and strikes frequent.

Comparatively: Trinidad and Tobago is as free as Venezuela, freer than Guyana, less free than Barbados.

TUNISIA

Economy: mixed capitalist   **Political Rights:** 5
Polity: dominant party   **Civil Liberties:** 5
Population: 6,800,000   **Status of Freedom:** partly free

A relatively homogeneous population

Political Rights. Tunisia has a dominant party system but is essentially under one-man rule. Elections to the assembly are contested primarily within the one-party framework, but opposition parties played a minor role in 1981 elections. Regional government is centrally directed; there is elected local government.

Civil Liberties. The private, party, and government press is under government pressure. Although frequently banned or fined, opposition papers are published. Broadcasting is government controlled. Private conversation is relatively free, but there is no right of assembly. Organizational activity is generally free, including that of the Tunisian Human Rights League. The courts demonstrate only a limited independence, but it is possible to win against the government. Unions have been relatively independent despite periods of repression. There are few if any long-term prisoners of conscience, but arrests for unauthorized political activity or expression occur. The unemployed young are drafted for government work. Overseas travel is occasionally blocked. Most private rights seem to be respected, including economic freedoms since doctrinaire socialism was abandoned and much of agriculture returned to private hands.

Comparatively: Tunisia is as free as Egypt, freer than Algeria, less free than Senegal.

T U R K E Y

Economy: capitalist-statist	**Political Rights:** 4
Polity: military nonparty	**Civil Liberties:** 5
Population: 49,155,000	**Status of Freedom:** partly free

An ethnic state with a major territorial subnationality

Political Rights. In 1980 Turkey came under military rule. The change was widely welcomed because of the severe internal security and financial situations and political crisis. The current president was confirmed in power on a questionable adjunct to a constitutional referendum in late 1982. Opposition campaigning was restricted and the vote not entirely secret. Controls on party formation and candidature were so severe as to greatly reduce the significance of the legislative election in November 1983. Subnationalities: Several million Kurds are denied self-determination; it is even illegal to teach or publish in Kurdish.

Civil Liberties. The press is private; the government controls the broadcasting system directly or indirectly. Suspensions and arrests by the new government have produced general self-censorship in all media. There remain many prisoners of conscience under martial law. Torture has been common, but the military government has made arrests of some accused torturers. Private rights are generally respected in other areas such as religion. Independent union activity has been curtailed; strikes are prohibited. Nearly fifty percent of the people are subsistence agriculturists. State enterprises make up more than half of Turkey's industry.

Comparatively: Turkey is as free as Singapore, freer than Yugoslavia, less free than Spain.

T U V A L U

Economy: noninclusive capitalist **Political Rights:** 1
Polity: traditional nonparty **Civil Liberties:** 2
Population: 9,000 **Status of Freedom:** free

A relatively homogeneous state

Political Rights. Tuvalu is a parliamentary democracy under the British monarch. Each island is represented; seats are contested individually. Opposition blocs have been formed in the assembly and have been able to achieve power. There are local councils for each island. Continued dependence on the United Kingdom is self-chosen.

Civil Liberties. Media are government owned but little developed. The rule of law is maintained in the British manner, alongside traditional ideals of justice. The economy is largely subsistence farming; much of the labor force is employed overseas.

Comparatively: Tuvalu is as free as Belize, freer than Mauritius, less free than New Zealand.

UGANDA

Economy: noninclusive capitalist-statist

Political Rights: 4

Polity: multiparty (military dominated)

Civil Liberties: 5

Population: 13,800,000

Status of Freedom: partly free

A transethnic heterogeneous state with major subnationalities

Political Rights. Uganda is ruled by an elected government with, at least until recently, the aid of the Tanzanian army. The 1980 election was not entirely free or fair, but parties opposed to the ruling group received a substantial number of seats. Since then many opposition leaders have been forced into violent opposition, imprisoned, or co-opted into the ruling party. Subnationalities: The population is divided among a wide variety of peoples, some of which are subnationalities based on kingdoms that preceded the present state. The most important of these was Buganda. Its Ganda people suffer from recurrent repression.

Civil Liberties. The largest circulation newspaper and radio and television are government owned. Political violence and an incomplete rule of law inhibit all expression. Critical newspapers have suffered recurrent pressure, but opposition leaders speak out. Assembly and travel are restricted within the country. Unions are weak and government influenced. Arbitrary arrests are frequent; opposition politicians are killed by the government or murdered by unknown assailants. Massacres accompany anti-guerrilla campaigns. Torture is widely reported. The courts have some independence. Religious freedom has been reestablished, and the churches play a balancing role to a limited extent. The economy has suffered severe dislocation: property is not secure, corruption is pervasive and costly, a black market flourishes.

Comparatively: Uganda is as free as Turkey, freer than Tanzania, less free than Brazil.

UNION OF

SOVIET SOCIALIST REPUBLICS

Economy: socialist
Polity: communist one-party
Population: 272,308,000

Political Rights: 6
Civil Liberties: 7
Status of Freedom: not free

A complex ethnic state with major territorial subnationalities

Political Rights. The Soviet Union is ruled by parallel party and governmental systems: the party system is dominant. Elections are held for both systems, but in neither is it possible for the rank and file to determine policy. Candidacy and voting are closely controlled, and the resulting asemblies do not seriously question the policies developed by party leaders (varying by time or issue from one individual to twenty-five). The Soviet Union is in theory elaborately divided into subnational units, but in fact the all-embracing party structure renders local power minimal.

Subnationalities. Russians account for half the Soviet population. The rest belong to a variety of subnational groupings ranging down in size from the forty million Ukrainians. Most groups are territorial, with a developed sense of subnational identity. The political rights of all of these to self-determination, either within the USSR or through secession, is effectively denied. In many cases Russians or other non-native peoples have been settled in subnational territory in such numbers as to make the native people a minority in their own land (for example, Kazakhstan). Expression of opinion in favor of increased self-determination is repressed at least as much as anticommunist opinion. Most of these peoples have had independence movements or movements for enhanced self-determination in the years since the founding of the USSR. Several movements have been quite strong since World War II (for example, in the Ukraine or Lithuania); the blockage of communication by the Soviet government makes it very difficult to estimate either the overt or latent support such movements might have. In 1978 popular movements in Georgia and Armenia led to the retention of the official status of local languages in the Republics of the Caucasus.

Civil Liberties. The media are totally owned by the government or party and are, in addition, regularly censored. Elite publications occasionally present variations from the official line, but significant deviations are found only in underground publications.

Recent cases of arrests and exile have forced nearly all criticism underground. Crimes against the state, including insanity (demonstrated by perverse willingness to oppose the state), are broadly defined; as a result political prisoners are present in large numbers both in jails and insane asylums. Nearly all imprisonment and mistreatment of prisoners in the Soviet Union are now carried out in accordance with Soviet security laws--even though these laws conflict with other Soviet laws written to accord with international standards. Since the Bolshevik Revolution there has never been an acquittal in a political trial. Insofar as private rights, such as those to religion, education, or choice of occupation, exist, they are de facto rights that may be denied at any time. Travel within and outside of the USSR is highly controlled; many areas of the country are still off-limits to foreigners-- especially those used as areal prisons for dissidents. Nearly all private entrepreneurial activity is outside the law; there are rights to nonproductive personal property. Other rights such as those to organize an independent labor union are strictly denied. Literacy is high, few starve, and private oppression is no more.

Comparatively: The USSR is as free as Malawi, freer than East Germany, less free than Hungary.

UNITED ARAB EMIRATES

Economy: capitalist-statist
Polity: decentralized nonparty
Population: 1,400,000

Political Rights: 5
Civil Liberties: 5
Status of Freedom: partly free

A relatively homogeneous citizenry

Political Rights. The UAE is a confederation of seven shaikhdoms in which the larger are given the greater power both in the appointed assembly and the administrative hierarchy. There is a great deal of consultation in the traditional pattern. Below the confederation level there are no electoral procedures or parties. Each shaikhdom is relatively autonomous in its internal affairs. The majority of the people are recent immigrants and noncitizens.

Civil Liberties. The press is private or governmental. There is self-censorship, but some criticism is expressed. Broadcasting is under federal or shaikhdom control. There are no political assemblies, but there are also few, if any, prisoners of conscience. The courts dispense a combination of British, tribal, and Islamic law. Labor unions are prohibited, but illegal strikes have occurred. Private rights are generally respected; there is freedom of travel. As in most Muslim countries there is freedom of worship for established religions, but only the favored Muslims may proselytize. Many persons may still accept the feudal privileges and restraints of their tribal position. The rights of the alien majority are less secure: "troublemakers" are deported. Private economic activity exists alongside the dominance of government petroleum and petroleum-related activities.

Comparatively: United Arab Emirates are as free as Bahrain, freer than North Yemen, less free than Kuwait.

U N I T E D   K I N G D O M

Economy: mixed capitalist   **Political Rights:** 1
Polity: centralized multiparty   **Civil Liberties:** 1
Population: 56,006,000   **Status of Freedom:** free

An ethnic state with major subnationalities

Political Rights. The United Kingdom is a parliamentary democracy with a symbolic monarch. Fair elections are open to all parties, including those advocating secession. There are elected local and regional governments, and their limited powers are gradually being increased. Subnationalities: Scots, Welsh, Ulster Scots, and Ulster Irish are significant and highly self-conscious territorial minorities. In 1978 parliament approved home rule for Scotland and Wales, but the Welsh and (more ambiguously) the Scots voters rejected this opportunity in 1979. Northern Ireland's home rule has been in abeyance because of an ethnic impasse, but is being reestablished. Ulster Scot and Irish live in intermixed territories in Northern Ireland. Both want more self-determination--the majority Ulster Scots as an autonomous part of the United Kingdom, the minority Ulster Irish as an area within Ireland.

Civil Liberties. The press is private and powerful; broadcasting has statuatory independence although it is indirectly under government control. British media are comparatively restrained because of strict libel and national security laws, and a tradition of accepting government suggestions for the handling of sensitive news. In Northern Ireland a severe security situation has led to the curtailment of private rights, to imprisonment, and on occasion to torture and brutality. However, these conditions have been relatively limited, have been thoroughly investigated by the government, and improved as a result. Elsewhere the rule of law is entrenched, and private rights generally respected. Unions are independent and powerful. In certain areas, such as medicine, housing, inheritance, and general disposability of income, socialist government policies have limited choice for some while expanding the access of others.

Comparatively: The United Kingdom is as free as the United States, freer than West Germany.

UNITED STATES OF AMERICA

Economy: capitalist
Polity: decentralized multiparty
Population: 234,193,000

Political Rights: 1
Civil Liberties: 1
Status of Freedom: free

An ethnically complex state with minor territorial subnationalities

Political Rights. The United States is a constitutional democracy with three strong but separate centers of power: president, congress, and judiciary. Elections are fair and competitive. Parties are remarkably weak: in some areas they are little more than temporary means of organizing primary elections. States, and to a less extent cities, have powers in their own rights; they often successfully oppose the desires of national administrations. Each state has equal representation in the upper house, which in the USA is the more powerful half of parliament.

Subnationalities. There are many significant ethnic groups, but the only clearly territorial subnationalities are the native peoples. The largest Indian tribes, the Navaho and Sioux, number 100,000 or more each. About 150,000 Hawaiians still reside on their native islands, intermingled with a much larger white and oriental population. Spanish-speaking Americans number in the millions; except for a few thousand residing in an area of northern New Mexico, they are mostly twentieth-century immigrants living among English-speaking Americans, particularly in the large cities. Black Americans make up over one-tenth of the U.S. population; residing primarily in large cities, they have no major territorial base. Black and Spanish-speaking Americans are of special concern because of their relative poverty; their ethnic status is quite comparable to that of many other groups in America, including Chinese, Japanese, Filipinos, Italians, or Jews.

Civil Liberties. The press is private and free; both private and public radio and television are government regulated. There are virtually no government controls on the content of the printed media (except in nonpolitical areas such as pornography) and few on broadcasting. There are no prisoners of conscience or sanctioned uses of torture; some regional miscarriages of justice and police brutality have political and social overtones. Widespread use of surveillance techniques and clandestine interference with radical groups or groups thought to be radical have occurred; as a reduction of liberties the threat has remained largely potential; in recent years these security excesses have been greatly attenuated if not eliminated. A new threat is control over the expression of former government employees. Wherever and whenever publicity penetrates, the rule of law is generally secure, even against the most powerful. The government often loses in the courts. Private rights in most spheres are respected. Unions are independent and politically influential. Although a relatively capitalistic country, the combination of tax loads and the decisive government role in agriculture, energy, defense, and other industries restricts individual choice as it increases majority power.

Comparatively: The United States is as free as Australia, freer than Italy.

UPPER VOLTA

Economy: noninclusive capitalist
Polity: military nonparty
Population: 6,800,000

Political Rights: 6
Civil Liberties: 5
Status of Freedom: partly free

A transethnic heterogeneous state

Political Rights. Upper Volta has suffered a succession of military coups, but there remain elements of consensus after each.

Civil Liberties. Media are both government and private; self-censorship is the rule. Private criticism is common. As a result of successive coups there are prisoners of conscience; freedom of assembly or of political organization is denied. At least until recently there has been a rule of law; within traditional limits

446

private rights are respected. Trade unions are active but under government pressure; they have a limited right to strike. External travel is restricted; internal movement is free. The economy remains dependent on subsistence agriculture, with the government playing the role of regulator and promoter of development.

Comparatively: Upper Volta is as free as Zambia, freer than Liberia, less free than Sierra Leone.

U R U G U A Y

Economy: mixed capitalist
Polity: military nonparty
Population: 3,000,000

Political Rights: 5
Civil Liberties: 4
Status of Freedom: partly free

A relatively homogeneous population

Political Rights. Uruguay is a military dictatorship supplemented by an appointed civilian head of state and appointed advisory council. The leading parties held elections in 1982, with results favoring opponents of the present system. Several parties and individuals could not compete. Recent elections suggest some balance of popular and military power.

Civil Liberties. The press is private, and broadcasting private and public. Both are under censorship and the danger of confiscation or closure, as are books and journals. No criticism of the military is permitted, but other criticism of government appears in the media; foreign media are also generally available. The right of assembly is restricted. The independence of the judiciary and the civil service has been curtailed. There are still hundreds of prisoners of conscience. Torture has been routinely used in the past, and may continue in some instances; convictions generally have been based on written confessions. Many parties have been banned, but there is political discussion of alternatives beyond the limits of the present system. All organizations, including unions, are under close government supervision. There is no inviolability of the home. Private rights are generally respected. The tax load of an overbuilt bureaucracy and emphasis on private and government monopolies in major sectors have also restricted choice in this now impoverished welfare state.

Comparatively: Uruguay is as free as Morocco, freer than Paraguay, less free than Brazil.

VANUATU

Economy: noninclusive capitalist-statist
Polity: decentralized mutiparty
Population: 100,000

Political Rights: 2
Civil Liberties: 4
Status of Freedom: partly free

A relatively homogeneous society with geographical subnationalities

Political Rights. Vanuatu has a parliamentary system with an indirectly elected president. Elections have been freely contested by multiple parties. Opposition exists between islands and between the French and English educated. Local government is elected; a decentralized federal system of regional government is being developed.

Civil Liberties. News media are limited and largely government owned; the only critical paper was closed by government order in 1983; radio is not free. The full spectrum of civil freedoms is observed, but in the aftermath of the suppression of a secessionist (largely French supported) movement at independence, many political arrests and trials occurred; mistreatment was reported. The judiciary is independent. Rights to political economic, and union organization are observed. There is a general right to travel.

Comparatively: Vanuatu is as free as Honduras, freer than Maldives, less free than Belize.

VENEZUELA

Economy: capitalist-statist
Polity: centralized multiparty
Population: 18,000,000

Political Rights: 1
Civil Liberties: 2
Status of Freedom: free

A relatively homogeneous population

Political Rights. Venezuela is a parliamentary democracy in which power has alternated between major parties in recent years. Campaigns and voting are fair and open. Regional and local assemblies are relatively powerful, but governors are centrally appointed. Each state has equal representation in the upper house.

Civil Liberties. The press is private and free; most broadcasting is also in private hands. Censorship occurs only in emergencies, but television scripts on certain subjects must be approved in advance, and there are recurrent attempts at government control. The rule of law is generally secured, except occasionally in areas of guerrilla actions. On rare occasions members of parliament have been arrested. However, there are no prisoners of conscience, and the government has taken steps to prevent torture. The court can rule against the government and charges are brought against the security forces. Most private rights are respected; government involvement in the petroleum industry has given it a predominant economic role. Human rights organizations are very active. Unions are well organized and powerful.

Comparatively: Venezuela is as free as France, freer than Ecuador, less free than Costa Rica.

VIETNAM

Economy: socialist
Polity: communist one-party
Population: 57,000,000

Political Rights: 7
Civil Liberties: 6
Status of Freedom: not free

An ethnic state with subnationalities

Political Rights, Vietnam is a traditional communist dictatorship with the forms of parliamentary democracy. Actual power is in the hands of the communist party; this is in turn dominated by a small group at the top. Officially there is a ruling national front as in several other communist states, but the noncommunist parties are facades. Administration is highly centralized, with provincial boundaries arbitrarily determined by the central government. The flow of refugees and other evidence suggest that the present regime is very unpopular, especially in the South which is treated as an occupied country. Subnationalities: Continued fighting has been reported in the Montagnard areas in the South. Combined with new resettlement schemes non-Vietnamese peoples are under pressure in both North and South Vietnam. Many Chinese have been driven out of the country.

Civil Liberties The media are under direct government, party, or army control; only the approved line is presented. While the people have essentially no rights against the state, there continues to be some public criticism and passive resistance, espe-

cially in the South. Arbitrary arrest is frequent. Severe
repression of the Buddhist opposition has led to many immo-
lations--pressure on the Hoa Hao and Catholics is comparable. In
spite of superficial appearances religious freedom is generally
denied. Perhaps one-half million persons have been put through
reeducation camps, hundreds of thousands have been forced to move
into new areas, or to change occupations; thousands are prisoners
of conscience or in internal exile. Former anticommunist and
other groups are regularly discriminated against in employment,
health care, and travel. There are no independent labor union
rights, rights to travel, or choice of education; many have been
forced into collectives.

Comparatively: Vietnam is as free as Iraq, freer than Cambodia,
less free than China (Mainland).

WESTERN SAMOA

Economy: noninclusive capitalist   **Political Rights:** 4
Polity: traditional nonparty   **Civil Liberties:** 3
Population: 160,000   **Status of Freedom:** partly free

A relatively homogeneous population

Political Rights. Western Samoa is a constitutional monarchy
in which the assembly is elected by 9,500 "family heads." There
have been important shifts of power within the assembly as the
result of elections, although there are no political parties. A
recent election was voided in the courts on a corruption issue.
Village government has preserved traditional forms and considerable autonomy; it is also based on rule by "family heads."

Civil Liberties. The press is private and government; radio is
government owned; television is received only from outside.
Government media have limited independence. There is general
freedom of expression, organization, and assembly. The judiciary
is independent and the rule of law and private rights are respected within the limits set by the traditional system. Most arable
land is held in customary tenure. Health and literacy standards
are very high for a poor country.

Comparatively: Western Samoa is as free as Mexico, freer than
Indonesia, less free than Nauru.

Y E M E N, N O R T H

Economy: noninclusive capitalist
Polity: military nonparty
Population: 5,700,000

Political Rights: 6
Civil Liberties: 5
Status of Freedom: not free

A complex but relatively homogeneous population

Political Rights. North Yemen is a military dictatorship supplemented by an appointive and elected advisory assembly. Leaders are frequently assassinated. The tribal and religious structures still retain considerable authority, and the government must rely on a wide variety of different groups in an essentially nonideological consensual regime. Recent local elections have allowed some competition. Political parties are forbidden. The country is divided between city and country, a variety of tribes, and two major religious groupings, and faces a major revolutionary challenge.

Civil Liberties. The weak media are largely government owned; the papers have occasional criticisms--the broadcast media have none. Foreign publications are routinely censored. Yet proponents of both royalist and far left persuasions are openly accepted in a society with few known prisoners of conscience. There is no right of assembly. Politically active opponents may be encouraged to go into exile. The traditional Islamic courts give some protection; many private rights are respected. There is no right to strike or to engage in religious proselytizing. Unions and professional associations are government sponsored. Economically the government has concentrated on improving the infrastructure of Yemen's still overwhelmingly traditional economy. Most farmers are tenants; half the labor force is employed abroad.

Comparatively: North Yemen is as free as Djibouti, freer than South Yemen, less free than Egypt.

Y E M E N, S O U T H

Economy: noninclusive socialist
Polity: socialist one-party
Population: 2,100,000

Political Rights: 6
Civil Liberties: 7
Status of Freedom: not free

A relatively homogeneous population

Political Rights. South Yemen considers itself a communist country governed according to the communist one-party model. It is doubtful that the party retains the tight party discipline of its exemplars; it is government by coup and violence. Parliamentary elections follow the one-party model; they allow some choice among individuals. Soviet influence in internal and external affairs is powerful.

Civil Liberties. The media are government owned or controlled, and employed actively as means of indoctrination. Even conversation with foreigners is highly restricted. In the political and security areas the rule of law hardly applies. Political imprisonments, torture, and "disappearances" have instilled a pervasive fear in those who would speak up. Death sentences against protesting farmers have been handed down by people's courts. Independent private rights are few, although some traditional law and institutions remain. Unions are under government control. Industry and commerce have been nationalized, some of the land collectivized.

Comparatively: South Yemen is as free as Malawi, freer than Somalia, less free than Oman.

YUGOSLAVIA

Economy: mixed socialist
Polity: communist one-party
Population: 22,800,000

Political Rights: 6
Civil Liberties: 5
Status of Freedom: partly free

A multinational state

Political Rights. Yugoslavia is governed on the model of the USSR, but with the addition of unique elements. These include: the greater role given the governments of the constituent republics; and the greater power given the assemblies of the self-managed communities and industrial enterprises. The Federal Assembly is elected indirectly by those successful in lower level elections. In any event, the country is directed by a small elite of the communist party. No opposition member is elected to state or national position, nor is there public opposition in the assemblies to government policy on the national or regional level.

Subnationalities. The several peoples of Yugoslavia live largely in their historical homelands. The population consists of forty percent Serbs, twenty-two percent Croats, eight percent

Slovenes, eight percent Bosnian Muslims, six percent Macedonians, six percent Albanians, two percent Montenegrins, and many others. The Croats have an especially active independence movement; Albanians have agitated for more self-determination. Yet there is a degree of authentic defense of cultural differences.

Civil Liberties. The media in Yugoslavia are controlled directly or indirectly by the government, although there is ostensible worker control. The range of ideas and criticism of government policy in domestic and available foreign publications is greater than in most communist states. There is no right of assembly, but some assemblies are allowed outside of government direction. Hundreds have been imprisoned for ideas expressed verbally or in print that deviated from the official line (primarily through subnationalist enthusiasm, anticommunism, or communist deviationism). Dissidents are even pursued overseas. Torture and brutality occur; psychiatric hospitals are also used to confine prisoners of conscience. As long as the issue is not political, however, the courts have some independence; there is a realm of de facto individual freedom that includes the right to seek employment outside the country. Travel outside Yugoslavia is often denied to dissidents, and religious proselytizing is forbidden. Labor is not independent, but has rights through the working of the "self-management" system; local strikes are common. Although the economy is socialist or communalist in most respects, agriculture in this most agricultural of European countries remains overwhelmingly private.

Comparatively: Yugoslavia is as free as Poland, freer than Romania, less free than Morocco.

ZAIRE

Economy: noninclusive capitalist-statist   **Political Rights:** 6

Polity: nationalist one-party (military dominated)   **Civil Liberties:** 7

Population: 31,300,000   **Status of Freedom:** not free

A transethnic heterogeneous state with subnationalities

Political Rights. Zaire is under one-man military rule, with the ruling party essentially an extension of the ruler's personality. Elections at both local and parliamentary levels are

453

restricted to one party, but allows for extensive choice among individuals. Regions are deliberately organized to avoid ethnic identity: regional officers all are appointed from the center, generally from outside of the area, as are officers of the ruling party.

Subnationalities. There are such a variety of tribes or linguistic groups in Zaire that no one group has as much as twenty percent of the population. The fact that French remains the dominant language reflects the degree of this dispersion. Until recently most of the Zaire people have seen themselves only in local terms without broader ethnic identification. The revolts and wars of the early 1960s saw continually shifting patterns of affiliation, with the European provincial but not ethnic realities of Katanga and South Kasai being most important. The most self-conscious ethnic groups are the Kongo people living in the west (and Congo and Angola) and the Luba in the center of the country. In both cases ethnicity goes back to important ancient kingdoms. There is continuing disaffection among the Lunda and other ethnic groups.

Civil Liberties. Private newspaper ownership remains only in name. Broadcasting is government owned and directed. Censorship and self-censorship are pervasive. There is no right of assembly, and union organization is controlled. Government has been arbitrary and capricious. The judiciary is not independent; prisoners of conscience are numerous, and execution and torture occurs. Ethnic organizations are closely restricted. Arrested conspirators have been forbidden their own lawyers. There is relative religious freedom; the Catholic church retains some power. Through the misuse of government power, the extravagance and business dealings of those in high places reduces economic freedom. Nationalization of land has often been a prelude to private development by powerful bureaucrats. Pervasive corruption and anarchy reduce human rights. There is also considerable government enterprise.

Comparatively: Zaire is as free as Vietnam, freer than Benin, less free than Zambia.

Z A M B I A

Economy: noninclusive
     mixed socialist
Polity: socialist one-party
Population: 6,000,000

Political Rights: 5

Civil Liberties: 6

Status of Freedom: partly free

A transethnic heterogeneous state

Political Rights. Zambia is ruled as a one-party dictatorship, although there have been elements of freedom within that party. Party organs are constitutionally more important than governmental. Although elections have some meaning within this framework, the government has suppressed opposition movements within the party. Expression of dissent is possible through abstention or negative votes. There are some town councils with elected members.

Civil Liberties. All media are government controlled. A considerable variety of opinion is expressed, but it is a crime to criticize the president, the parliament, or the ideology. Foreign publications are censored. There is a rule of law and the courts have some independence; cases have been won against the government. Political opponents are often detained, and occasionally tortured, yet most people talk without fear. Traditional life continues. The government does not fully accept private or traditional rights in property or religion; important parts of the economy, especially copper mining, have been nationalized. Union, business, and professional organizations are under government pressure but retain significant independence.

Comparatively: Zambia is as free as Chile, freer than Angola. less free than Morocco.

Z I M B A B W E

Economy: noninclusive capitalist-
     statist
Polity: centralized
     dominant party
Population: 8,400,000

Political Rights: 4

Civil Liberties: 5

Status of Freedom: partly free

An ethnically complex state with a territorial subnationality

Political Rights. Zimbabwe is a parliamentary democracy. The ruling party came to power in 1980 through elections marked by considerable coercion of the electorate. The whites retain special minority political rights in a transitional phase. All military forces are still not controlled. Pressure to form a one-party state is growing with the increasing repression of the main opposition party. Subnationalities: The formerly dominant white, Indian, and colored populations (five percent altogether) are largely urban. The emerging dominant people are the majority Shona-speaking groups (seventy-four percent). The Ndebele (eighteen percent) are territorially distinct and politically self-conscious. Their allegiance to a minority party is being violently reduced.

Civil Liberties. The press is indirectly government owned and follows the government line except occasionally as in the letters columns. The government-owned broadcast media are active organs of government propaganda. The rule of law is increasingly threatened; opposition politicians have been forced into exile or imprisoned. Acquittals are regularly followed by rearrests. Racial discrimination is officially outlawed, especially in residence, occupation, and conscription. Many citizens live in fear of the nationalist parties and their former guerrilla forces. Unions and private associations retain some independence, but are increasingly being unified under government direction. The economy has capitalist, socialist, and statist aspects. The white population still wields disproportionate economic power.

Comparatively: Zimbabwe is as free as Singapore, freer than South Africa, less free than Botswana.

Table 9
Ratings of Nations Since 1973[1]

Country	73	74[2]	75	76	77	78	79	80	81	82
Afghanistan	4	7	7	7	7	7	7	7	7	7
	5	6	6	6	6	6	7	7	7	7
	PF	NF	NF	NF	NF	NF	NF	NF	NF	NF
Albania	7	7	7	7	7	7	7	7	7	7
	7	7	7	7	7	7	7	7	7	7
	NF	NF	NF	NF	NF	NF	NF	NF	NF	NF
Algeria	6	6	6	7	6	6	6	6	6	6
	6	6	6	6	6	6	6	6	6	6
	NF	NF	NF	NF	NF	NF	NF	NF	NF	NF
Angola[3]	7		6	6	6	7	7	7	7	7
	6		4	6	6	7	7	7	7	7
	NF		PF	NF*	NF	NF	NF	NF	NF	NF
Antigua & Barbuda[3]	2		2	2	2	2	2	2	2	2
	3		3	3	3	2	2	2	2	2
	F		F	F	F	F	F	F	F	F*
Argentina	6	2	2	2	6	6	6	6	6	6
	3	2	4	4	5	6	5	5	5	5
	PF	F	PF	PF	NF	NF	NF	NF	NF	NF
Australia	1	1	1	1	1	1	1	1	1	1
	1	1	1	1	1	1	1	1	1	1
	F	F	F	F	F	F	F	F	F	F
Austria	1	1	1	1	1	1	1	1	1	1
	1	1	1	1	1	1	1	1	1	1
	F	F	F	F	F	F	F	F	F	F
Bahamas	2	1	1	1	1	1	1	1	1	1
	2	2	2	2	2	2	2	2	2	2
	F	F*	F	F	F	F	F	F	F	F
Bahrain	6	6	4	6	6	6	6	6	5	5
	5	5	4	4	4	4	4	4	4	5
	NF	NF	PF	PF	PF	PF	PF	PF	PF	PF
Bangladesh	2	4	4	7	7	6	4	3	3	3
	4	4	4	5	4	4	4	3	3	4
	PF	PF	PF	NF	PF	PF	PF	PF	PF	PF
Barbados	1	1	1	1	1	1	1	1	1	1
	1	1	1	1	1	1	1	1	1	1
	F	F	F	F	F	F	F	F	F	F
Belgium	1	1	1	1	1	1	1	1	1	1
	1	1	1	1	1	1	1	1	1	1
	F	F	F	F	F	F	F	F	F	F
Belize (British Honduras)	2		1	1	1	1	1	1	1	1
	2		2	2	2	2	2	2	2	2
	F		F	F	F	F	F	F	F	F*

Notes to the Table

* indicates year of independence.

1. Ratings are from the January-February issues of *Freedom at Issue*. Ratings for political rights are on the first line, civil liberties are on the second line, and status of freedom are on the third line.
2. Ratings for many former dependencies are not available for 1974.
3. Angola, Mozambique, and Guinea-Bissau (formerly Portuguese Guinea) evaluated together as Portugal Colonies (A), and Cape Verde Islands and Sao Tome and Principe evaluated as Portugal (B) until 1975. Antigua and Barbuda, Dominica, and St. Lucia evaluated together as West Indies Associated States until 1978; Grenada was also included until 1975. Comoro Islands and Djibouti (formerly French Territory of the Afars and Issas) evaluated as France: Overseas Territories until 1975. Kiribati and Tuvalu evaluated together as Gilbert and Ellice Islands until 1977. Cyprus (G) and Cyprus (T) evaluated together as Cyprus until 1981.
4. 1973 ratings for South Africa were (white): 2,3 F and (black): 5,6 NF.
5. Ratings for North Vietnam for 1973 through 1976 were 7,7 NF; those for South Vietnam for 1973 through 1975 were 4,5 PF, and for 1976 were 7,7 NF.

Country	73	74[2]	75	76	77	78	79	80	81	82
Benin	7	7	7	7	7	7	7	7	7	7
(Dahomey)	5	5	6	7	7	7	7	6	6	6
	NF	NF	NF	NF	NF	NF	NF	NF	NF	NF
Bhutan	4	4	4	4	4	4	4	5	5	5
	4	4	4	4	4	4	4	5	5	5
	PF	PF	PF	PF	PF	PF	PF	PF	PF	PF
Bolivia	5	5	6	6	6	6	5	3	7	7
	4	4	5	5	4	4	3	3	5	5
	PF	PF	NF	NF	PF	PF	PF	PF	NF	NF
Botswana	3	2	2	2	2	2	2	2	2	2
	4	3	3	3	3	3	3	3	3	3
	PF	F	F	F	F	F	F	F	F	F
Brazil	5	5	4	4	4	4	4	4	4	4
	5	5	4	5	5	5	4	3	3	3
	PF	PF	PF	PF	PF	PF	PF	PF	PF	PF
Bulgaria	7	7	7	7	7	7	7	7	7	7
	7	7	7	7	7	7	7	7	7	7
	NF	NF	NF	NF	NF	NF	NF	NF	NF	NF
Burma	7	7	7	6	6	7	7	7	7	7
	5	5	5	6	6	6	6	6	6	6
	NF	NF	NF	NF	NF	NF	NF	NF	NF	NF
Burundi	7	7	7	7	7	7	7	7	7	7
	7	7	7	6	6	6	6	7	6	6
	NF	NF	NF	NF	NF	NF	NF	NF	NF	NF
Cambodia	6	6	6	7	7	7	7	7	7	7
(Kampuchea)	5	5	6	7	7	7	7	7	7	7
	NF	NF	NF	NF	NF	NF	NF	NF	NF	NF
Cameroon	6	6	6	6	7	6	6	6	6	6
	4	4	4	4	5	5	5	6	6	6
	PF	PF	PF	PF	NF	NF	NF	NF	NF	NF
Canada	1	1	1	1	1	1	1	1	1	1
	1	1	1	1	1	1	1	1	1	1
	F	F	F	F	F	F	F	F	F	F
Cape Verde Is.[3]	5		5	5	6	6	6	6	6	6
	6		5	5	6	6	6	6	6	6
	NF		PF	PF*	NF	NF	NF	NF	NF	NF
Central African	7	7	7	7	7	7	7	7	7	7
Republic	7	7	7	7	7	7	7	6	6	5
	NF	NF	NF	NF	NF	NF	NF	NF	NF	NF
Chad	6	6	6	7	7	7	6	7	6	7
	7	7	7	6	6	6	6	6	6	6
	NF	NF	NF	NF	NF	NF	NF	NF	NF	NF
Chile	1	7	7	7	7	7	6	6	6	6
	2	5	5	5	5	5	5	5	5	5
	F	NF	NF	NF	NF	NF	NF	PF	PF	PF
China (M)	7	7	7	7	7	6	6	6	6	6
	7	7	7	7	7	6	6	5	6	6
	NF	NF	NF	NF	NF	NF	NF	NF	NF	NF
China (T)	6	6	6	6	5	5	5	5	5	5
	5	5	5	5	4	4	5	6	5	5
	NF	NF	NF	NF	PF	PF	PF	PF	PF	PF
Colombia	2	2	2	2	2	2	2	2	2	2
	2	2	2	3	3	3	3	3	3	3
	F	F	F	F	F	F	F	F	F	F
Comoros[3]	4		2	5	4	5	4	4	4	4
	4		2	2	3	3	4	4	5	5
	PF		F	PF*	PF	PF	PF	PF	PF	PF
Congo	7	5	5	5	5	7	7	7	7	7
	7	6	6	6	6	6	6	7	7	6
	NF	PF	PF	PF	PF	NF	NF	NF	NF	NF

Country	73	74[2]	75	76	77	78	79	80	81	82
Costa Rica	1	1	1	1	1	1	1	1	1	1
	1	1	1	1	1	1	1	1	1	1
	F	F	F	F	F	F	F	F	F	F
Cuba	7	7	7	7	7	7	6	6	6	6
	7	7	7	7	6	6	6	6	6	6
	NF	NF	NF	NF	NF	NF	NF	NF	NF	NF
Cyprus (G)[4]	2	2	4	4	3	3	3	3	3	1
	3	3	4	4	4	4	4	4	3	2
	F	F	PF	PF	PF	PF	PF	PF	PF	F
Cyprus (T)[4]										4
										3
										PF
Czechoslovakia	7	7	7	7	7	7	7	7	7	7
	7	7	7	6	6	6	6	7	6	6
	NF	NF	NF	NF	NF	NF	NF	NF	NF	NF
Denmark	1	1	1	1	1	1	1	1	1	1
	1	1	1	1	1	1	1	1	1	1
	F	F	F	F	F	F	F	F	F	F
Djibouti[3]	4		4	4	3	2	2	3	3	3
	4		3	3	3	2	3	4	4	5
	PF		PF	PF	PF	F*	F	PF	PF	PF
Dominica[3]	2		2	2	2	2	2	2	2	2
	3		3	3	3	2	3	2	2	2
	F		F	F	F	F	F*	F	F	F
Dominican Republic	3	3	4	4	4	4	2	2	2	2
	2	2	2	2	3	2	2	3	3	3
	F	F	PF	PF	PF	PF	F	F	F	F
Ecuador	7	7	7	7	6	6	5	2	2	2
	3	4	4	4	4	4	3	2	2	2
	PF	PF	PF	PF	PF	PF	PF	F	F	F
Egypt	6	6	6	6	5	5	5	5	5	5
	6	6	4	4	4	4	5	5	5	6
	NF	NF	PF	PF	PF	PF	PF	PF	PF	PF
El Salvador	2	2	2	2	3	3	4	5	6	5
	3	3	3	3	3	3	4	3	4	5
	F	F	F	F	PF	PF	PF	PF	PF	PF
Equatorial Guinea	6	6	6	6	6	7	7	7	7	7
	6	6	6	7	7	7	7	6	6	6
	NF	NF	NF	NF	NF	NF	NF	NF	NF	NF
Ethiopia	5	5	6	7	7	7	7	7	7	7
	6	6	5	6	6	7	7	7	7	7
	NF	PF	NF	NF	NF	NF	NF	NF	NF	NF
Fiji	2	2	2	2	2	2	2	2	2	2
	2	2	2	2	2	2	2	2	2	2
	F	F	F	F	F	F	F	F	F	F
Finland	2	2	2	2	2	2	2	2	2	2
	2	2	2	2	2	2	2	2	2	2
	F	F	F	F	F	F	F	F	F	F
France	1	1	1	1	1	1	1	1	1	1
	2	2	2	2	1	1	2	2	2	2
	F	F	F	F	F	F	F	F	F	F
Gabon	6	6	6	6	6	6	6	6	6	6
	6	6	6	6	6	6	6	6	6	6
	NF	NF	NF	NF	NF	NF	NF	NF	NF	NF
Gambia	2	2	2	2	2	2	2	2	2	3
	2	2	2	2	2	2	2	2	2	4
	F	F	F	F	F	F	F	F	F	PF
Germany (E)	7	7	7	7	7	7	7	7	7	7
	7	7	7	7	7	7	6	7	6	7
	NF	NF	NF	NF	NF	NF	NF	NF	NF	NF

Country	73	74[2]	75	76	77	78	79	80	81	82
Germany (W)	1	1	1	1	1	1	1	1	1	1
	1	1	1	1	1	1	2	2	2	2
	F	F	F	F	F	F	F	F	F	F
Ghana	6	7	7	7	7	6	6	4	2	2
	6	6	5	5	5	5	4	4	3	3
	NF	NF	NF	NF	NF	PF	PF	PF	F	F
Greece	6	7	2	2	2	2	2	2	2	1
	6	5	2	2	2	2	2	2	2	2
	NF	NF	F	F	F	F	F	F	F	F
Grenada	2		2	2	2	2	2	4	5	6
	3		4	4	4	3	3	5	5	5
	F		PF*	PF	PF	F	F	PF	PF	NF
Guatemala	2	2	4	4	4	4	3	3	5	6
	3	2	3	3	3	4	4	5	6	6
	F	F	PF	PF	PF	PF	PF	PF	PF	NF
Guinea	7	7	7	7	7	7	7	7	7	7
	7	7	7	7	7	7	7	7	7	7
	NF	NF	NF	NF	NF	NF	NF	NF	NF	NF
Guinea-Bissau[3]	7		6	6	6	6	6	6	6	6
	6		6	6	6	6	6	6	6	6
	NF		NF*	NF	NF	NF	NF	NF	NF	NF
Guyana	2	4	4	4	3	3	4	4	4	5
	2	2	3	3	3	3	3	4	4	4
	F	PF	PF	PF	PF	PF	PF	PF	PF	PF
Haiti	7	6	6	6	6	7	7	6	6	7
	6	6	6	6	6	6	6	5	6	6
	NF	NF	NF	NF	NF	NF	NF	NF	NF	NF
Honduras	7	6	6	6	6	6	6	6	4	3
	3	3	3	3	3	3	3	3	3	3
	PF	PF	PF	PF	PF	PF	PF	PF	PF	PF
Hungary	6	6	6	6	6	6	6	6	6	6
	6	6	6	6	5	5	5	5	5	5
	NF	NF	NF	NF	NF	NF	NF	NF	NF	NF
Iceland	1	1	1	1	1	1	1	1	1	1
	1	1	1	1	1	1	1	1	1	1
	F	F	F	F	F	F	F	F	F	F
India	2	2	2	2	3	2	2	2	2	2
	3	3	3	5	5	2	2	2	3	3
	F	F	F	PF	PF	F	F	F	F	F
Indonesia	5	5	5	5	5	5	5	5	5	5
	5	5	5	5	5	5	5	5	5	5
	PF	PF	PF	PF	PF	PF	PF	PF	PF	PF
Iran	5	5	5	6	6	6	6	5	5	6
	6	6	6	6	6	5	5	6	5	6
	NF	NF	NF	NF	NF	NF	PF	PF	PF	NF
Iraq	7	7	7	7	7	7	7	7	6	6
	7	7	7	7	7	7	6	7	7	7
	NF	NF	NF	NF	NF	NF	NF	NF	NF	NF
Ireland	1	1	1	1	1	1	1	1	1	1
	2	2	2	2	1	1	1	1	1	1
	F	F	F	F	F	F	F	F	F	F
Israel	2	2	2	2	2	2	2	2	2	2
	3	3	3	3	3	3	2	2	2	2
	F	F	F	F	F	F	F	F	F	F
Italy	1	1	1	1	2	2	2	2	1	1
	2	2	2	2	1	1	2	2	2	2
	F	F	F	F	F	F	F	F	F	F
Ivory Coast	6	6	6	6	6	6	6	6	6	5
	6	6	6	5	5	5	5	5	5	5
	NF	NF	NF	NF	NF	NF	NF	PF	PF	PF

Country	73	74[2]	75	76	77	78	79	80	81	82
Jamaica	1	1	1	1	1	2	2	2	2	2
	2	2	2	2	3	3	3	3	3	3
	F	F	F	F	F	F	F	F	F	F
Japan	2	2	2	2	2	2	2	2	1	1
	1	1	1	1	1	1	1	1	1	1
	F	F	F	F	F	F	F	F	F	F
Jordan	6	6	6	6	6	6	6	6	6	6
	6	6	6	6	6	6	6	6	6	6
	NF	NF	NF	NF	NF	NF	NF	NF	NF	NF
Kenya	5	5	5	5	5	5	5	5	5	5
	4	4	4	5	5	5	5	4	4	4
	PF	PF	PF	PF	PF	PF	PF	PF	PF	PF
Kiribati[3]	2		2	2	2	2	2	2	2	2
(Gilbert Islands)	2		2	2	2	2	2	2	2	2
	F		F	F	F	F	F	F*	F	F
Korea (N)	7	7	7	7	7	7	7	7	7	7
	7	7	7	7	7	7	7	7	7	7
	NF	NF	NF	NF	NF	NF	NF	NF	NF	NF
Korea (S)	5	4	5	5	5	5	5	4	5	5
	6	6	6	5	5	5	5	5	6	6
	NF	PF	PF	PF	NF	PF	PF	PF	PF	PF
Kuwait	4	4	4	4	6	6	6	6	6	4
	4	3	3	3	5	4	3	4	4	4
	PF	PF	PF	PF	NF	PF	PF	PF	PF	PF
Laos	5	5	5	6	7	7	7	7	7	7
	5	5	5	6	7	7	7	7	7	7
	PF	PF	PF	NF	NF	NF	NF	NF	NF	NF
Lebanon	2	2	2	4	4	4	4	4	4	4
	2	2	2	4	4	4	4	4	4	4
	F	F	F	PF	PF	PF	PF	PF	PF	PF
Lesotho	7	5	5	5	5	5	5	5	5	5
	4	3	4	4	4	4	4	5	5	5
	NF	PF	PF	PF	PF	PF	PF	PF	PF	PF
Liberia	6	6	6	6	6	6	6	6	6	6
	6	5	3	4	4	4	4	5	6	6
	NF	NF	PF	PF	PF	PF	PF	PF	NF	NF
Libya	7	7	7	7	7	7	6	6	6	6
	6	7	7	6	6	6	6	6	6	7
	NF	NF	NF	NF	NF	NF	NF	NF	NF	NF
Luxembourg	2	2	2	2	2	1	1	1	1	1
	1	1	1	1	1	1	1	1	1	1
	F	F	F	F	F	F	F	F	F	F
Madagascar	5	5	5	5	6	5	5	6	6	6
(Malagasy	3	4	4	5	5	5	5	6	6	6
Republic)	PF	PF	PF	PF	NF	PF	PF	NF	NF	NF
Malawi	7	7	7	7	7	7	6	6	6	6
	6	6	6	6	6	6	6	7	7	7
	NF	NF	NF	NF	NF	NF	NF	NF	NF	NF
Malaysia	2	2	3	3	3	3	3	3	3	3
	3	3	3	4	4	4	3	4	4	4
	F	F	PF	PF	PF	PF	PF	PF	PF	PF
Maldives	3	3	3	4	4	4	5	5	5	5
	2	2	2	4	4	4	5	5	5	5
	PF	PF	PF	PF	PF	PF	PF	PF	PF	PF
Mali	7	7	7	7	7	7	7	7	7	7
	6	6	6	7	7	7	7	6	6	6
	NF	NF	NF	NF	NF	NF	NF	NF	NF	NF
Malta	1	1	1	1	1	2	2	2	2	2
	2	1	1	1	2	2	2	2	3	3
	F	F	F	F	F	F	F	F	F	F

Country	73	74[2]	75	76	77	78	79	80	81	82
Mauritania	6	6	5	6	6	6	6	6	7	7
	6	6	6	6	6	6	6	6	6	6
	NF	NF	NF	NF	NF	NF	NF	NF	NF	NF
Mauritius	3	3	3	3	3	2	2	2	2	2
	2	2	2	2	2	2	4	4	4	3
	F	F	F	F	F	F	PF	PF	PF	F
Mexico	5	4	4	4	4	4	4	3	3	3
	3	3	3	3	4	4	4	3	4	4
	PF	PF	PF	PF	PF	PF	PF	PF	PF	PF
Mongolia	7	7	7	7	7	7	7	7	7	7
	7	7	7	7	7	7	7	7	7	7
	NF	NF	NF	NF	NF	NF	NF	NF	NF	NF
Morocco	5	5	5	5	5	4	3	3	4	4
	4	5	5	5	5	3	4	4	4	5
	PF	PF	PF	PF	PF	PF	PF	PF	PF	PF
Mozambique[3]	7		6	6	7	7	7	7	7	7
	6		6	6	7	7	7	7	7	7
	NF		NF	NF*	NF	NF	NF	NF	NF	NF
Nauru	2	2	2	2	2	2	2	2	2	2
	2	2	2	2	2	2	2	2	2	2
	F	F	F	F	F	F	F	F	F	F
Nepal	6	6	6	6	6	6	6	5	3	3
	5	5	5	5	5	5	5	4	4	4
	NF	NF	NF	NF	NF	NF	NF	PF	PF	PF
Netherlands	1	1	1	1	1	1	1	1	1	1
	1	1	1	1	1	1	1	1	1	1
	F	F	F	F	F	F	F	F	F	F
New Zealand	1	1	1	1	1	1	1	1	1	1
	1	1	1	1	1	1	1	1	1	1
	F	F	F	F	F	F	F	F	F	F
Nicaragua	4	5	5	5	5	5	5	5	5	6
	3	4	4	4	5	5	5	5	5	5
	PF	PF	PF	PF	PF	PF	PF	PF	PF	PF
Niger	6	6	7	7	7	7	7	7	7	7
	6	6	6	6	6	6	6	6	6	6
	NF	NF	NF	NF	NF	NF	NF	NF	NF	NF
Nigeria	6	6	6	6	6	5	5	2	2	2
	4	4	4	5	4	4	3	3	3	3
	PF	PF	PF	PF	PF	PF	PF	F	F	F
Norway	1	1	1	1	1	1	1	1	1	1
	1	1	1	1	1	1	1	1	1	1
	F	F	F	F	F	F	F	F	F	F
Oman	7	7	7	7	6	6	6	6	6	6
	6	6	6	6	6	6	6	6	6	6
	NF	NF	NF	NF	NF	NF	NF	NF	NF	NF
Pakistan	3	3	3	5	4	6	6	6	7	7
	5	5	5	5	5	4	5	6	5	5
	PF	PF	PF	PF	PF	PF	PF	NF	NF	NF
Panama	7	7	7	7	7	6	5	5	4	4
	6	6	6	6	6	5	5	5	4	4
	NF	NF	NF	NF	NF	NF	PF	PF	PF	PF
Papua New Guinea	4		3	3	2	2	2	2	2	2
	2		2	2	2	2	2	2	2	2
	PF		PF	PF*	F	F	F	F	F	F
Paraguay	4	5	5	5	5	5	5	5	5	5
	6	5	5	5	6	6	5	5	5	5
	PF	PF	PF	PF	NF	NF	PF	PF	PF	PF
Peru	7	7	6	6	6	6	5	5	2	2
	5	5	6	4	4	4	4	4	3	3
	NF	NF	NF	PF	PF	PF	PF	PF	F	F

Country	73	74[2]	75	76	77	78	79	80	81	82
Philippines	4	5	5	5	5	5	5	5	5	5
	6	5	5	5	5	5	5	5	5	5
	PF	PF	PF	PF	PF	PF	PF	PF	PF	PF
Poland	6	6	6	6	6	6	6	6	6	5
	6	6	6	6	6	5	5	5	4	4
	NF	NF	NF	NF	NF	NF	PF	PF	PF	PF
Portugal	5	5	5	5	2	2	2	2	2	2
	6	6	3	3	2	2	2	2	2	2
	NF	NF	PF	PF	F	F	F	F	F	F
Qatar	6	6	6	6	5	5	5	5	5	5
	5	5	5	5	5	5	5	5	5	5
	NF	NF	NF	NF	PF	PF	PF	PF	PF	PF
Romania	7	7	7	7	7	7	7	7	7	7
	6	6	6	6	6	6	6	6	6	6
	NF	NF	NF	NF	NF	NF	NF	NF	NF	NF
Rwanda	7	7	7	7	7	7	6	6	6	6
	6	6	5	5	5	5	5	6	6	6
	NF	NF	NF	NF	NF	NF	NF	NF	NF	NF
St. Lucia[3]	2		2	2	2	2	2	2	2	2
	3		3	3	3	3	3	3	3	2
	F		F	F	F	F	F	F*	F	F
St. Vincent	2		2	2	2	2	2	2	2	2
	2		2	2	2	2	2	2	2	2
	F		F	F	F	F	F	F*	F	F
Sao Tome & Principe[3]	5		5	5	5	6	6	6	6	6
	6		5	5	5	5	5	6	6	6
	NF		PF	PF	PF	NF	NF	NF	NF	NF
Saudia Arabia	6	6	6	6	6	6	6	6	6	6
	6	6	6	6	6	6	6	6	6	6
	NF	NF	NF	NF	NF	NF	NF	NF	NF	NF
Senegal	6	6	6	6	6	5	4	4	4	4
	6	6	5	4	4	3	3	3	4	4
	NF	NF	NF	PF	PF	PF	PF	PF	PF	PF
Seychelles[3]	3		2	2	1	6	6	6	6	6
	2		2	2	2	3	4	5	6	6
	PF		F	F	F*	PF	PF	PF	NF	NF
Sierra Leone	4	6	6	6	6	5	6	5	5	5
	5	5	5	5	5	5	5	5	5	5
	PF	PF	PF	PF	PF	PF	PF	PF	PF	PF
Singapore	5	5	5	5	5	5	5	5	5	4
	5	5	5	5	5	5	5	5	5	5
	PF	PF	PF	PF	PF	PF	PF	PF	PF	PF
Solomon Is.	4		4	3	2	2	2	2	2	2
	2		2	2	2	2	2	2	2	2
	PF		PF	F	F	F	F*	F	F	F
Somalia	7	7	7	7	7	7	7	7	7	7
	6	6	6	6	7	7	7	7	7	7
	NF	NF	NF	NF	NF	NF	NF	NF	NF	NF
South Africa[4]		4	4	4	4	5	5	5	5	5
		5	5	5	5	6	6	6	6	6
		PF	PF	PF	PF	PF	PF	PF	PF	NF
Spain	5	5	5	5	5	2	2	2	2	2
	6	6	5	5	3	2	3	2	3	3
	NF	NF	PF	PF	PF	F	F	F	F	F
Sri Lanka	2	2	2	2	2	2	2	2	2	2
	3	3	3	4	3	2	3	3	3	3
	F	F	F	PF	F	F	F	F	F	F
Sudan	6	6	6	6	6	6	5	5	5	5
	6	6	6	6	6	5	5	5	5	6
	NF	NF	NF	NF	NF	NF	PF	PF	PF	PF

Country	73	74²	75	76	77	78	79	80	81	82
Suriname	2		2	2	2	2	2	2	7	7
	2		2	2	2	2	2	2	5	5
	F		F	F*	F	F	F	F	NF	NF
Swaziland	4	6	6	6	6	6	6	5	5	5
	2	4	4	4	4	4	5	5	5	5
	PF	PF	PF	PF	PF	PF	PF	PF	PF	PF
Sweden	1	1	1	2	1	1	1	1	1	1
	1	1	1	1	1	1	1	1	1	1
	F	F	F	F	F	F	F	F	F	F
Switzerland	1	1	1	1	1	1	1	1	1	1
	1	1	1	1	1	1	1	1	1	1
	F	F	F	F	F	F	F	F	F	F
Syria	7	7	6	6	6	5	5	5	5	5
	7	7	7	7	6	6	6	6	6	6
	NF	NF	NF	NF	NF	PF	PF	PF	NF	NF
Tanzania	6	6	6	6	6	6	6	6	6	6
	6	6	6	6	6	6	6	6	6	6
	NF	NF	NF	NF	NF	NF	NF	NF	NF	NF
Thailand	7	6	5	2	6	6	6	4	3	3
	5	3	3	3	6	5	4	3	4	4
	NF	PF	PF	F	NF	NF	PF	PF	PF	PF
Togo	7	7	7	7	7	7	7	7	7	7
	5	5	6	6	6	6	6	6	6	6
	NF	NF	NF	NF	NF	NF	NF	NF	NF	NF
Tonga	4	5	5	5	5	5	5	5	5	5
	2	3	3	3	3	3	3	3	3	3
	PF	PF	PF	PF	PF	PF	PF	PF	PF	PF
Transkei					6	6	5	5	5	5
					5	5	5	6	6	6
					NF*	NF	PF	PF	PF	PF
Trinidad & Tobago	2	2	2	2	2	2	2	2	2	2
	3	2	2	2	2	2	2	2	2	2
	F	F	F	F	F	F	F	F	F	F
Tunisia	6	6	6	6	6	6	6	6	6	5
	5	5	5	5	5	5	5	5	5	5
	NF	NF	NF	NF	NF	NF	NF	PF	PF	PF
Turkey	3	2	2	2	2	2	2	2	5	5
	4	4	3	3	3	3	3	3	5	5
	PF	PF	F	F	F	F	F	F	PF	PF
Tuvalu³ (Ellice Islands)	2		2	2	2	2	2	2	2	2
	2		2	2	2	2	2	2	2	2
	F		F	F	F	F	F*	F	F	F
Uganda	7	7	7	7	7	7	7	6	5	5
	7	7	7	7	7	7	7	6	5	5
	NF	NF	NF	NF	NF	NF	NF	NF	PF	PF
USSR	6	6	6	7	7	7	7	6	6	6
	6	6	6	6	6	6	6	6	7	7
	NF	NF	NF	NF	NF	NF	NF	NF	NF	NF
United Arab Emirates	7	6	6	6	5	5	5	5	5	5
	5	5	5	5	5	5	5	5	5	5
	NF	NF	NF	NF	PF	PF	PF	PF	PF	PF
United Kingdom	1	1	1	1	1	1	1	1	1	1
	1	1	1	1	1	1	1	1	1	1
	F	F	F	F	F	F	F	F	F	F
United States	1	1	1	1	1	1	1	1	1	1
	1	1	1	1	1	1	1	1	1	1
	F	F	F	F	F	F	F	F	F	F
Upper Volta	3	3	6	6	5	5	2	2	6	6
	4	4	4	4	5	4	3	3	5	5
	PF	PF	PF	PF	PF	PF	F	F	PF	PF

Country	73	74[2]	75	76	77	78	79	80	81	82
Uruguay	3	5	5	5	6	6	6	6	5	5
	4	5	5	5	6	6	6	6	5	5
	PF	PF	PF	PF	NF	NF	NF	NF	PF	PF
Vanuatu (New Hebrides)	4		4	4	3	3	3	3	2	2
	3		3	3	3	3	3	3	3	3
	PF		PF	PF	PF	PF	PF	PF	F*	F
Venezuela	2	2	2	2	1	1	1	1	1	1
	2	2	2	2	2	2	2	2	2	2
	F	F	F	F	F	F	F	F	F	F
Vietnam[5]					7	7	7	7	7	7
					7	7	7	7	7	7
					NF	NF	NF	NF	NF	NF
Western Samoa	4	4	4	4	4	4	4	4	4	4
	2	2	2	2	2	2	2	2	3	3
	PF	PF	PF	PF	PF	PF	PF	PF	PF	PF
Yemen (N)	4	5	5	6	6	6	6	6	6	6
	4	4	4	5	5	5	5	5	5	5
	PF	PF	PF	NF	NF	NF	NF	NF	NF	NF
Yemen (S)	7	7	7	7	7	7	7	6	6	6
	7	7	7	7	7	7	7	7	7	7
	NF	NF	NF	NF	NF	NF	NF	NF	NF	NF
Yugoslavia	6	6	6	6	6	6	6	6	6	6
	6	6	6	6	6	5	5	5	5	5
	NF	NF	NF	NF	NF	NF	NF	NF	NF	NF
Zaire	7	7	7	7	7	7	7	6	6	6
	6	6	6	7	6	6	6	6	6	6
	NF	NF	NF	NF	NF	NF	NF	NF	NF	NF
Zambia	5	5	5	5	5	5	5	5	5	5
	5	5	4	5	5	5	5	5	6	6
	PF	PF	PF	PF	PF	PF	PF	PF	PF	PF
Zimbabwe (Rhodesia)	6	6	6	6	6	6	5	4	3	3
	5	5	5	5	5	5	5	5	4	5
	NF	NF	NF	NF	NF	NF	PF	PF	PF	PF

Index

See also Country Summaries, pages 326–456, and Tables 1–9.

Index

Index